NEW TAIWAN, NEW CHINA

NEW TAIWAN, NEW CHINA

Taiwan's changing role in the Asia-Pacific region

GARY KLINTWORTH

 LONGMAN

ST. MARTIN'S PRESS
NEW YORK

Longman Australia Pty Ltd
Longman House
Kings Gardens
95 Coventry Street
Melbourne 3205 Australia

Offices in Sydney, Brisbane, Perth, and associated companies
throughout the world.
Copyright © Longman Australia Pty Ltd 1995

First published 1995

Designed by Rob Cowpe
Set in Palatino
Printed in Singapore through Longman Singapore

National Library of Australia
Cataloguing-in-Publication data

ISBN 0 312 12550 X

Klintworth, Gary, 1945–   .
     New Taiwan, New China: Taiwan's changing role in the Asia-Pacific region
     Bibliography
     Includes index.
     ISBN 0 582 80245 8

1. Taiwan – Foreign relations – Asia. 2. Asia – Foreign relations – Taiwan. 3. Taiwan – Foreign relations –
Pacific Area. 4. Pacific Area – Foreign relations – Taiwan. 5. Taiwan – Politics and government – 1988-   .
I. Title. (Series : Key topics in Asian history, politics and internation relations).

     327.5124905

New Taiwan New China
Copyright © 1995 Garry Klintworth

Library of Congress Cataloging-in-Publication Data

Klintworth Gary
     NEW TAIWAN, NEW CHINA: TAIWAN'S CHANGING ROLE IN
     THE ASIA-PACIFIC REGION/ by Gary Klintworth
     336 p.   23.4 x 15.6 cm.
     Includes bibliographical references and index.
     ISBN 0-312-12550-X

1. Taiwan – Economic conditions – 1957- 2. Taiwan – Politics and government – 1988- 3. Taiwan –
Foreign economic relations – Pacific Area. 4. Pacific Area – Foreign economic relations – Taiwan. 5.
China – Economic conditions – 1976- I. Title.
HC430.5.H35 1995
337.5124'9–dc20

First edition 1995
First published in the United States of America 1995 by
Scholarly and Reference Division,
ST. MARTIN'S PRESS, INC.,
175 Fifth Avenue,
New York, N.Y. 10010

Contents

Acknowledgements

The advice and assistance at various times of Peter Chen, Samuel Shih-Liang Chen, C.K. Cheng, James Chu, James Cotton, Kay Dancey, Mark Elvin, Edmund Fitzgerald, Ross Garnaut, Brett Kunkel, Li Xinhua, Andrew Macdougal, Michelle Marginson, Bruce Major, Alastair Morrison, Barbara Owen-Jones, Lynne Payne, Marilyn Popp, Robin Ward, Chris Wilson, Zhang Yuhe and Zou Junyu is much appreciated. The contributions and facilities provided by the Australian National University, the Department of International Relations, the Australia Japan Research Centre and the Northeast Asia Program were also considerable. The assistance of the ANU Press Editorial Committee (Subsidy Group) is also gratefully acknowledged.

Foreword

I have long been concerned that we should be devoting more time and attention to the phenomenon of Taiwan and the implications of its emergence as one of Pacific Asia's newly industrialising economies. For the first time in this century, Taiwan finds itself in a position where it is able to enjoy constructive relations simultaneously with the three biggest powers in the Asia–Pacific region. At the same time, it continues to pose dilemmas for countries, especially for its regional neighbours, in balancing their relations with the Peoples' Republic of China (PRC) and Taiwan.

Gary Klintworth's detailed study of Taiwan is a substantial response to that concern and an important contribution to a greater understanding of where Taiwan fits in the geopolitical pattern of the region. The book follows a multidisciplinary approach to the subject. It examines the historical, economic, cultural, strategic and political forces that propelled Taiwan from obscurity to prominence as a rich, industrialised Chinese democracy. The analysis of Taiwan's unique relationship with Japan, China and the United States is particularly interesting and, in my view, original.

In a sense, Taiwan is drawing power from the point where the geopolitical interests of China, Japan and the United States intersect. One result is that, while the West is facilitating rapid political and social change in the PRC, an important contribution to those changes is being made through Taiwan. This has profound consequences for Taiwan and the development of a greater China. It foreshadows a new confidence and stability in Pacific Asia that has accompanied the withdrawal of the European powers from the region, and from China's doorstep in particular.

The book is the culmination of a major research effort over the period from 1989 to 1994 conducted under the auspices of the Northeast Asia

Program in the Research School of Pacific and Asian Studies at the Australian National University. It will, I am confident, make an important contribution to the study of how Taiwan arrived at what now seems to be its natural role — joining up with the mainland in the Asia–Pacific region whilst keeping the PLA at arm's length.

Stuart Harris,
Convenor,
Northeast Asia Program,
Research School of Pacific and Asian Studies,
Australian National University.

1 Introduction

Background

The confident, wealthy, modern, sometimes influential, often vulnerable island of Taiwan is emerging as the newest middle power in the Asia-Pacific region. Whether the yardstick is economic, military or diplomatic, it is difficult to ignore Taiwan's growing status as a significant force in the politics of the Asia-Pacific region. The Republic of China on Taiwan, as Taipei claims to be, is emerging as an independent regional actor after an ambiguous existence as a colony and a refuge for more than a century.

In the last twenty years, the world community has given little attention to Taiwan in terms of its claim to be the Republic of China. In fact, for most governments, it has been an established policy to avoid contact with the Republic of China, as Taiwan wanted to be known, in deference to the one China principle demanded by both Beijing and Taipei. In the last decade, however, Taiwan has given up any claim to represent mainland China and now demands recognition for what, in practical terms, it has become — an independent, sovereign Chinese state, recognisable in international law. Many countries privately feel that the time may be ripe for Taiwan to present itself as Taiwan — still Chinese, but culturally, economically, politically and physically separated from mainland China. Taiwan has established itself with an international identity as the Republic of China on Taiwan, a successful international trading nation that is as distinct from China as Singapore. Had Taiwan been located anywhere else in the world, it would have been entitled to (and there is little doubt that it would have been granted) recognition as the Republic of China on Taiwan.

But whether as the Republic of China on Taiwan, or as simply Taiwan or as part of some notion of one China, the island is being treated as an independent entity disconnected from the historical and cultural ties that many thought made it an integral part of mainland China. It has been rediscovered by governments, bankers, strategic analysts, aerospace corporations and international economists, as well as academics seeking confirmation of their theories on economic development and regime-change in newly industrialising economies.

It is not in the interests of any government in the Asia-Pacific region to maintain a hands-off policy towards Taiwan. Its geo-economic and cultural influence, its mainland China connections, its foreign exchange reserves, its strong defences and its record of successful trade-led economic development make it too important to ignore. Rather than being the Orphan Annie of the Asia-Pacific region, Taiwan is, so to speak, taking on the role of an orphan billionaire, getting richer, more popular and more influential as it dispenses portions of its wealth to countries in need and neighbours, including mainland China. Those countries which are too cautious in contacts with Taiwan may miss out on commercial opportunities and/or risk delays in investment projects and even cuts made to their quota of apples and beef.

It would seem that the main reason behind the dramatically revised world view of Taiwan is that Taiwan's economy literally took off. After 1953, Taiwan's GNP growth rates in real terms averaged around 9 per cent per annum, more than twice the rate for industrialised countries such as Japan, the United States, Canada, Sweden, Britain, Italy, France and Germany.[1] Today, Taiwan ranks 20th or 21st in the world in terms of GNP and twelfth in terms of world trade. For many countries, Taiwan is a more important trading partner than China.[2] By the end of the century, on present trends, Taiwan is likely to become one of the world's ten largest trading states.

Few countries can match Taiwan's record of sustained trade-led economic development, low unemployment, low rates of inflation, trade surpluses, low foreign debt, high savings and large foreign exchange reserves. High GNP growth rates have been accompanied by unusually equitable income distribution.[3] There have been heavy costs, including 40 years of martial law, clogged transport systems and a polluted environment. Nonetheless, Taiwan has developed from being a neglected Chinese island refuge, a Japanese colony and an American satellite into a leading industrialised economy. With Hong Kong, it has become a catalyst for change in China and for economic development in Southeast Asia. As the only example of a democratised industrialised Chinese society, many Chinese on both sides of the Strait see Taiwan as a model for the mainland under a non-communist system. Taiwan, in short, is a wealthy, dynamic, outward looking, internationalised economy.

As a successful economy, trading state and source of aid and investment funds, Taiwan has become a desirable member of international organisations dealing with copyright, trade and economic co-operation, including organisations or institutions like Asia-Pacific Economic Cooperation (APEC), GATT, the ADB, the OECD, the IMF, the UN's economic agencies and the South Pacific Forum. It is a prospective dialogue partner in the ASEAN Regional Forum and, indeed, in any regional economic or security mechanism that forms in the Asia-Pacific region, such as the East Asian Economic Caucus and the Conference on Security Cooperation in the Asia-Pacific (CSCAP). It is lobbying to become a member of the United Nations, although the route and Taiwan's nomenclature have yet to be determined.[4]

Ironically, the shift by the world community towards accepting and working with what is essentially a two Chinas solution to a one China policy coincides with growing economic and political linkages between Taiwan and the mainland. Complementarities between China and Taiwan have made them mutually important trading partners via trade through Hong Kong and direct Taiwanese investment in mainland enterprises. There are obvious benefits accruing to both sides from co-operation in other areas such as science and technology, law enforcement and transportation. One consequence of this is that Taiwan's separatist tendencies are being offset by the attractions of integration into some form of greater Chinese economic community. This issue is discussed further in Chapter 7.

The plunge into Hong Kong and southern China in the late-1980s is the third occasion in the last century that Taiwan's position between the three great Pacific powers of Japan, China and the United States has been adjusted. Taiwan broke away from China in 1895 and joined Japan. From 1950, Taiwan tilted towards the United States and then, from around 1986–87, it established commercial linkages with mainland China. Unlike the earlier positional shifts, Taiwan now finds itself located at a point almost equidistant between the three poles of gravity posed by Japan, China and the United States (see Figure 1). Previously, Taiwan had been pulled towards control or protection by one or the other of them and, until the late 1980s, was never in a position where it could exploit a relationship with all three at one and the same time.

I would argue that Taiwan's rise to prominence, and ultimately its move towards a kind of independence, can be seen as a long and complicated process deriving from the mix of historical, geographic, political and economic circumstances that have prevailed in the Western Pacific over the last few centuries. It was not simply a matter of the developments that occurred in East Asia or on Taiwan after 1950, such as the American intervention or the implementation of Sun Yatsenism.

Taiwan's break towards an independent existence of its own — neither Chinese, Japanese nor American, but thriving on the synergism generated by all three — is partly due to its location, its strong economy, its strong defences and its status as a world trader. It is also a consequence of the historical balance that has been struck between Japan, China and the

United States, the three greatest influences on the political economy of the Western Pacific, after two centuries of intense rivalry, war, readjustment and, finally, a strategic accommodation. The last-mentioned circumstance is due in part to the rejuvenation and modernisation of mainland China after 1949, the defeat of Japan in World War II and the post-Vietnam retreat of American military power from the Western Pacific.

Figure 1
The emergence of Taiwan:
The historical and strategic dimension 1895–1995

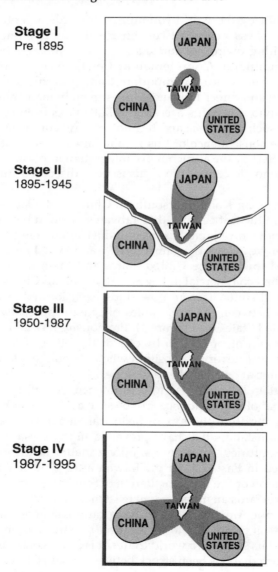

Before proceeding to discuss Taiwan's relationships with China, Japan and the United States, it may be useful to review Taiwan's history and geography. These factors go a long way towards explaining how and why the great powers of the Pacific took such a deep interest in Taiwan and how this interest then contributed to Taiwan's rapid economic development.

History

Before the late fifteenth century, Taiwan was seen as a no-man's land — almost *terra nullius* — waiting to be discovered and colonised. While it may not have been ignored altogether by successive Chinese dynasties, there are very few references to Taiwan in official Chinese historical sources except as an island occupied by 'barbarians'.[5] Some Chinese are reputed to have moved to Taiwan as early as the Sui dynasty (AD 581–618). But there were only a few Chinese expeditions to Taiwan between the seventh and fourteenth centuries and the Chinese made no effort to establish permanent settlements.[6] Recent authoritative studies confirm that Taiwan was not associated with traditional Chinese territory in any formal way until the Ch'ing dynasty and the claim that Taiwan was part of 'the sacred territory of China since ancient times' is difficult to sustain.[7]

Taiwan was inhabited by head-hunting aboriginal tribes of uncertain origin. Their descendants today inhabit the remote mountain regions of Taiwan and number about 350 000, or less than 2 per cent of the total population of 21 million.[8] Recent archaeological research points to a Stone Age culture in Taiwan while other evidence suggests the aborigines of Taiwan were closely related to the people of mainland China.[9] Physically and linguistically, however, the aborigines resemble the Malays from Southeast Asia.[10] They were essentially food-gatherers and hunters, but practised a rudimentary form of agriculture.[11]

The first significant influx of foreign settlers arrived on Taiwan in the late fifteenth to early sixteenth centuries. They were landless adventurers and fugitives from the mainland or pirate traders from Japan and China. These early pirates, in fact, pioneered Taiwan's later role as a centre of regional trade: their ships visited Borneo, Malacca, Annam, Siam, Tonkin, Cambodia and the Philippines.[12]

The Chinese and Japanese were followed by European traders. En route to establishing a presence in Macau in the 1550s, the Portugese paused long enough to call the island Formosa, a name that remained in common use until the mid-twentieth century.[13] In 1598, Japan's Tokugawa shogunate attempted to conquer the island (as well as Korea).[14] Further attempts to bring Taiwan under Japanese rule were made in 1609, 1616 and 1628.[15] Thereafter, the Japanese did not again seek control of Taiwan until the late nineteenth century.

Taiwan, according to a recent study, remained unclaimed by China throughout this period: the Pescadores, and not Taiwan, were administered by authorities in Fujian.[16] In 1623, local Chinese authorities in Fujian offered to cede Taiwan to the Dutch provided they withdrew from the Pescadores in the Taiwan Strait.[17] The Dutch agreed and moved to Taiwan in August 1624.[18] The Chinese population on the island then numbered around 25 000, with perhaps several hundred Japanese. They were outnumbered by a population of around 70 000 aborigines. In 1626, the Spaniards arrived and built a trading base in Keelung in northern Taiwan. King Philip IV issued a decree on 2 October 1627 declaring that Taiwan belonged to Spain. The Spanish, however, were evicted by the Dutch in 1642.

The Dutch East India Company built fortifications at Zeelandia, near present-day Tainan in southwest Taiwan, and ruled Taiwan until January 1662. European administration on Taiwan attracted a steady influx of Chinese immigrants.[19] This period became what George Kerr described as Formosa's relatively prosperous 'European half century'.[20] Foreshadowing the island's pivotal trading role after World War II, Dutch-ruled Taiwan became a profitable base for regional trading operations by Chinese, Japanese and Europeans.[21] Taiwan in fact became one of the most lucrative Asian colonies for the Dutch East India Company, partly from taxes on the local Chinese population and partly from exporting Chinese porcelain to Europe and exchanging Chinese silk for Japanese silver at Nagasaki.[22] At the height of their rule in 1650, the Dutch East India Company employed 1800 Dutch personnel and 2000 soldiers at Zeelandia.[23] They exercised jurisdiction over almost 300 villages, including some on the remote east coast.[24] Taiwan's Chinese population, then numbering around 100 000, was mostly employed growing sugar cane for export by the Dutch to Persia.[25] Taiwan might have remained a Dutch colony if the Dutch had not been so preoccupied with maximising their profits that they 'refused to expend the money necessary to make themselves secure against a Chinese invasion'.[26]

In 1644, Beijing fell to the Ch'ing and the Ming government fled south. Cheng Ch'eng-kung (Koxinga), a Ming loyalist, took Formosa from the Dutch in 1662 as part of his resistance strategy. The Cheng treated the island as a military colony and, like the Kuomintang during their takeover of Taiwan after World War II, were fairly ruthless towards the local Taiwanese.[27] According to William Limbrey, an English trader who visited the island in 1672:

> the people were generally poor and discontented and kept in subjection by a high hand; they (i.e. the Cheng) came here only with swords in their hands to conquer and mouths to devour other men's labour.[28]

In 1682, the Cheng and most of Taiwan's population of around 200 000 surrendered to Ch'ing Manchu rule.[29] However, many thousands of Ming loyalists fled to Dutch-ruled Batavia near Jakarta.[30]

Taiwan became a prefecture of Fujian province with its capital at Tainan. However, the Manchu were an inland people, and, unlike the Ming, they had little knowledge of or interest in the sea and its potential.[31] Taiwan was 'a trifling place — taking it would add nothing, relinquishing it would not be a loss', according to the Ch'ing Emperor K'ang Hsi.[32] Indeed, the only reason the Ch'ing attacked Taiwan was to eliminate the anti-Ch'ing Ming loyalists.[33] Thereafter, immigration from the mainland to Taiwan was prohibited and the extent of Ch'ing adminstrative control on Taiwan was less than what it had been under the Ch'eng.[34] For the next two centuries, Taiwan remained a static, often rebellious, Chinese peasant society consisting of a series of rather isolated towns and villages that maintained better links with the mainland across the Taiwan Strait than with each other.[35] Neglected by Beijing, Taiwan wallowed along as a lawless frontierland.[36] Poor Chinese migrants continued to trickle across the Strait from Fujian and Guangdong. The island became 'an abode for a race of outlaws — thieves, swindlers and murderers who had been forced to fly from the [mainland]'.[37] Most smoked opium.[38] They pushed the aboriginal peoples off the arable lowlands and fought with them in a pattern of intermittent, brutal warfare similar to that waged by whites against Indians in America's Wild West.[39] Shipwrecked Japanese and European sailors were usually killed. With Ch'ing China weakened by dynastic decay, Taiwan was ripe for seizure by Japan or a European power wanting to protect its nationals or establish an East Asian trading base.

In 1855 American traders established a stockade at Kaohsiung and ran up the American flag.[40] When China was defeated by an Anglo-French army in 1858, Anping (near Tainan) was opened up as a treaty port to Western traders and missionaries under the terms of the Treaty of Tientsin.[41] Another port at Tamsui (near Taipei) was opened under the Treaty of Peking in 1860. In 1863, Keelung and Takao (present-day Kaohsiung) were opened.[42] In 1884–85, the French attempted to seize control of Keelung, known for its high-grade coal deposits.[43] At around the same time, Germany contemplated the occupation of Taiwan, but chose instead Shantung on the mainland.[44]

Meanwhile, Meiji Japan was beginning to emerge as an expansionist Asian power intent on acquiring an overseas empire. Japan had plans to occupy the eastern half of Taiwan in 1874 and in 1884 it contemplated seizing Taiwan and half of Fujian province.[45]

Such attention awakened Beijing to Taiwan's strategic importance. Taiwan was made an autonomous province in 1887. The newly appointed governor, Liu Ming-ch'uan, set about strengthening the island's defences. He built schools, reformed the tax system and set up government bureaus to control the camphor, salt, sulphur and coal industries.[46] Liu introduced a Western-style postal system and had a cable laid between the island and the mainland.[47] Rail and port facilities were built.[48] Electric lighting, a sewer and public baths were built in Taipei, making it 'a model city'.[49] However, progress ceased in 1891 when

Liu was forced to resign.[50] Economically, the island was still a backward traditional agricultural society.[51] The population was then between 2.5 and 3 million, mainly Chinese peasant farmers and aborigines.[52]

In 1892 the American Consul, James W. Davidson, described Taiwan as 'a land of tea, camphor, savages and fever'.[53] Two years later, in 1894, China went to war with Japan and was defeated. Under the terms of the 1895 Treaty of Shimonoseki, Taiwan and the Pescadores were ceded to Japan.

Geography and location

Taiwan's history in the crossfire or interface of Chinese, European and Japanese imperial interest and its later period of modern economic development owes much to its island geography, its physical size and its location (see Figure 2). It is located close to Japan, the industrialising pioneer of Northeast Asia, and it is close to China, the country with the most conservative civilisation and the biggest population in the Asia-Pacific. Taiwan would never have become a powerful economic entity if it had not been located close to the central coastal provinces of China, the point where the Pacific interests of Japan, China and the United States intersect.[54] Nor would it have become rich and successful had it fallen under direct mainland Chinese control.

Adjacent to China, Taiwan's history, traditions, culture, language, racial origins, politics and security have been very much bound up with the course of events on the mainland. It is on that basis that Taiwan was and is assumed to be Chinese and therefore part of China. However, the Taiwan Strait, 142 kilometres wide at its narrowest point, has served as a moat that has shielded and separated Taiwan from the mainland, like the Channel that protected England from Napoleon and Hitler. Historically, the strong sea currents in the Taiwan Strait and the steep sea cliffs on the east made access to Taiwan difficult. This sea barrier has contributed to an ambiguity about Taiwan's precise status that is the basis of Taipei's bid for membership of the United Nations today.[55]

Taiwan's small size was conducive to economic reform.[56] Taiwan is a small island with an area of 35 751 square kilometres, about 0.375 per cent of the size of the mainland. Strong central government was easily applied in Taiwan because it was a 'tight little isle', small and hence easier to manage and control than the diversity of mainland China or sprawling archipelagoes like the Philippines and Indonesia.[57] Moreover, a small compact island like Taiwan can reap disproportionate benefits from an efficient transportation system. Taiwan's transport infrastructure, first built by the Japanese, has been constantly improved and expanded by the Taiwanese. As Adam Smith observed, fast, cheap and efficient transport systems are essential for rapid economic development.[58] By the mid-1980s the island was served by an integrated transport complex of all-weather roads and highways, rail linkages, ports, airports and mass transit facilities — all of which are being further modernised and upgraded.

Taiwan's small size and its refurbished transport network contributed to the decentralisation of industry and this in turn contributed to a relatively equitable distribution of the fruits of modernisation throughout rural Taiwan. Rural-based industries absorbed surplus farm labour and offered seasonal or part-time jobs, improving the income of farmers.[59] At the same time, industry decentralisation has kept labour costs down and minimised the high social and economic costs of urbanisation.[60] Ranis describes the dispersed rural character of Taiwan's industrialisation as a case of 'developing agriculture by means of industry and fostering industry by virtue of agriculture'.[61] It was, he claims, one of the keys to Taiwan's successful growth and export substitution performance.[62]

Figure 2
Taiwan: In the centre of the Asia-Pacific region

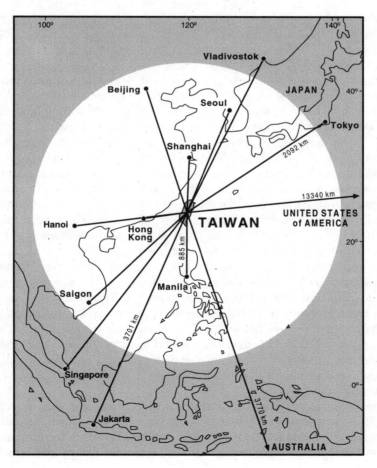

Small size and surrounding water barriers also make Taiwan militarily defensible. The administrative area of Taiwan includes several smaller islands including Quemoy (146 square kilometres) and Matsu (both within artillery range of the mainland), the Pescadores (a group of islands 40 kilometres off the west coast of Taiwan), the Pratas group (near Hong Kong) and the disputed Spratlys in the South China Sea. With the Tiaoyutais (Senkakus) in the East China Sea (between Taiwan and Japan), these offshore islands give the Chinese on both sides of the Strait a shared interest in the notion of a greater China encompassing the mainland and its maritime approaches.

Topographically, Taiwan is divided into two parts. The arable lowland on the west coast (23 per cent of the total area) was the first destination of Chinese boat people migrating from the mainland. Taiwan has a warm, sub-tropical climate with a long hot summer and a short mild winter that made it conducive to self-sufficiency in rice and agricultural products such as sugar, pineapples, bananas and tea.[63] With intensive irrigation, scientific management and heavy use of chemical fertilisers, Taiwan's lowlands could provide substantial surpluses of food and agricultural products. Most Taiwanese (presently 21 million, or less than 2 per cent of the mainland's 1.2 billion people) live on the western side of Taiwan in densities surpassed by few countries.

Taiwan's east coast is screened from the west — and hence from China — by the Central Mountain Range, a north–south ridge containing many peaks over 3000 metres, with Mount Yushan (3950 metres) the highest in East Asia.[64] The eastern two-thirds of Taiwan consist of mainly mountainous terrain covered by forests. These forests became the retreat of aborigines pushed out of the lowlands by incoming Chinese in the seventeenth to nineteenth centuries. The shoreline on Taiwan's east coast features steep sea cliffs, amongst the highest in the world, with no natural harbours and no shallow beaches that might be suitable for an amphibious landing.[65] It is not surprising, therefore, that Taiwan's most important airbase for dealing with a mainland attack has been built into the mountainside on Taiwan's northeast coast (near Hualien).

As an island a few hours by sea from the mainland, yet safely beyond the immediate reach of mainland authority, Taiwan was a natural refuge for pirates, landless peasants and those who had lost their mandate to rule on the mainland. In 1949, refuge on Taiwan was the only option other than surrender for Chiang Kai-shek's defeated Kuomintang forces. Equally, however, Taiwan provided an island bastion where losers on the mainland might retreat, recuperate and dream of a counter-attack.[66] Taiwan's island character and location made it an ideal launch pad for regional military operations.

Given Taiwan's geographic centrality in East Asia and the Western Pacific, it is not surprising that possession of it was, until recently, strenuously contested by the big Pacific powers. Taiwan's location as a platform for regional trade and a stepping stone for forays into Southeast Asia and the China coast made it a valuable prize for great powers competing against each other in the Western Pacific. Its small size was an advantage because it made it relatively easier to snatch away from the mainland. Comparable islands like Sri Lanka and Hainan lack Taiwan's special geographical and cultural attributes: Taiwan is on the doorstep of China and Japan; it is inhabited by Chinese; like Hong Kong and Singapore, it is located at a maritime crossroads; it absorbed great waves of foreign influence and, because of its strategic importance, it became the receptacle for large amounts of United States and Japanese economic aid.

As a small defensible island, centrally located in East Asia and agriculturally self-sufficient, Taiwan was destined to become a colony, a stopping place, a trading base and a military outpost for the Spanish, the Dutch, the English, the Japanese and the Americans.

As a Japanese colony, Taiwan was a support and resupply base for Japanese armies in Southeast Asia, mainland China and the South Pacific during World War II. Japanese-built naval bases at Kaohsiung and Keelung and airfields on the western plain provided the jumping-off places for Japanese attacks on the Philippines and the Dutch East Indies in 1941.[67] Taiwan was an important staging area for supplying and processing industrial materials for the 'immense Japanese military drive into South Asia and Indonesia, towards India and towards Australia' during the Pacific War.[68] After 1950, Taiwan became 'an unsinkable aircraft carrier' in the United States strategy to attack, deter and then contain Chinese communism. As a discrete, defensible piece of territory close to the mainland, Taiwan became an important link in America's Pacific perimeter that stretched around mainland China from South Korea through Japan to the Philippines, South Vietnam and Australia.

Another more recent metaphor about the island is that it has become a beacon lighting up the contrast between Taiwan's capitalist modernisation experience and the socialism of mainland China. In this modern guise, Taiwan has combined several of its former roles as an outpost, a bastion, a launch pad, a place beyond Beijing's grasp, and yet a place that is able to influence developments on the mainland precisely because it is Chinese, because of its proximity to the mainland and because it has critical Japanese and American support.

As an island surrounded by seas, Taiwan is insulated and separate from the Chinese mainland. The seas, however, also served to connect Taiwan to the wider world. Like Hainan island and Xinjiang, Taiwan was able to escape Beijing's bureaucratic centralism because of its distance from the centre. Historically, it has been one of the few parts of the Chinese empire that enjoyed the freedom to rebel, to experiment, to innovate and to interact with the rest of the world. As an island, Taiwan has had even greater exposure to the West than historically independent provinces in China's south, such as Guangdong and Fujian.

China is traditionally regarded as the Middle Kingdom of the Western Pacific. But Taiwan is even more centrally located when it comes to dealing with the Asia-Pacific's Chinese community on the mainland, in Hong Kong, in North America, in Indochina and in Southeast Asia. Taiwan is located midway between Northeast and Southeast Asia. It is adjacent to the richest coastal provinces of the China mainland. It is 142 kilometres by sea from Fujian, 600 kilometres from Hong Kong, 1216 kilometres from South Korea, 1400 kilometres from Vietnam, 1150 kilometres from Japan and 370 kilometres from the Philippines. It is a natural stopping place on the way to and from Hong Kong and China. It straddles the maritime crossroads between North America and East Asia, and between Northeast Asia and Southeast Asia. It is, as Michael Handels puts it, located 'on a strategic highway for great powers on the march', which for Taiwan, as for other small powers, means there are great benefits as well as liabilities.[69]

Taiwan's comparative advantage over other nations of a similar physical size is based on this duality of easy access to the sea and pivotal location in East Asia, advantages that have been compounded by Taiwan's impressive technical and financial resources. Federal Express Asia wants to turn Taiwan into its regional air cargo transport hub.[70] Not surprisingly, the biggest container shipping company in the world, the Evergreen Line, is Taiwanese and leading parcel delivery companies like DHL, TNT, Federal Express and United Parcel Service all have regional headquarters in Taipei. Companies such as McDonnell Douglas, Boeing, British Aerospace, Westinghouse, Aerospatiale, Rolls Royce, Pratt and Whitney, General Dynamics, Hughes Aircraft and Airbus Industries are establishing footholds in Taiwan as a regional base for tapping the growing East Asian aerospace market. Microsoft chose Taiwan as its headquarters for forays into China and the East Asian region.

Historically, however, Taiwan's location and its island character made it, like Hong Kong, a disposable piece of territory whenever the central government in Beijing came under pressure from predatory states. It was, in relative terms, a long way from the Forbidden City and became a territory of national importance on only two or three occasions totalling less than a few decades during the course of the last several centuries. When Taiwan was taken by the Dutch in the mid-seventeenth century, it was beyond the reach and interest of Beijing. It might have remained a Dutch colony and followed the route to independence of other Dutch colonies, such as Indonesia, had it not become a base for rebel Ming forces challenging the legitimacy of the Ching dynasty. Beijing took a brief interest in Taiwan in the late 1880s when it was about to be lost to Japan. After 1895, Taiwan was lost to China until 1945 and even then it remained of peripheral interest to the protagonists on the mainland until it became the refuge of a Nationalist government that dared to challenge the legitimacy of Mao's new China.

Disposition after World War II

Before proceeding to examine the external and domestic factors that created modern Taiwan, we should note Taiwan's disposition in the aftermath of World War II as this has a bearing on the choices open to Taiwan, on relations between Taiwan and the mainland and on Taiwan's international legal status.

Taiwan was destined to be returned to China after World War II, under the terms of the Cairo Declaration of 1943 and the Potsdam Proclamation of 1945 whereby China, Britain, the United States and the Soviet Union agreed that 'all the territories Japan had stolen from the Chinese, such as Manchuria, Formosa and the Pescadores, shall be returned to the Republic of China'.[71]

After Japan's surrender in September 1945, the Taiwanese initially welcomed the return of Taiwan to China 'with great enthusiasm'.[72] The Taiwanese, however, were soon in open revolt against a mainland administration characterised by corruption and violence.[73] Nationalist officials allegedly behaved like carpetbaggers 'occupying enemy territory'.[74] The Governor, Chen Yi, systematically plundered Taiwan. Junks left the former Japanese colony every day loaded with food, scrap metal, machine tools, consumer goods and other booty seized for sale on the mainland.[75] Taiwan's problems in the late 1940s were compounded by 'a vicious whirlpool of circumstances' that included a war-damaged economy, obsolete machinery, no fertiliser for agriculture, a loss of markets in Japan, a lack of foreign exchange and a breakdown in health and education services.[76] Inflation reached 10 000 per cent between October 1945 and December 1946, with food shortages which had never occurred in all the 50 years of Japanese rule.[77]

Before long, unrest and resentment led to demands that the 'Chinese go home' and agitation for a 'Formosa for the Formosans'.[78] A minor incident on 28 February 1947 flared into an open revolt with the Taiwanese seizing control of the island's nine largest cities.[79] Martial law was imposed and ruthlessly enforced.[80] Estimates of the number of Taiwanese killed or executed range between 10 000 and 20 000 in what was alleged to have been 'a systematic effort . . . to eliminate the principal native leaders' on Taiwan.[81] While these massacres destroyed trust between the mainlanders and the Taiwanese, they also eliminated any potential opposition to the mainland regime. With no local ties or loyalties, the Kuomintang administration was unchallenged in the exercise of its authority over Taiwan, its land and resources and the population.

Taiwan's 1945 population of about 5 million was swollen to over 7 million by 1949 with the addition of almost 2 million Kuomintang refugees.[82] Despite the accompanying disorganisation and demoralisation, the influx included an army of 500 000 and a professional technocratic elite of over 200 000 that brought with it all the mainland's gold reserves and many of its art treasures and valuables.[83] According to Gustav Ranis, these not-so-ordinary refugees filled the gaps left by the Japanese in economic management and internal security and were to prove essential for Taiwan's later reconstruction.[84]

However, by 1949, Taiwan was on the verge of falling under the direct administrative authority of Beijing for the first time since 1887. The United States, the only Pacific power in a position to determine Taiwan's future, was inclined to abandon the island to Mao Zedong. But after the start of the Korean War on 25 June 1950, the United States reversed its hands-off policy. Taiwan, under threat of amphibious assault by PLA forces, was pulled inside the American defence perimeter. Because of its unique central location close to the East China coast and because it was occupied by vehemently anti-communist forces, Taiwan became a logical part of America's anti-China policy.

The Americans began to build on the foundations established by the Japanese in the preceding half-century. Massive aid, philosophical advice, rich markets and protection by the United States ensured that Taiwan not only recovered from World War II but went on to prosper on two fronts — as a rapidly developing internationalised economy and as a modern, Westernised society. Both trends served to weaken Kuomintang nostalgia for the mainland and any hopes it held of achieving one China.

We can say, therefore, that Taiwan has been under the effective administrative control of a government in Beijing for no more than one or two decades in the last several centuries. Taiwan was China's for a few years in the 1660s and from 1887 to 1891. For most of the rest of its time in modern history, Taiwan was controlled by the Dutch, the Japanese or the Americans, or largely neglected by the mainland Chinese. Put another way, Taiwan drifted away from or was removed from the gravitational pull of China in four historical periods: 1624–62, before 1887, between 1895 and 1945, and from 1949 up to the present.

Thus disentangling China, or at least giving it roughly the same weight as the influences exerted by Japan and the West, Taiwan's economic, social and political development might be divided up as follows:

- **Pre-1624** — Taiwan was *terra nullius* or at most a frontier land, inhabited mainly by aborigines.
- **From 1624 to 1662** — Taiwan was controlled and exploited by European trading companies.
- **From 1662 to 1894** — China exercised perfunctory control over the lowlands of Taiwan.
- **From 1895 to 1945** — Japan exercised exclusive and effective political and economic control over a predominantly Chinese-populated Taiwan.
- **From 1945 to 1949** — Taiwan was treated as conquered territory by the Kuomintang.

- **From 1950 to 1972** — Taiwan was dominated by the United States. It rebuilt its economic links with Japan but remained cut off from China.
- **After 1972** — An isolated Republic of China adapted to its status as the Republic of China on Taiwan.
- **From the late 1980s** — Taiwan improved relations with China, and maximised its importance to the three big Pacific powers.

Viewed from this perspective, Taiwan's debut as the Republic of China on Taiwan in the 1990s can be seen as the culmination of four centuries of frequently turbulent history, sometimes as a frontierland, a colony, a fortress, an island retreat and an aid recipient, together with a century of intense state-managed economic development. The Chinese were important, but so too were the Japanese and the Europeans.

From an historical viewpoint, therefore, Taiwan's development as a modern Chinese state has been very much determined by its character as an island territory and its location in the centre of a triangle formed by China to the west, Japan to the north and the United States to the east.

Like Hong Kong, Taiwan is, in a sense, too close to China and is therefore vulnerable to its moods and responses to external pressure. On the other hand, much of Taiwan's postwar success and its future prospects can be attributed to this very proximity. Taiwan derives power and influence, both economic and strategic, from being close to China. It is sufficiently distant to be out of artillery range, yet it is close enough to serve as an important military base or as a trading place, or to fill both roles simultaneously if necessary. It has strong family connections with China, a country that on present trends is forecast to become the Pacific region's third economic locomotive and the world's next superpower. At the same time, Taiwan retains close economic, historical and cultural links with Japan and the United States — the current locomotives of the Pacific economy, and, over the last century, the two leading military powers in Pacific Asia. Taiwan is strategically important to both Japan and the United States precisely because of its influential yet independent role near the China mainland.

In the past, China, Japan and the United States were often fierce rivals for power and influence in the Western Pacific around Taiwan. Sometimes they have been at war with each other; sometimes two of them have been allies against the third. Consequently, the fortunes of Taiwan, a small vulnerable island territory, oscillated back and forth at the interface of the triangular dynamics of trade, rivalry and tension between China, Japan and the United States (see Figure 1, p. 4). As a small island territory, Taiwan became the centre of a contest between China and Japan in the late nineteenth century. It was a pawn in World War II when the United States and China were allied against Japan. And American possession of Taiwan was contested by China during the Taiwan Straits crises of 1954, 1958 and 1962. But Taiwan's location in the

centre of the triangle sometimes offered opportunities to exercise disproportionate leverage, as in the 1950s when tension between China
and the United States was high. Conversely, there were dangers when
tension was replaced by a rapprochement, as occurred between China
and the United States following President Nixon's visit to Beijing in
1972. For Taiwan, peace, prosperity, security and independence only
evolved after China, Japan and the United States each adjusted to the
reality and power of the other two.

In other words, Taiwan's historical trajectory has not been an aimless
one. It was almost destined to evolve into an independent, influential,
secure and wealthy island power for the last few centuries precisely
because of its location between the three dominant Pacific powers. If it
has moved closer to the best position for a small state in such a great
power triangle, it is because Japan, China and the United States have
each pulled back from contesting the claims to Taiwan of the other two.
All three powers seem satisfied with the current power balance around
Taiwan, at least for the time being (see Figure 1, p. 4).

This has left Taiwan in the middle with room to manoeuvre and enjoy
the fruits of its geographic location and the advantages of a simultaneous
relationship with the three most important powers in the Pacific. Taiwan,
in a sense, lies at the apex of a triangular dynamic created by the interaction of China, Japan and the United States. The triangle is presently in
equilibrium because none of the three players is in a position to dominate
the other two, either singly or in alliance with one of the others. All three,
therefore, are in a sense donating power to the point where their interests
intersect in East Asia (i.e. off the China coast at roughly the point where
Taiwan, Shanghai and Hong Kong are located). Taiwan has an advantage
over Hong Kong in this regard because it is beyond the control of Beijing,
whereas Hong Kong is overshadowed by 1997 while Shanghai has yet to
loosen the grip of Beijing.

Taiwan's history as a small state caught between the three great
Pacific powers has been and remains complicated by China's territorial
claims to Taiwan, Japan's economic stake, the American strategic interest and Taiwanese nationalism. The underlying trend, however, is for
Taiwan to consolidate its independence from the mainland by drawing
on its connections with two corners of the triangle — the United States
and Japan — while increasing its economic and even political exchanges
with mainland China in the third corner. In fact, Taiwan's independence
from mainland China has been facilitated by Taipei's willingness to
develop a new relationship with the mainland. Ironically, the cumulative effect — whether by design or by accident — is to strengthen
Taiwan's negotiating position in the event of reunification with China. It
is doing this in two ways: first, Taiwan is becoming stronger and more
influential in the international arena; and second, Taiwan is hastening
the process of social and political change on the mainland. These themes
are examined in Chapter 9.

Waves of civilisation

Explanations of Taiwan's success have tended to concentrate on domestic political factors, the role of government or economic factors, and most notably land reform.[85] I would argue, however, that the cultural, economic, political and strategic influence of China, Japan and the West have been just as important, if not more so.

Taiwan's ethnic and cultural base is Chinese, formed after several centuries of haphazard Chinese migration across the Taiwan Strait, mainly from Fujian province. The Taiwanese are a composite of the descendants of these migrant-refugees and an additional two million or more who arrived in a mass exodus in the years 1945–49. They form an underlay of 'Chineseness' that is an essential part of Taiwan's modernisation formula. The significance of this Chinese underlay on Taiwan's character and development is examined in Chapter 4.

As well as its basic 'Chineseness', Taiwan has been exposed to two additional overlays. There was a 50-year period of Japanese colonialism, infrastructural development and cultural influence from 1895 to 1945. Japanese colonial rule fertilised Taiwan's roots as a society and state beyond the grip of mainland China. It was a period when the Taiwanese, taught to speak and think like Japanese, worked and produced for the Japanese market. This overlay is examined in Chapter 2.

Then, for two decades or so from 1950 to the 1970s, Taiwan's Sino-Japanese heritage was subjected to the intense cultural influences that accompanied United States-led reconstruction and direction of the island's economy and its future. American domination of Taiwan was important not only because the United States was a rich and powerful benefactor, but also because it followed closely on the heels of Taiwan's Japanese period. United States domination of Taiwan provided the island with a second consecutive period of exposure to non-Chinese ways of economic development, business management and reform. Taiwan's American interlude and its continuing significance are examined in Chapter 3.

Given the advantages of its location, and the addition of these three cumulative waves of foreign economic and cultural influence, management, aid and protection, Taiwan's rise as a successful internationalised trading post in East Asia can be seen as just a matter of time. Each wave left the Taiwanese with a distinctive cumulative legacy so that today the island retains its predominantly Chinese roots and a smattering of its Japanese heritage. At the same time, it has been Westernised to a degree matched only by Hong Kong and Singapore.

These layers of foreign influence were capped by an evolving Taiwanese style of government. It was an amalgam of Chinese authoritarianism, Kuomintang ideology, the trauma of Chiang Kai-shek's mainland failure and the spur of the PLA threat. Martial law was imposed after World War II and remained in place until 1987. It guaranteed political stability and strong government, thereby underpinning Taiwan's economic recovery and its subsequent economic growth. In the 1970s, Taiwan's economic growth accelerated at the same time as its international diplomatic support collapsed. This forced the Kuomintang to adapt to strategic realities. Taiwan's separate Taiwanese identity was almost ready to be unveiled. It simply awaited a Kuomintang leadership transition, more flexible domestic and external policies and the end of the mainland's threat to use force to achieve reunification.

By the mid-1980s the Kuomintang had decided on a major course correction with profound implications for the conduct of Taiwan's foreign policy, its relations with the mainland and domestic politics. One consequence was the willingness of the Taiwanese to research their historical roots and investigate their Eurasian heritage. There was a growing interest in Taiwan's non-Chinese history, its architecture, the culture of the indigenous people and Taiwanese art and literature. A recent major study on Taiwan's history referred to 'a powerful burgeoning of native consciousness in Taiwan'.[86] Taiwanese writers are beginning to deny that Taiwanese literature is simply a branch of mainland Chinese literature. According to Taiwanese literary critic Yeh Shih-tao, Taiwan's culture stems from the mainland in terms of geographical and blood ties, but the cultural influences that the island received from the Spanish, the Dutch, the Japanese and other settlers formed 'a unique cultural system'.[87]

Contemporary Taiwan

Taiwan is still a small, vulnerable state. It is not a member of any military alliance system or of any significant regional political organisation other than the Asia-Pacific Economic Community (APEC). It lacks formal diplomatic relations with all countries in the Asia-Pacific region apart from a few South Pacific states that are hard to find on a map of the world.[88]

However, orthodox political diplomacy, alliance relationships and simple military might are not the only means for exercising national power and influence in Asia. Taiwan has impressive military capabilities (discussed in Chapter 8) and it retains informal defence ties with the United States through the *Taiwan Relations Act* of 1979.[89] In addition, however, Taiwan is one of the best equipped actors in the Asia-Pacific region if the definition of security and state power is broadened to include such measures as technology, capital, marketing skills, business acumen and access to regional networks.[90]

As a world trading economy with a large infrastructural development budget, a large domestic consumer market and plenty of surplus capital, Taiwan has developed into one of the most influential small states in a region where 'the name of the game is economics'.[91] This strength is reinforced by Taiwan's location next to China and by important economic and leadership relationships with Japan and the United States. Being wealthy, well-educated and Chinese, the Taiwanese have the additional advantage of being able to exploit personal or family connections amongst the over-seas Chinese in government, banks, business and academia in Hong Kong, Indochina and Southeast Asia. Being Chinese gives Taiwan access to levers of political influence at critical points in government in Southeast Asia and on the mainland. That translates into an important commerical advantage over competitors from Japan, South Korea and the rest of the world. These commercial and cultural channels of communication are in many ways more practical and effective in the business of trade, market-ing and investment than the embassies and consulates that are used by non-Chinese actors. Indeed, the lack of formal diplomatic relations with the rest of the world has honed Taiwan's survival skills and made it adept at analysing technical knowledge and exploiting market trends through semi-official commercial offices in capitals around the world.

As a leading world trading economy, Taiwan is a logical member of the GATT, the ASEAN Regional Forum, the OECD and ultimately the United Nations. It was a natural and desirable candidate for membership in Asia-Pacific Economic Cooperation once that forum was established in 1989. By the 1990s, Taiwan was seen to be too central in the Asia-Pacific region and too critically important in the greater China context to remain on the sidelines. Taiwan's debut as the Republic of China on Taiwan is partly a consequence of Beijing's acquiescence in a practical approach to the one China principle. The struggle between Beijing and Taipei over the last four decades, like the confrontation between Seoul and Pyongyang on the Korean peninsula, has produced a political stalemate in which both sides accept the existence, if not the de facto legitimacy, of the other. China has been less hard-nosed about Taiwan in international forums; Taiwan has ceased to regard the Chinese Communist Party as a rebel regime. Both are willing to trade and look for mutually beneficial eco-nomic solutions. The new Sino-Taiwanese detente was symbolised by the historic meeting between China's Association for Relations Across the Taiwan Straits and Taiwan's Straits Exchange Foundation in Singapore in April 1993. The net result has been that lines drawn between the two sides during the Cold War have become more or less fixed — in effect, they have become new international boundaries between two Chinas.

Taiwan's separateness has been strengthened by the end of Cold War tensions in East Asia, the consequent decline in the strategic importance of China and the contrast between Taiwan's domestic political reforms and the bloody events in Beijing in June 1989. These events coincided with the worldwide economic slump of the late 1980s and the lure of Taipei's announcement in 1989 of a six-year infrastructure development plan worth US$300 million (since cut by 22 per cent). Coincidentally, looming unemployment in the arms industries of Europe and the United States helped clear the way for lifting controversial bans on sales to Taiwan of modern fighter aircraft, warships and possibly submarines. Taiwan's international status has been further enhanced by the limits to state sover-eignty imposed by changing attitudes towards such principles as the uni-versality of human rights and the right of people to self-determination.

Taiwan is not governed by Beijing, nor is it a province of mainland China. It is physically much further away from the mainland than Hong Kong, although it is not as far from China as Singapore. Is Taiwan a Chinese island state like Singapore? Or is it part of China, like Hong Kong? Is it part of one China in which there are two political systems and several governments in Macao, Hong Kong, Beijing and Taipei? Or is it an undefined entity that is both state-like and a non-state, both Chinese and Westernised, both independent from China while nominally part of it? Should it be part of a greater China? Should it be the Republic of Taiwan or the Republic of China on Taiwan? The question is, does it matter? The categorisation of Taiwan as a state, a province of China, an economy or an entity has become a matter of diminished importance in the age of geo-economics. Indeed, one could argue that any attempt to sharply define Taiwan's status and identity would jeopardise its immediate national interests. Taiwan's survival depends, for the time being, on preserving the ambiguity of its status. Besides, Taiwan, China and the international community have been able to defer making a judgment because flexible arrangements, such as those practised in APEC and the PECC, have been devised and accepted by the regional Asia-Pacific community to overcome barriers imposed by state-based diplomatic protocol.

While Taiwan is a Chinese place, it has a Taiwanese identity that is distinct and separate from the mainland. It is an identity that makes Taiwan an international trading state and an international economic entity. Yet, even as Taiwan drifts towards a kind of ambiguous, independent status — one accepted in Taiwan, internationally and, arguably, in Beijing as well — the island's economic ties with mainland China are growing closer.

Which trend will predominate in the end? This question might be better put another way, given that mainland China's 'socialism with Chinese characteristics' is making the mainland more and more like Taiwan. Economically, socially and politically, southern China is becoming indistinguishable from Hong Kong and Taiwan. In other words, the attraction and proven success of the Taiwanese model is slowly but inexorably transforming the mainland. The question about Taiwan's future, therefore, might be posed in terms of the Taiwanisation of Chinese communism. That is, can China be reunified with Taiwan on Taiwanese terms? Is Taiwan's past likely to become China's future? The answer to this question will be discussed more fully in Chapter 7.

Notes

1   Shirley W.Y. Kuo, Gustav Ranis and John C.H. Fei, *The Taiwan Success Story*, Westview, Boulder, 1981, p. 9.

2   In 1991, Britain, Holland, Japan, the United States, Australia, India, Fiji, Indonesia, Malaysia, South Korea, Thailand, Singapore, New Zealand, the Philippines and Brunei conducted more trade with Taiwan than with China: International Monetary Fund, *Direction of Trade Statistics Yearbook 1992*, Washington DC, 1992.

3   ibid.

4   Gary Klintworth, 'Taiwan's United Nations Membership Bid', *Pacific Review*, vol. 7, no. 3, 1994, p. 283.

5   Christine Vertente, Hsu Hsueh-chi and Wu Mi-cha, *The Authentic Story of Taiwan*, Mappamundi Publishers, Knokke (Belgium), 1991, pp. 18, 39, 51.

6   Joseph W. Ballantine, *Formosa*, The Brookings Institution, Washington, 1952, p. 9.

7   Vertente, Hsu and Wu, *The Authentic Story of Taiwan*, p. 34. But see Chen Qimao, 'The Taiwan Issue and Sino-US Relations', *Asian Survey*, vol. XXVII, no. 11, November 1987, pp. 1161, 1163, who claims that Taiwan was traditional Chinese territory and that, but for the interference of the United States, Taiwan would have been united with the mainland and there would today be no question that it is an inalienable part of China.

8   Department of Mines and Technical Surveys, *Taiwan (Formosa)*, Foreign Geography Information Series No. 5, Ottawa, Canada, 1952, p. 1.

9   Vertente, Hsu and Wu, *The Authentic Story of Taiwan*, p. 19.

10   ibid.

11   Ballantine, *Formosa*, p. 7.

12   Yosaburo Takekoshi, *Japanese Rule in Formosa*, Longman, London, 1907, p. 52.

13   ibid., p. 54.

14   F.A. Lumley, *The Republic of China Under Chiang Kai-shek: Taiwan Today*, Barrie & Jenkins, London, 1976, p. 43.

15   Derek Massarella, Chinese, Tartars and Thea or a Tale of Two Companies: the English East India Company and Taiwan in the Late Seventeenth Century, unpublished paper, Princeton University, February 1993.

16   Vertente, Hsu and Wu, *The Authentic Story of Taiwan*, p. 39.

17   James W. Davidson, *The Island of Formosa Past and Present*, Macmillan and Co., London, 1903, p. 12.

18   ibid., p. 13.

19 Vertente, Hsu and Wu, *The Authentic Story of Taiwan*, p. 75.

20 George H. Kerr, *Formosa Betrayed*, Eyre & Spottiswoode, London, 1966, p. 3.

21 Samuel P.S. Ho, *Economic Development of Taiwan 1860–1970*, Yale University Press, New Haven, 1978, p. 8.

22 From Massarella; and Vertente, Hsu and Wu, *The Authentic Story of Taiwan*, p. 78.

23 Vertente, Hsu and Wu, *The Authentic Story of Taiwan*, pp. 78, 102.

24 ibid.

25 Ho, *Economic Development of Taiwan*, p. 9.

26 Davidson, *The Island of Formosa Past and Present*, p. 29

27 Massarella.

28 Quoted in Massarella. This contrasts with other accounts suggesting that Cheng Ch'eng-kung treated everybody on Taiwan, including the aborigines, with great kindness and consideration and that his son and successor, Ch'eng Ching, dedicated himself to making the island more prosperous: Vertente, Hsu and Wu, *The Authentic Story of Taiwan*, pp. 107–8.

29 Ho, *Economic Development of Taiwan*, p. 10.

30 Vertente, Hsu and Wu, *The Authentic Story of Taiwan*, p. 127.

31 In the fifteenth century, Ming Admiral Cheng Ho led several state-supported voyages of exploration to Southeast Asia, India and Africa.

32 Quoted in Vertente, Hsu and Wu, *The Authentic Story of Taiwan*, p. 130.

33 ibid.

34 ibid.

35 Neil H. Jacoby, *US Aid to Taiwan*, Praeger, New York, 1966, p. 72.

36 ibid.

37 Department of Mines, *Taiwan (Formosa)*, p. 1.

38 There were 152 044 opium smokers on Taiwan in 1875 and opium was the single largest import by value, accounting for 45–75 per cent of total imports: Ho, *Economic Development of Taiwan*, p. 15.

39 Department of Mines, *Taiwan (Formosa)*, p. 1.

40 Peng Ming-min, *A Taste of Freedom, Memoirs of a Formosan Independence Leader*, Holt Rinehart and Winston, New York, Chicago and San Francisco, 1972, p. 4.

41 Department of Mines, *Taiwan (Formosa)*, p. 1.

42 Ho, *Economic Development of Taiwan*, p. 13.

43 Vertente, Hsu and Wu, *The Authentic Story of Taiwan*, p. 136.

44 The German geographer, Ferdinand Richthofen, recommended Shantung instead of Taiwan because the latter's harbours were regarded

as poor and its inhabitants too rebellious: Shinkichi Eto, 'An Outline of Formosan History' in Mark Mancall, *Formosa Today*, Praeger, New York, 1964, pp. 43, 49.

45 Hsu Chieh-lin, 'The Republic of China and Japan' in Yu San Wang (ed.), *Foreign Policy of the Republic of China on Taiwan*, Praeger, New York, 1990, pp. 45, 46.

46 Ballantine, *Formosa*, p. 20.

47 Jacoby, *US Aid to Taiwan*, p. 73.

48 ibid.

49 Vertente, Hsu and Wu, *The Authentic Story of Taiwan*, p. 143.

50 Jacoby, *US Aid to Taiwan*, p. 73.

51 Ho, *Economic Development of Taiwan*, p. 24.

52 Ho, ibid., p. 11, gives a figure of 3.2 million.

53 Davidson, *The Island of Formosa Past and Present*, p. 254–58, observed that the flesh of slaughtered savages was sold like pork with desirable portions like 'the kidney, liver, heart and soles of the feet . . . ordinarily cut up into very small pieces, boiled and eaten somewhat in the form of soup'.

54 See Edwin A Winckler, 'Mass Political Incorporation 1500–2000' in Edwin A. Winckler and Susan Greenhalgh (eds), *Contending Approaches to the Political Economy of Taiwan*, M.E. Sharpe, New York, 1988, pp. 41, 47ff.

55 See Klintworth, 'Taiwan's United Nations Membership Bid'.

56 Bela Belassa, *The Newly Industrialising Countries of the World Economy*, Pergamon Press, New York, 1981, p. 2.

57 Leonard Unger, 'Chiang Kai-shek's Second Chance', *Policy Review*, vol. 50, Fall 1989, p. 26.

58 Edwin Cannan (ed.), Adam Smith, *The Wealth of Nations*, The Modern Library, New York, 1937, Book I, Chapter III, p. 17ff.

59 In 1964 non-agricultural income made up 32 per cent of total farm family income and by 1972 the proportion was in excess of 50 per cent: Gustav Ranis 'Industrial Development' in Walter Galenson (ed.), *Economic Growth and Structural Change in Taiwan*, Cornell University Press, Ithaca, 1979, pp. 224–25.

60 ibid., p. 229.

61 ibid., pp. 214–15.

62 ibid., p. 222.

63 Jon Woronoff, *Asia's 'Miracle Economies'*, M.E. Sharpe Inc., New York, 1986, p. 63; also Ho, *Economic Development of Taiwan*, p. 14.

64 Department of Mines, *Taiwan (Formosa)*, p. 6.

65 Ballantine, *Formosa*, p. 4.

66   Department of Mines, *Taiwan (Formosa)*, p. 42.

67   ibid.

68   Kerr, *Formosa Betrayed*, p. 11.

69   Michael Handel, *Weak States in the International System*, Frank Cass, London, 1981, pp. 72, 74.

70   For an anlysis of Taiwan's plans to develop itself as a regional transport hub, see Peter Rimmer, 'Taiwan's Future as a Regional Transport Hub', in Gary Klintworth (ed.), *Taiwan in the Asia-Pacific in the 1990s*, Allen & Unwin/Department of International Relations, ANU, Canberra, 1994, pp. 214ff.

71   In E. Lauterpacht, 'Effect of the Cairo and Potsdam Declarations 1943 and 1946', *British Yearbook of International Law*, vol. VIII, no. 1, January 1959, pp. 182, 186.

72   Mark Mancall, 'Introduction', in Mancall, *Formosa Today*, pp. 1, 4.

73   Ong Joktik, 'A Formosan's View of the Formosan Independence Movement' in Mancall, ibid., p. 163.

74   Peng, *A Taste of Freedom, Memoirs of a Formosan Independence Leader*, pp. 52, 61, 62.

75   ibid., p. 52.

76   Ballantine, *Formosa*, p. 60; Department of Mines, Taiwan (Formosa), p. 18.

77   C.L. Chiou, 'The Uprising of 28 February 1947 on Taiwan: the Official 1992 Investigation Report', *China Information*, vol. VII, no. 4, Spring 1993, pp. 1–16.

78   Ong Joktik, 'A Formosan's View of the Formosan Independence Movement', p. 164.

79   Peng, *A Taste of Freedom, Memoirs of a Formosan Independence Leader*, p. 70.

80   C.L. Chiou, 'The Uprising of 28 February 1947'.

81   Ballantine, *Formosa*, p. 63.

82   Department of Mines, *Taiwan (Formosa)*, p. 36.

83   ibid., pp. 36–38.

84   Ranis 'Industrial Development', p. 211.

85   The domestic sources of Taiwan's modernisation are examined in Chapter 6.

86   Yang Chung-sen, Director, National Central Library, preface to Vertente, Hsu and Wu, *The Authentic Story of Taiwan*, p. 7.

87   'Taiwan Literature Seen From Both Sides', *Sinorama*, December 1992, pp. 123, 129.

88   Nauru, the Solomon Islands, Tonga and Tuvalu.

89   The Act and its current significance are discussed in Chapter 3.

90 From Peter Polomka, 'Asia Pacific Security Beyond the Cold War: Trends and Issues for the 1990s', paper presented to ISIS-SDSC Conference Security & Prosperity in Pacific Asia Beyond the Cold War, Chiang Mai, Thailand, 29–31 July 1990.

91 US Under-Secretary of Defence, Paul Wolfowitz, *Backgrounder: US Plans Phased Troop Reduction in Asia-Pacific*, USIS Wireless File, Canberra, 25 April 1990, p. 19.

2 Taiwan's Japanese Foundations

Some of the roots of Taiwan's modern identity and certainly its economic foundations can be traced directly to the contribution made by the Japanese. Together with China and the United States, Japan is one of the three external powers to dominate Taiwan's history, economy, culture and security over the last two hundred years. Japan's particular importance stems from the opportunity it gave Taiwan to disconnect itself from the misfortunes that have plagued mainland China for most of the last one hundred years.

Taiwan was launched out of what had been hitherto a rather haphazard orbit around China. For a period of 50 years between 1895 and 1945, it was reshaped into a likeness of Japan. After the Korean War, the United States' goal of containing communism guaranteed Taiwan's non-return to China, enabling it to slip back into a Japanese sphere of influence. There it remained beyond the reach of China for another several decades. Japan was able — and was encouraged by the United States and its own policy inclinations — to recover and expand its economic influence over Taiwan. In consequence, the Japanese origins and connections in Taiwan that might otherwise have withered in the face of a Chinese restoration were renewed, developed and expanded. Taiwan continued to enjoy the benefits of a subordinate yet mutually beneficial association with an ascendant Japan. This association, under the protection of the United States (discussed in the next chapter), gave the Kuomintang the freedom to concentrate on governing Taiwan and refurbishing its economy, undistracted by China. It had a significant impact on Taiwan in terms of nation-building and shaping Taiwan's Taiwanese identity.

Taiwan's often admired rapid economic development was given a critical advantage by Japan. It was Japanese colonial rule that, according to Shirley W.Y. Kuo, 'left behind an excellent physical and human infrastructure upon which Taiwan could later build growth in agriculture and industry'.[1]

Taiwan's development was also boosted by the momentum created by 50 years of relatively amicable and successful Japanese colonisation. Taiwan, unlike China, did not have to start afresh in its relationship with Japan. It simply followed and expanded on a well-established relationship. Taiwan, therefore, was exceedingly well-placed to benefit from Japan's rapid postwar economic development and the great business partnership that developed between Japan and the United States after the Korean War.

According to Bruce Cumings, Japanese imperialism is the definitive starting point for understanding Taiwan's subsequent development as a core part of a dynamic Northeast Asian economic community.[2] Indeed, he says that it was only after the Japanese took charge in 1895 that Taiwan's modern future began to take shape.[3] Influential Japanese concur.[4] So do many Taiwanese and American writers.[5] They argue that Japan's colonial administration, to a greater or lesser degree, laid the physical and societal foundations for Taiwan's development after 1950. Taiwan's modern industry, transportation and educational infrastructure — and, it is claimed, even the seeds of democracy — were sown during the Japanese period.[6] Leonard Unger, the last United States ambassador to the ROC (1974–78), said that when the KMT took over from the Japanese, Taiwan was ready for the 'takeoff stage of economic development'.[7]

This chapter will focus on Taiwan's Japanese connections and examine how and why the rise, fall and later recovery of Japanese power and influence affected Taiwan's evolution as an independent entity in the Western Pacific. In doing so, we need to bear in mind our analytical framework. That is, Taiwan's evolution towards becoming a modern industrialised state can be viewed in terms of its drift within a Pacific triangle of power and influence formed by Japan to the north, a forward-deployed United States in the east, with China immediately to the west. This chapter is about Taiwan's drift away from China towards Japan.

In looking at Taiwan, one instinctively associates the island with China and the Chinese. Taiwan, as noted in the previous chapter, is an island located just off the richest part of the China coast to the west. It is physically close to China and it was settled by Chinese people.

But Taiwan also has a distinct Japanese heritage. Geographically, Taiwan can be viewed as a natural prolongation of the Japanese archipelago and the Ryukyu islands. It is approximately 1159 kilometres southwest of Japan, or a few days' journey by ship across the East China Sea. As the crow flies, Taipei is almost the same distance from Tokyo as it is from Beijing. That is, Taiwan is roughly the same distance away from the capitals of two of the three centres of political and military power in the Western Pacific. However, Tokyo has been open and accessible to the

Taiwanese since 1895. Today it takes three hours by air to reach Taipei from Tokyo or vice versa, whereas air travel to or from Beijing via Hong Kong takes up to a day and a half and was only possible after 1987.

For Japan, as for China and the West, Taiwan is strategically located in the centre of East Asia. This explains the frequent attempts by the Japanese — and the Chinese — to occupy Taiwan and the large number of expeditions there by Japanese explorers, traders and pirates in the sixteenth and seventeenth centuries. The island was well known to the Japanese and several hundred had settled there by the time Taiwan came under Dutch rule in the early seventeenth century. Cheng Ch'eng-kung (Koxinga), who evicted the Dutch from Taiwan in 1662, was the son of a Formosan-Japanese pirate chief.[8]

As a nearby territory, one which Japan had previously attempted to acquire and which China was willing to shed when necessary, and being at the time of relatively low priority for the European powers, Taiwan was a logical target for the empire-building ambitions of Meiji Japan in the late nineteenth century.

The orthodox view is that Taiwan was Chinese before 1895 and was returned to China at the end of World War II. There is, however, an alternative — Japanese — viewpoint. Japanese influence on Taiwan and the exclusion of China can be seen as a continuum of two almost consecutive periods: the first from 1895 to 1945; the second extending from the period after the Korean War began up until the late 1980s. In the first period, Japan exercised a comprehensive economic, social, military and political influence over Taiwan, while in the second period its influence was reinforced by America's Pacific strategy. From this Japanese perspective, Taiwan was never fully or formally returned to Chinese control after being a Japanese colony from 1895 to 1945. When World War II ended, there were a few years of uncertainty between 1945 and 1949, but mainland China remained strictly off-limits for Taiwan, even though it was Chinese and physically closer to the mainland than Japan. Indeed, the two sides of the Taiwan Strait were at war with each other and individual Taiwanese could be arrested and imprisoned for visiting mainland China as recently as 1986. During the second period, therefore, historical association, ideological inclination, American direction and economic necessity drove Taiwan towards re-establishing strong trade, technological and strategic links with Japan rather than China. For almost the whole of the last century, therefore, Taiwan has had almost continuous exposure to Japanese influence and, relatively speaking, little or no interaction with mainland China. Consequently, Taiwan has become more Japanified, Westernised and internationalised than any other part of China, with the exception of Hong Kong.

This century of association with Japan, and its sequel of independence from mainland China, has been a profitable period for Taiwan. It has been an era of sustained economic development, the first half of which gave Taiwan an opportunity for real economic development after centuries of neglect under Chinese rule.[9] In other words, while analysis of

Taiwan's modernisation often starts from 1952, Japan had already pro-pelled Taiwan 'to the threshold of becoming a modern economy' by 1940.[10] All that a new administration had to do after the war — whether American–Kuomintang or Taiwanese — was to pick up the reins where they had been left by the Japanese.

The Kuomintang faltered initially because they were preoccupied with the civil war on the mainland. However, after that war was lost, and once the United States intervened to separate Taiwan from the mainland, the Kuomintang's task on Taiwan was relatively easy. As Samuel Ho acknowledges, Taiwan was left with crucial advantages gained from its colonial experience, including an educated workforce, a well-ordered society, an infrastructure that, despite war damage, made Taiwan one of the most developed areas of China, an agricultural sector that was 'the most advanced' in the region, repairable industries and revivable institu-tions such as farmers' co-operatives, agricultural experimental stations and banking facilities.[11] The habit of using the network of rural co-opera-tives established by colonial Japan was of critical importance for Taiwan's postwar agricultural recovery.[12]

In this light, therefore, one can perceive Taiwan developing on a track that has run behind, but in many ways parallel to, that of Japan. It was a path temporarily interrupted by the aftermath of World War II but, with an injection of American aid and protection, Taiwan's development in Japan's wake resumed as soon as the latter's postwar economic recovery got underway.[13] Japan's recovery in turn was galvanised by the Korean War and United States procurement orders for all manner of goods that could be produced by Japanese industries.[14] By 1952, Japan was again the dominant trading partner for Taiwan, taking over half of its exports and supplying over 30 per cent of its imports. By 1965, Japan supplied around 40 per cent of Taiwan's imports and still took 30 per cent of its exports.[15] On the other hand, indirect trade and contacts between Taiwan and mainland China did not commence until 1987.

This is not to underestimate the importance of Taiwan's Chineseness, the consequences of its proximity to the mainland and the significance for Taiwan of the People's Liberation Army, whether in Korea or across the Taiwan Strait.[16] But in terms of Taiwan's infrastructural development, economic management, export orientation, market linkages and indus-trial technology over the last hundred years, it is Japan rather than China which has played the critical role in Taiwan's ascent. Throughout Taiwan's modern period, therefore, we can say that Japan, not China, has been the dominant influence on Taiwan's social, political and economic development.

Pre-Japanese Taiwan was a poorly governed traditional rural economy with few cash crops apart from tea, sugar and camphor distillation.[17] Aborigines practised slash and burn agriculture on the mountain slopes.[18] Intra-island commerce was limited and roads and infrastructure were generally poor.[19]

Taiwan's location made it an ideal stepping stone for Japan's longer term regional ambitions. It was seized by Japan in 'a ruthless and bloody act of conquest' for later use as a military base to launch the Japanese empire in East Asia.[20] Yet the Japanese also appreciated Taiwan's under-utilised agricultural potential. Taiwan had land, a good subtropical climate and an undirected peasant labour force.[21] According to many accounts, Japan developed Taiwan into a model Japanese colony. Indeed, Thomas B. Gold suggests that Japan's colonisation of Taiwan reflected a desire to demonstrate that Japan could be just as effective as a colonial power as the Europeans.[22] For whatever combination of reasons, Japanese control gave Taiwan an historically rare opportunity for nation-building. The Taiwanese economy was integrated into a regional system to support Japan's home islands on the basis of an 'industrial Japan and an agricultural Taiwan'.[23] Yet this control also freed Taiwan from Chinese bureaucratic inertia and the neglect of a government too far away and beset by too many problems to manage or direct the island's agricultural potential.

Unlike Japan in the nineteenth century, China was 'an intensely conservative society' ruled by bureaucrats who 'resisted at every step, not merely the enterprise of the Westerners, but Western civilisation itself, its technology, and its very idea of material progress'.[24] Despite the overthrow of the Ch'ing dynasty in 1910, China remained in disarray for several more decades, with ongoing civil and military strife and the complication of war with Japan. Even when the People's Republic of China was established in 1949, self-reliance, socialist economics and ideological barriers precluded interaction with the outside world. It was only after the death of Mao Zedong in 1976 that China adopted an open door policy towards the rest of the world and began to follow the path pioneered by Taiwan.

In contrast to China's generally negative response to contacts with the West, Japan embraced change. Compared with China, Japan was ambitious, efficient and goal-oriented.[25] Determined from the outset to become a modern industrial state, its rise as a great East Asian power was marked by its victories over China in 1894–95 and Russia in 1905.[26]

By coming under the control and protection of a strong imperial power like Japan, and later the United States, Taiwan was able to avoid the great turbulence and uncertainty that swept China for the first half of this century. As Peng Ming-min commented, 'while the Chinese on the mainland proper endured fifty years of revolution, warlordism and civil war', Taiwan was driven in the opposite direction by imperial Japan.[27]

> [Under] Japanese reorganisation and direction [Taiwan's] economy made spectacular gains, and our living standards rose steadily until among Asian countries we were second only to Japan in agricultural and industrial technology, in communications, in public health, and in provisions for the general public welfare. Our grandparents had witnessed this transformation from a backward, ill-gov-

erned, disorganised island, nominally dependent on the Chinese. They did not like the Japanese, but they appreciated the economic and social benefits of fifty years of peace which they enjoyed.[28]

It was perhaps fortunate for Taiwan — and, in the long historical perspective, for China too — that Japan was able to recast Taiwan into a successful model of economic development. In doing so, Japan had more than a free hand in dismantling and rebuilding the Taiwanese economy and society. While the Taiwanese Chinese and aborigines resisted Japan's takeover — and there were sporadic anti-Japanese uprisings as late as 1930 — Japanese rule was well entrenched by 1902.[29] Order was enforced by a pervasive security apparatus based on the *pao-chia* system of collective family responsibility introduced in 1898. It was backed up by the use of informants, an extensive police force and severe punishments.[30] The compactness of Taiwan's island geography helped make Japan's task of social control relatively easy, supplying what Robert Wade calls an 'enabling condition'.[31] That is, it enabled Japan to impose strict social and political controls, to organise Taiwan's resources and to accomplish the kind of comprehensive, deep-rooted economic change that great size and enormous population made difficult if not impossible for an outside power to achieve on the mainland. In smaller Taiwan, the Japanese had access to virtually every village, whereas on the mainland, Japan's penetration was mainly confined to coastal enclaves like Hong Kong and Shanghai.

Where Japan was able to physically isolate a natural region of China, as it did with Taiwan and later Manchukuo, it could implement a detailed long-term economic plan.[32] For Taiwan, Japan was able to draw on lessons learned from its own modernisation experience after the Meiji Restoration in 1868, including reforms in agriculture, the concentration of economic power in the hands of the state, strict social controls and the exercise of 'efficiency of economic administration at the centre', or what Bruce Cumings termed 'sharp administrative guidance'.[33] By the 1930s, there were around 300 000 Japanese managers, teachers and technicians in Taiwan advising, training and managing the Taiwanese.[34]

The development of an efficient transportation system was recognised by the Japanese as a prerequisite for economic development, whether in Japan, Taiwan or Manchukuo. An efficient transportation network made it possible for what had been a village economy to cast off its age-old shell of self-sufficiency, enlarge the market for its products and increase gains from the division of labour.[35] Not surprisingly, the centrepiece of Japan's development policy in Taiwan, as in Manchukuo, was the rapid construction of a transport and communications system, including airfields, ports and telephone lines.[36] Most of Taiwan's modern railway mileage was built by the Japanese between 1905 and 1935.[37] Taiwan's first north–south railway line was built by the Japanese in 1899.[38] It connected Keelung and Kaohsiung, which were subsequently developed into two of the busiest ports in the Asia-Pacific region. Then, as they are today,

Keelung and Kaohsiung were connected to Japanese ports like Osaka, Tokyo, and Yokohama rather than to ports on the China coast.[39] As well as railway lines and harbours, the Japanese built a network of roads and telephone lines.[40] This transportation network then became the basic framework for harnessing the surrounding agricultural land and its resources, extracting the surplus and shipping it back to Japan. Even today, building efficient transport systems connecting Taiwan's cities to each other and the outside world remains a high priority for the govern-ment of President Lee Teng-hui.

An essential precondition for capital formation in the early stages of Japan's industrial development was to get agriculture on the right track.[41] This experience was simply transplanted to Taiwan during the colonial period.[42] Japanese rural institutions based on credit co-operatives and a network of farmers' associations helped boost rural productivity by dis-seminating technical knowledge and providing credit services.[43] Japan-ese fertilisers, training, crop rotation, seed technology and irrigation works that covered half of Taiwan's arable land, together with guaran-teed Japanese markets combined to offer Taiwanese farmers such power-ful incentives that great, productive energy was unleashed.[44] Taiwan's growth in agricultural output over the period 1903–40 averaged (in con-stant prices) around 45 per cent per decade, a phenomenal result.[45] Sugar production rose from 45 391 tonnes in 1902 to 498 460 tonnes in 1925.[46] Taiwan also produced large quantities of bananas, pineapples, citrus fruit, tobacco, jute, sisal and other agricultural or forest products (like paper pulp and camphor). The rapid expansion of Taiwan's agricultural output led to the establishment of Japanese-controlled food and timber processing industries.[47]

According to one Taiwanese, the revolution in Taiwan's agricultural productivity achieved during Japan's colonial administration was noth-ing short of remarkable.[48] The island soon became 'a granary for the Japanese homeland' and 'Japan's sugar bowl'.[49] Half of Taiwan's annual rice crop and nearly all of its sugar and pineapple production — canned or refined — went to Japan.[50] In the 1930s, when Taiwan's trade with Japan comprised around 60 per cent of GDP, Taiwan supplied Japan with nearly 75 per cent of its sugar and 30 per cent of its imported rice.[51] Although Taiwan was exploited as a food source by Japan, it acquired a sound physical basis for future agricultural development, the habits of being an efficient export-oriented economy and strong links with Japan.

Japanese-developed agricultural industries and a highly productive Japanese-trained agricultural labour force sustained Taiwan's economy after the Japanese departed. With growth rates of 10.2 per cent per annum between 1946 and 1951, Taiwan's agricultural output had sur-passed its prewar peak by 1952.[52] In 1953, Taiwan's agriculture sector employed over 55 per cent of Taiwan's workforce and, while this ratio declined as manufacturing industries expanded, Taiwan's agricultural industries continued to provide around half the employment opportunities on the island, even in the mid-1960s.[53] Sugar continued as the dominant industry in Taiwan and made up about half of Taiwan's exports throughout the 1950s and around 30 per cent in 1964.[54] Other leading exports in the 1950s were rice, tea, bananas and canned food products, all of which had been established during Japan's colonial period.

When the Japanese completed their withdrawal from Taiwan in 1946, the Kuomintang simply stepped into their shoes and took over all the Japanese levers of industrial, economic and political power. As Wade comments, they reinforced a pre-existing centralised structure of government.[55] As the successor regime to the Japanese, the Kuomintang inherited 25 per cent of the best agricultural land in Taiwan, making the task of land reform that much easier.[56] A successful land reform program in turn contributed to increased agricultural productivity. This helped keep the price of food and real wages down while providing surplus capital and a supply of low-cost labour for Taiwan's new manufacturing industries.[57]

As well as investing in agriculture, Japan developed Taiwan industrially after 1935 'to fulfil more adequately its position as an advance base of Japanese imperialism' in East Asia.[58] Taiwan's manufacturing industries were mainly processing, canning and refining agricultural products, or were industries related to agriculture, like chemical fertilisers.[59] But Japan gradually developed basic industries and by the 1930s, Taiwan was producing aluminium, cement, chemicals, petroleum and steel. From 1914 to 1941, factory employment rose from 21 800 to 127 700 and mining employment from 6500 to 53 700.[60] A hydro-electric power plant with an output of 100 000 megawatts was built to support the industrialisation of Taiwan's west coast.[61] By 1940, aluminium plants at Kaohsiung and Hualien were supplying Japan with one-sixth of its aluminium imports.[62] Taiwan's Japanese-founded industries were all rehabilitated and modernised and their productive capacity was expanded by the Kuomintang in 1949.[63]

Japan's prime concern, like that of other colonial powers, was to maximise its returns from Taiwan.[64] Over the period 1911–40, Japan took around 85 per cent of Taiwan's exports and supplied 74 per cent of its imports, mainly fertilisers and machinery destined to boost the agricultural surplus for Japan.[65] Taiwanese workers were confined to rural, manual or semi-skilled jobs, while those in industry were paid a fraction of the wages received by workers in similar industries in Japan.[66] Japanese nationals were appointed to most of the managerial and skilled jobs in manufacturing, industry, communications, transport, trade, government and professional services.[67] The overall result was a colony that was 'a conspicuous object lesson in profitable imperialism'.[68]

As in agriculture, virtually all of Taiwan's industrial mining and service enterprises were controlled and operated by Japanese *zaibatsu* like Mitsui, Mitsubishi, Yasuda and Sumitomo.[69] As the successor regime to the Japanese, the Kuomintang obtained a ready supply of industrial assets that could be used to compensate Taiwanese landowners who lost their land through the Kuomintang's land reform program in the 1950s.[70]

Japan's colonial policy discriminated against the Taiwanese and exploited the island's resources, but there were opportunities for upward social mobility.[71] Japanese rule was also efficient, enterprising and 'rarely tainted with corruption or malfeasance'.[72] William Chamberlin concluded that it was not a colonial policy of 'the decadent, parasitic type'.[73] Sometimes Japanese rule was relatively benevolent, at least in its early phase.[74] Many observers were impressed by the probity and earnestness of purpose of the majority of the higher Japanese officials on Taiwan.[75] Han Lih-wu concludes that, while order was enforced by a strong police system, 'there was both promptness and effectiveness and also a good deal of fairness in the execution of law and the maintenance of order'.[76]

The result was an absence of animosity between the Japanese and the Taiwanese, and even a degree of tolerance and goodwill — with positive consequences for the post-colonial relationship. It was enhanced by Japanese policies that brought literacy, health and a degree of prosperity to most Taiwanese.[77] Byron Weng and C.L. Chiou recall that many older-generation Taiwanese look back on Taiwan's Japanese period with a mixture of respect and admiration, despite the fact that punishments, even for children, could be very harsh when the rules were infringed.[78]

The Japanese invested in a public health scheme and improved sanitation and sewage. Plague and cholera were brought under control by 1920 and the death rate was halved between 1906 and 1940.[79] One visitor, albeit Japanese, wrote in 1904 that Taipei, formerly 'a Chinese city of sewage-filled alleys', had been transformed into a clean and spacious metropolis in the European style.[80] Another visitor wrote that Japan's Taiwan had made striking progess in 'such matters as municipal cleanliness and sanitation, communication facilities, hygienic measures calculated to root out infectious diseases [and] freedom from banditism and piracy'.[81] The Japanese also introduced standardised weights and measures, a single currency and a ban on opium.[82]

Even though wages were held back to about half the increase in productivity in industry and agriculture, the real income and quality of living of the Taiwanese rose steadily during the Japanese colonial period.[83] The Taiwanese enjoyed an increase in the number of bicycles and per capita cloth consumption, as well as improved calorific intake, life expectancy and educational opportunities.[84] According to Alice Amsden, the social welfare of many of the Taiwanese may have been better than that of many Japanese living in Japan.[85]

The Japanese were sensitive to the financial and social benefits of a skilled workforce.[86] A modern universal education system was introduced. Vocational schools and specialised colleges to produce Taiwanese trained in agriculture, forestry, commerce, engineering and various trades were established.[87] Some Taiwanese were selected for higher education in Japan.[88]

Most Taiwanese were obliged to learn Japanese.[89] In the 1930s, a more thorough and compulsory Japanese language program was implemented in schools, government, banking and the media.[90] Some Taiwanese responded positively.[91] These educational, linguistic and training opportunities stood the Taiwanese in good stead after 1945; many who had worked in Japanese companies in the 1930s and 1940s became Taiwan's future entrepreneurs.[92]

According to one commentator, Japanese policies on Taiwan were carried out in a way 'worthy of observation by contemporary development administrators'.[93] Japan, according to George Barclay, 'transformed Taiwan from a backward and neglected land into a thriving region . . . a success that would satisfy most . . . countries striving for modernisation'.[94]

Overall, then, Japanese rule on Taiwan can be said to have been positive and successful. The result was a lack of hostility by the Taiwanese towards the Japanese. They did not regard the Japanese as cruel, oppressive colonial overlords and were not thinking of rebellion or collaboration with the Allies. On the contrary, 220 000 Taiwanese served in the Japanese Imperial Army during World War II and those who survived appear not to have regretted the experience.[95] In consequence, the reestablishment of a special Taiwanese relationship with Japan was a smooth affair. It did not require spending a lot of time, emotion and effort to negotiate a reconciliation, as is the case with South Korea and Japan.

After the war, however, Taiwan faced huge problems, not least the damage to infrastructure caused by wartime bombing.[96] There were bloody mistakes made by a harsh Kuomintang administration that treated Taiwan as conquered territory and the Taiwanese as Japanese collaborators.[97] If a choice had been possible, many Taiwanese would have preferred union with Japan rather than the rule of the Kuomintang.[98] There was a flood of refugees from the mainland. Machinery was worn out or obsolete. Taiwan's guaranteed markets in Japan were temporarily lost and a Japanese managerial elite numbering up to 400 000 was withdrawn in 1946.[99] The island was in 'complete ruin', according to Kwohting Li, one of the architects of Taiwan's postwar renaissance.[100] Industrial and agricultural output had dropped sharply.[101] Rice production was less than half its peak production, electric power was down to 16 per cent of its peak and sugar, one the largest industries, was 8 per cent of its 1940 peak.[102] In addition, the Nationalists were losing the Chinese civil war.

But without the contribution made by Japan, Taiwan would have been much less viable as a refuge for the Kuomintang and the United States may have been much less willing to intervene, as they did in 1950, to shield Taiwan from China's PLA. As Lieutenant-General Albert C. Wedemeyer observed in his report on Taiwan to the United States Secretary of State on 14 August 1947:

> the Japanese had efficiently electrified even remote areas and also established excellent railroad lines and highways. Eighty per cent of

the people can read and write, the exact antithesis of conditions prevailing in the mainland of China.[103]

With America's intervention after the outbreak of the Korean War, Taiwan was able to rebuild its Japanese foundations which, even in 1945, made Taiwan more advanced agriculturally, commercially and industrially than any of the provinces of China.[104]

Japan had given Taiwan a practical economic blueprint, a period of relative peace and political stability, ports, airfields, railways, roads, electric power, irrigation works and other infrastructure, an export-orientation, Japanese technology and management skills, an educated population and a disciplined workforce, as well as the enduring benefits of a close and, on the whole, a successful association with a powerful neighbouring economy. These attributes coalesced to give Taiwan a headstart in economic development over much of the rest of the Asia-Pacific region. There was no comparable large-scale transfer of foreign technology and assistance to the mainland until the 1950s when China received an unprecedented infusion of Soviet aid, materials, technology and skills.[105]

Mainland China's development, however, was still afflicted by the 'blind groping, false starts and frustrations' of revolutionary Chinese communism.[106] Taiwan, in contrast, had the benefits of 50 years of effective administration, a disciplined society, law and order and systematic economic management.[107] Whatever the extent of the physical damage suffered by Taiwan during World War II bombing raids, the intangible aspects of Taiwan's Japanese-derived heritage were left unscathed. These included habits of:

> hard work, discipline and social order . . . a receptivity to technological change and an appetite for progress . . . an agricultural population schooled in fairly advanced techniques of intensive farming and a small group of Taiwanese with technical training in education, medicine, engineering, construction and skilled trades. Japan also left Taiwan modern banking and financial institutions that were useful to its further development . . . the farmers' associations, agricultural experiment stations, credit unions, government enterprises and monopolies — including a food bureau and banking and marketing organisations. Japan reoriented Taiwan's agriculture from a subsistence to a market level . . . [with] profound social implications. It initiated gradual changes in traditional forms of communal and family life on the land. It triggered the emergence of an urbanised middle class, which later came to dominate the private industrial and commercial sector.[108]

To this list of intangible assets left by the Japanese, Thomas Gold would add the practice of state-led capitalist economic development by a merit-based administrative staff.[109] Samuel Ho's list of critical intangibles includes exposure of the Taiwanese to scientific techniques, machine technology and modern business practices and the gains from a broadly based education system that provided a basic education for 71 per cent of Taiwanese children.[110] Alice Amsden concludes that such 'social over-heads' were amongst the most important and enduring legacies of Taiwan's Japanese period.[111]

It is hard to quantify the significance of these intangibles for Taiwan's subsequent economic development. One can say, however, that it definitely contributed to the likelihood that Taiwan could succeed because the Taiwanese were familiar with the Japanese language and were at home with Japanese management methods. Many Taiwanese looked to Japan for inspiration, guidance and education. President Lee Teng-hui, for example, studied at Kyoto Imperial University, speaks Japanese and thought of himself as a Japanese before he reached the age of 22 (in 1945, when Japan surrendered).[112]

The natural affinity between the Taiwanese and the Japanese was based on Taiwan's Japanese roots. These were nurtured by the Americans and reinforced by mainland China's hostility towards Taiwan. This made it relatively easy for Taiwan to continue learning from Japan and emulating its business style. One of the key factors in Taiwan's postwar competitiveness was the smooth transfer of Japanese-style plant management, use of market information, and know-how on process innovation such as how to operate more efficiently, raise quality, cut administrative costs and eliminate wasteful use of energy and materials. In this area, the Taiwanese were particularly adept and learned a lot from the Japanese (in contrast to the Koreans).[113] In fact, the Taiwanese became very similar to the Japanese in developing the organisational skills necessary to maintain a competitive and efficient edge in the production of consumer goods for the world market.[114] Not surprisingly, Taiwan's postwar economic success reflects many of the features of the Japanese model: a market-based economy with strong state planning, high savings, making use of comparative advantages in cheap labour, emphasis on efficiency in the production line, moving up the technology ladder by importing and processing technology, export-oriented industrialisation, a growth strategy that was dependent on selling to the United States and, later, internationalising.

In other words, Taiwan gained a headstart on the region as a newly industrialising Pacific economy because of its Japanese connections, linguistic heritage and general orientation towards Japan. As a neighbour and a former colony that was culturally attuned to the Japanese, Taiwan was destined to become an integral part of the Northeast Asian economic and security system built around Japan by the United States after the Korean War. As Taiwan did not suffer under Japanese rule to the same degree as Korea and Manchuria, it could embrace the idea of a postwar business partnership with Japan more easily than the Koreans and more quickly than the mainland Chinese.[115] Inevitably, the spectacular recovery and expansion of the Japanese economy after World War II had a profound impact on Taiwan, its former colony. Japan's annual GNP growth rates in real terms averaged over 9 per cent in the 1950s and 12 per cent in the period 1965–70, surpassing the United States, the United Kingdom and most European countries.[116] Such rapid growth in Japan was a significant factor in the high growth rates of Taiwan from the early 1950s to the early 1970s.[117]

Japan dominated Taiwan's export trade throughout the 1950s and 1960s. In 1952, it took over half of Taiwan's exports. In 1955, the proportion had risen to almost 60 per cent and although it declined thereafter, it was still around 25 per cent in 1966 and 15 per cent in 1974 (see Tables 9 and 10). The ratio continued to decline, however, as Taiwan made the transition from being an agricultural supplier to Japan to a manufacturer of consumer goods for export to the United States.

As Taiwan made this shift, it became increasingly dependent on Japan for the technology, components and industrial raw materials that became the basis of its export-oriented manufacturing economy. Indeed, many of Taiwan's early export industries, especially footwear and electronics, were started on orders made by Japanese trading enterprises that were catering for the United States market.[118] By the mid-1960s, Taiwan was firmly entrenched in a division of labour in Northeast Asia that had Japan exporting middle-level technology and intermediate goods to Taiwan for processing and assembly into goods to be re-exported to markets in the United States and Europe.

Imported Japanese technology has become essential for the survival of Taiwan's electronics, machinery, appliance and information industries — that is, its export industries. Japan is the first or second largest supplier to Taiwan of capital goods, precision machinery, electrical equipment, electronic components, metal products, transportation equipment, base metals, chemicals and metals. It has been estimated that goods made in Taiwan derived from Japanese technology, spare parts, components and raw materials account for more than 60 per cent of all of Taiwan's exports.[119] Taiwan depends on Japan for around 45 per cent of its imported technology, while almost two-thirds of all technology co-operation agreements signed by Taiwan have been with Japan.[120] For example, although Taiwan is the seventh largest computer manufacturer in the world, accounting for over 3 per cent of the global trade in computers, almost 40 per cent of the components, including LCDs and central processing units, are Japanese.[121] Similarly with the car industry, where Taiwan's twelve car makers have strong business links with Japanese auto makers and depend on them for key components, including the engines. Kuozui, for example, is 49 per cent owned by Toyota; Yulon is 25 per cent Nissan; Taching is tied to Subaru; Nan Tang is tied to Honda and China Motor Company is linked to Mitsubishi.

Many of these linkages were formed during the prewar period, so that after the war it was often simply a matter of resuming old ties. This is what happened between Japan's giant Marubeni trading company and Taiwan's Evergreen Corporation (now the world's largest container shipping group), and many of the joint ventures and technical tie-ups between Japanese and Taiwanese corporations in the electronics industry.[122] In a sense, despite the end of the colonial era, Taiwan is still very much a Japanese satellite, functioning in a new form as a sub-contractor to Japanese corporations like Mitsubishi, Marubeni and Mitsui, Canon, Sony and Hitachi.

As in the colonial period, the Japanese objective is to increase sales of Japanese products and maximise profits rather than to facilitate the technology base of a potential competitor like Taiwan. The Japanese control the quality and the price of the technology and the components and materials that they are prepared to supply to Taiwan. Advanced technology in areas such as electronics and pharmaceuticals is kept secret.[123] Most Japanese technology transferred to Taiwan is at the lower end of the scale. But Japanese technology and distribution channels have been critical to the growth of Taiwanese exports in almost all areas of the Taiwanese economy.[124] Japan provides the technology, production equipment and intermediate goods and components that are then processed in Taiwan for re-export. Taiwanese products enter world markets through distribution channels controlled by Japanese trading companies. Japanese marketing firms are estimated to control 50 per cent of Taiwan's exports, even to the United States.[125] Another estimate goes as high as 70 per cent.[126]

Nonetheless, although the quality of Japanese technology transferred to Taiwan may be at the lower end of the scale, Taiwan has became so efficient in its niche role as a subcontractor and exporter that it has recorded a large surplus in its balance of trade in almost every year since 1970 and has accumulated one of the world's largest reserves of foreign exchange. Taiwan has done this by moving up a notch in the world economic hierarchy. Instead of being on the periphery as a supplier of agricultural products to Japan, Taiwan has moved closer to the Japanese industrial heartland. It has built its fortunes on importing agricultural products and raw materials from more efficient producers around the world, such as Australia, while exploiting its comparative advantages. Amongst these, the most important are its central location, skilled labour and physical and historical proximity to Japan. Taiwan has specialised in a sub-contractor role in which it imports secondary technologies and components mainly from Japan for manufacture, assembly or processing into electronic goods and appliances that are re-exported under Japanese, North American or European brand names to the rest of the world. Taiwanese-made commodities are now competing with Japanese-made goods at the lower end of the technology scale.

Growth in Taiwan's wealth has depended on an expansion of exports. Increased Taiwanese exports (mainly to North America, China/Hong Kong and Europe) have been supported by increased imports from Japan, Taiwan's second largest trading partner. However, while Japan has been Taiwan's most important source of imports, supplying around

30 per cent of all imports over the period 1950–91, it only ranks ninth as an export market, taking 12 per cent of total exports in 1991 (down from the peak of 60 per cent in 1955). So while Taiwan has been steadily accumulating surpluses in its overall trade, and in particular with the United States and China/Hong Kong, its trade deficit with Japan has continued to grow — and indeed, has been in deficit every year since 1955.

Taiwan's persistent trade imbalance with Japan and its surplus with the rest of the world reflect the extent to which Taiwan has become integrated with the Japanese economy. It can be interpreted as a sign of dependency, but equally as a mark of Taiwan's success in following along in Japan's wake. In other words, the price of Taiwan's postwar growth has been increased dependence on Japan, the world's second largest economy. According to Kiyoshi Kojima, such dependence was the only path open to Northeast Asian countries such as Taiwan and South Korea.[127] Bruce Cumings also maintains that the economic development of Taiwan and Korea can only be explained as part of a regional phenomenon that has Japan as its core.[128]

However, dependency on Japan has led to recurrent complaints from Taipei and frequent attempts to diversify sources of imports and restrict Japanese imports. Taiwanese leaders have exhorted business to upgrade technologies so as to reduce their reliance on Japanese-made machinery parts and components. Japanese industrialists have been called on to liberalise technology transfers. But these demands, and 'Buy American' campaigns, bans on imported Japanese cars and restraints on Japanese bids for Taiwanese infrastructure projects have not stemmed the tide. On the contrary, the gap has widened. Taiwan's deficit in trade with Japan more than doubled from US$4.8 billion in 1987 to US$14.2 billion in 1993 (see Table 9). The trouble is that Japanese technologies in key areas for Taiwanese export industries such as industrial ceramics, semiconductors, automated production facilities and parts for computerised numerically controlled machine tools are superior, cheaper, more readily available and of a better quality than comparable technologies from Western countries.[129]

Many Japanese enterprises transferred to Taiwan in the 1960s and 1970s simply because because of Taiwan's comparative advantage in labour costs and the appreciation of the yen against the US dollar. However, they were also influenced by cultural factors such as language and lifestyle. The Japanese 'feel comfortable' in Taiwan because many older-generation Taiwanese speak Japanese, as do many of Taiwan's political elite, such as the President, Lee Teng-hui; Chiang Pin-kung, Minister of Economic Affairs; Hsu Shui-te, formerly Minister of the Interior; and Shirley Kuo and Huang Shih-cheng, Ministers of State in the Executive Yuan.[130] The Taiwanese legal system is based on Japanese laws borrowed from Japan during the colonial period or brought back by Taiwanese lawyers trained in Japan, such as Liang Su-yung, former President of the Legislative Yuan, who studied at Meiji University; and Liu Kuo-tsai, a former President of the Legislative Yuan who studied law at Kyoto Imperial University.[131] Japanese is the most popular foreign language in Taiwanese schools after English. The Japanese dominate Taiwan's foreign visitor arrival statistics (around 900 000 Japanese visit Taiwan annually, compared with 220 000 from the United States in 1990).[132]

Japan was the biggest investor in Taiwan over the period 1952–92 in terms of both value and the number of projects.[133] Japanese investment grew from 5 per cent of total DFI in 1965 to 28.6 per cent in 1992, matching the decline in importance of United States investment, which fell from 96 per cent of the total in 1955 to 12.5 per cent in 1992.[134] Japanese investment in Taiwan over the period 1952–92 was worth US$4 778 222, or 29 per cent of the total of $US16 491 409 in DFI, compared with US$4 484 683, or 27 per cent from the United States.[135] This is more than twice the amount of Japanese investment in mainland China.[136] Over the same period, the number of Japanese projects was 2287, or around twice the figure for the United States of 1188.[137] That is, of the 3400 or so joint ventures set up in Taiwan since 1952, 61 per cent have been with Japanese firms, well ahead of United States firms with 23 per cent and European firms with 13 per cent.[138] Japanese investment has tended to be in smaller enterprises and has been concentrated in manufacturing, especially electronics, electric appliances and machinery, the industries which have led Taiwan's export sector.

Taiwan's share of Japanese investment in Asia in the period 1951–90 was, however, only 2.2 per cent of the total, with most Japanese funds going to Indonesia, Hong Kong, Singapore and South Korea.[139] In world terms, in the period 1951–90, Japanese foreign investment in Taiwan was barely one-tenth of the amount received by Australia.[140]

The current Taiwan–Japan relationship has preserved and expanded Japan's earlier economic domination of Taiwan. The indigenous Taiwanese who comprise the majority on Taiwan are more powerful economically than the mainlanders and can often speak Japanese. They tend to look towards Japan whereas the mainlanders favour business and academic connections with the United States.

Common strategic interests

Taiwan is of considerable strategic importance to Japan. It is part of Japan's inner perimeter in strategic, economic and historical terms.

Taiwan is undoubtedly one of Japan's most important trading partners. In 1994, two-way trade between Taiwan and Japan totalled US$34 billion. Taiwanese exports to Japan in 1994 were worth US$23.8 billion, while imports were worth US$23.8 billion. Japan is Taiwan's third largest market, while Taiwan is Japan's fourth largest market. (By way of comparison, Japanese exports to China in 1994 were worth US$18.6 billion and imports US$27.5 billion.)[142]

Strategically, Taiwan sits astride Japan's sea and air lines of communication to Hong Kong, Southeast Asia and oil routes from the Middle East. The Japanese defence plan that envisages protection of sea lines of communication (SLOC) out to a distance of 1000 nautical miles from Tokyo takes in Kaohsiung, Taiwan's southernmost port, and Taiwan's shipping routes to Japan across the East China Sea. The Taiwanese, predictably, often remind Japan (and the United States) of the implications for regional peace and security, and for Japan's SLOCs, if Taiwan is reunified with a communist China.[143] For their part, Japanese naval officers have said that if the mainland attacked Taiwan, Japan might be prepared to intervene if other countries such as Australia joined in, perhaps under United Nations auspices.[144] Japan anticipates a probable United States intervention under the terms of the 1979 *Taiwan Relations Act* and the 1960 Japan–United States Treaty of Mutual Co-operation and Security.[145]

Taiwan is not as important to Japan as China is, but it assumes a particular importance in the China context. Japan's historical preference has been for a Taiwan that is separate from China and this has not changed. There is a strong group in the Japanese Diet supportive of Taiwan remaining as Taiwan and not becoming part of China. Taiwan and Japan indeed share a common interest in preventing a communist China from becoming the dominant power in East Asia. More basically, however, Japan would not like to see Taiwan integrated into a greater China that might then be in a position to claim regional dominance at Japan's expense. In fact, the Japanese Foreign Ministry would probably be willing to recognise Taiwan's independence once a consensus supporting such a move emerged in the world community. Not surprisingly, groups once banned in Taiwan for calling for independence were able to operate freely in Japan.

Japan's appreciation of Taiwan's strategic importance was reaffirmed in November 1969 and September 1972. In 1969, Prime Minister Eisaku Sato signed a joint communiqué with President Nixon declaring that 'the maintenance of peace and security in the Taiwan area was a most important factor for the security of Japan' and that Taiwan was 'within Japan's defence zone'.[146] In September 1972, when Japan established diplomatic relations with Beijing, it renounced any claims it may have had to Taiwan. However, the Japanese Foreign Ministry maintained that, while Japan fully understood and respected China's claims to Taiwan, it did not regard the island as legally part of the People's Republic of China.[147] The wording of the Sino-Japanese communiqué of 29 September 1972 accords with Japan's view that Taiwan's international status has yet to be determined in international law.[148] This Japanese view of Taiwan's de facto existence as an independent state and its strategic importance for Japan's maritime approaches has been reaffirmed by Japan's leading security-oriented research institute and officials in the Japanese Defence Agency.[149]

Japan was the first country in the world to implement the now widely accepted diplomatic policy of one China in principle and two Chinas in practice. It has maintained its economic and political ties with Taiwan through a semi-official representative office in Taipei and Kaohsiung called the Interchange Association of Japan. The Interchange Association took over the functions and many of the diplomatic immunities and privileges of what had hitherto been an embassy and consulate. Staff are government officials who have retired or are on secondment. In 1991, Japan upgraded relations with Taiwan with the appointment of a senior diplomat to head its Taipei office. In 1992, as part of an upgrading of Taiwan's representation throughout the Asia-Pacific region, Taipei was given permission to change the name of its representative office in Tokyo from the innocuous-sounding Association of East Asia Relations Office to the more specific title of Taipei Economic and Cultural Association. For the moment, the two Chinas and Japan are satisfied with the way the present relationship works but Taiwan is putting increasing pressure on Japan to further upgrade relations.

Conclusions

For Taiwan, Japan was first a coloniser and moderniser and then became the core of a regional economic hegemony that incorporated Taiwan, though less directly than in the colonial era. The result has been a Taiwan that has been Japanified over an extended period — a period that consolidated Taiwan's non-Chineseness and exposed the Taiwanese to many foreign influences. Japan modernised Taiwan's agriculture, infrastructure, education, industry and management and gave it familiarity with and connections in Japan.

Left untouched by Japan, Taiwan might have stumbled along as an undeveloped, neglected island on the periphery of a society beset by dynastic decay, mismanagement, fragmentation, civil war and revolutionary communism. Tied to the fortunes of mainland China, Taiwan's development from 1895 to 1993 would have fallen well behind that of the rest of East Asia. Instead, Taiwan joined forces with the region's most efficient and dynamic economy and became one of the dragon economies of East Asia. In historical perspective, therefore, association with Japan was perhaps the best possible arrangement available for Taiwan. It gained half a century, or the equivalent of two generations, of political stability and immersion in the Japanese way of economic management. It remains closely associated with the success of Japan, the most powerful economic locomotive in the Asia-Pacific, and possibly the de facto leader of an Asia-Pacific economic community in a posthegemonic world.[150]

While Taiwan has become rich and successful, it has also remained dependent on Japan, and in many ways the Taiwanese are pro-Japanese. This has ensured that the barriers between Taiwan and the mainland have remained substantially intact while the possibility and the attractions of an existence separate from mainland China have grown stronger.

Notes

1   John C.H. Fei, Gustav Ranis and Shirley W.Y. Kuo, *Growth with Equity: The Taiwan Case*, Oxford University Press, New York, 1979, p. 21.

2   Bruce Cumings, 'The Origins and Development of the Northeast Asian Political Economy: Industrial Sectors, Product Cycles and Political Consequences', in Frederic C. Deyo (ed.), *The Political Economy of the New Asian Industrialism*, Cornell University Press, Ithaca, 1987, pp. 45, 53

3   ibid., p. 52.

4   Akio Morita and Shintaro Ishihara, *The Japan That Can Say 'No'*, Kobunsha, Kappa-Holmes, 1990, p. 73.

5   Shirley W.Y. Kuo, formerly a Minister for Finance, suggests that Taiwan's successful agricultural program was in large part due to Japanese investment in agricultural infrastructure during the colonial period: Shirley W.Y. Kuo, Gustav Ranis and John C.H. Fei, *The Taiwan Success Story: Rapid Growth with Improved Distribution in the Republic of China 1952–1979*, Westview, Boulder, Col., 1981, p. 37. According to Samuel P.S. Ho, Taiwan's Japanese-built infrastructure made it one of the most developed areas of China after World War II, despite war damage: Samuel P.S. Ho, *Economic Development of Taiwan 1860–1970*, Yale University Press, New Haven, 1978, p. 104. Neil H. Jacoby, in *US Aid to Taiwan*, Praeger, New York, 1966, p. 71, argues that Taiwan's era of sustained development began in 1895, so that by the time the United States began its aid program in 1950, Taiwan had already undergone half a century of development under Japanese tutelage.

6   Emma Wu, 'Local Scholars Take a Closer Look at Home', *Free China Review*, March 1992, pp. 6, 8.

7   Leonard Unger, 'Chiang Kai-shek's Second Chance', *Policy Review*, vol. 50, Fall 1989, p. 26.

8   Koxinga's Japanese origins formed part of the basis for Japan's claim to Taiwan in 1895: Frank P. Morello, *The International Legal Status of Formosa*, Martinus Nijhoff, The Hague, 1966, p. 13.

9   Jon Woronoff, *Asia's 'Miracle Economies'*, M.E. Sharpe Inc., New York, 1986, p. 64.

10   Gustav Ranis 'Industrial Development' in Walter Galenson (ed.), *Economic Growth and Structural Change in Taiwan*, Cornell University Press, Ithaca, 1979, p. 206–9.

11   Ho, *Economic Development of Taiwan 1860-1970*, p. 104. See also Robert Wade, *Governing the Market Economic Theory and the Role of Government in East Asian Industrialisation*, Princeton University Press, Princeton, New Jersey, 1990, p. 108.

12   Ranis in Galenson, *Economic Growth and Structural Change in Taiwan*, p. 211; and Yu-kang Mao, 'Land and Agricultural Policies in the

Process of Economic Development in the Republic of China on Taiwan', *Conference on Successful Economic Development Strategies of the Pacific Rim Nations*, Chung Hua Institution for Economic Research, Conference Series No. 10, Taipei, 1988, p. 91.

13 The rapidity of Japan's economic recovery in the period 1953–60, with GNP growth rates averaging close to 10 per cent per annum, was matched by few other countries: G.C. Allen, *Japan's Economic Policy*, Macmillan Press, London, 1980, p. 127.

14 Takeshi Hayashi, *The Japanese Experience in Technology*, United Nations University Press, Tokyo, 1990, pp. 11–12.

15 *Taiwan Statistical Data Book*, (hereafter TSDB), Council for Economic Planning and Development, Taipei, 1989, p. 222.

16 The China leg in Taiwan's modern period is discussed in Chapter 4.

17 Supra, note 4.

18 Department of Mines and Technical Surveys, *Taiwan (Formosa)*, Foreign Geography Information Series No. 5, Ottawa, Canada, 1952.

19 ibid.

20 Andrew Fraser, *First Fruits of Empire: Japan's Colonial Administration in Taiwan 1895–1934*, Papers on Far Eastern History, No. 38, Canberra, September 1988, pp. 93–95.

21 Taiwan's population in 1905 was around three million: Ho, *Economic Development of Taiwan 1860–1970*, p. 26.

22 Thomas B. Gold, 'Colonial Origins of Taiwanese Capitalism', in Edwin A Winckler and Susan Greenhalgh (eds), *Contending Approaches to the Political Economy of Taiwan*, M.E. Sharpe Inc., New York, 1988, pp. 101, 103. The Japanese were apparently so impressed by the idea of a crown colony like Hong Kong that they designed their colonial policy on Taiwan along the lines of a plan drawn up by a British consultant, W.M.H. Kirkwood: Christine Vertente, Hsu Hsueh-chi and Wu Mi-cha, *The Authentic Story of Taiwan*, Mappamundi Publishers, Knokke (Belgium), 1991, p. 156.

23 Vertente, Hsu and Wu, *The Authentic Story of Taiwan*, p. 159.

24 Allen, *Japan's Economic Policy*, p. 85. See also Ssu-yu Teng and John K. Fairbank, *China's Response to the West: a Documentary Survey 1839–1923*, Atheneum, New York, 1969, pp. 1–21.

25 Allen, *Japan's Economic Policy*, p. 181.

26 Edwin O. Reischauer, John K. Fairbank, Albert M. Craig, *East Asia: The Modern Transformation*, George Allen & Unwin, London, 1967, p. 180.

27 Peng Ming-min, *A Taste of Freedom: Memoirs of a Formosan Independence Leader*, Holt, Rinehart & Winston, New York 1972, pp. 59–60.

28 ibid.

29 See generally Joseph W. Ballantine, *Formosa*, The Brookings Institution, Washington, 1952, Chapter 1. In 1930 the Japanese allegedly

used poison gas to help suppress a major uprising by aborigines rebelling against Japanese brutality: Hsu Chieh-lin, 'The Republic of China and Japan', in Yu San Wang (ed.), *Foreign Policy of the Republic of China on Taiwan*, Praeger, New York, 1990, pp. 45, 46.

30 John Copper, *Taiwan: Nation, State or Province*, Westview, Boulder, Col., 1990, p. 24.

31 Robert Wade, 'State Intervention in Outwards-looking Development: Neoclassical Theory and Taiwanese Practise', in Gordon White (ed.), *Developmental States in East Asia*, St Martin's Press, New York, 1988, p. 36.

32 Samuel Pao-San Ho, 'Colonialism and Development: Korea, Taiwan and Kwantung', in Ramon Myers and Mark R. Peattie (eds), *The Japanese Colonial Empire 1895–1945*, Princeton University Press, Princeton, 1984, p. 386.

33 Allen, *Japan's Economic Policy*, p. 134. Bruce Cumings, 'The Origins and Development of the Northeast Asian Political Economy' in Deyo, *The Political Economy of the New Asian Industrialism*, pp. 45, 52.

34 There were 60 000 Japanese in a population of about three million in 1905. This number increased to around 271 000 in 1935: Shinkichi Eto, 'An Outline of Formosan History', in Mark Mancall (ed.), *Formosa Today*, Praeger, New York, 1964, p. 53. By 1940 there were 312 386 Japanese in Taiwan: Ho, *Economic Development of Taiwan 1860–1970*, p. 81.

35 Saburo Okita, *Japan in the World Economy*, The Japan Foundation, Tokyo, 1975, p. 169.

36 On the Japanese experiment in Manchukuo, see F.C. Jones, *Manchuria Since 1931*, Oxford University Press, London, 1949.

37 Jacoby, *US Aid to Taiwan*, p. 75.

38 Vertente, Hsu and Wu, *The Authentic Story of Taiwan*, p. 156.

39 Peter Rimmer, 'Taiwan's Future as a Regional Transport Hub', in Gary Klintworth (ed.), *Taiwan in the Asia-Pacific in the 1990s*, Allen & Unwin/Department of International Relations, ANU, Canberra, 1994, p. 217.

40 Roads multiplied from 164 kilometres in 1899 to 4456 kilometres in 1935: Eto, 'An Outline of Formosan History' in Mancall, *Formosa Today*, pp. 43, 50.

41 Rong-I Wu, 'Infrastructure and Economic Development', *Conference on Successful Economic Development Strategies of the Pacific Rim Nations*, supra, note 12, p. 451.

42 Okita, *Japan in the World Economy*, p. 168.

43 Erik Thorbecke, 'Agricultural Development', in Galenson, *Economic Growth and Structural Change in Taiwan*, p. 138.

44 Jacoby, *US Aid to Taiwan*, p. 74.

45 Ho, *Economic Development of Taiwan 1860–1970*, pp. 26, 28.

46 Eto, 'An Outline of Formosan History' in Mancall, *Formosa Today*, p. 55.

47 Ranis, 'Industrial Development', in Galenson, *Economic Growth and Structural Change in Taiwan*, pp. 206–9:

48 Ramon H. Myers and Adrienne Ching, 'Agricultural Development in Taiwan Under Japanese Colonial Rule', *Journal of Asian Studies*, vol. XXIII, no. 4, August 1964.

49 See William Henry Chamberlin, *Japan Over Asia*, Duckworth, London, 1938, p. 81; Ho, *Economic Development of Taiwan 1860–1970*, p. 63; Department of Mines, *Taiwan (Formosa)*, p. 15.

50 Department of Mines, *Taiwan (Formosa)*, pp. 21–22.

51 Ho, *Economic Development of Taiwan 1860–1970*, p. 31 and Ho, 'Colonialism and Development', in Myers and Peattie, *The Japanese Colonial Empire 1895–1945*, p. 369.

52 Yu-kang Mao, 'Land and Agricultural Policies', *Conference on Successful Economic Development Strategies of the Pacific Rim Nations*, p. 91.

53 *Economic Statistics Annual (Taiwan Area)*, The Republic of China, Department of Statistics, Ministry of Economic Affairs, Taipei, 1992, p. 3.

54 TSDB, p. 227.

55 Wade, *Governing the Market*, p. 195; Bruce Cumings 'The Origins and Development of the Northeast Asian Political Economy: Industrial Sectors, Product Cycles and Political Consequences', *International Organization*, vol. 38, no. 1, Winter 1984, pp. 1, 11.

56 Ho, 'Colonialism and Development' in Myers and Peattie, *The Japanese Colonial Empire 1895–1945*, pp. 371–73.

57 Fei, Ranis and Kuo, *Growth with Equity: The Taiwan Case*, p. 31.

58 Department of Mines, *Taiwan (Formosa)*, p. 16.

59 In 1930, 64 per cent of Taiwanese factories were engaged in food processing: Ho, *Economic Development of Taiwan 1860–1970*, p. 71.

60 ibid.

61 Vertente, Hsu and Wu, *The Authentic Story of Taiwan*, p. 159.

62 Ho, *Economic Development of Taiwan 1860–1970*, p. 75.

63 Jacoby, *US Aid to Taiwan*, p. 201.

64 Liu, Paul K.C., *Economic Development and Population in Taiwan Since 1895: An Over-view*, The Institute of Economics, Academica Sinica, Taipei, 1972, pp. 1–6.

65 Chamberlin, *Japan Over Asia*, p. 153; Jacoby, *US Aid to Taiwan*, p. 77.

66 Chamberlin, *Japan Over Asia*, pp. 51, 151; and Ho, 'Colonialism and Development', in Myers and Peattie, *The Japanese Colonial Empire 1895–1945*, p. 377.

67 Ho, *Economic Development of Taiwan 1860–1970*, p. 81.

68 Chamberlin, *Japan Over Asia*, p. 150 .

69 Ho, 'Colonialism and Development', in Myers and Peattie, *The Japanese Colonial Empire 1895–1945*, pp. 87, 375; Liu, *Economic Development and Population*, pp. 16.

70 Fei, Ranis and Kuo, *Growth with Equity: The Taiwan Case*, p. 37.

71 Taiwanese employees made up 55 per cent of the civil service of 84 995 in 1945, with just 2 per cent, or 2336, in the two highest grades: Ballantine, *Formosa*, p. 102.

72 Mark R. Peattie, Introduction to Myers and Peattie, *The Japanese Colonial Empire 1895–1945*, p. 27.

73 Chamberlin, *Japan Over Asia*, p. 152.

74 For example, the first Governor General, Kodama Gentaro, adopted a policy of tolerance towards local customs and offered material incentives to help quell guerrilla resistance: Vertente, Hsu and Wu, *The Authentic Story of Taiwan*, p. 156.

75 Ballantine, *Formosa*, p. 48.

76 Han Lih-wu, *Taiwan Today*, Cheng Chung Book Company, Taipei, 1988, p. 31.

77 E. Patricia Tsurumi, 'Colonial Education in Korea and Taiwan', in Myers and Peattie, *The Japanese Colonial Empire 1895–1945*, pp. 275, 309.

78 Personal conversations on Taiwan's identity with Byron Weng, Professor of Government and Public Administration, Chinese University of Hong Kong, and C.L. Chiou, Reader in Politics, University of Queensland, in Fremantle, 21–23 September 1993. Both were taught Japanese as children in pre-1945 Taiwan.

79 Ho, 'Colonialism and Development' in Myers and Peattie, *The Japanese Colonial Empire 1895–1945*, pp. 348, 352.

80 Quoted in Vertente, Hsu and Wu, *The Authentic Story of Taiwan*, p. 156.

81 Chamberlin, *Japan Over Asia*, p. 151.

82 Eto, 'An outline of Formosan History', in Mancall, *Formosa Today*, p. 43, 50ff.

83 Jacoby, *US Aid to Taiwan*, p. 80. From 1910–39, agricultural labour productivity increased by an average of 3 per cent per annum, while wages increased by 1.3 per cent per annum in real terms; and in manufacturing, productivity rose by 3.3 per cent per annum while wages were held to about 1.5 per cent per annum: Ho, 'Colonialism and Development' in Myers and Peattie, *The Japanese Colonial Empire 1895–1945*, p. 93.

84 The people:bicycle ratio improved from 698:1 in 1911 compared with 17:1 in 1940: Ho, *Economic Development of Taiwan 1860–1970*, pp. 99–

100. See also Ho, 'Colonialism and Development' in Myers and Peattie, *The Japanese Colonial Empire 1895–1945*, p. 379.

85 Alice H. Amsden, 'Taiwan's Economic History: A Case of Etatisme and a Challenge to Dependency Theory', *Modern China*, vol. 5, no. 3, July 1979, pp. 341, 348. See also Gold, 'Colonial Origins of Taiwanese Capitalism' in Winckler and Greenhalgh, *Contending Approaches to the Political Economy of Taiwan*, p. 116.

86 Ho, 'Colonialism and Development', in Myers and Peattie, *The Japanese Colonial Empire 1895–1945*, pp. 347, 354.

87 Tsurumi, 'Colonial Education in Korea and Taiwan', in Myers and Peattie, *The Japanese Colonial Empire 1895–1945*, pp. 287–88.

88 The flow of Taiwanese students to Japan reached 2400 in 1922 and over 7000 in 1942: Tsurumi, ibid., p. 292.

89 ibid., p. 289.

90 Ballantine, *Formosa*, pp. 33, 34.

91 Tsurumi, 'Colonial Education in Korea and Taiwan', in Myers and Peattie, *The Japanese Colonial Empire 1895–1945*, p. 287.

92 Denis Fred Simon, 'External Incorporation and Internal Reform', in Winckler and Greenhalgh, *Contending Approaches to the Political Economy of Taiwan*, pp. 138, 145.

93 Jacoby, *US Aid to Taiwan*, pp. 73–74; Paul Liu, on the other hand, rejects the consensus view that, overall, Japanese colonial rule brought about improvements to standards of living and instilled modern attitudes amongst the general population: Liu, *Economic Development and Population*, pp. 1–13.

94 George Barclay, *Colonial Development and Population in Taiwan*, Princeton University Press, Princeton, 1954, p. 7.

95 *Sinorama*, July 1993, p. 119.

96 While there was extensive war damage to military targets and oil refineries, John Copper claims that 'Taiwan sustained little damage to its economic infrastructure': Copper, *Taiwan: Nation State*, p. 76. Gustav Ranis offers a contrary view, claiming that much of Taiwan's transportation infrastructure, industrial plant, oil refineries, power stations and hydroelectric and irrigation systems had been heavily damaged by United States bombing raids and that three-quarters of Taiwan's industrial capacity, two-thirds of its power and half of the transport network were out of commission — Ranis, 'Industrial Development' in Galenson, *Economic Growth and Structural Change in Taiwan*, p. 209. Peng Ming-min concedes that the port of Keelung near Taipei was virtually destroyed and Kaohsiung was heavily damaged, but says that Taiwan's railways, basic industrial infrastructure, power plants and sugar mills were not, while warehouses were full of sugar, rice, chemicals, rubber and other raw materials: Peng, *A Taste of Freedom*, pp. 47–48, 61.

97 See Chapter 1; Peng, *A Taste of Freedom*, p. 70; and Ballantine, *Formosa*, p. 63. Ironically, the only reconciliation necessary on Taiwan was not that between the Japanese and the Taiwanese. Instead, it was a matter of healing the rift between the mainland Chinese and the Taiwanese, many of whom had been killed and ill-treated by the mainland administration when it took over the island. That reconciliation took nearly 40 years to achieve.

98 Mark Mancall, Introduction, in Mancall, *Formosa Today*, p. 27.

99 Department of Mines, *Taiwan (Formosa)*, p. 38.

100 Kwoh-ting Li, *Economic Transformation of Taiwan*, Shepheard-Walwyn, London, 1988, p. 218.

101 Liu, *Economic Development and Population*, pp. 1–13.

102 Han Lih-wu, *Taiwan Today*, p. 10.

103 Quoted by Ballantine, *Formosa*, p. 66.

104 Wade, *Governing the Market*, p. 74.

105 A. Doak Barnett, *China and the Major Powers in East Asia*, The Brookings Institution, Washington, 1977, p. 29; and O. Edmund Clubb, *China and Russia: The Great Game*, Columbia University Press, New York, 1971, p. 408.

106 Ballantine, *Formosa*, p. 49.

107 ibid., p. 49.

108 Jacoby, *US Aid to Taiwan*, p. 83.

109 Gold, 'Colonial Origins of Taiwanese Capitalism' in Winckler and Greenhalgh, *Contending Approaches to the Political Economy of Taiwan*, pp. 101, 116–17.

110 Ho, *Economic Development of Taiwan 1860–1970*, p. 100.

111 Amsden, 'Taiwan's Economic History' in Modern China, pp. 341, 348. See also Gold, 'Colonial Origins of Taiwanese Capitalism' in Winckler and Greenhalgh, *Contending Approaches to the Political Economy of Taiwan*, p. 116.

112 Xinhua, *Beijing*, commentary on Lee Teng-hui, 18 June 1994, in Foreign Broadcast Information Service China, 20 June 1994, p. 66.

113 Masato Hayashida, *Entrepreneurship in Taiwan and Korea: A Comparison*, IIGP Policy Paper No. 109E, International Institute for Global Peace, Tokyo, May 1993; and personal correspondence, 16 July 1993.

114 ibid.

115 ibid.

116 Okita, *Japan in the World Economy*, p. 21.

117 Simon Kuznets, 'Growth and Structural Shifts', in Galenson, *Economic Growth and Structural Change in Taiwan*, pp. 15, 49. It was not the sole reason, however, because the real value of Taiwan's exports

over the period 1952–75 rose by nearly 14 per cent per annum, whereas Taiwanese exports to Japan rose by only 7.5 per cent per annum: Ian M.D. Little 'An Economic Reconnaissance', in Galenson, ibid., pp. 448, 464.

118 Mitchell Bernard, *Northeast Asia The Political Economy of a Postwar Regional System*, Joint Centre for Asia Pacific Studies, Asia Papers No. 2, University of Toronto–York University, 1989, p. 15.

119 Chiang Hsiao-wu, 'Republic of China's Representative to Tokyo', article in *Sinorama*, April 1991, p. 115.

120 *Monthly Statistics of Exports and Imports (Taiwan Area)*, The Republic of China, Ministry of Finance, Taipei, December 1990. See also Denis Fred Simon, 'Technology Transfer and National Autonomy', in Winckler and Greenhalgh, *Contending Approaches to the Political Economy of Taiwan*, pp. 206, 213–14, 222; Tran Van Tho, *Direct Investment and Technology: Japan and Northeast and Southeast Asia*, Japan Centre for Economic Research, Research Report Series No. 56, 1986; and Toru Nakakita, 'The Takeoff of the East Asian Economic Sphere', in *Japan Review of International Affairs*, vol. 5, no. 1, Spring/Summer 1991, pp. 62, 77.

121 *China Post*, 24 March 1992.

122 Bernard, 'Northeast Asia The Political Economy of a Postwar Regional System', p. 17.

123 Gold, 'Colonial Origins of Taiwanese Capitalism', in Winckler and Greenhalgh, *Contending Approaches to the Political Economy of Taiwan*, p. 197.

124 Denis Fred Simon, 'The Orbital Mechanics of Taiwan's Technological Development: An Examination of the Gravitational Pushes and Pulls', in Klintworth, *Taiwan in the Asia-Pacific in the 1990s*, pp. 195, 201.

125 Huang Chi, The State and Foreign Capital: A Case Study of Taiwan, PhD Thesis, Department of Political Science, Indiana University, February 1986, p. 189, cited in Walden Bello and Stephanie Rosenfeld, *Dragons in Distress: Asia's Miracle Economies in Crisis*, Food First, San Francisco, 1990, p. 243.

126 Denis Simon, *Taiwan, Technology Transfer and Transnationals: The Political Management of Dependency*, PhD Thesis, University of California, Berkeley, 1980, p. 327, cited in Bello and Rosenfeld, *Dragons in Distress*, p. 244.

127 Kiyoshi Kojima, *Japan and a New World Economic Order*, Tuttle, Tokyo, 1977, p. 179.

128 Cumings, 'The Northeast Asian Political Economy', *International Organization*, pp. 1, 4.

129 Osman Tseng, 'Talking Fair Trade', *Free China Review*, August 1991, pp. 54, 56.

130 C.L. Chiou, Reader in Politics, University of Queensland, personal interview, 21 September 1993.

131 ibid.

132 TSDB, p. 123.

133 *Statistics on Overseas Chinese and Foreign Investment*, Investment Commission, Ministry of Economic Affairs, Republic of China, Taipei, 1992.

134 TSDB (1993 edition), pp. 244–46.

135 *Statistics on Overseas Chinese and Foreign Investment*, Investment Commission, Ministry of Economic Affairs, Republic of China, Taipei, 1993.

136 US$2.2 billion up to 1990: Ma Zongshi,'China's Role in the Emerging Multipolar Asia-Pacific Scene', *Contemporary International Relations*, no. 6, China Institute of Contemporary International Relations, Beijing, February 1991, p. 14.

137 *Statistics on Overseas Chinese and Foreign Investment*, Investment Commission, Ministry of Economic Affairs, Republic of China, 1993.

138 Tseng, 'Talking Fair Trade', pp. 54, 58.

139 Ministry of Finance, Government of Japan, 1991.

140 ibid.

141 International Monetary Fund, *Direction of Trade Statistics Yearbook*, IMF, Washington, DC, 1992.

142 ibid.

143 John Copper claims that in 'frequent meetings with conservative Japanese leaders, particularly those with ties to the Japanese military', Taiwanese leaders had pointed out the problems Japan might experience if China took over Taiwan, such as dislocation of its oil SLOCs, disruption of its trade and a reduction of its influence in the region: John Copper, 'Taiwan's Strategy and America's China Policy', *Orbis*, vol. 21, no. 2, Summer 1977, pp. 261, 269 . See also Chiao Chiao Hsieh, *Strategy for Survival*, The Sherwood Press, London, 1985, p. 238.

144 Interviews, Tokyo, 15 April 1991.

145 The Japan–United States Defence Treaty is subject to different interpretations but there is scope for Japanese–United States co-operation in the event of a threat to Taiwan. The preamble of the Treaty states that the United States and Japan have a common concern in the maintenance of international peace and security in the Far East while Article 4 states that they will consult together whenever the security of Japan or international peace and security in the Far East are

threatened: Japanese Defence Agency, *Defence of Japan*, Tokyo, 1992, p. 220. On the significance of the *Taiwan Relations Act*, see Chapter 3.

146 *New York Times*, 22 November 1969, p. 14.

147 The operative paragraph of the Sino-Japanese Joint Communiqué states that: 'The Government of the People's Republic of China reaffirms that Taiwan is an inalienable part of the territory of the People's Republic of China. The Government of Japan fully understands and respects this stand of the Government of China and adheres to its stand of complying with Article 8 of the Potsdam Declaration.' The Potsdam Declaration of 26 July 1945, issued by United States President Truman and British Prime Minister Winston Churchill, with the concurrence of China's Chiang Kai-shek, stated that Japan's postwar sovereignty was to be limited 'to the islands of Hokkaido, Honshu, Shikoku and Kyushu and such minor islands as the Allies determine': in Keesings, *Contemporary Archives 1971–72*, London, 1972, p. 25517.

148 Cable from Tokyo, 5 December 1972, on Australian Department of Foreign Affairs and Trade file 519/3/1, part 14, Formosa — External Relations with Australia (General), Department of Foreign Affairs and Trade, Canberra.

149 Research Institute for Peace and Security, *Asia Security 1979*, Tokyo, 1979, pp. 93–94; Research Institute for Peace and Security, *Asia Security 1980*, Tokyo, 1980, p. 107, cited in A. James Gregor, 'US Interests in Northeast Asia and the Security of Taiwan', *Strategic Review*, Winter 1985, pp. 52, 54. Also author interviews, Japanese Defence Agency, Tokyo, April 1990.

150 David Arase, 'Japan in East Asia', in Tsuneo Akaha and Frank Langdon (eds), *Japan in the Posthegemonic World*, Lynne Rienner Publishers, Boulder and London, 1989, pp. 113, 131.

3 Taiwan's American Interlude

There are three countries that are central to any consideration of Taiwan's development and identity: Japan, the United States and China. The Japanese provided the economic base. China provided the threat. This chapter is about the American input and Taiwan's special and ongoing relationship with Washington. The United States supplied the economic aid, the military guarantees, the markets, the technology, the training and education, fluency in English and exposure to United States market practices that underpinned Taiwan's postwar takeoff. It was a period in which Taiwan was to a large degree Americanised.

Taiwan's separation from the mainland was poised to end in 1948–49. The Japanese administration had been withdrawn in 1946. The PLA were massing forces in Fujian in preparation for crossing the Strait. Only the United States could preserve Taiwan's autonomy, but the United States government had written off the 'helpless and hopeless' Chiang Kai-shek because, said Secretary of State Dean Acheson, he had 'completely lost the support of the Chinese people, despite huge amounts of American aid'.[1] The United States State Department had in any case decided that Taiwan held no strategic significance for America.[2] On 5 January 1950, President Truman announced that the United States would not become involved in China's civil war.[3]

By 1949, Taiwan was on the verge of collapse from the weight of runaway inflation, chaotic social and political conditions, the loss of Japanese technicians, a war-damaged infrastructure, a lack of fertilisers and insecticides, a shortage of foreign exchange, deep hostility between mainlanders and Taiwanese and a government in disarray after its mainland debacle.[4] The mainlanders, moreover, had to feed and house an oversized army and almost two million refugees.

Had Taiwan reverted to Chinese control, its subsequent development path would probably have resembled that of Hainan island, surrendered to the PLA by the Kuomintang in March 1949. Hainan is comparable to Taiwan in its agricultural potential, size, island geography, climate and offshore location. It is perhaps too far to the south of China's richest coastal provinces and, with the Qiongzhou Strait just 25 kilometres wide, it is much closer to the mainland than Taiwan. Unlike Taiwan, Hainan has never been free of mainland control and was never exposed to sustained foreign mercantile or colonial influences. Apart from its military functions during the Second Indochina War, Hainan's distance from Beijing and its island characteristics left it, until recently, a relatively backward and undeveloped part of China.

However, United States security concerns about the spread of world communism preserved Taiwan from Hainan's fate. Following the outbreak of the Korean War on 25 June 1950, the United States reversed its hands-off policy. Taiwan almost overnight became 'an important anchor in the defensive chain from the Aleutians to Australia'.[5] President Truman ordered the Seventh Fleet to prevent a mainland attack on Taiwan as occupation of Taiwan by Communist forces was held to be a direct threat to the United States' national interest.[6]

Taiwan was given twenty years of security by United States Seventh Fleet warships, which patrolled the Taiwan Strait until September 1969. The neutralisation of the Taiwan Strait prevented a mainland attack on Taiwan and preserved Taiwan's separateness. At the same time, the Kuomintang's armed forces were prevented from launching operations against the mainland.[7]

The United States intervention in China's civil war restrained the two sides from attacking each other and, in effect, forced them to go their separate ways. It reinforced Taiwan's previous history of separatism and independence from the mainland, it allowed the Kuomintang to concentrate on the economic development of Taiwan and it helped hasten Taiwan's integration into the mainstream of the Asia-Pacific's capitalist political economy. In the long run, it also undermined the insistence of the Kuomintang that Taiwan was part of one China.

In other words, the American shield between Taiwan and the mainland consolidated Taiwan's status as an island unconnected with the mainland, meaning that the separation of Taiwan from the mainland that had been pioneered by Japan was guaranteed by the United States, the leading hegemonic power in East Asia since 1945. These consecutive periods of Japanese and United States control over Taiwan's fortunes, to the exclusion of China, reinforced Taiwan's drift towards an existence that is separate and independent from the mainland. This autonomy is the basis of Taiwan's bid for United Nations membership today.

America's Taiwan policy has been, and in many ways still is, refracted through Washington's approach to mainland China. The United States has been at odds with, or mistrusted, China for much of the postwar period. In that context, Taiwan has been treated as a part of China, yet physically and ideologically separate from the mainland. Because Taiwan was a strategic asset, Kuomintang violations of human rights were overlooked while the island was given privileged treatment in terms of military support, material and financial aid and market access. Behind an American shield, Chiang Kai-shek could confidently claim to represent all of China and disregard the demands of the majority of Taiwanese who were excluded from the political process and who had been subjected to rule by martial law.[8]

The United States followed in Japan's footsteps vis-a-vis Taiwan for many of the same reasons that prompted Japan to seize the island in 1895. That is, Taiwan was a physical asset: a strategically placed, defensible island in the centre of the western Pacific. And it was adjacent to China, then allied to the Soviet Union and thus regarded by Washington as an enemy state. In this context, an anti-communist Taiwan was an important ally in the United States-led struggle against world communism. Taiwan's location made it 'a vital link' in a United States security chain in the western Pacific.[9] For General Douglas Macarthur, Taiwan was 'an unsinkable aircraft carrier and submarine tender ideally located for offensive or defensive operations'.[10] He said:

> Formosa's geographical location was such [that] in the hands of a power unfriendly to the United States, it constituted a salient in the very centre of America's strategic frontier and to abandon Formosa would completely expose friends in the Philippines, Australia, New Zealand, Indonesia and in Japan and other areas.[11]

A staunchly pro-Western Taiwan, on the other hand, would complicate military planning by the PLA.[12]

The United States Joint Chiefs of Staff therefore recommended a resumption of economic and military aid to Taiwan and United States involvement in reorganisation and training of the Nationalist armed forces.[13] By the 1960s, when it had emerged as a major support base for United States military operations in Southeast Asia, up to 10 000 United States military personnel were based in Taiwan.[14]

United States aid and protection of Taiwan was critically important for Taiwan's development as a newly industrialising economy in East Asia. It gave the Kuomintang time — in fact, several decades — to establish itself as a viable state that might be expected to survive independently. Ironically, United States policy towards China in the 1950s resulted in Taiwan being pushed back towards its old colonial overlord, Japan. As Frederic Deyo explains, the United States transformed Taiwan into one of several 'developmentalist, authoritarian anti-communist states in a newly revived, Japan-centred, capitalist regional economy'.[15]

The political wounds left during this period are still being healed, but the economic results were 'astounding'.[16] As Neil Jacoby suggests, large-scale United States assistance in the period 1950–65 succeeded 'superlatively well'.[17] Between 1950 and 1965, Taiwan received between 15 and 25 per cent of all United States regional aid in East Asia in most years and up to 47 per cent in 1954 when the United States–ROC Mutual Defence Treaty was signed.[18] It was perhaps 'the richest United States economic aid programme in East Asia' and averaged about 6.4 per cent of Taiwan's GNP and about 34 per cent of total gross investment in Taiwan over the period 1951–65.[19] In June 1965, United States aid ceased because the Taiwanese economy had graduated from 'deep dependence to self-sustained rapid growth'.[20]

Much has been written about the reasons for Taiwan's successful economic development and which particular factors were more or less important.[21] The great expansion of world trade during the 1950s and 1960s, Confucianism, Sun Yatsenism, location and geography, transnational linkages to the biggest and strongest market in the world, foreign investment, lessons from the mainland, getting inflation under control, cheap labour, a successful land reform program, government intervention and high-quality leaders are all important factors in the explanation for Taiwan's rapid postwar development.[22] So was Taiwan's Japanese infrastructure.[23] As well as material aid, United States markets played an important role in Taiwan's rapid economic development. United States political support helped Taiwan establish its creditworthiness with international financial institutions and gain technical assistance from the United Nations and its agencies.[24] United States aid and protection was important for Japanese, United States and overseas Chinese investment in Taiwan.

However, the entire experiment in nation-building on Taiwan was underwritten by the credibility of the United States military commitment to defend Taiwan against external attack. Japan, South Korea and South Vietnam were given similar assurances by the United States.[25] According to United States Secretary of State John Foster Dulles, if Chiang Kaishek's government collapsed, it would so jeopardise America's offshore defences that 'it would really be a matter of time before [the United States] was forced back to Hawaii or the West Coast'.[26] That is, an essential precondition for Taiwan's economic recovery, development and take-off and for its political stability was the United States military guarantee. Without it, Taiwan would never have prospered. Without similar, albeit unwritten, United States military guarantees today, Taiwan's future would be bleak.

Several decades have elapsed since the United States last hinted at the possible use of tactical nuclear weapons to ensure that Taiwan survived as a separate, sovereign independent state.[27] While the United States may acknowledge that the Chinese on both sides of the Taiwan Strait claim to be part of one China, Washington retains a strategic and political interest in Taiwan's separation from a communist China. This may be one reason why the United States has never clarified its position on China's claim of sovereignty over Taiwan, an omission noted by Chinese scholars in Beijing.[28]

In the 1950s, when relations between China and the United States were particularly hostile, Taiwan's separation from the mainland looked like a permanent feature on East Asia's geopolitical landscape. However, Chiang Kai-shek's ambition to recover the mainland helped preserve a degree of ambiguity about Taiwan's status. Chiang Kai-shek was in a sense pulling Taiwan towards the mainland, and away from the West. Once the Chinese civil war was accepted as having come to an end, Taiwan's separateness from mainland China and the Taiwanisation of the Kuomintang might be expected to accelerate in the absence of some new gravitational pull from mainland China.

Even in the 1950s, however, the objective of United States allies like Australia was to recognise geopolitical realities, contrary to the wishes of Chiang Kai-shek. Both the United States and Australia wanted a physical separation of the warring parties. Australia wanted Chiang Kai-shek to abandon the offshore islands, cease launching attacks on the mainland and recognise the limits of his sovereignty to Taiwan. At the same, Beijing had to be persuaded to accept the fact of Taiwan's separation from the mainland.[29]

In December 1954, the United States and Taiwan signed a Mutual Defence Treaty intended to deter China and restrain the Nationalists.[30] The treaty was bolstered by the Formosa Resolution of January 1955 which authorised the United States President 'to employ the Armed Forces of the United States as necessary' to protect Taiwan, the Pescadores and other islands in Nationalist hands such as Matsu and Quemoy.[31] However, the support of the United States encouraged Chiang to persist in launching raids on the mainland from Quemoy and Matsu. Crises over the islands occurred in 1954, 1958 and 1962, as China responded to what were acts of brinkmanship practised by Chiang Kai-shek. While the official United States position was to avoid involvement in any attempt to recover the mainland, Washington felt obliged to tolerate Chiang's mainland pretensions and provocations.[32] The net result was to prolong the civil war and the debate over whether or not Taiwan was a part of China.

Although Sino–United States relations remained in stalemate for the next decade, with the United States bogged down in Vietnam, and China preoccupied with the Cultural Revolution, the ground rules for future Sino-United States and Sino-Taiwanese relations had been established: the United States would not intervene militarily if China did not use force against Taiwan and Taiwan would not be allowed to launch attacks on or otherwise provoke the mainland. This was a satisfactory working arrangement for both the United States and for China. It defused a civil war by separating the two warring parties; it also helped to consolidate Taiwan's separate identity.

Secure behind the Seventh Fleet, Taiwan was revived, modernised and transformed in accordance with a Japanese-style development plan. According to Neil Jacoby, the United States implemented a sequence of development strategies on Taiwan beginning with financial and social stability and strong defences, a rapid increase in agricultural productivity, the development of Taiwan's infrastructure, its human resources and industry and, in 1960, an emphasis on fostering private enterprise and promoting exports.[33]

In the beginning, the United States supplied the daily necessities of life and material aid, including the large amounts of chemical fertiliser, wheat, cotton and raw materials that were needed to revive the economy. This was complemented by financial assistance to stabilise inflation and pay for the import of essential capital goods, machinery and technical services.[34] What amounted to 'massive injections' of American economic and military assistance then 'enabled Taiwan to transmute domestic saving into productive investment'.[35] Nearly 40 per cent of the island's gross domestic capital formation and 30 per cent of Taiwan's essential imports in the 1950s were financed by United States financial aid.[36]

Almost half of the United States aid program was devoted to vital infrastructural development such as construction of roads, harbours, railways, thermal and hydroelectric power stations, communications and other infrastructure needed to attract foreign investment.[37] There was substantial investment in industries started by the Japanese, such as fertilisers, chemicals and food processing. These improvements provided the catalyst for the rapid expansion of Taiwanese industry around the key port cities of Taipei/Keelung and Kaohsiung.[38] As Joseph Ballantine concluded in 1952, American rehabilitation and expansion of productive industries and the improvement of transportation facilities provided the foundations for Taiwan's subsequent economic and political stability.[39]

United States military aid, meanwhile, equipped Taiwan's defence forces at a time of foreign exchange shortages and high defence expenditure. Total United States military assistance to Taiwan during the period 1951–65 was worth at least twice as much as the $1.465 billion given by the United States in civil aid over the same period.[40] The United States provided most of Taiwan's heavy military equipment, including ammunition, artillery, aircraft, tanks, ships and vehicles as well as budgetary support, technical training and advice, airfields, roads and telecommunications facilities.

As Samuel Ho observes, United States aid enabled Taiwan to pursue the conflicting objectives of rapid economic growth and stable prices, and at the same time possess a strong military force.[41] According to Neil Jacoby, United States aid over the period 1950–65 had such significant multiplier effects on GNP growth rates that Taiwan reached living standards in 1964 that it otherwise would have taken until 1995 to achieve.[42] During the fifteen-year period of United States aid to Taiwan, Taiwan achieved an average annual compound rate of growth in real GNP of around 7.5 per cent while per capita GNP increased at the astonishing annual compound rate of 4.2 per cent per annum despite high defence expenditure and a high rate of population growth.[43] Without United States aid and protection, therefore, Taiwan could not have survived and thrived.

The Sino-American Joint Commission on Rural Reconstruction (JCRR), a powerful United States-run 'superministry of agriculture', which took about one-third of all United States aid to Taiwan, was of particular importance in this regard.[44] It often overruled Kuomintang objections to reform by a mixture of incentives and threats to withhold aid.[45] It was the catalyst for a great number of projects, including the planning and implementation of land reform, crop improvement, soil conservation, irrigation, product diversification, pest control, scientific cropping, research and education, biological and technical innovations, land consolidation, farmers' organisations, animal husbandry, rural health, fisheries, agricultural credit, rural economics and a farm radio service.[46] Like the Japanese, the JCRR provided a variety of support services to upgrade agriculture, including co-ordination of research, education and extension activities throughout Taiwan. It synchronised an island-wide rat control campaign that eliminated approximately 27 610 000 rats.[47]

The overall package — Taiwan's comparative advantage in labour, Japanese agricultural foundations and United States aid and direction — resulted in a 'green revolution' that formed the basis for Taiwan's successful industrialisation.[48] The surplus transferred from agriculture to industry through a rice/fertiliser exchange mechanism amounted to 22 per cent of total agricultural production in 1950–55 and around 15 per cent between 1956 and 1969.[49]

Additional funds came from United States multinationals like General Electric, ITT, RCA, United States Steel, General Motors, General Instruments, Texas Instruments, Union Carbide and Kodak. They and 600 other United States companies placed US$4.26 billion or 28.4 per cent of total foreign investment of US$15 billion in Taiwan between 1952 and 1991.[50] In 1992, Taiwan received around 2.7 per cent of all United States foreign investment in the Asia-Pacific.[51] Around 60 per cent of investments by United States multinationals was concentrated in Taiwan's electronic and electrical appliance export industries. Japan rivals the United States' overall DFI today, but the latter was the dominant source of foreign investment capital in Taiwan's formative decades with over 90 per cent of the total in the 1950s, over 60 per cent for the period 1952–70 and 27.5 per cent in the period 1952–90.[52]

United States aid and investment in Taiwan was accompanied by the transfer of some vitally important intangibles to Taiwan: the philosophy of the free market, familiarity with the English language and advanced technical training.[53]

The majority of the well-educated workers, technical staff and senior engineers involved in Taiwan's development over the last four decades were trained in the United States.[54] Like access to United States markets, Taiwanese access to training opportunities in the United States educational system was one of the keys to Taiwan's rapid economic growth.[55] President Lee Teng-hui, Premier Lien Chan and over half of Taiwan's cabinet ministers received their postgraduate training in the United States and are at home with the English language (in contrast to many in the Chinese leadership, such as Premier Li Peng and Party Secretary General Jiang Zemin, who were trained in the former Soviet Union and speak Russian). According to Neil Jacoby, United States influence was instrumental in promoting the institutions of private property, individual incentives, freedom of enterprise, competitive markets, the liberalisation of foreign trade, realistic exchange rates and the elimination of government red tape and subsidies.[56] American movies, music and fast food became part of Taiwan's popular culture.[57] American values, American standards and American practices saturated 'almost every major social institution, public and private, of the Republic of China' right down to 'the grass roots of society'.[58] These American free enterprise values were 'the key to Taiwan's fast growth' in Jacoby's view.[59]

Equally important, however, was Taiwanese access to the United States as an export market for its expanding industrial and manufacturing sector without any obligation to open up its own market to United States exports.[60] Taiwan was the largest beneficiary of the United States Generalised System of Preferences from 1976 to 1988. The GSP permitted 3000 Taiwan-made products to enter the United States duty free.[61] The United States was the largest, most reliable and most open market in the world and it provided ample opportunities for the expansion of Taiwanese exports.[62] The Taiwanese currency was undervalued and Taiwanese industries were protected by high tariffs. Between 1952 and 1988, exports as a percentage of Taiwan's economic growth increased from 8.6 per cent to 50.3 per cent.[63] The United States' share of Taiwanese exports (mainly electrical and electronic goods, textiles and clothing, footwear, toys and sporting goods) jumped from 3.5 per cent in 1952 to 11.5 per cent in 1960, 21.9 per cent in 1961, 38 per cent in 1969 and a peak of 48.8 per cent in 1984 (see Table 10). Taiwan's exports to the United States grew at a rate of more than 22 per cent per annum between 1954 and 1984, whereas imports grew by around 16 per cent per annum. International trade contributes about 90 per cent of Taiwan's GNP so nearly a quarter of Taiwan's GNP and most of its accumulated trade surplus stems from trade with the United States.[64]

Michael Hsiao suggests that Taiwan was fortunate to 'hit the market' in the United States in the 1960s, a time when the limits of growth in agricultural exports to Japan and elsewhere had been reached.[65] Over the period 1952–84, the share of agriculture in Gross Domestic Product declined from 32.2 per cent to 6.3 per cent (see Table 6), whereas over the same period manufacturing rose from 12.9 per cent to 37.6 per cent. Taiwan, in effect, was able to change horses in midstream. Instead of depending on exports of mainly agricultural products to Japan (which took 59.5 per cent of all exports in 1955), Taiwan was able to switch to exporting manufactured goods to the United States (which took 48.8 per cent of all exports from Taiwan in 1984).

The United States aimed to create a model capitalist Chinese economy in Taiwan that would contrast with mainland communism and in this regard it might be said that the United States succeeded very well. American political pressure, aid, values and markets created a Taiwanese private sector that became 'the mainspring in Taiwan's economy'.[66] Chalmers Johnson goes so far as to suggest that 'without the initial American pressure . . . it is hard to see how the Kuomintang would ever have invented the capitalist developmental state on its own'.[67]

As well as aid, investment and market access, Taiwan was in a position to benefit from its status as a client state of the United States by becoming a supplier of equipment, food and ammunition for American military operations in the Asia-Pacific region.[68]

But by 1965, the United States terminated its aid program to Taiwan. In 1967, Richard Nixon foreshadowed his intention to normalise relations with China if he became President.[69] In July 1971, Nixon's National Security Adviser, Henry Kissinger, travelled to Beijing via Pakistan. With that signal, Taiwan's claim to represent China became untenable and it withdrew from the United Nations and its key agencies in October 1971. For United States allies like Australia and Canada, China was a political reality and an increasingly important market.[70] For the United States, friendship with China presented opportunities that could be used to extricate America from its involvement in Indochina. In February 1972, President Richard Nixon made his historic visit to China. The United States, however, continued to guarantee Taiwan's security by maintaining diplomatic ties and its Defence Treaty with Taipei for the rest of the decade. The Formosa Resolution of 1955, committing the United States to defend Taiwan and its offshore islands, was not repealed until 1974 and there were still 1100 American military personnel based in Taiwan in 1977.[71]

By the late 1970s, however, Soviet–United States antagonism had become particularly tense. The United States perceived a shift in the balance of strategic weaponry in favour of the Soviet Union. The Soviet Navy was active in the Indian Ocean and had developed naval facilities in the Horn of Africa. By 1977, the Soviet Navy had obtained access to Cam Ranh Bay in Vietnam. In November 1978, Vietnam signed a Treaty of Friendship and Co-operation with the Soviet Union and on 25 December 1978 it invaded Cambodia. President Carter and his advisers saw a China card as the central element in dealing with an expansionist Soviet Union.[72] In that larger strategic game, Taiwan was a dispensable pawn.

Sino-United States normalisation was announced on 15 December 1978, with effect from 1 January 1979. The United States State Department instructed its ambassador in Taipei to give one hour's notice to the Republic of China. As of 1 January 1979, the United States formally recognised Beijing, withdrew diplomatic recognition from Taipei and gave notice of the abrogation of the United States–ROC Mutual Defence Treaty as of 31 December 1979.

Strategically, Taiwan looked to be very vulnerable. It had been dealt a devastating blow to its self-esteem, its confidence and its aspirations to be the Republic of China. It was effectively on its own, a circumstance that forced the Kuomintang to drastically rethink its calculus for survival, and particularly its attitude towards one China, its view of Beijing and its approach to Taiwanese politics. The end result was to hasten the Taiwan-isation of the Kuomintang and Taiwan's emergence as an independent country.[73]

At the time, it was expected that, without strong United States guaran-tees, Taiwan had few options other than to 'seek some form of accommoda-tion with Peking, leading to an eventual reversion of the island to Peking's jurisdiction'.[74] Taiwan had become an obstacle to Washington's pursuit of its main game with Beijing. Like other governments of the day, the Carter Administration was very sensitive to any adverse reaction from the PRC over Taiwan. It insisted that Taiwan close all its consulates in America.[75]

However, China was in no position to take advantage of Taiwan's vul-nerability for three reasons. First, the PLA's General Staff Department concluded that China was not strong enough militarily. Second, China was dependent on the United States vis-a-vis the Soviet Union in a three-way triangular dynamic. The same strategic considerations that drove the United States into an alliance of convenience with Beijing at Taiwan's expense also served to restrain China. In March 1979, Russian warships made their first port call to Cam Ranh Bay (the first by Russian warships since April 1905) while in December 1979, the Soviet Union invaded Afghanistan. Perceiving itself to be the target of a Soviet encirclement strategy in Asia, Beijing needed the United States as much as the United States needed China. Beijing could not afford, therefore, to alienate the United States and key allies, such as Japan, by even hinting at a threat to use force against Taiwan. Third, the United States Congress passed a spe-cial *Taiwan Relations Act* (TRA) in April 1979. The Act was intended to reassure the Taiwanese and deter mainland China from any attempt to use force against Taiwan. The Act, as an Act of Congress, has proved to be very close to the spirit and intent of the United States–ROC Mutual Defence Treaty. The Act, passed by the United States Congress in April 1979, states *inter alia* that it is United States policy:

> to make clear that the United States decision to establish diplomatic relations with the PRC rests upon the expectation that the future of Taiwan will be determined by peaceful means; . . . to consider any effort to determine the future of Taiwan by other than peaceful means . . . a threat to the peace and security of the Western Pacific area and of grave concern to the United States; to provide Taiwan with arms of a defensive character; [and] to maintain the capacity of the United States to resist any resort to force or other forms of coer-cion that would jeopardize the security or social or economic system of the people of Taiwan.[76]

Section 2(c) of the Act provides that:

> The preservation and enhancement of the human rights of all the people on Taiwan are hereby reaffirmed as objectives of the United States.[77]

Section 3 provides that the United States:

will make available to Taiwan such defense articles and defense ser-vices as may be necessary to enable Taiwan to maintain a sufficient self-defence capability [and that the] President is directed to inform Congress promptly of any threat to the security of the social or eco-nomic system of the people on Taiwan, and any danger to the inter-ests of the United States arising therefrom . . . The President and the Congress shall determine the nature and quantity of such defence articles and services based solely upon their judgement of the needs of Taiwan.[78]

The Act was intended to be part of a transitional mechanism pending the settlement of the mainland–Taiwan unification issue. It was to become 'a relic of the past' as contacts between Taiwan and the mainland developed.[79] Read literally, however, the Act left open the possibility of renewed United States military protection and assistance to safeguard Taiwan's interests and deter mainland China if and when it was deemed necessary.[80] That was how the Act was interpreted at the time by the Japanese.[81] It is how the Act was interpreted by the United States in Sep-tember 1992 when President Bush announced his decision to sell aircraft to Taiwan. In this sense, the ambiguity of the *Taiwan Relations Act* proved to be a very useful (although because it is so 'dangerously vague' it invites miscalculation in a prospective crisis).[82]

As well as its implicit expression of an ongoing United States commit-ment to protect Taiwan from attack by the mainland, Section 4(b) of the Act ensured that some 46 treaties in existence before December 1978 remain in force today (with the main exception of the Defence Treaty, ter-minated on one year's notice in December 1979). The United States, in other words, undertook to treat and has subsequently treated, the Kuom-intang government in Taipei — not the government of the PRC in Beijing — as the authority that is in effective administrative control of Taiwan.

Under the Act, Taiwan was, for the purposes of United States domestic law, accorded treatment equivalent to that of a sovereign state. The Act has allowed trade negotiations over issues such as Taiwanese trade prac-tices, drift-net fishing, copyright and intellectual property 'to be addressed and dealt with as effectively as if there were a recognised gov-ernment on the other side'.[83] The Act allowed Taiwanese exporters to benefit from key economic statutes in the United States such as Most Favoured Nation and the Generalised System of Preferences for develop-ing countries (until it graduated to developed country status in 1989).[84] Since 1979, over 50 additional agreements in aviation, trade, commerce, fisheries, education, defence technology and other areas have been signed between Taiwan's Coordination Council of North American Affairs (CCNAA, redesignated 'Taipei Economic and Cultural Represen-tative Office' in September 1994) in Washington and its counterpart, the American Institute in Taiwan (AIT) in Taipei. Both offices represent their respective countries, are staffed by career diplomats and carry out all the diplomatic 'functions previously performed by the embassies and con-sulates', including the issue of visas.[85] As well as Washington, Taiwan has offices in twelve American cities, including New York, Los Angeles, Chicago, Houston, Atlantic City, Seattle, San Francisco and Honolulu — seven consulate-equivalent offices more than it had as the Republic of China in 1979.

Under the *TRA*, Taiwan has obtained judicial recognition as a state enti-tled to the benefits of the *Foreign Sovereign Immunities Act* in several United States court cases involving Taiwan or Taiwanese interests. That is, the Act effectively sustains Taiwan's right to choose between the options of reuni-fication with the mainland, independence, or something in between that can adapt to the state of Taiwan's relations with the mainland.[86]

Of course, these options were not so clearcut in 1980. The United States was then preoccupied in dealing with 'the major strategic problem for the next decade — the containment of expanding Soviet military power and influence in world affairs'.[87] Reagan's first Secretary of State, Alexander Haig, and other influential voices in the United States Department of Defence 'believed absolutely in the necessity of a secure relationship, per-haps ultimately a strategic relationship with China, the better to confront the Soviet Union'.[88] The United States interest in strengthening the Chi-nese navy was reflected in United States naval ship visits to China and sales of naval engine technology, ASW torpedoes and ship-borne air defence systems.[89] The United States also pursued defence co-operation in other areas, such as intelligence exchanges and the modernisation of China's F-8 fighter aircraft.[90] American concern about the Soviet threat gave China leverage to demand an end to United States arms sales to Taiwan, particularly the F-16 fighter aircraft and Harpoon anti-ship mis-siles.[91] In November 1981, the Pentagon decided that Taiwan did not need a fighter aircraft as advanced as the F-16.[92] On 17 August 1982, the United States and China issued a Joint Communiqué which said:

> The United States government states that it does not seek to carry out a long-term policy of arms sales to Taiwan, that its arms sales to Taiwan will not exceed, either in qualitative or in quantitative terms, the level of those supplied in recent years since [1979] and that it intends to gradually reduce its sales of arms to Taiwan, leading over a period of time to a final resolution.[93]

The contradictory intent of the 1979 *Taiwan Relations Act* and the 17 August 1982 Joint Communiqué reflected United States uncertainty and reservations in Washington about China as a strategic partner. The *Taiwan Relations Act* was an expression of United States Congressional concern about Taiwan, while the communiqué was a commitment under-taken by the United States President, Ronald Reagan.

While China may have had an expectation that United States arms sales to Taiwan would eventually be terminated over a period of time, the United States side always claimed to have had a different view.[94] Its bottom line was that arms sales to Taiwan might decline but would not necessarily terminate. After signing the Joint Communiqué, President Reagan said America's 'future actions would be conducted' in accordance with China's statement that its fundamental policy was to find a peaceful solution to the Taiwan question.[95]

The United States, in fact, continued to be the principal supplier of modern arms, defence technology and equipment to Taiwan. Sales declined very gradually from around US$830 million in 1979 to around US$670 million in 1990.[96] Taiwan and the United States circumvented restrictions against United States arms sales by supplying technology which was not explicitly caught by the 17 August 1982 Joint Communiqué. The Reagan administration claimed, moreover, that arms sales to Taiwan had to be indexed for inflation.[97] At such a rate, the value might only approach zero after about 30 years — that is, in the year 2020. Even then there was no guarantee that arms sales might not be resumed.

By 1988–89, any strategic need for the United States to defer to Beijing over Taiwan lost its rationale through a combination of several factors, including the end of the Cold War, the collapse of the Soviet Union, the state of the American economy and a growing rift in Sino-United States relations over the Tiananmen massacre, human rights, Chinese missile sales, the bilateral trade imbalance and China's image as the world's last bastion of communism.

Taiwan, on the other hand, was in a strong position economically, morally and strategically. Taiwan's importance grew, relatively speaking, once the criteria for power and influence were measured in terms of political reform, economics and trade. Taiwan's ruling Kuomintang had launched a program of democratisation in 1987 in an effort to broaden its domestic political base. This shift, a response to the impact of the earlier Sino-United States rapprochement, allowed Taiwan to capitalise on the international condemnation of China that accompanied the Tiananmen affair. Taiwan, moreover, was the fourteenth largest trading entity in the world, with the world's largest or second largest reserves of foreign exchange.

Taiwan is the fifth largest trading partner of the United States, after Canada, Japan, Mexico and Germany and ahead of China (in tenth place in 1991). The United States has been Taiwan's most important trading partner for the last few decades with enormous influence over Taiwan's trade policies and domestic prosperity. It is Taiwan's most important market, and second largest source of imports. Taiwan–United States trade in 1985 totalled US$22.4 billion, more than twice the level of United States trade with China in that year (US$8 billion). In 1989, Taiwan–United States trade was $US36.9 billion, compared with China–United States trade of US$18.7 billion.[98] In 1991, Taiwan–United States trade was US$37 billion, 40 per cent greater more than United States–China trade of US$26.5 billion. By 1993, Taiwan–United States trade was worth more than US$40 billion, which was still twice the level of United States–China trade.[99] Taiwan is also the eleventh largest investor in the United States, mainly in computers, electronics, plastics, trading and financial commodities. US$10 billion in 2460 projects, or 40 per cent of all Taiwanese investment in the Asia-Pacific region, has gone to the United States.[100] They are in a sense natural commercial and strategic partners.

Additionally, Taiwan has invested considerable time and effort in maintaining a special relationship with the United States, despite the ups and downs of the last two decades.[101] Taiwan has always enjoyed a core of support in the United States Congress.[102] It has built a new form of strategic alliance based on trade, investment and ideological and sentimental ties. United States agriculture has been given preferential treatment over other suppliers, like Australia and New Zealand. Taiwanese companies breaching United States intellectual property rights have been prosecuted. To ease complaints about the ballooning trade deficit, Taipei has launched many 'buy American' campaigns with importers of United States products given preferential treatment in loans and taxes and exporters to the United States market encouraged to increase imports from the United States. United States firms have been invited to tender for development projects. Goods from the United States, such as cars, radios, television sets, machinery and equipment, and agricultural products such as soybeans, corn, beef, tobacco leaf, apples, barley and poultry, are given preferential tariff treatment whereas Japanese goods are subject to quotas and other import restrictions.

In an effort to ease American criticism of Taiwan's persistent surplus in its trade with the United States, Taiwan has diversified away from the United States, liberalised its market, appreciated the NT$ against the US dollar by 40 per cent since 1985, and reduced tariffs from an average of 32 per cent in 1986 to 19 per cent in 1988.[103] In 1989, the average nominal tariff was reduced to 9.7 per cent. As a result, Taiwan managed to halve its surplus in trade with the United States from US$16 billion in 1987 to US$8 billion in 1991, albeit mainly by locating labour-intensive export industries in mainland China rather than through its tariff reduction policy.[104]

Taiwan's impressive, if bloated, six-year infrastructure development budget and its defence expenditure plans have been used to attract the interest of influential American business and political leaders. Taiwan invites over one thousand influential Americans to Taiwan each year, all expenses paid. Most are policy-makers such as members of Congress and their families, legislative assistants, state and local officials, important persons and academics.[105] Taipei is reported to now have access to nearly all senators and a majority of the members of the House of Representatives in the United States Congress.[106] Like Israel, the Taiwanese understand the importance of lobbying influential members of the United States Congress. Taiwan has a massive network of pro-Taiwan organisations and pro-Taiwan Chinese news media sources at its disposal in the United States. It has established sister-state agreements with 35 American states, twenty of whom have trade offices in Taipei. It has invited political figures such as former Presidents Gerald Ford and George Bush, and defence officials such as former Secretary of Defence Caspar Weinberger to Taipei, and carefully cultivated up-and-coming politicians such as Bill Clinton (who visited Taiwan four times as Governor of Arkansas). Academic conferences are also an important vehicle for consolidating Taiwan's influence on the American political scene.

Meanwhile, China's strategic value to the West vis-a-vis the former Soviet Union declined with the end of the Cold War. China lost its leverage in the United States over United States arms sales to Taiwan and its immunity on human rights and arms sales issues. Previously, the United States rarely if ever referred to Tibet or human rights in China. It exercised restraint in arms sales to Taiwan and was deeply involved in the modernisation of China's navy and airforce. After Tiananmen and the collapse of the Soviet Union, democracy and the rule of law, geo-economics and the fashion of an Asia-Pacific economic community dominated the regional political agenda. This resulted in a reassessment and recognition of Taiwan's regional and global importance in contrast to the rash of sensitive issues that broke out in Sino–United States relations.[107]

The shift in United States policy on China and Taiwan is reflected in reports to Congress by the United States Department of Defence. In 1990, the Pentagon made no mention of Taiwan in its Report to Congress except to note in passing that Taiwan was an unresolved Chinese territorial issue along with the Spratly and Paracel Islands.[108] In July 1992, in contrast, the United States Defence Department stated that:

> Taiwan continues to be a political and economic success story. Our sixth largest trading partner in the world, with hard currency reserves over $80 billion, Taiwan is an essential factor in the economic health of Asia and has played a constructive role in the region. United States unofficial relations with Taiwan have been strong and mutually beneficial.[109]

Under the sub-head 'Sources of East Asian and Pacific Regional Instability', the Report referred to the Taiwan Strait. It said:

> The situation in the Taiwan Strait is peaceful, and the relationship between Beijing and Taipei is improving with increasing trade, contact and tourism. It is in our interests to encourage these trends. United States policy remains as defined in the *Taiwan Relations Act* and the three communiqués. In keeping with this policy, we will sustain our efforts to enable Taiwan to maintain a sufficient self-defence capability.[110]

Legal advice from the State Department reinforced an emerging view that the United States government could, if it chose, maintain or even increase arms sales to Taiwan.[111] In early 1992, the United States Defence Department commenced a major review of the military balance in East Asia and and its obligations to meet Taiwan's defence needs under the *Taiwan Relations Act*.[112]

In August 1992, the United States approved the sale to Taiwan by General Dynamics of 207 Standard surface-to-air missiles, with parts and support in a deal worth US$126 million.[113] In September 1992, Washington announced the sale of twelve SH2F light airborne multi-purpose helicopters to Taiwan worth US$161 million.[114] These announcements were capped by the decision to sell F-16 fighter aircraft to Taiwan in a deal worth US$5.8 billion. President Bush said the United States would permit General Dynamics to sell Taiwan 150xF-16 A/B fighter aircraft, 40 spare aircraft engines, 900 Sidewinder and 600 Sparrow AAMs, 500 000 rounds of 20 mm ammunition, spare parts, technical documentation, personnel training, and related logistics and technical services. The deal was based ostensibly on the grounds that China had acquired sophisticated Su-27 fighter aircraft from the Soviet Union and because the mainland had not renounced the use of force as an option for the reunification of Taiwan.[115] Taiwan's existing fighter aircraft (F-104s and F-5s) were said to be 'stuff that was 35, 40 years old and needed to be replaced' by the F-16 to allow Taiwan to maintain its air defence capability.[116] Taiwan's F-16s are to be upgraded with a new mission computer and avionics systems so that they can in fact outperform the later C/D model that Taiwan preferred. Deliveries start in 1995.[117]

Just coincidentally, the F-16 contract preserves up to 3000 American jobs, a reflection of where United States priorities lie in the post-Cold War period and Taiwan's comparative advantage over China in political and economic terms.

Subsequently, the United States announced that it would also sell Taiwan 41 Harpoon anti-ship missiles (range 128 kilometres or 80 miles) for US$68 million and that it was co-operating in a deal worth $1.3 billion to give Taiwan a Modified Aid Defence System (MADS) based on the Patriot missile.[118]

The United States has also sold to Taiwan four Grumman E-2T airborne early warning aircraft. Japan, Egypt, Israel and Singapore are the only other countries to have acquired this aircraft, which is capable of monitoring six million square miles of air space and 150 000 square miles of the sea surface.[119] The Pentagon claimed that these decisions would not affect the basic military balance in the region and that they were consistent with United States law and policy.[120] Contracts for additional United States sales of modern weapons to Taiwan, including Stinger portable anti-aircraft missiles, naval munitions and MK-46 ASW torpedoes, have subsequently multiplied.

Taken together, these contracts represent a significant departure from previous United States policy towards Taiwan. Hitherto, the United States had gradually reduced arms sales to Taiwan and had limited its involvement in capital items, such as the IDF jet fighter and the Perry-class frigate, to the supply of design technology and components. In both quantitative and qualitative terms, the sales of the F-16, the Harpoon and the Patriot are a breach of the 17 August 1982 Joint.Communiqué, one of the three communiqués regarded by China as central to the Sino-United States relationship.[121] The United States rationale is that it is helping Taiwan upgrade obsolete defence equipment and that, in any case, it has an overriding obligation under the *Taiwan Relations Act*. In fact, the United States Senate Foreign Relations Committee passed an amendment to the Act in July 1993 affirming that, as a public law of the United States, the *Taiwan Relations Act* superseded the 17 August 1982 Joint Communiqué.[122]

By reaffirming the *Taiwan Relations Act* and effectively discarding the 17 August 1982 Joint Communiqué, the United States defence contracts represent a United States tilt towards supporting Taiwan as Taiwan and also supporting Taiwan as a counter to a greater China. In America's post-Cold War strategic outlook, China, while not a foe, is also not the friend it was seen to be in the early 1980s. Caspar Weinberger, former Secretary of Defence in the Bush administration, said that Chinese purchases of weapons that were 'mainly offensive in nature' were seen in Washington as 'the largest threat to peace and stability in Asia'.[123] Weinberger added that the United States arms sales indicated America's continuing strategic interest in maintaining 'a strong and free' Taiwan in the Pacific.[124]

The change in United States policy towards Taiwan and China is reflected in United States support for Taiwan's application for GATT membership and its participation in APEC and increased high-level contacts with Taipei. Almost half of the United States Senate supports a shift in the United States policy on Taiwan. Forty-four senators signed a letter expressing their support for Taiwan's membership of the United Nations and its agencies.[125] Other influential figures, such as Newt Gingrich and Jesse Holms, have called on the United States administration to resume diplomatic relations with Taipei. These perceptions of Taiwan, as they gather strength, will have profound strategic and political implications for the future of Taiwan and Sino-United States relations.

The *Taiwan Relations Act*, rather than any previous presidential undertaking about Taiwan being part of one China, is the basis for United States–Taiwan relations today. It neither endorses nor precludes eventual reunification of Taiwan with the PRC or Taiwan's separation from China, but demands that any resolution should be achieved by peaceful means. The Act avoids the form but, as it currently stands, it preserves the substance of diplomatic and military relations between Taiwan and the United States.[126] Taiwanese Foreign Minister Fredrick Chien claimed that 'if the PRC used force against Taiwan, the Taiwanese [would] expect Washington to intervene because of the Act'.[127]

As well as treating Taiwan for what it has become since 1972 — a successful and important economic entity in the Pacific Community and one of the largest trading nations in the world — the United States views

Taiwan as an integral part of its China policy and its vision of a new Pacific Community in the 1990s. The United States has recognised the strategic and economic importance of preserving and supporting Taiwan's separateness in the Asia-Pacific region precisely because of its Chineseness and the impact it can have on China, the largest remaining communist country left in the world. As President Bill Clinton said in his address to the United Nations General Assembly in September 1993, the overriding purpose of the United States was 'to expand and strengthen the world's community of market-based democracies'.[128] He said that United States policy in the post-Cold War era was to 'seek to enlarge the circle of nations that live under free institutions'.[129] If, as it seems, the promotion of free market democracies has risen to near the top of the United States foreign policy agenda, and if, as it also seems, repressive communist regimes like China have become the target of United States foreign policy, then Taiwan is an ideal candidate for renewed American support. In a sense, it would appear that, since 1992, the United States State Department has reallocated to Taiwan the role of a bastion or island base located to contain, balance and bring about the transformation of communism on the mainland. That is, the United States' perception of Taiwan in 1994 is not so different from the view it held in 1958, *viz*:

> United States policy in Asia, as elsewhere in the world, is to promote the domestic welfare and to strengthen the independence of free nations. Because of the proximity of many Asian nations to mainland China and the disparity in size and power between them and mainland China, this can be done only if the the communist threat is neutralised . . . The United States has sought to accomplish this by military assistance to the nations directly in the path of Chinese Communist expansion . . . Taiwan is steadily developing its political, economic and military strength. The Government of the Republic of China controls the strategic island of Taiwan and through its possession of a sizeable military force — one of the largest on the side of the free world in Asia — presents a significant deterrent to renewed Chinese Communist aggression. Continued United States recognition and support of the Republic of China enables it to challenge the claim of the Chinese Communists to represent the Chinese people and keeps alive the hopes of those Chinese who are determined eventually to free their country of communist rule.[130]

In this sense, therefore, the United States and Taiwan still share common strategic and economic interests — in effect, a strategic alliance. Taiwan's role is to counterbalance and neutralise communist China and, in the longer term, to transform its communism. The United States, therefore, has a vested policy interest in supporting a strong, confident Taiwan rather than to permit Taiwan to weaken and thereby 'invite adventurism' from the PLA.[131]

For the United States, as for Japan, a Taiwan that is separate from the mainland is preferable to a Taiwan integrated into a greater and more powerful Chinese state. This shift in United States policy on China and Taiwan suggests that the hundredth anniversary of Taiwan's separation from the mainland in 1995 will not be the last. The United States, after all, remains pre-eminently the strongest military and economic power in the world. Moreover, as former United States President Gerald Ford observed, there 'remains a strong bipartisan belief in the United States that we have a moral commitment to assist Taiwan to meet its defence requirements and to resist any coercion from the outside'.[132]

China, meanwhile, is physically large and it no longer needs an alliance with the United States to protect it against Soviet encirclement. China's economic modernisation depends on access to Western markets, especially in the United States, as well as Western finance and technology. Militarily, China lags well behind the kind of precision firepower that the United States demonstrated during the Gulf War. The United States, however, does not want a confrontation with China over Taiwan.[133] Its preference is for Taiwan to maintain the present ambiguity of its status — de facto independence within a one China framework — rather than provoking Beijing by, for example, applying to join the United Nations as the Republic of China on Taiwan or as the Republic of Taiwan.

As well as a re-evaluation of Taiwan in a China context, there is renewed American economic interest in Taiwan as an important trading entity. Taiwan is the sixth largest trading partner of the United States. Few countries wield its buying power for aircraft, ships, nuclear power generators and transport equipment. Taiwan's economic clout was recognised in the December 1992 visit by United States Trade Representative Carla Hills, the first senior Administration official to visit Taipei since 1980. Her interests were Taiwan's policy on protection of intellectual property rights and the liberalisation of Taiwanese markets for United States agricultural products. Hills added, however, that the United States also recognised Taiwan as one of the Asia-Pacific's more important economic powers.[134]

Notes

1   Joseph W. Ballantine, *Formosa*, The Brookings Institution, Washington, 1952, p. 120; and Bruce Cumings, 'Telltale Taiwan', in Bruce Cumings (ed.), *The Origins of the Korean War: Volume II The Roaring of the Cataract*, Princeton University Press, Princeton, N.J., 1990, pp. 508, 533–36.

2   United States, Department of State, Policy Memorandum on Formosa, 23 December 1949, in *Military Situation in the Far East, Hearings before the Committee on Armed Services and the Committee on Foreign Relations*, United States Senate, 82nd Congress, 1st Session, Part III, United States Government Printing Office, Washington, 1951, p. 1668; and Ballantine, *Formosa*, pp. 118–19, 130.

3   Ballantine, *Formosa*, p. 120.

4   Jon Woronoff, *Asia's 'Miracle Economies'*, M.E. Sharpe Inc., New York, 1986, p. 66.

5   United States Senate, Committee on Foreign Relations, *Report on Mutual Defence Treaty with the Republic of China*, 8 February 1955, Senate, 84th Congress, 1st Session, Executive Report No. 2, United States Government Printing Office, Washington, 1955, p. 8.

6   Ballantine, *Formosa*, p. 127.

7   ibid.

8   Frank B. Cooper, Ambassador to Taipei, despatch to the Minister for External Affairs, Paul Hasluck, 24 April 1967 on Department of Foreign Affairs and Trade, file No. 519/3/1, *Formosa: External Relations with Australia: General*.

9   Neil H. Jacoby, *US Aid to Taiwan*, Praeger, New York, 1966, p. 30; and Ballantine, *Formosa*, p. 183.

10 *Current Notes on International Affairs*, vol. 22, no. 7, 1951, p. 375.

11 ibid.

12 The Nationalists proposed sending troops to Korea and Vietnam and often dabbled in clandestine operations in China's eastern provinces. A recently published secret cable from Mao Zedong to Josef Stalin in 1950 (reported in the *New York Times*, 26 February 1992) revealed Mao's fears of a two-pronged strategy against China launched by the United States in Korea and the Nationalists in Taiwan.

13 Ballantine, *Formosa*, pp. 131, 141, 142, 145.

14 Michael Armacost, Deputy Assistant Secretary, United States Department of State, Hearings, Committee on Foreign Relations, United States Senate, 96th Congress, United States Government Printing Office, Washington DC, February 1979, p. 668.

15 Frederic C. Deyo, 'Introduction' in Frederic C. Deyo (ed.), *The Political Economy of the New Asian Industrialism*, Cornell University Press, Ithaca, 1987, p. 18.

16 Cal Clark, *Taiwan's Development: Implications for Contending Political Economy Paradigms*, Greenwood Press, Connecticut, 1989, p. 4.

17 Jacoby, *US Aid to Taiwan*, pp. 84, 157.

18 ibid., p. 11.

19 ibid., p. 38.

20 ibid., pp. 84, 157.

21 For example, Robert Wade, *Governing the Market: Economic Theory and the Role of Government in East Asian Industrialisation*, Princeton University Press, Princeton, N.J., 1990; Bruce Cumings 'The Origins and Development of the Northeast Asian Political Economy: Industrial Sectors, Product Cycles and Political Consequences', *International Organization*, vol. 38, no. 1, Winter 1984, p. 1; Shirley W.Y. Kuo, Gustav Ranis and John C.H. Fei, *The Taiwan Success Story: Rapid Growth with Improved Distribution in the Republic of China 1952–1979*, Westview, Boulder, Col., 1981; and Frederic C. Deyo (ed.), *The Political Economy of the New Asian Industrialism*, Cornell University Press, Ithaca, 1987.

22 Discussed in Chapters 5 and 6.

23 Discussed in Chapter 2.

24 Jacoby, *US Aid to Taiwan*, p. 35.

25 United States policy failed in South Vietnam partly because the country was adjacent to sanctuaries in Indochina. Japan, South Korea and Taiwan, in contrast, had the sea around them — or at least on three sides.

26 United States Department of State, *Foreign Relations of the United States 1955–1957*, Volume II, United States Government Printing Office, Washington, 1987, pp. 62, 80.

27 Gordon H. Chang, 'To the Nuclear Brink: Eisenhower, Dulles and the Quemoy–Matsu Crisis', *International Security*, vol. 12, no. 4, Spring 1988, pp. 97, 98; Ralph N. Clough, *Island China*, Harvard, Cambridge, Mass., 1978, pp. 12–13. Suggestions endorsed by the president that the United States might resort to nuclear weapons to defend Taiwan were made by the United States Secretary of State, John Foster Dulles, in a radio broadcast on 8 March 1955: *Current Notes on International Affairs*, vol. 26, no. 7, 1955, p. 173.

28 Guo Changlin, 'Sino-US Relations in Perspective', *Contemporary International Relations*, vol. 2, no. 7 (Beijing), July 1992.

29 Garry Woodard, 'Australian Foreign Policy on the Offshore Island Crisis of 1954–55 and Recognition of China', *Australian Journal of International Affairs*, vol. 45, no. 2, November 1991, pp. 242, 244,

246–47, 251, 255. Today, the opposition Democratic Progressive Party wants to achieve the same result by handing over control of the off-shore islands to Beijing: Central News Agency, Taipei, 5 September 1993.

30 United States Department of State, *Foreign Relations of the United States, 1952–1954, Vol. XIV*, United States Government Printing Office, Washington, 1987, pp. 870–80.

31 *United States Statutes at Large*, vol. 69 (1955), p. 7 in Hungdah Chiu, *China and the Taiwan Issue*, Praeger, New York, 1979, p. 231. This resolution was repealed in 1974.

32 However, key United States advisers such as Admiral Arthur Radford, Chairman of the Joint Chiefs of Staff, favoured 'giving the Communists a bloody nose' and launching pre-emptive, even nuclear, strikes against the mainland: H.W. Brands 'Testing Massive Retaliation: Credibility and Crisis Management in the Taiwan Strait', *International Security*, vol. 12, no. 4, Spring 1988, pp. 124, 150; and Motoyuki Takamatsu, 'The United States and China: the Crises of 1954 and 1958', The China Academy, *Sino-American Relations*, vol. XIV, no. 1, Taipei, Spring 1988, pp. 59–84.

33 Jacoby, *US Aid to Taiwan*, pp. 34, 192, 244.

34 ibid., pp. 152–53.

35 ibid., pp. 83, 152; Woronoff, Asia's 'Miracle Economies', p. 66; and Samuel P.S. Ho, *Economic Development of Taiwan 1860–1970*, Yale University Press, New Haven, 1978, pp. 111–13.

36 Ho, *Economic Development of Taiwan 1860–1970*, p. 115.

37 Jacoby, *US Aid to Taiwan*, pp. 174, 176.

38 ibid., p. 177.

39 Ballantine, *Formosa*, p. 111.

40 Jacoby, *US Aid to Taiwan*, pp. 38, 118–19; Sheppard Glass, 'Some Aspects of Formosa's Economic Growth', in Mark Mancall (ed.), *Formosa Today*, Praeger, New York, 1964, pp. 84–85.

41 Ho, *Economic Development of Taiwan 1860–1970*, p. 107.

42 Jacoby, *US Aid to Taiwan*, pp. 38, 152.

43 ibid., p. 85.

44 ibid., pp. 172, 182.

45 Susan Greenhalgh, 'Supranational processes of Income distribution', in Edwin A. Winckler and Susan Greenhalgh (eds), *Contending Approaches to the Political Economy of Taiwan*, M.E. Sharpe Inc., New York, 1988, pp. 67, 94; Denis Fred Simon 'External Incorporation and Internal Reform', in Winckler and Greenhalgh, pp. 138, 139, 149; and Richard E. Barrett, 'Autonomy and Diversity in the American State on Taiwan' in Winckler and Greenhalgh, pp. 121, 135–36.

46 Erik Thorbecke, 'Agricultural Development', in Walter Galenson (ed.), *Economic Growth and Structural Change in Taiwan*, Cornell University Press, Ithaca, 1979, p. 182; Jacoby, *US Aid to Taiwan*, pp. 172, 181; and Yu-Kang Mao, 'Agricultural development policy and performance in Taiwan', in *Lessons from Taiwan: Pathways to Follow and Pitfalls to Avoid*, ISIS Malaysia, 1986, pp. 58ff.

47 T.H. Shen, *Agricultural Development on Taiwan since World War II*, Cornell University Press, Ithaca, 1964, p. 148.

48 Thorbecke, 'Agricultural Development' in Galenson (ed.), *Economic Growth and Structural Change in Taiwan*, pp. 132, 138, 139, 203.

49 From T.H. Lee, 'Strategies for Transferring Agricultural Surplus under Different Agricultural Situations in Taiwan', JCRR mimeo, July 1971, cited in Thorbecke, ibid., p. 203.

50 American Institute in Taiwan, *Foreign Economic Trends and their Implications for the United States*, Taipei, various issues; and Investment Commission, Ministry of Economic Affairs, *Statistics on Overseas Chinese and Foreign Investment*, Taiwan, December 1992. This is approximately the same amount that United States firms subsequently invested in China: in mid-1992 the amount of United States investment in China was estimated at US$4.7 billion: Guo, 'Sino–US Relations in Perspective', p. 6.

51 China News Agency (Taipei), 27 September 1993.

52 American Institute in Taiwan, *Foreign Economic Trends and their Implications for the United States*, Taipei, various issues; and Investment Commission, Ministry of Economic Affairs, *Statistics on Overseas Chinese and Foreign Investment*, Taiwan, December 1992.

53 United States military training programs stimulated the civilian economy by giving instruction in areas such as radio, engine and aerospace maintenance, petroleum production and medicine: Jacoby, *US Aid to Taiwan*, p. 120.

54 Samuel Shieh, Governor of the Central Bank of China, quoted in the *Free China Journal*, 14 May 1993.

55 ibid. There are currently 37 000 Taiwanese students in America.

56 Jacoby, *US Aid to Taiwan*, pp. 130, 140–41; and Wade, *Governing the Market: Economic Theory and the Role of Government in East Asian Industrialisation*, p. 83.

57 Ralph Clough, *Reaching Across the Taiwan Strait*, Westview, Boulder, 1993, p. 181.

58 Jacoby, *US Aid to Taiwan*, p. 165.

59 ibid., p. 129.

60 Jui-meng Chang, *The Determinants of Trade Policies in Taiwan*, Chung-Hua Institution for Economic Research Economic Monograph No. 18, CIER, Taipei, 1987, p. 25.

61 Paul T.K. Yen, 'Sino-American Relations in the 1980s: An Economic Review', *Sino-American Relations*, vol. XVI, no. 4, Winter 1990, pp. 9, 11.

62 ibid.

63 Jiann-jong Guo and Raymond Jui-meng Chang, 'Taiwan's Economic Relations with the US', in Gary Klintworth (ed.), *Modern Taiwan in the 1990s*, Canberra Papers on Strategy and Defence, No. 75, Strategic and Defence Studies Centre, Canberra, 1990, pp. 106, 107.

64 Szu-yin Ho, 'The Republic of China's Policy Toward the United States 1979–1989', in Yu San Wang (ed.), *Foreign Policy of the Republic of China on Taiwan*, Praeger, New York, 1990, pp. 29, 35.

65 Hsin-Huang Michael Hsiao, 'An East Asian Development Model: Empirical Explorations', in Peter Berger (ed.), *In Search of An East Asian Development Model*, Transaction Books, New Brunswick, 1988, pp. 12, 14.

66 Jacoby, *US Aid to Taiwan*, p. 138.

67 Chalmers Johnson, in Deyo, *The Political Economy of the New Asian Industrialism*, pp. 155–56.

68 The United States spent over US$120 billion on the war in Vietnam between 1965 and 1973: Stanley Karnow, *Vietnam: A History*, Penguin, New York, 1983, p. 24. This expenditure stimulated Taiwan's economy.

69 Richard Nixon, 'Asia After Vietnam in Foreign Affairs', in *Foreign Affairs*, October 1967, p. 49.

70 See Gary Klintworth, *Australia–Taiwan Relations 1942–1992*, Department of International Relations, ANU, 1993, p. 56.

71 Clough, *Reaching Across the Taiwan Strait*, p. 27.

72 Zbigniew Brzezinski, *Power and Principle*, Farrer Straus, Giroux, New York, 1983, pp. 197–200.

73 From Hungdah Chiu, *The Taiwan Relations Act and Sino-American Relations*, Occasional Papers No. 5, School of Law, University of Maryland, 1990, p 13.

74 John F. Copper, 'Taiwan's Strategy and America's China Policy', *Orbis*, vol. 21, no. 2, Summer 1977, pp. 161–62.

75 Chiu, *The Taiwan Relations Act and Sino-American Relations*, p. 20.

76 *Taiwan Relations Act*, Congressional Record-House 125, no. 38, 16 March 1979: H1668-70.

77 ibid.

78 ibid.

79 Lori Fisler Damrosch, *The Taiwan Relations Act After Ten Years*, Occasional Papers No. 4, School of Law, University of Maryland, 1990, p. 2.

80 See Lin Bih-jaw, 'Taipei-Washington Relations: Moving Towards Institutionalisation', in Chang King-yuh (ed.), *ROC–US Relations*

Under the Taiwan Relations Act: Practice and Prospects, Institute of International Relations, Taipei, 1989, p. 40.

81 Japanese sources, cited by A. James Gregor, 'US Interests in Northeast Asia and the Security of Taiwan', *Strategic Review*, Winter 1985, pp. 52, 54.

82 Richard K. Betts, 'Wealth, Power and Instability: East Asia and the United States after the Cold War', *International Security*, vol. 18, no. 3, Winter 1993/94, pp. 34, 37.

83 Damrosch, *The Taiwan Relations Act After Ten Years*, p. 11.

84 Cited in Damrosch, ibid., p. 7.

85 *China Yearbook 1980*, Taipei, 1980, p. 348.

86 Damrosch, *The Taiwan Relations Act After Ten Years*, pp. 19–21.

87 Robert Sutter, 'Domestic Complications in US China Policy and their Implications for Taiwan' in Yu-ming Shaw (ed.), *ROC–US Relations: A Decade After the Shanghai Communique*, The Asia and World Institute, Taipei, 1983, pp. 52, 53.

88 Harvey J. Feldman, 'The Development of US–Taiwan Relations 1948–1987', in Harvey J. Feldman et al. (eds), *Taiwan in a Time of Transition*, Paragon House, New York, 1988, pp. 129, 156.

89 Gary Klintworth, *China's Modernisation and the Strategic Implications for the Asia-Pacific Region*, AGPS, Canberra, 1989, p. 88.

90 ibid.

91 Martin Lasater, 'The PRC's Force Modernisation: Shadow Over Taiwan and US Policy', *Strategic Review*, Winter 1984, pp. 51, 57.

92 Jaw-ling Joanne Chang, 'Negotiation of the 17 August 1982 US–PRC Communique: Beijing's Negotiating Tactics', in Steven W. Mosher (ed.), *The United States and the Republic of China*, Transaction Publishers, New Brunswick, 1992, pp. 129, 137.

93 ibid., p. 129.

94 For an informed discussion of differing interpretations about what the TRA and the August Communique meant to Congress and the president, see Richard Bush, 'Helping the Republic of China to Defend Itself', in Ramon Myers (ed.), *A Unique Relationship: The United States and the Republic of China Under the Taiwan Relations Act*, Hoover, Stanford, 1989, pp. 78, 79ff.

95 *Weekly Compilation of Presidential Documents 1983*, United States Government Printing Office, Washington, 1983, pp. 1040–41.

96 Ho, 'The Republic of China's Policy Toward the United States 1979–1989', in Wang, *Foreign Policy of the Republic of China on Taiwan*, pp. 29, 32.

97 Stephen P. Gilbert, 'Safeguarding Taiwan's Security', *Comparative Strategy*, vol. 8, no. 4, 1989, pp. 425, 439.

98 International Monetary Fund, *Direction of Trade Statistics Yearbook*, IMF, Washington, 1994, p. 402.

99 ibid.

100 *Free China Journal*, 4 December 1992.

101 Graphing its course over the last four decades, one can see a peak in the 1950s and 1960s, a decline in the 1970s, a slump in the early 1980s and a resurgence in the late 1980s.

102 Many members of Congress were critical of Carter's policy change on Taiwan in 1979 and independent polls indicated that a majority of Americans opposed closer ties with Beijing at the expense of Taipei. A *New York Times*–CBS poll just after Carter's 15 December 1979 announcement found that 45 per cent of Americans opposed and 27 per cent supported closer ties with the PRC at the expense of Taiwan: cited in Chiu, *The Taiwan Relations Act and Sino-American Relations*, p. 3.

103 Lena H. Sun, 'US Optimistic on Relations Despite Tension on Agriculture', *International Herald Tribune*, 21 April 1988, p. 13. See also Jiannjong Guo and Raymond Jui-meng Chang, 'Taiwan's Economic Relations with the US', in Klintworth, *Modern Taiwan in the 1990s*, p. 106.

104 China's trade surplus with the United States in 1991 was US$12.5 billion. By 1993 it was estimated to have doubled to US$24 billion.

105 Ho, 'The Republic of China's Policy Toward the United States 1979–1989', in Wang, *Foreign Policy of the Republic of China on Taiwan*, p. 39.

106 ibid., p. 40.

107 Set out in Kerry B. Dumbaugh, *China–US Relations in the 1990s: Issues for Congress*, Foreign Affairs and National Defense Division, Congressional Research Service, the Library of Congress, Washington, 24 January 1992.

108 United States Department of Defence, *A Strategic Framework for the Asia Pacific Rim, Looking Towards the 21st Century*, Washington, 1990, p. 8.

109 United States Defence Department, *A Strategic Framework for the Asia-Pacific Rim*, Report to Congress, Washington, 1992, p. 11.

110 ibid.

111 Cited in Bush, 'Helping the Republic of China to Defend Itself', in Myers (ed.), *A Unique Relationship: The United States and the Republic of China Under the Taiwan Relations Act*, p. 89; also comments by Hungdah Chiu, quoted in *China News Agency* (Taipei), 3 September 1992.

112 *Defence News*, Washington, 2026 July 1992, p. 3.

113 Pentagon News Release, Washington, 5 August 1992.

114 USIS Wireless File, Canberra, 23 September 1993.

115 USIS Wireless File, Canberra, 14 September 1992.

116 United States Secretary of State, Dick Cheney, Interview, Indianapolis, USIS Wireless File, 4 September 1992.

117 *Business Week*, 14 September 1992.

118 *China Post*, 6 August 1993 and 8 September 1993; and *Free China Journal*, 10 September 1993.

119 *China Post*, 18 September 1993.

120 *China Post*, 6 August 1993.

121 Guo, 'Sino-US Relations in Perspective'. The others are the 1972 Shanghai Communiqué and the 1979 Communiqué on the Establishment of Diplomatic Relations.

122 The initiator of the resolution was Republican, Frank Murkowski: *China Post*, 19 July 1993.

123 Quoted during his visit to Taiwan: *China Post*, 21 October 1993.

124 ibid.

125 China News Agency (Taipei), 5 October 1993.

126 See Damrosch, *The Taiwan Relations Act After Ten Years*.

127 *South China Morning Post*, Hong Kong, 9 October 1991.

128 President Bill Clinton, address to the UN General Assembly, New York, 27 September 1993 in USIS Wireless File, Canberra, 29 September 1993.

129 ibid.

130 State Department, 'Memorandum on US Policy regarding Non-recognition of Communist China', 11 August 1958, in *Current Notes on International Affairs*, vol. 29, 1958, p. 512.

131 James Lilley, speaking in Taipei, quoted in *China Post*, 22 May 1993.

132 Gerald R. Ford, 'The US–Taiwan Connection', an address to the 13th Joint USA–ROC Business Conference, Honolulu, Hawaii, 18 November 1989, in *Sino-American Relations*, vol. XVI, no. 2, Summer 1990, pp. 3, 5.

133 Dick Cheney, former Secretary of Defence in the Bush Administration, said the United States did not regard China as an adversary and that while the United States was committed to Taiwan's security under the terms of the TRA, he could not promise direct United States military involvement: it would only commit forces if and when it decided a military solution was feasible and necessary: speaking in Taipei, quoted in the *China Post*, 14 May 1993.

134 Carla Hills, speech in Taipei, USIS Wireless Report, Canberra, 8 December 1992.

4 The China Factor and Taiwan

In one way or another, it was China that provided the basic ingredients for Taiwan's rise to fame and fortune. Japan built the economic foundations of modern Taiwan and the United States supplied critical financial aid and military protection to speed it on its way. But it was from China that the Chinese people migrated and derived their Chineseness. China supplied the lessons learned by the Kuomintang. Later, the threat from China dominated Taiwan's security outlook, spurred its economic development and shaped its modern identity. Today, ironically, the Chinese hinterland has given a new lease of life to Taiwan's labour-intensive manufacturing industries, such that Taiwan derives half of its trade surplus with the rest of the world from its trade with the mainland.

The China factor — whether as a threat, a reminder of the past, the promise of the future or its ethnicity — has always been central to the nation-building objectives of Taiwan and its ruling elite. Chiang Kai-shek's aim of reconquering the mainland was regarded by many governments in the Asia-Pacific as a narrow, potentially dangerous and thoroughly impractical mission.[1] However, his dream of recovering the mainland became an article of faith for Kuomintang policy-makers during Taiwan's formative years between 1950 and 1975. They devised ambitious long-term development plans accordingly. Their vision for Taiwan and China has been maintained by the successors to Chiang Kai-shek, even though the means to achieve it have been revised and any sense of urgency disappeared when Chiang died in 1975. Long-term national goals that integrated the security of Taiwan with a reunified China had profound implications for the direction, priorities and shape of Taiwan's economic development. They became a central reference point for the diplomacy and the politics of the Kuomintang between 1949 and 1989.

The China threat, the quest for national survival and the struggle for reunification produced an authoritarian mission-oriented regime usually found only in wartime or in small states with a strong sense of vulnerability like South Korea, Israel and Singapore. Taiwan developed a national purpose and a resolve to succeed, both key ingredients in nation-building.[2] By putting Taiwan on what amounted to a war footing, the Kuomintang could pursue urgent national goals, introduce sweeping reforms and direct the economy in a ruthless executive style of government that would be unacceptable in a democratic Western society.

Such a regime demanded social stability, national consolidation, long-term economic development, an indoctrinated armed force, a disciplined workforce and, as it eventuated, rule by martial law. The Kuomintang's 'enlightened authoritarianism', it is claimed, was an important factor behind Taiwan's successful economic development: if Taiwan needed a super-highway, Chiang Kai-shek simply ordered one to be built.[3]

The spur of mainland failure

The explanations for Taiwan's rapid economic growth are many and varied. They include the government's land reform policies, American aid, Confucian ethics, labour-intensive export-oriented manufacturing and the habit of government intervention.

One of the underlying factors was the trauma of the Kuomintang's mainland experience of high inflation, peasant unrest, factionalism and a civil war capped by an unseemly rout and retreat. Failure on the mainland shocked and pained Chiang Kai-shek, but it cleared his mind, with positive consequences for the way in which the Kuomintang subsequently managed Taiwan's affairs — notwithstanding the initial mistakes made by Governor Ch'en Yi in February 1947.[4]

Mainland failure honed Chiang's vision, ability and leadership.[5] He became a 'more determined and stronger leader'.[6] The Kuomintang, 'baptised by the bitter experience of its defeat on the mainland', gave up much of its old arrogance and seemed ready to undertake genuine reform of the kind that it had been unable or unwilling to implement on the mainland.[7] It worked hard on Taiwan in making sure it had the right policies in place at the right time.

More specifically, the Kuomintang was acutely conscious of the fact that it had lost the mainland because it failed to carry out land reform and had not done enough to control the labour unions, inflation, corruption and party discipline. It was determined not to repeat those mistakes. Chiang Kai-shek purged the Kuomintang of undisciplined elements, including Governor Ch'en Yi. He also strengthened the organisational hierarchy to ensure that individuals were subordinate to the majority.[8]

He ruled by martial law and prohibited the formation of trade unions, the right to strike, a free press and political dissent.

Price stability became an ingrained government concern. The experience of inflation on the mainland made financial stability on Taiwan an overriding priority.[9] The Kuomintang followed conservative financial policies throughout the 1950s: it undertook monetary reform, minimised borrowing, balanced the government budget and encouraged high savings with high interest rates on deposits. It became 'receptive to ideas that were highly unorthodox at the time'.[10] Under martial law, disrupting the money market was one of ten offences punishable by death.[11] Hyperinflation was brought under control and dropped to less than 9 per cent in the 1950s and to around 2 per cent in the 1960s. This early success in controlling inflation made an important contribution to domestic and foreign business confidence and the subsequent rapid economic growth of Taiwan.

Chiang remained committed to 'national recovery'. This policy envisaged a counter-attack on the mainland, the defeat of Chinese communism and the rejuvenation of China under the Nationalist flag. That goal spurred the Kuomintang to do better and to strive harder to build Taiwan into a support base and to justify the claim that Chiang had been cheated out of his rightful place in Chinese history. Taiwan was thus developed into a showcase for the kind of free China that the Kuomintang had failed to achieve on the mainland.[12]

Land reform

The Kuomintang's successful land reform program of 1949–53 is often cited as the underlying reason for Taiwan's subsequent economic take-off.[13] It dramatically increased agricultural productivity, provided a surplus that funded industrialisation, fed a growing urban population, alleviated unemployment and supplied cheap labour for Taiwan's new factories.[14] It stimulated social change and modernisation. It was the first and perhaps the most important foray by the Kuomintang government into economic reconstruction and management and it underpinned the legitimacy of Kuomintang rule in the countryside where the majority of the population lived.

The architect of land reform was the governor of Taiwan, Chen Cheng. He was committed to Sun Yat-sen's principle of people's livelihood and the idea that land reform was a prerequisite to domestic economic development.[15] However, the Kuomintang land reform program was implemented primarily because of the Kuomintang's fear of a peasant revolt.[16] And it was easy to execute because the mainland Kuomintang was relatively neutral to sectoral or regional interests in Taiwan and could take a more detached view of its development.[17]

The post-1945 system on Taiwan deprived peasants of security of tenure, charged extortionate rents (up to 70 per cent of the annual harvest) and imposed a range of other taxes.[18] In 1948, the Kuomintang perceived rural Taiwan to be resentful and susceptible to communist propaganda.[19] The Kuomintang believed that failure to carry out land reform on Taiwan would mean 'the communists could just as easily . . . grab this last foothold' of China.[20] Land reform, therefore, was 'implemented vigorously' to prevent the communists from 'fishing in troubled waters'.[21] T.H. Shen, Chairman of the Joint Commission on Rural Reconstruction in Taiwan, observed that the Kuomintang was 'sincerely sorry' for not carrying out Dr Sun Yat-sen's land to the tiller idea in China.[22] Basically, however, the policy of land to the tiller and land rent reductions was intended to build 'a new social order' in Taiwan's rural areas so as to deprive the communists of 'propagandistic weapons'.[23]

In 1949, rents were reduced by up to two-thirds to a maximum of 37.5 per cent of the value of the crops produced. Then public land, land compulsorily acquired from landlords and land confiscated from the Japanese (amounting to 20–25 per cent of the total cultivated area)[24] was sold to tenants at a reasonable price on easy terms. Landlords were compensated with shares in large agro-industrial enterprises (Taiwan Cement Corporation, Taiwan Pulp and Paper Corporation, Taiwan Industrial and Mining Corporation and Taiwan Agriculture and Forestry Development Corporation). By 1953, the proportion of land farmed by tenants was down to 17 per cent compared with 56 per cent in 1939.[25]

Giving peasants responsibility for their own land encouraged multiple cropping, crop diversification and improved farming techniques. Taiwan's agricultural takeoff was supported by a lavish use of chemical fertilisers, an impressive agricultural research and training program and reactivated rural co-operatives that disseminated information on credit, new crop strains, new crops, new technology and new pesticides.[26] A basic infrastructure of roads and irrigation works was built or repaired. Yields rose sharply with significant gains in rural prosperity.[27] Over the period 1948–59, owner-cultivators were six to seven times better off in terms of average annual income than if they had remained as tenants without land reform and rent reduction.[28] The success of the Kuomintang's land reform program in the countryside — where most of the population lived in the 1950s — thus helped consolidate the political power and prestige of the Kuomintang.

As well as achieving its political purposes, the Kuomintang squeezed large profits out of a revitalised agricultural sector. Basically it sold dear and bought cheap by acquiring half the annual rice crop at lower than market rates, collecting various taxes and exploiting its monopoly on the supply of overpriced fertiliser.[29] By this method, the government was able to transfer a significant slice of wealth — estimated at 22 per cent of total agricultural production between 1950 and 1955 and around 15 per cent between 1956 and 1969 — from the agricultural sector to manufacturing.[30] In this way, agriculture played a key role in providing the capital resources for Taiwan's subsequent industrialisation.

Considerable credit should go to the Japanese, who laid the foundations for the land reform progam, and to the United States, which provided the Kuomintang with the funds to compensate the landlords through its Joint Sino-American Commission on Rural Reconstruction and otherwise helped to modernise Taiwan's rural sector. However, if there had been no lessons from the mainland and no threat from the PLA, the Kuomintang may not have been forced to implement its land reform program. Taiwan may then have ended up like the Philippines: with an impoverished peasant class supporting a small corrupt urban elite.

The threat from the mainland

The significance of the Kuomintang's mainland failure for its nation-building efforts in Taiwan was reinforced by the ongoing civil war with China and the constant threat of invasion — or at least the threat of use of force — by China. The threat from China made Taiwan look west to the United States. It adopted many positive aspects of Western culture, including the English language, technology, military strategy and education. The China threat brought support for Taiwan from America, the world's strongest military power. This in turn gave Chiang Kai-shek considerable international and domestic legitimacy.

But as Kwoh-ling Li has remarked, some nations become stronger because they are under pressure from isolation, hardship and adversity.[31] Indeed, Chiang Kai-shek often compared Taiwan to Britain after Dunkirk.[32] Taiwan's security, under constant pressure from China as a threat or a rival since 1949, was made more precarious because of a lack of natural resources, its small size, the uncertainty of United States support and its dependence on imported energy. Survival depended on profitable export industries and a nimble response to the international marketplace. Adversity in the 1970s was compounded by threats of protectionism, competition from other NIEs and a rise in oil prices that led the government to assert its 'economic leadership and political control even more strongly than before'.[33]

Chiang Kai-shek's mission of converting Taiwan into an island bastion and recovering the mainland became the common national goal — the *raison d'etre* for all Chinese on Taiwan.[34] The air of tension, urgency and confrontation used to sustain the threat syndrome was compounded by crises in the 1950s over Matsu and Quemoy, offshore islands in the Taiwan Strait. These islands are located close to the mainland, but are physically occupied by the Taiwanese. They were the object of mainland artillery bombardments in 1955–56, 1958 and 1962, as well as occasional air engagements, infiltration and verbal threats, often initiated by Chiang Kai-shek's forces.[35] Since then, the China threat has been the dominant factor in Taiwan's strategic outlook and its domestic political affairs. Taiwan was prodded along by its loss of the China seat at the United Nations in 1971 and United States recognition of Beijing in 1979. In March 1990, the PLA conducted massive military exercises along the Fujian coast at the height of the presidential nomination crisis in Taiwan.[36]

As a beleaguered economy in a hostile world, the Kuomintang needed a strong military force and that presupposed the rapid development of the Taiwanese economy. The Kuomintang was thus forced to administer Taiwan efficiently. It had to draw up a long-term strategic plan for nation-building and orchestrate the island's scarce economic and financial resources and, where necessary, take the lead and play a critical entrepreneurial role.[37]

It nurtured domestic industry through a strong protectionist policy. There were strict rules on domestic content (of up to 90 per cent) for television sets, cars, telephones, motorcycles and light buses and a range of protection offsets, such as tariff rebates and privileged access to the domestic market, that were intended to encourage exports.[38] Such a program of sheltered growth, administered by the state, was calculated to protect domestic producers and help 'transform Taiwan from an agricultural into an industrial society'.[39] Tariff policy gave an effective rate of protection for manufacturing of around 23 per cent in 1969 and supplied between 19 per cent and 25 per cent of government revenue annually between 1954 and 1980.[40]

Police state

The one China myth, the civil war with Mao Zedong, the threat from the PLA and Chiang's wish to recover the mainland required close control and direction of Taiwan's economy. Taiwan's rapid economic development occurred under a regime that ruled by martial law from May 1949 until July 1987. This was one of the critical keys to Taiwan's successful economic development.[41] The Kuomintang monopolised the media, the banks, the government, the police, security forces and other instruments of political power. The Kuomintang established a strong security force to ensure 'law and order' and social stability and preserve its monopoly of political power. As Chiang Kai-shek said in a message to the Kuomintang on 24 November 1974, the Republic of China was in the middle of a revolutionary struggle with the mainland.[42] While China's revolution required sacrifice, bloodshed, mobilisation, indoctrination, national reconstruction and national recovery, it could not afford Western-style democracy.[43] Instead, the Kuomintang followed the principle of 'organised democracy and disciplined freedom'. In practice, this amounted to a certain ruthlessness that was supported by legislation such as the 18 April 1948 'Temporary Provisions Effective During the Period of Communist Revolution'. The Temporary Provisions, in force until 1991, effectively suspended the Constitution and allowed Chiang Kai-shek to rule by decree. The need to 'take emergency measures to avert an imminent danger to the security of the state' from the PLA was then used as justification to stamp out political dissent.

Under Chiang Kai-shek, Taiwan was a police state in which the government practised 'what might be called the politics of national emergency'.[44] Until the 1970s, any person endangering 'the national interest' could be arbitrarily arrested, tortured, executed or sentenced to more than ten years in prison.[45]

Those who suggested reconciliation with the mainland or who voiced criticism of Chiang Kai-shek would come under surveillance and risked being charged with treason.[46] Attempts to organise political parties were quickly nipped in the bud.[47] In fact, there were no legitimate opposition political parties in Taiwan other than the Kuomintang until the DPP announced its formation in September 1986. People who dared to discuss independence sometimes died in mysterious circumstances.[48] Trade unions and strikes were banned.

Frank Cooper wrote that, despite its progressive features, especially in land reform, the Kuomintang had many 'unsavoury' ones.[49] Basic freedoms did not exist and even to discuss the 28 February 1947 massacre was forbidden because it was regarded as treason.[50] After visiting Taiwan in 1963 and 1964, Stephen Fitzgerald wrote that, although there were fewer executions than in the early 1950s, each year still brought new arrests, closed military trials and long prison sentences.[51] The Taiwanese, he said, had been imprisoned, executed and cowed into submission by systematic surveillance, torture, strict censorship and tight political controls.[52]

Political stability

Until he died in 1975, Chiang Kai-shek could be described as a dictatorial ruler who always 'insisted on tighter authoritarian controls'.[53] But the Chinese-Taiwanese were used to such authoritarianism and had grown up with it under the Japanese for 50 years. There was in any case no experience of parliamentary democracy in Chinese tradition. Such authoritarianism gave Taiwan political stability and industrial peace.[54] It was one of Sun Yatsen's principles for good government and in any case it was a lesson learned from the Kuomintang's mainland experience and the urgency imposed by the threat from the PLA.

Kuomintang rule was unopposed from 1945–87 because any local Taiwanese political opposition had been eliminated or intimidated by the 1947 massacres and arrests, and landlords and peasants had been neutralised or bought off by the land reform program.[55] Other avenues for political dissent were stifled or closed off by a pervasive security apparatus. Meanwhile, the war, the influx of refugees, the land reform program, the United States influence and the threat from the mainland contributed to a fluid class structure that was easily manipulated by the Kuomintang.[56]

This meant that the power of the state was almost unchallengeable. According to Haggard and Cheng, the Kuomintang had power that in the West was 'normally exercised only by naval commanders of isolated warships'.[57]

Authoritarianism allowed the Kuomintang to resist pressure from sectional interests and pursue long-term goals without the disharmony and diffusion of political energy that can accompany the practice of regular elections in a pluralist democratic society, as in the Philippines. The Kuomintang was able to give its economic technocrats the leeway to implement 'a more systematic approach' to industrial planning and economic management than might otherwise have been the case.[58] A similar opportunity was available to the government of Kim Il Sung in North Korea, but the critical difference was that Taiwan was an internationalised market economy. That is, Taiwan combined the strengths of communism and capitalism and avoided their weaknesses, as Sun Yatsen envisaged. According to Chalmers Johnson, the Kuomintang perfected the Japanese model of combining absolutist state power with capitalist economics.[59]

Cheap labour

Under rule by martial law, unauthorised workers' associations, strikes, stoppages or labour unrest to seek better conditions and higher wages were illegal. The repression of labour by direct legislation (the 1947 'Measures for Handling Labour Disputes during the Period of National Mobilisation for the Suppression of Rebellion') gave priority to the prompt settlement of disputes, eliminated the right to strike and gave local government extensive powers in mediation and arbitration.[60] Even today, Taiwan has restrictions on the freedom of association by workers and their right to strike.[61] Taiwan indeed has one of the lowest unionised workforce ratios in the Pacific region, with around 17 per cent of workers belonging to a union, compared with 50 per cent in Australia (in 1991) and over 50 per cent in New Zealand.[62] Non-unionised labour gave Taiwan (and other East Asian NIEs) a formidable advantage over workers in more advanced countries.[63] There was no central wage-fixing system and no powerful nationally organised council of trade unions as in Australia. Wage rates were set by free competition in the labour market. Workers' rights, basic labour standards, safety and hygiene were not enforced.[64] A new comprehensive *Basic Labour Standards Law* was only passed in July 1984, but few companies have bothered to abide by its provisions.[65] Many of Taiwan's business leaders feared the law would raise their costs by 10–30 per cent and create a less flexible anti-entrepreneurial labour structure.[66] Expenditure on social welfare, public health, safety and the environment was kept to a minimum so as to preserve Taiwan's competitiveness on the world market.[67] Only soldiers, civil servants and teachers — or less than 10 per cent of the population — were covered by social welfare. Workers had to rely on family, savings and hard work to support themselves. Piecemeal social assistance for those in need was first made available in the early 1960s.[68] By 1985, just over four million workers, or 21 per cent of the total population, were covered under the *Labour Insurance Act* for death, sickness, injury or other forms of disability.[69] Taiwanese workers, in short, needed to be self-reliant. They have had to work harder for longer hours — six days a week — in more sweated conditions for less money than workers in other countries.[70] In 1972, for example, the relative wage rate for a worker in the textile or electronics industries was 20 US cents per hour in Taiwan, 22 cents in South Korea, $1.20 in Japan, $1.90 in Germany and $2.75 in the United States.[71] In 1974, workers in most services and industries worked a six-day week with an average of more than 50 hours per week.[72] In 1990, wages for computer engineers were 35–40 per cent of world levels.[73]

Low-cost, disciplined, non-unionised labour that would not strike and which would not upset industrial peace in the factories and EPZs was the key to Taiwan's export competitiveness and industrialisation.[74] As Shirley Kuo observed recently, the labour market in Taiwan has been in a state close to perfect competition.[75] With cheap flexible wages, mobile labour, political stability and industrial peace, Taiwan was an attractive destination for foreign investors seeking a comparative advantage in labour-intensive manufacturing.

There was clearly room for an adverse political reaction if the regime was too oppressive. The Kuomintang's solution, however, complemented its anti-union, police state authoritarianism by spreading rewards for landlords and peasants through the land reform program; offering educational opportunities to all Chinese in Taiwan; giving pensions, subsidies and other social welfare benefits to teachers, the civil service and the army; and stimulating a rapid expansion in job opportunities. Full employment, in fact, led to a steady increase in real wages for workers that averaged between 7 and 12 per cent annually between 1961 and 1992.[76] The Kuomintang thereby won broad community support because it achieved economic growth, financial stability and growth with a fair degree of equity. With rapid export-oriented industrialisation, average GNP per capita income rose by 8.8 per cent per annum between 1951 and 1992, up from US$145 to over $10 000 (at current prices).[77]

Mainland textile industries

Failure on the mainland brought a windfall to Taiwan's economic development. Many of the 735 000 or so refugees who fled to Taiwan from China between 1947 and 1956 were technical, professional and administrative personnel. They eased 'the skill constraint typical of developing countries', had clear ideas about Taiwan's future economic development and had no vested social or political interests 'as between rural and urban groups or between different rural groups such as landlords and tenants'.[78] They easily filled the managerial gap left by the departing Japanese.[79]

Many of the refugees who arrived in Taiwan from the mainland came with substantial assets and considerable expertise in managing a large-scale business enterprise. There were many common soldiers but the core comprised an entrepreneurial, intellectual and industrial elite. Some were men of vision, like K.Y. Yin, T.C. Liu, K.T. Li, T.S. Tsiang and K.C. Yeh. They played a key role in directing Taiwan's economy towards an export-oriented culture.[80] As Minister for Economic Affairs and head of the Industrial Development Commission in the mid-1950s, K.Y. Yin promoted Taiwan's new industries and, above all, the textile industry.[81] Many refugees from the mainland brought experience and skills in textile manufacturing and, in some cases, the looms and other equipment that were subsequently used in establishing Taiwan's textile and clothing industries. Given this headstart and Taiwan's cheap non-unionised labour, it was not surprising that the textile and clothing industries were systematically promoted by the government.[82] In 1976, one-third of the top 106 business groups in Taiwan had a textile firm at their core.[83] With competition from textile manufacturing in China closed off, and privileged access to the United States market, Taiwan easily developed an impressive comparative advantage in the production of textiles and apparel. Growth was boosted by government assistance with capital, tax benefits, foreign exchange, raw materials and protection from imported yarns.[84] The creation of export processing zones was especially helpful in facilitating the inflow of textile-related foreign capital and technology, most of it Japanese.[85] Taiwan's textile and clothing industries boomed and textile exports, mainly to the United States, dominated Taiwan's export earnings until overtaken by electronic machinery in 1984.[86]

Competition with the mainland

The Kuomintang and the CCP have been rivals since the 1920s. This rivalry has acted as a spur to economic and political development in Taiwan. The Kuomintang has constantly sought to demonstrate that communism is an alien and unworkable ideology and that the Taiwanese model, based on a Sun Yatsenism and a free market economy, are more appropriate for China. Chiang Kai-shek wanted Taiwan to develop as a 'showcase of Chinese development under free economic institutions'.[87] In speeches on 1 March and 14 August 1950, Chiang announced his grand strategy of building Taiwan as a base for the recovery of the mainland and a prosperous model province that would serve as 'a prototype for the recovered mainland'.[88] He was joined by others with a similar vision, such as Minister of Economic Affairs K.T. Li, Vice President Ch'en Ch'eng, Prime Minister C.K. Yen, Minister for Communications Sun Yun-suan, Bank of China chief Yu Kuo-hua and, the architect of Taiwan's industrial policies in the 1950s, K.Y. Yin. As Robert Wade suggests, Taiwan's ruling elite developed an ideology around their competition with the mainland and their conviction that the Nationalists would eventually win back the right to rule on the mainland once the communists squandered their 'mandate of heaven'.[89]

Taiwan's course, therefore, was to build a strong free-market economy, a strong army and a sound political base. It was forced to show the world and, in particular, to prove to its American benefactor that it could survive, modernise, develop, compete, change and reform and that it was not a lost cause. Taiwan's land reform, its export-led industrialisation, its virulent anti-communism and the reverence for Confucius and Sun Yatsen were born out of this competitive dynamic. Taiwan became preoccupied with trends and developments in political and economic life on the mainland. Indicators of the quality of life and economic progress or setbacks on the mainland are used to highlight the success of Taiwanese capitalism and the failure of Chinese socialism. Taiwan prides itself on the fact that the mainland is 55 times the size of Taiwan in terms of population, and 270 times in area, yet Taiwan's GNP grew from one-fifth of the size of the mainland in 1985 to about half in 1991.[90] Their rivalry is reflected in their approach to several major policy issues such as land reform, material incentives, foreign investment, export processing zones and international trade. In the case of land reform, Taiwan emulated the mainland. In most other cases, the mainland has followed Taiwan's lead. Taiwan's experiment with political reform and its attention to human rights are in part a product of the rivalry between the two governments, over which one can morally claim to best represent all Chinese. The irony is that the more that China competes with Taiwan, the more like Taiwan it becomes. Leaders like Deng Xiaoping often refer to Taiwan's rapid progress as a ground for speeding up the pace of mainland reform.[91] The Kuomintang, therefore, has a strong interest in maintaining its lead over China and using the so-called Taiwan experience in economic and political development as a catalyst for change on the mainland.

We are all Chinese

As well as the lessons of failure in China, the threat from the PLA and the spur of rivalry with the mainland, Taiwan has developed a strong sense of obligation to help the Chinese on the mainland. The Taiwanese have always held themselves out as a beacon of hope for oppressed Chinese on the mainland. Scoffed at in the 1970s, this metaphor lost its air of unreality with the retreat from communism that Deng Xiaoping began in 1978 and China's shift towards 'socialism with Chinese characteristics' — a euphemism for

Taiwanese-style economics. This shift has been strengthened by the cultural and economic exchanges that have flourished between the two Chinas since 1987. The Taiwanese believe that Taiwan should help the mainland make the transition — they were, after all, Chinese, and:

> all plans have been conceived with the future of all of China in mind. Taiwan and the mainland are indivisible parts of China's territory, and all Chinese are compatriots of the same flesh and blood . . . [and] should work together to seek . . . our common goal of national reunification.[92]

Previously, Taiwanese policy aimed at widening the gap between Taiwan and the mainland so that Taiwan would be in a stronger position to topple the communist government. This has changed and Taiwan now aims to narrow the gap.[93] According to the Guidelines for National Unification:

> The unification of China is meant to bring about a strong and prosperous nation with a long-lasting bright future for its people; it is the common wish of Chinese people at home and abroad . . . to establish a democratic, free and equitably prosperous China.[94]

Sun Yatsenism

Sun Yatsen's ideals for the revival of China — notably 'land to the tiller', social justice, state intervention, a return to Confucian and Mencian virtues, loyalty to the state, rejection of materialism and the rights of the individual, gradualism, mass education, a concern for people's livelihood and guided democracy — were an important influence on Kuomintang ideology.[95] Sun Yatsenism was a response to China's weakness and its internal disarray in the face of pressure from the West. It was first conceived in 1905 and written down in 1924.[96] In other words, as James Gregor suggests, Taiwan's successful post-1949 economic development stemmed from principles of government devised in China several decades earlier.[97] According to Ramon Myers, Sunist thought combined Confucianist moral values, Western advances and respect for the social authority of the ruling elite.[98] It was a philosophy intended to rejuvenate China by Western means without discarding Chinese values. For Chiang Kai-shek, Sun Yatsen's philosophy was 'the crystallization of China's ancient culture and the virtues of the nation' as well as 'the inevitable trend of the modern world' and it was to be China's future guiding principle.[99]

According to Gregor, the Nationalist program was 'not only infused with the developmental spirit characteristics of Sun's ideology, it embodied most of its critical programmatic components' as well.[100] Under Sun Yatsenism, Taiwan's was to be 'neither a capitalist system nor a communist one'.[101] It was, rather, 'a planned free economy' that combined the strength of the two systems in the principle of people's livelihood, a notion that paid 'more attention to the attainment of equity of distribution than capitalism and more attention to freedom of choice than communism'.[102] It preserved the efficiency of the free market and drew on the strategic advantages of centralised long-term planning and government intervention. It imposed a duty on the state to satisfy people's basic needs by developing national enterprises and protecting private ownership while, at the same time, it restrained private wealth and prevented 'the capitalistic control of the people's livelihood'.[103]

China would not adopt *laissez-faire* principles, said Chiang Kai-shek.[104] This meant, as Sun envisaged, state guidance of a market economy — 'the development [of China] would be inspired and directed by the interventionist state controlling private capital and foreign trade through a comprehensive policy that would ensure balanced growth, decentralised industry, substantial equality in income distribution, opportunities for private economic initiatives and competitiveness in the international market'.[105] It also meant the adoption of Sun's ideas on the regulation of private and state capital, encouragement of savings and protective tariffs and import controls to assist new labour-intensive industries.

All that remained was to find a place, an opportunity and a strong leader to apply Sun's principles. American aid and protection provided the opportunity, Taiwan became the locale and Chiang Kai-shek was the strong leader.

Chiang Kai-shek: Man of vision

Chiang built a national ideology that was adapted from the philosophy of Sun Yatsen, drew on lessons learned from losing the mainland and stressed traditional Chinese values. This had 'a becalming, affirmative and even integrating impact on Taiwan'.[106] It was underpinned by the support of the United States and enforced by a powerful security apparatus. By suspending the Constitution and operating a kind of paternalistic old boy network — a community of modernisers — Chiang sought to avoid the tangle of red tape and the delays and wrangling inherent in a fragile democratic system.[107] Things got done. There was none of the political wrangling and compromise between different factions within the Kuomintang or between the Kuomintang and the DPP as, it is claimed, is often the case today.[108]

Chiang's vision was to achieve in Taiwan what he had failed to achieve on the mainland. He purged the Kuomintang of corrupt and incompetent officials in favour of able tertiary-educated scientists and engineers like Vice President and Premier Ch'en Ch'eng, K.Y. Yin (an electrical engineer), C.K. Yen and K.T. Li (a nuclear physicist).[109] Like Mao Zedong, Chiang was authoritarian, but unlike Mao, he was quiet, practical, consistent, willing to delegate economic matters to experts, ideologically flexible and tolerant of specialists.[110]

Transformed Confucian virtues

One of the most important inheritances that the Chinese brought to Taiwan from China was their sense of Chinese tradition, history and values. The six cardinal virtues in Chinese society are filial piety, respect for elders, cordial relations between neighbours, a good education for sons and grandsons, diligence and frugality, and law and order. Hong-chao Tai and others suggest that this cultural baggage — defined loosely as Confucianism (although it might include the influence of Taoism and Legalism)[111] — does much to explain the success of Taiwan and other East Asian states.[112]

But the fact that traditional Confucianism frowned on initiative and emphasised passivity, social equilibrium, rote learning of the Confucian classics and a rigid bureaucratic hierarchy has led many observers to question such claims.[113] China's dynastic histories suggest, on the contrary, that Confucianism has been a hindrance to entrepreneurship and dynamic economic development.[114]

Taiwan, however, adapted and refined Confucianism to suit its new circumstances.[115] First, it was able to break away from centralised authority in Beijing, and thus detached and protected by the West, it could absorb capitalist ethics.[116] In a sense, as Wang Gungwu suggests, Taiwan became a liberated Confucian society.[117]

Second, as Koh Byong-ik suggests, the sense of siege and the urgency of Taiwan's economic and strategic circumstances in the 1950s transformed old Confucian values into an energising ideology.[118] The Kuomintang developed a strong sense of nationalism:

> The nation was constantly inculcated for dedication to the national cause, order and discipline, frugality and hard work and vocational education. Dedication to the national cause in turn, implies loyalty to the nation, subduing self-interest and individual rights, endurance, conciliation, and even sacrifice. Emphasis on order and discipline calls for submissiveness, conformity and deference to superiors and authority.[119]

The Taiwanese also retained useful habits of mind — for instance, a philosphical and long-term view of fortune, relationships and government, an attitude reflected in the Taiwanese approach to planning the economy in three-, four-, six- and ten-year cycles; and the common conviction, certainly amongst the Kuomintang, that communism in China would not last. They also retained instinctive Confucian values that are invaluable for a Westernising Chinese society, such as diligence, pragmatism, thrift, family loyalty, respect for elders, social harmony/equity, benevolence, eating at round tables (sharing information), the pursuit of learning, modesty, the primacy of the group, a preference for law and order, and a sense of hierarchy.[120] These virtues were a key part of the school curriculum.[121] The aim was to teach students to respect teachers and how to become:

> a civilised person . . . to become an active and vigorous student . . . to teach the student to love his or her country and compatriots, to get along well with others and to serve others, and to take on responsibilities and to obey rules and regulations, and to become an upright Chinese citizen whose conduct manifests sound Chinese moral and cultural values.[122]

Lin Bih-jaw refers to the avoidance of individualism and overt conflict in favour of co-ordination, consultation and harmony; and discipline, single-minded dedication, hard-work and loyalty as the social norms of people living in Taiwan.[123] Hofheinz and Calder speak of a propensity to sacrifice individual interests to those of the group, or what they call 'together-ness'.[124] Yi-ting Wong suggests that Chinese cultural traits such as industriousness, thrift, social harmony and pursuit of education made it easy for the Taiwanese to accumulate surplus capital and technology skills.[125]

The Confucianist emphasis on harmony is one of the main reasons cited for Taiwan's economic success: harmony means social stability, the avoidance of political confrontation and industrial peace. Lucian Pye suggests that the Taiwanese became a disciplined, hardworking society, like others in Asia, because of their habit of respect for authority and rules.[126] Confucian traits, in other words, made Taiwan a fertile ground for the seeds of modernisation.[127] They were not the primary cause of rapid development in Taiwan, but factors such as a belief in social harmony and group loyalty and acceptance of virtuous dictators were an essential conditioning element.[128] Confucianism provided political and social stability, forming a base that was then reinforced by universal conscription, mass indoctrination, government control of the media and a strong security apparatus.

Of course, social stability was enhanced by a discernible improvement in the material wellbeing of the general population. Rising per capita income and improved living standards assuaged any inclination for widespread anti-government political unrest. Increased prosperity and greater economic opportunities across the whole country (because of its size and good transport network) tended to give the majority of people a vested interest in continued stability and enabled them to be patient in the face of an authoritarian Kuomintang.[129]

As well as the important habit of social harmony, three other Confucian traits stand out as being of particular importance: family loyalty, savings and the emphasis on education.

Family

Family loyalty has been an important and positive aspect in Taiwanese business practice. Susan Greenhalgh suggests that Taiwan was 'partly preadapted to capitalism' because of its traditional family-based loyalty and cohesiveness.[130] That is, the Chinese are naturally small-business minded: it is in their blood. In business, they tend to be small, flexible and quick to respond to market signals.[131] In fact, much of the success of Taiwan's export-oriented industrialisation is based on such nimble family-run enterprises. They have specialised in the manufacture of toys, bicycles, sewing machines, watches, umbrellas, leather goods, travel goods, shoes, clothing, electronic goods, sporting goods, plastic goods, textiles, chemicals, precision machinery, metalwork and publishing services. Greenhalgh argues that the family unit helped promote Taiwan's rapid growth and its integration into the world economy because it was flexible and efficient, had dedicated workers and was able to draw on personal family networks in Taiwan, in China and in Southeast Asia.[132] It could easily pool financial resources by calling on family members.[133] Employees are usually hardworking family members who are committed to making the business work and are willing to work in harsh conditions for long hours.[134] There are 730 000 small to medium family-run business enterprises in Taiwan, representing over 95 per cent of all companies, and they employ around 85 per cent of the workforce and supply more than 60 per cent of Taiwan's exports.[135]

Being small, highly competitive and export oriented, Taiwanese enterprises were quick to adapt to new trends, to copy from each other or borrow from new technologies, styles and materials that became available in the United States, Taiwan's chief benefactor and export market. International copyright law was frequently ignored in the drive to obtain a competitive advantage.[136]

Savings

The Taiwanese might be un-Confucian about savings when there is no incentive, or they might be extremely thrifty and frugal simply because of their relative poverty, a meagre social welfare system and uncertainty about the financial system.

Whatever the reasons, however, the Chinese do appear to have a propensity for savings. This propensity has often been mentioned as one of the personal traits that lie behind Taiwan's economic success.[137] Savings were low until the government eased inflationary expectations in the 1950s (as a consequence of sound government economic policies). Only then did Taiwanese savings bank deposits as a proportion of the total money supply begin to rise.[138] In the 1950s, there was a severe shortage of investment capital, despite United States aid, and any propensity to save had to be stimulated by government intervention.[139] Consumption was cut by floating the exchange rate and savings were encouraged by measures such as the Statute for Encouragement of Investment in 1960. National savings subsequently increased from around 5 per cent of GNP in 1950 to 12.6 per cent in 1960. In 1963, the rate was boosted by measures such as tax exemptions on interest earned on term deposits.[140] Term deposits, mostly held by households, increased by a factor of over 40 between 1953 and 1971.[141] The savings rate as a percentage of GNP rose to 25.8 per cent in 1970, 30 per cent in 1980 and over 38 per cent in 1987. It declined subsequently to just under 30 per cent but it is still one of the highest in the world (and compares with 16 per cent in Australia).[142]

The difference between savings and investment (22.5 per cent of GNP in 1991) meant Taiwan did not have to borrow from abroad to speed up national development and modernise its infrastructure. Its 'great accumulation of domestic savings' enabled it to attain rapid self-sustained growth from within its own resources, without large external debts, trade deficits or inflation, despite international financial instability and the end of United States aid in 1965.[143] As real income increased with Taiwan's rapid economic development, average savings per capita in Taiwan also increased and are today around US$17 250, or over US$360 billion.[144] Private savings and windfalls from land reform (see above) provided an abundance of relatively cheap capital that made it easy for new businesses to start up.[145] Taiwan's surplus in savings was, moreover, sufficient to make it a capital exporting country as early as 1975.

Education

It is hard to quantify the significance of education as a factor in Taiwan's development, or to demonstrate that acquiring an education was uniquely Chinese because of the 'Confucian reverence for learning'.[146] Another more basic explanation is that a skilled, well-indoctrinated disciplined workforce was an economic and political necessity. A long-term strategic plan to develop a clever country was essential if Taiwan was to make its way in the world and improve the people's livelihood.

Education was an important building block for Taiwan because it allowed for a rapid upgrading of the technology skills of the workforce. The government consulted specialists in the academic community on national development issues and it put more effort into education than many other countries. Its 1947 Constitution is one of the few in the world that pays attention to schools and education. Article 164, for example, provides that expenditure on education, science and cultural services is to be at least 15 per cent of the total national budget.[147] Expenditure reached 17 per cent of the budget in 1991.[148] In Australia, by comparison, education took 8.1 per cent of total budget outlays in 1991–92, or less than half the proportion allocated in Taiwan.[149] In 1984, Taiwan's education budget was 5.46 per cent of GNP, a level on a par with Australia's education expenditure of about 5.3 per cent of GNP in 1989–90.[150]

Education was free and compulsory for all children up to sixth grade.

In 1968, Taiwan became the second country in Asia after Japan to extend compulsory education to a ninth year to meet the demand for higher quality skilled labour. The literacy rate for persons six years and older increased from 45 per cent in 1949 to 93 per cent in 1990. Vocational and technical education were expanded on a large scale. New technical colleges, institutes and universities were established as a national priority as the Kuomintang spent increasing amounts on education, up from 11.6 per cent of government expenditure in 1955–56 to 20.5 per cent in 1970–71.[151] According to Woronoff, Taiwan's education system was soon 'one of the best in Asia'.[152]

In addition, the Kuomintang targeted the kind of university graduates it wanted — technicians, engineers, scientists and agronomists rather than arts–law graduates.[153] Today, Taiwan has 42 universities and 75 polytechnics graduating 37 000 engineers and 136 000 technicians each year.[154] Of the 535 064 Taiwanese in higher education in Taiwan in 1989–90, 43 901 were listed as students of the humanities or fine arts, 6416 were studying law and 179 495 were listed under engineering.[155] One in four candidates for a PhD in electrical engineering at American universities is Taiwanese.[156] Taiwanese Chinese — more than 26 000 of them — are in the United States undertaking postgraduate studies, mostly in the sciences.[157]

Kwoh-ling Li claims that one of Taiwan's greatest assets was a well educated workforce that was receptive to new ideas.[158] Half the economic growth achieved by Taiwan over the period 1952–79 stemmed from gains in technology, skill levels and the improved output that accompanied advanced knowledge.[159]

Overseas Chinese

Being Chinese has advantaged Taiwan in other ways. It gave the Taiwanese an edge over other competitors in doing deals or starting businesses in the region. It was important for attracting investment funds from overseas Chinese businesspeople in Hong Kong, Singapore and the Philippines in the 1950s and 1960s. The overseas Chinese are the third largest source of investment funds in Taiwan, and were particularly important in Taiwan's early period. Of total foreign investment of US$16.5 billion over the period 1952–92, 29 per cent came from Japan, 27 per cent came from the United States, 15 per cent came from the Overseas Chinese and 14 per cent came from European sources.[160] Taiwan has been advantaged by its Chinese connections in more recent years since becoming a net exporter of capital and a significant investor in Southeast Asia and mainland China. Taiwan's Chineseness has also been an important factor in the drive to attract Chinese-born and Western-trained scientists to return or contribute to Taiwan's science and technology base.

Conclusion

Taiwan has become a modern society with a successful and competitive internationalised economy. Taiwan's Chinese character, population, connections and values have been an important part of the formula. So too has been its proximity to China, the dynamics that this entailed and the lessons that were brought to Taiwan from mainland China by the defeated Nationalists.

Notes

1 Australia, for example: see Gary Klintworth, *Australia's Taiwan Policy 1942–1992*, Australian Foreign Policy Papers, Australian National University (ANU), Canberra, 1993, p. 48.

2 Lucian Pye, 'The New Asian Capitalism: A Political Portrait', in Peter Berger and Hsin-Huang Hsiao (eds), *In Search of an East Asian Development Model*, Transaction Books, New Brunswick and Oxford, 1986, p. 89.

3 David Chen, 'Whither Taiwan's democratisation?', *Free China Journal*, 2 February 1993, p. 7.

4 See C.L. Chiou, 'The Uprising of 28 February 1947 on Taiwan: The Official 1992 Investigation Report', *China Information*, vol. VII, no. 4, Spring 1993, p. 1.

5 Chalmers Johnson, 'Political Institutions and Economic Performance: the Government–Business Relationship in Japan, South Korea and Taiwan', in Frederic C. Deyo (ed.), *The Political Economy of the New Asian Industrialism*, Cornell University Press, Ithaca, 1987, p. 156.

6 Han Lih-wu, *Taiwan Today*, Cheng Chung Book Company, Taipei, 1988, pp. 4–5.

7 Lucian Pye, *Asian Power and Politics*, Belknap Press, Cambridge, Mass., 1985, p. 234.

8 J. Bruce Jacobs, 'Paradoxes in the Politics of Taiwan: Lessons for Comparative Politics', *Politics*, vol. 13, no. 2, pp. 239–47.

9 Kwoh-ting Li, *Economic Transformation of Taiwan*, Shepheard-Walwyn, London, 1988, p. 26.

10 Stephan Haggard, *Pathways from the Periphery: The Politics of Growth in the Newly Industrialising Countries*, Cornell University Press, Ithaca and London, 1990, p. 84.

11 Robert Wade, *Governing the Market: Economic Theory and the Role of Government in East Asian Industrialisation*, Princeton University Press, Princeton, New Jersey, 1990, p. 263.

12 Neil H. Jacoby, *US Aid to Taiwan*, Praeger, New York, 1966, p. 140.

13 Chen Cheng, *Land Reform in Taiwan*, China Publishing Co., Taipei, 1961, p. xii; Kuo-Shu Liang and Ching-ing Hou Liang, 'The Industrial Policy of Taiwan' in Hiromichi Mutoh et al., *Industrial Policies for Pacific Economic Growth*, Allen & Unwin, Sydney, 1986, pp. 104–5; Jacoby, *US Aid to Taiwan*, p. 109; A. James Gregor, 'Sun Yat-sen and the Economic Development of Taiwan', in A. James Gregor and Maria Hsia Chang, *Essays on Sun Yat-sen and the Economic Development of Taiwan*, Occasional Papers in Contemporary Asian Studies No. 1, 1983, School of Law, University of Maryland, pp. 34–35; and Li, *Economic Transformation of Taiwan*, p. 43.

14 Samuel Shieh, Governor of the Central Bank of China, quoted in the *Free China Journal*, 14 May 1993, p. 7.

15 Chen Cheng, *Land Reform in Taiwan*.

16 ibid., pp. xiii, 47.

17 Samuel P.S. Ho, *Economic Development of Taiwan 1860–1970*, Yale University Press, New Haven, 1978, p. 251.

18 Chen Cheng, *Land Reform in Taiwan*, p. 9.

19 T.H. Shen, *The Sino-American Joint Commission on Rural Reconstruction*, Cornell University Press, Ithaca, 1970, pp. 56–57.

20 Martin M.C. Yang, *Socio-Economic Results of Land Reform in Taiwan*, East West Center Press, Honolulu, 1970, pp. 14–15.

21 Chen Cheng, *Land Reform in Taiwan*, pp. 47–48.

22 Shen, *The Sino-American Joint Commission on Rural Reconstruction*, pp. 56–57.

23 ibid.

24 Samuel Pao-San Ho, 'Colonialism and Development: Korea, Taiwan and Kwantung', in Ramon H. Myers and Mark R. Peattie (eds), *The Japanese Colonial Empire 1895–1945*, Princeton University Press, Princeton, 1984, pp. 347, 372.

25 Ho, *Economic Development of Taiwan 1860–1970*, pp. 162–64.

26 ibid., pp. 178–79; Yu-Kang Mao, 'Agricultural Development Policy and Performance in Taiwan', in *Lessons from Taiwan Pathways to Follow and Pitfalls to Avoid*, ISIS Malaysia 1986, pp. 58, 63, 73.

27 Paul K.C. Liu, *Economic Development and Population in Taiwan since 1895: An Overview*, The Institute of Economics, Academica Sinica, Taipei, 1972, pp. 1–20; and Jacoby, *US Aid to Taiwan*, pp. 181–82.

28 According to Ho, *Economic Development of Taiwan 1860–1970*, pp. 271–74.

29 Ho, *Economic Development of Taiwan 1860–1970*, p. 181; see also Alice Amsden, 'Taiwan's Economic History — A Case of Etatisme and a Challenge to Dependency Theory', *Modern China*, vol. 5, no. 3, July 1979, pp. 357–58.

30 Ho, *Economic Development of Taiwan 1860–1970*, p. 182; and Yu Kang Mao, 'Agricultural Development Policy and Performance in Taiwan', in *Lessons from Taiwan Pathways to Follow and Pitfalls to Avoid*, p. 83.

31 Kwoh, *Economic Transformation of Taiwan*, p. 11. The siege factor is something that all the East Asian NIEs and Japan have in common: Gustav Papaanek 'The New Asian Capitalism: An Economic Portrait', in Berger and Hsiao, *In Search of an East Asian Development Model*, pp. 27, 76–77. Roy Hofheinz Jr and Kent E. Calder, *The Eastasia Edge*, Basic Books, New York, 1982, p. 47 suggest that the drive for economic survival and growth is spurred on by adversity and insecurity, as evidenced, for example, in 1965, when Taiwan established its first EPZ in Kaohsiung just after United States aid ceased.

32 ibid.

33 Wade, *Governing the Market*, p. 96.

34 President Chiang Kai-shek's Last Testament, *China Yearbook 1975*, China Publishing Co., Taipei, 1975.

35 For a comprehensive summary of the situation, see Chien-min Chao, 'China's Policy Towards Taiwan' in *Pacific Review*, vol. 3, no. 2, 1990, p. 125.

36 David Chen, 'Coastal Military Exercise Admitted', *South China Morning Post*, 20 March 1990.

37 Ho, *Economic Development of Taiwan 1860–1970*, p. xviii.

38 Han Herderschee, *Incentives for Exports: The Case of Taiwan*, Working Paper No. 91/9, National Centre for Development Studies (NCDS), ANU, Canberra, 1991; and Han Herderschee, *Protection and Exports A Comparison of Taiwan and Thailand*, Working Paper No. 91/11, NCDS, ANU Canberra, 1991.

39 Chiang Kai-shek, 'Chapters on National Fecundity, Social Welfare, Education and Health and Happiness', supplement to *San Min Chu-I*, China Publishing, Taipei, cited in Gregor, 'Sun Yat-sen and the Economic Development of Taiwan', in Gregor and Chang, *Essays on Sun Yat-sen and the Economic Development of Taiwan*, p. 38.

40 Herderschee, *Incentives for Exports*, pp. 4–5, 8.

41 Alice Amsden, 'The State and Taiwan's Economic Development', in Peter Evans et al. (eds), *Bringing the State Back In*, Cambridge University Press, Cambridge, 1985, pp. 79, 100–101. Authoritarianism is a necessary condition for economic development: Thomas W. Robinson, 'Democracy and Development in East Asia — Toward the Year 2000' in Thomas W. Robinson (ed.), *Democracy and Development in East Asia*, AEI Press, Washington, 1991, p. 279. Haggard, *Pathways from the Periphery*, p. 255, raises the hypothesis that a disciplined society under an authoritarian political system is better at promoting long-term economic growth in a developing country than the democractic alternative.

42 President Chiang Kai-shek, Message to the Fifth Plenary Session of the Tenth Central Committee on the 80th Anniversary of the Kuomintang, 24 November 1974, in *China Yearbook* 1975, China Publishing Company, Taipei, 1975, p. 687.

43 ibid.

44 Peng Ming-min, *A Taste of Freedom Memoirs of a Formosan Independence Leader*, Holt Rinehart and Winston, New York, Chicago and San Francisco, 1972, p. 237.

45 John Copper, 'Ending Martial Law in Taiwan: Implications and Prospects', *Journal of Northeast Asian Studies*, vol. VII, no. 2, Summer 1988, pp. 1, 5. The *China Post* of 15 June 1993 reported the discovery of the graves of 163 dissidents who had been executed and buried during 'the white terror' of the early 1950s. See also Lori Fisier Damrosch, *The Taiwan Relations Act After Ten Years*, Occasional Papers in Contemporary Asian Series, No. 4, School of Law, University of Maryland, 1990, pp. 15, 16.

46 John Israel, 'Politics on Formosa', in Mark Mancall (ed.), *Formosa Today*, Praeger, New York, 1964, pp. 59, 64–65.

47 Hung-mao Tien, 'Social Change and Political Development in Taiwan', in Harvey Feldman et al. (eds), *Taiwan in a Time of Transition*, Paragon House, New York, 1988, pp. 1, 18.

48 Ch'en Wen-ch'eng, for example, was arrested on his return to Taiwan in July 1981 for allegedly supporting Taiwanese independence movements in the United States. His body was later found on the campus of Taiwan National University: F. Gilbert Chan, *China's Reunification and the Taiwan Question*, Asia Research Service, Hong Kong, 1984, p. 29. See also Lori Fisler Damrosch, *The Taiwan Relations Act After Ten Years*, Occasional Papers in Contemporary Asian Series No. 4 (1990), School of Law University of Maryland, pp. 15, 16.

49 Frank Cooper, Australian ambassador to Taiwan, Despatch No. 2/67, 24 April 1967, Department of Foreign Affairs and Trade, file 519/3/1 *Formosa: External Relations with Australia — General*.

50 ibid.

51 Stephen Fitzgerald, memo from Hong Kong, 6 August 1964, Department of Foreign Affairs and Trade, File No. 519/3/1, *Formosa: External Relations with Australia — General*. Fitzgerald's impressions were published in two articles in *The Australian*, 16 and 17 March 1967.

52 ibid.

53 Ralph N. Clough, *Island China*, Harvard, Cambridge, Mass., 1978, p. 45.

54 Alan P.L. Liu, *The Political Basis of the Economic and Social Development in the Republic of China 1949–1980*, Occasional Papers No. 1, School of Law, University of Maryland, 1984, p. 3.

55 Anthony Y.C. Koo, 'Into the Twenty-first Century: The Challenge of Development of Social Welfare Programs in Taiwan', in Paul K.C. Liu et al., *Economic Development and Social Welfare in Taiwan*, Academica Sinica, Taipei, 1988, p. 3.

56 ibid.

57 Stephan Haggard and Tuan-jen Cheng, 'State and Foreign Capital in the East Asian NICs', in Deyo, *The Political Economy of the New Asian Industrialism*, p. 249.

58 Haggard, *Pathways from the Periphery*, p. 76.

59 Johnson in Deyo, *The Political Economy of the New Asian Industrialism*, p. 138.

60 Haggard, *Pathways from the Periphery*, p. 81.

61 United States State Department, '1993 Human Rights Report', January 1993 in *Free China Journal*, 29 January 1993.

62 *Canberra Times*, 23 November 1993; *The Pacific Basin: An Economic Handbook*, Euromonitor Publications, London, 1987, p. 116. Union labour ratios in East Asian NICs are: South Korea — 7 per cent; Singapore — 16 per cent; and Hong Kong — 14.2 per cent.

63 Jon Woronoff, *Asia's 'Miracle' Economies*, M.E. Sharpe Inc., New York, 1986, p. 211.

64 Yeong-chin Su, 'The Current Situation of the Basic Labor Standards Law and Industrial Relations in the Republic of China', in Liu, *Economic Development and Social Welfare in Taiwan*, pp. 496, 514–16.

65 ibid., p. 515.

66 ibid.

67 Koo, 'Into the Twenty-first Century: The Challenge of Development of Social Welfare Programs in Taiwan', in Liu, *Economic Development and Social Welfare in Taiwan*, p. 4.

68 Hou-sheng Chan, 'Perspectives of the Social Security System in Taiwan', in Liu, *Economic Development and Social Welfare in Taiwan*, p. 115.

69 ibid.

70 Yeong-chin Su, 'The Current Situation of the Basic Labor Standards Law and Industrial Relations in the Republic of China', in Liu, *Economic Development and Social Welfare in Taiwan*, p. 496.

71 Maurice Scott, 'Foreign Trade', in Walter Galenson (ed.), *Economic Growth and Structural Change in Taiwan*, Cornell University Press, Ithaca, 1979, p. 360.

72 Council for Economic Planning and Development, *Taiwan Statistical Data Book* (TSDB), Taipei, 1989, p. 17.

73 Stan Shih, of Acer Computers, quoted in *The Economist*, 14 July 1990, p. 20.

74 Frederic Deyo, 'State and Labour: Modes of Political Exclusion in East Asian Development', in Deyo, *The Political Economy of the New Asian Industrialism*, p. 183.

75 Shirley Kuo, 'The Taiwan Economy in the 1990s', in Gary Klintworth (ed.), *Taiwan in the Asia-Pacific in the 1990s*, Allen & Unwin/Department of International Relations, ANU, Canberra, 1994, pp. 89, 97.

76 ibid., Table 6.1, p. 106.

77 Samuel Shieh, Governor of the Central Bank of China, quoted in *Free China Journal*, 14 May 1993.

78 Erik Thorbecke, 'Agricultural Development' in Galenson, *Economic Growth and Structural Change in Taiwan*, p. 204.

79 Jacoby, *US Aid to Taiwan*, p. 82.

80 Ian M. D. Little, 'An Economic Reconnaissance', in Galenson, *Economic Growth and Structural Change in Taiwan*, pp. 448, 475.

81 Maurice Scott, 'Foreign Trade' in Galenson, *Economic Growth and Structural Change in Taiwan*, pp. 308, 315; see also Haggard, *Pathways from the Periphery*, pp. 83–88.

82 Chung-in Moon, 'Trade Friction and Industrial Adjustment: The Textiles and Apparel in the Pacific Basin', in Stephan Haggard and Chung-in Moon (eds), *Pacific Dynamics: The International Politics of Industrial Change*, CIS-Inha University Inchon/Westview, Col., 1989, pp. 185–86.

83 Thomas Gold, 'Entrepreneurs, Multinationals and the State', in Edwin A. Winckler and Susan Greenhalgh (eds), *Contending Approaches to the Political Economy of Taiwan*, M.E. Sharpe, New York, 1988, pp. 175, 188.

84 Wade, *Governing the Market*, p. 79.

85 Moon, 'Trade Friction and Industrial Adjustment: The Textiles and Apparel in the Pacific Basin', in Haggard and Moon, *Pacific Dynamics: The International Politics of Industrial Change*, p. 202.

86 Council for Economic Planning and Development, TSDB, Taipei, 1989, p. 227.

87 Jacoby, *US Aid to Taiwan*, p. 36.

88 Keiji Furuya, *Chiang Kai-shek: His Life and Times*, St John's University, New York, 1981, pp. 913–14.

89 Wade, *Governing the Market*, p. 235.

90 Ma Ying-jeou, Vice Chairman of the Mainland Affairs Council, speech 'Regional Stability in East Asia: Implications of Taipei–Peking Relations', Munich, in *Free China Journal*, 19 February 1993, p. 7.

91 *Selected Works of Deng Xiaoping, 1975–1982*, Foreign Language Press, Beijing, 1983, p. 225.

92 Lee Teng-hui, *Creating the Future: Towards a New Era for the Chinese People*, Government Information Office, Taipei, 1993, p. 7.

93 Ma, speech, 'Regional Stability in East Asia: Implications of Taipei–Peking Relations'.

94 In Lee, *Creating the Future: Towards a New Era for the Chinese People*, p. 175.

95 On Sun Yatsenism and China generally, see King-yuh Chang (ed.), *The Impact of the Three Principles on the People of China*, English Monograph Series No. 34, Institute of International Relations, National Chengchi University, Taipei, 1988; and King-yuh Chang (ed.), *Ideology and Politics in Twentieth Century China*, English Monograph Series No. 32, Institute of International Relations, National Chengchi University, Taipei, 1988.

96 Samuel C. Chu, 'The Three Principles of the People and Political Developments: Thoughts on Democracy in the Republic of China and the People's Republic of China', in Chang, *The Impact of the Three Principles on the People of China*, pp. 1, 3–4.

97 Gregor, 'Sun Yat-sen and the Economic Development of Taiwan', in Gregor and Chang, *Essays on Sun Yat-sen and the Economic Development of Taiwan*, pp. 50–51. On the other hand, Johnson in Deyo, *The Political Economy of the New Asian Industrialism*, p. 137 suggests that Taiwan and South Korea simply refined the Japanese development model by combining Leninist authoritarianism with Anglo-American free-enterprise market capitalism. Robert Wade also makes it appear as though the role of the state in Taiwan's economic development is a novel post-1949 phenomenon or what he terms 'the governed market theory of East Asian economic success': Wade, *Governing the Market*, p. 297.

98 Ramon H. Myers, 'Introduction: A Unique Relationship' in Ramon H. Myers (ed.), *A Unique Relationship: The United States and the Republic of China under the Taiwan Relations Act*, Hoover Institution Press, Stanford, 1989, p. 6. See also Yang, *Socio-Economic Results of Land Reform in Taiwan*, pp. 11–17.

99 Chiang Kai-shek, *China's Destiny and Chinese Economic Theory*, Dennis Dobson Ltd, London, 1947, pp. 221–23.

100 Gregor, 'Sun Yat-sen and the Economic Development of Taiwan', in Gregor and Chang, *Essays on Sun Yat-sen and the Economic Development of Taiwan*, p. 32.

101 Li, *Economic Transformation of Taiwan*, pp. 79, 85, 399.

102 ibid.

103 Chiang, *China's Destiny and Chinese Economic Theory*, p. 277.

104 ibid., p. 221.

105 Gregor, 'Sun Yat-sen and the Economic Development of Taiwan', in Gregor and Chang, *Essays on Sun Yat-sen and the Economic Development of Taiwan*, p. 27.

106 Liu, *The Political Basis of the Economic and Social Development in the Republic of China 1949–1980*, p. 4.

107 ibid., p. 12.

108 David Chen, 'Whither Taiwan's democratisation?', *Free China Journal*, 2 February 1993, p. 7.

109 Liu, *The Political Basis of the Economic and Social Development in the Republic of China 1949–1980*, p. 15

110 ibid., p. 6.

111 Hofheinz and Calder, *The Eastasia Edge*, p. 41.

112 Hung-chao Tai (ed.), *Confucianism and Economic Development: An Oriental Alternative?*, The Washington Institute Press, Washington, 1989.

113 For example, William McCord, 'An East Asian Model of Development: Growth with Equity' in *Pacific Review*, vol. 2, no. 3, 1989, p. 209; Woronoff, *Asia's 'Miracle' Economies*, pp. 178–79; and Jacoby, *US Aid to Taiwan*, p. 184.

114 Koh Byong-ik, 'Confucianism in Asia's Modern Transformation', in *Korea Journal,* vol. 32, no. 4, Winter 1992, p. 61.

115 Pye, 'The New Asian Capitalism: A Political Portrait', in Berger and Hsiao (eds), *In Search of an East Asian Development Model*, pp. 86–89.

116 Pye, ibid., pp. 84–85 suggests that Confucianism in modern Taiwan incorporated rule by a technocracy, worship of the marketplace and other elements of Western capitalism. Koh, 'Confucianism in Asia's Modern Transformation', *Korea Journal*, p. 46, suggests that Confucianism helped Asia's NIEs because it was a passive way of thinking that was not hostile to foreign influence and ideas: it was able to absorb and adapt foreign ideas, unlike the Hindus or the Moslems who were more religiously inclined and exclusivist.

117 Wang Gungwu, *China and the Overseas Chinese*, Times Academic Press, Singapore, 1991, p. 271 .

118 Koh Byong-ik, 'Confucianism in Asia's Modern Transformation', *Korea Journal*, p. 60.

119 ibid.

120 Peter Berger, 'An East Asian Development Model?', in Berger and Hsiao, *In Search of An East Asian Development Model*, pp. 3, 7–8. Ian M. D. Little, 'An Economic Reconnaissance' in Galenson, *Economic Growth and Structural Change in Taiwan*, p. 461 suggests that Confucian virtues also include a willingness to work hard for long hours. See also S. Gordon Redding, *The Spirit of Chinese Capitalism*, Walter de Gruyter, Berling, New York, 1990.

THE CHINA FACTOR AND TAIWAN 107

121 Huang-ping Huang and Lian-Hwang Chiu, 'Moral and Civic Education', in Douglas C. Smith (ed.), *The Confucian Continuum: Educational Modernisation in Taiwan*, Praeger, New York, 1991, pp. 367, 371.

122 ibid., p. 376.

123 Lin Bih-jaw, paper, 'Thinking about Taiwan's Experience', Institute of International Relations, National Chengchi University, Taipei, 1990.

124 Hofheinz and Calder, *The Eastasia Edge*, pp. 23, 25, 48; see also Pye in Berger and Hsiao, *In Search of an East Asian Development Model*, pp. 86–87.

125 Yi-ting Wong, 'Republic of China's Experiences with Economic Development' in Tai, *Confucianism and Economic Development: An Oriental Alternative?*, pp. 115, 123, 124. Behind the Confucian facade, however, there lurks a very materialist Chinese society. In the late 1980s, for example, four million Taiwanese, or one-fifth of the population, engaged in a bout of gambling which saw stock and land prices and the crime rate skyrocket: Tzong-shian Yu, 'Current Conditions and the Prospects for Taiwan's Economy', paper, Chung-Hua Institution for Economic Research, Taipei 1990, pp. 7–8. An editorial in the *China Post* bemoaned the loss of Confucian virtues and what it claimed was a blind obsession with foreign goods and materialism. It called for more time to be spent reading the Chinese Classics, Chinese history and Dr Sun Yatsen's Three Principles of the People: *China Post*, 16 March 1992.

126 Pye, *Asian Power and Politics*, p. viii; see also Hsin-huang Michael Hsiao, 'An East Asian Development Model: Empirical Explorations', in Berger and Hsiao, *In Search of an East Asian Development Model*, pp. 12, 18; and Herman Kahn, *World Economic Development: 1979 and Beyond*, Croom Helm, London, 1979, p. 332. Wade, *Governing the Market*, p. 230, refers to Taiwan's 'cultural disposition towards a single source of authority and a restriction of interest group pluralism'.

127 For a discussion of 'industrial neo-Confucianism' in Taiwan, see Ezra F. Vogel, *The Four Little Dragons: The Spread of Industrialisation in East Asia*, Harvard University Press, Cambridge, Mass., 1991.

128 Hsiao, 'An East Asian Development Model: Empirical Explorations', in Berger and Hsiao, *In Search of an East Asian Development Model*, pp. 12, 20, 22. See also S.B. Linder, *The Pacific Century: Economic and Political Consequences of Asian-Pacific Dynamism*, Stanford University Press, Stanford, 1986, p. 26.

129 Woronoff, *Asia's 'Miracle' Economies*, p. 172; and Jacoby, *US Aid to Taiwan*, p. 164.

130 Susan Greenhalgh, 'Families and Networks in Economic Development', in Winckler and Greenhalgh, *Contending Approaches to the Political Economy of Taiwan*, pp. 224, 239.

131 Philippe Regnier, 'The Development of Small and Medium-Sized Enterprises in the Asian NIEs', in Manfred Kulessa (ed.), *The Newly Industrialising Economies of Asia — Prospects for Co-operation*, Springer-Verlag, Berlin, 1990, pp. 184–85.

132 Susan Greenhalgh, 'Families and Networks in Taiwan's Economic Development', in Winckler and Greenhalgh, *Contending Approaches to the Political Economy of Taiwan*, p. 224.

133 The Overseas Chinese contributed around 30 per cent of DFI in Taiwan in the period 1950–80.

134 Susan Greenhalgh, 'Families and Networks in Economic Development', in Winckler and Greenhalgh, *Contending Approaches to the Political Economy of Taiwan*, pp. 229, 239.

135 ibid.

136 Woronoff, *Asia's 'Miracle' Economies*, p. 232.

137 Li, *Economic Transformation of Taiwan*, p. 403; see also Papaanek, 'The New Asian Capitalism: An Economic Portrait' in Berger and Hsiao, *In Search of an East Asian Development Model*, pp. 27, 31.

138 Jacoby, *US Aid to Taiwan*, pp. 95–96.

139 Li, *Economic Transformation of Taiwan*, pp. 3–4.

140 S.C. Tsiang, 'Reasons for Taiwan's Economic Takeoff', in *Lessons from Taiwan Pathways to Follow and Pitfalls to Avoid*, pp. 11–17.

141 Ho, *Economic Development of Taiwan 1860–1970*, pp. 242–25.

142 *South China Morning Post*, 12 March 1991 and *The Age*, 30 June 1993.

143 Li, *Economic Transformation of Taiwan*, pp. 5–6, 91; also Yuan-li Wu, 'Taiwan in the Regional Economy of the Pacific Basin', in Feldman, *Taiwan in a Time of Transition*, pp. 39, 57.

144 China News Agency (Taipei), 12 July 1993.

145 Linda Y.C. Lim and Pang Eng Fong, *Foreign Direct Investment and Industrialisation in Malaysia, Singapore Taiwan and Thailand*, OECD, Paris, 1991, p. 141.

146 Erwin H. Epstein and Wei-fan Kuo, 'Higher Education' in Smith, *The Confucian Continuum*, pp. 167, 175.

147 Article 165 requires the state to increase the remuneration of teachers and others engaged in education. Article 166 requires the state to encourage scientific discoveries and inventions.

148 *Taiwan Yearbook 1993*, Government Information Office, Taipei, 1993, p. 337.

149 *The Defence Corporate Plan 91–95*, Australian Government Publishing Service, Canberra, 1991, p. 18.

150 *Education and Training in Australia*, Australian Bureau of Statistics, Cat. No. 4224.0, 1992, p. 162.

151 Wade, *Governing the Market*, p. 174; and Epstein and Kuo, 'Higher Education' in Smith, *The Confucian Continuum*, pp. 167, 214.

152 Woronoff, *Asia's 'Miracle' Economies*, p. 88.

153 Papaanek, 'The New Asian Capitalism: An Economic Portrait' in Berger and Hsiao, *In Search of an East Asian Development Model*, p. 67.

154 *The Economist*, 16 November 1991, p. 17.

155 Council for Economic Planning and Development, TSDB Taipei, 1990, p. 284.

156 *The Economist*, 16 November 1991, p. 17.

157 Council for Economic Planning and Development, TSDB, Taipei, 1990, p. 208.

158 Li, *Economic Transformation of Taiwan*, p. 18.

159 Epstein and Kuo, 'Higher Education' in Smith, *The Confucian Continuum*, pp. 168, 176–79; see also Kirby Chaur-shin Yung and Frederick G,. Welch, 'Vocational and Technical Education', in Smith, ibid., p. 230.

160 Investment Commission, Ministry of Economic Affairs, Taipei, *Statistics on Overseas Chinese and Foreign Investment, Technical Cooperation, Outward Investment, Outward Technical Cooperation*, December 1992, pp. 1–4.

5 How It All Came Together

The geo-politics of Taiwan's position between China, Japan and the United States over the last century provided the critical setting for Taiwan's development and its niche-role as a specialised mediator manoeuvring between Japan, the United States and China, the three leading commercial, cultural and/or military powers of Northeast Asia.

Taiwan's more recent re-linkage with China was contingent upon the economic, strategic and political foundations that Taiwan had built through prior linkages, first to Japan and then to the United States. Support and protection given to Taiwan by the United States in turn was hinged on its interest in keeping Taiwan at arm's length from the mainland for the duration of the Sino-United States Cold War. This provided a window of opportunity for Taiwan in the period from the 1950s to the 1970s. It allowed Taiwan three decades or so to consolidate its military strength, develop itself into a modern industrialised state and subsequently deal with the mainland from a position of strength.

Taiwan's industrialisation began with exports to Japan of processed food and agricultural products. It shifted to labour-intensive, low-technology, small-scale manufacturing for export, mainly to the United States. Indeed, throughout its modern post-1949 period, Taiwan has been dependent on these two powers. They provided almost two-thirds of all foreign investment in Taiwan since 1949. More than half of Taiwan's trade since 1952 has been with Japan and the United States.

In the 1950s, Japan took 50 per cent of all Taiwanese exports, then mainly agricultural products. By the 1970s, the United States took 40 per cent of Taiwan's exports, mainly manufactured goods. Between 1952 and 1992, Japan and the United States supplied up to 75 per cent of all Tai-

wanese imports and provided the markets for up to 50 per cent of all Taiwanese exports. Today, most Taiwanese imports come from Japan (30 per
cent in 1991) and most exports go to the United States. With its linkages
to Japan and the United States well established and secure, Taiwan is
poised to exploit the greater China market as an exporter and investor.

China has emerged as Taiwan's fastest growing export market and,
together with Hong Kong, is Taiwan's second largest export market after
the United States. Although direct exports to the United States have
fallen (from 49 per cent of the total in 1984 to 30 per cent in 1991), the
decline has been offset by increased exports to the United States from Taiwanese factories based in China. In 1992, China and Hong Kong took
around 19 per cent of Taiwan's total exports, mainly in the form of materials for labour-intensive Taiwanese-owned factories manufacturing
clothing and footwear in China for export to the United States.

In previous chapters, I disaggregated the most important conditioning
factors that lie behind Taiwan's development — its geography, the Japanese base and temporal sequencing after Japan's takeoff, American aid
and military protection, the impact of China's proximity and the significance of Chinese cultural values. Few other countries had such privileged access to a Japanese-led economic hierarchy and a United States
dominated geo-political system.[1] Few other cultures were as thoroughly
internationalised by constant exposure to the pressures and incentives of
business, war and politics in the Pacific region. As well, one must add the
global postwar recovery and the boom in international trade led by
Taiwan's ally and benefactor, the United States, and the stimulus to the
regional economy of United States defence spending on major wars in
Korea and Indochina. The United States provided hegemonic stability,
leadership and support for Taiwan as part of a free trade liberal economic
order in the Western Pacific. These were important conditions that contributed to Taiwan's rapid industrialisation.[2]

Each of these factors would not have been sufficient to sustain
Taiwan's rapid economic development. Cumulatively, however, they
formed a unique ongoing synergy that has given Taiwan special advantages over other developing economies.

This chapter is about the way the Kuomintang brought all its advantages together.

Explanations of the Taiwan puzzle have become many and varied.[3]
Some writers stress the importance of state intervention and downplay
Taiwan's geo-political advantages. James Reidel, for example, concludes
that government played a crucial role in determining economic performance in Taiwan and the other industrialising economies of East Asia.[4]
Alice Amsden, meanwhile, argues that while there were historical and
geopolitical circumstances that made Taiwan's development unique,
these explanations are 'dwarfed by those that focus on the forceful
manipulation of Taiwan's political economy by the state'.[5] Bruce Cumings calls it state-controlled capitalism by a bureaucratic authoritarian

industrialising regime.[6] Robert Wade describes the formula as 'the governed market theory of East Asian economic success'.[7] According to Masato Hayashida, Taiwan's postwar growth was 'an export-led expansion under the guidance of a powerful government leadership that created a development autocracy'.[8] Whatever the formula might be, clearly the role of government was important for Taiwan's takeoff. However, government in Taiwan after 1949 was very much a creature of local history, geography and international politics.

I am inclined to the view that the simplest explanation for Taiwan's development — that is, political stability and the practical adaptation of a carefully selected mix of the right policies to suit Taiwan's local circumstances and its unique geopolitical circumstances — is the best.[9] Some credit is due to the quality, motivation and commitment of the Kuomintang leaders in solving problems and pursuing the right policies, but their choices were fairly predictable, given the KMT's anti-communist stance, lessons from the mainland, the colonial experience with Japan, Taiwan's precarious security situation, its dependence on America, a limited domestic market, the lack of mineral resources, limited arable land and the low cost of labour.

The Nationalists, moreover, always intended to directly manage Taiwan's economy according to Sun Yatsen's Principle of People's Livelihood. Under *min-sheng* (people's livelihood), all major productive enterprises were to be under the control of the state.[10] Sun Yatsen's ideal of a rejuvenated Chinese government envisaged state control and management of large projects that were beyond the resources of private enterprise or which ought to be under the direction of the state for the public good.[11] Sun Yatsenism called for the government to play a central role in the management and co-ordination of resources, personnel, politics and long-term economic planning. Taiwan, moreover, had few natural assets other than its island geography and location, a relatively low-cost and docile labour force and the fact that it was of strategic importance to the United States and Japan. Since the Kuomintang's future rested on sustaining United States support and finding a way to sell goods to the United States, the future for Taiwan was fairly obvious: authoritarian government and land reform to guarantee political stability; an ideological commitment to 'free world' political values and, conversely, active opposition to communism in China; and rapid economic development based on the productive use of cheap labour and state intervention to start up domestic industries, boost exports and make Taiwan an attractive destination for United States investors.

Like the government in Beijing, the Nationalists provided a motivated visionary leadership with a commitment to build a new China. Chiang Kai-shek had a point to prove. He was under enormous pressure to succeed and to do so quickly because of the threat from the PLA; his rivalry with Mao Zedong to demonstrate the best form of government for all of China; the goal of mainland recovery; the need to demonstrate that if the

Nationalists had lost the mainland, it was for reasons other than ineptitude; and pressure from an activist United States aid mission.[12] Chiang was forced to devise and enforce successful long-term nation-building goals.

When Taiwan's China card lost its strategic and political value after Beijing's admission to the United Nations in 1971, the government gave renewed emphasis to an export-oriented survival strategy with support for industries such as petrochemicals, electrical machinery, electronics, precision machine tools and computer terminals.[13] After Washington abandoned its embassy in Taipei in favour of normalised relations with Beijing in 1980, the Kuomintang's survival strategy again shifted, this time towards domestic political reforms and the development of a practical working relationship with mainland China. This required the Kuomintang to strive even harder to consolidate its domestic and international position in anticipation of reunification negotiations with the mainland.

In other words, since 1949 there has been relentless pressure on the Kuomintang to outperform the mainland and to do well economically. For Taiwan, this presupposed a policy of state economic management and, as the Nationalists were ideologically bound to oppose socialism and uphold capitalist ethics, Taiwan inevitably became a crucible for a mix of capitalism side by side with the kind of long-range central planning and direction more typical of a socialist state.

How did the Kuomintang pull it all together?

One of the foundation stones was political, fiscal and industrial stability. The state (i.e. the Kuomintang) was in an unchallengeable position to manipulate Taiwan's economy and the Taiwanese because it was so ruthless and single-minded in its administration. Native Taiwanese leaders had been systematically exterminated and although by 1964 there was not 'as much shooting as there was in the early 1950s, each year still brought new arrests, closed military trials, and long prison sentences'.[14] The Nationalists were supported materially and morally by the United States and were not subject to the kind of agenda on human rights and democracy that prevails in the conduct of United States foreign policy today. They could justify their repressive politics on the grounds of an imminent external threat. They had also learned from the mistakes they had made on the mainland in allowing their domestic political control system to run down.[15]

Once on Taiwan, the Kuomintang gave priority to establishing an intrusive domestic security apparatus and a tight party network that stretched from the standing committee at the top to cells in schools, universities, factories, neighbourhoods and the bureaucracy.[16] The armed forces were controlled by a political control system similar to that used in the Soviet Union and mainland China.[17]

To question the authority of the Kuomintang was to risk arrest and imprisonment. As noted in the previous chapter, the Taiwanese had been cowed into submission by systematic surveillance, torture, strict censorship and tight political controls.[18] There were no independent labour unions, newspapers or opposition political parties.[19] Speculators were liable to arrest and imprisonment.

But the people of Taiwan were apparently used to such a style of government. At least, as Lucian Pye observes, they were culturally attuned to obeying the authority of a strong centralised government.[20] Besides, while the Kuomintang did not tolerate political dissent, it recognised and rewarded merit and technical skills and generally encouraged rapid national economic development. It combined authoritarianism with what Thomas Metzger and Ramon Myers call 'modern Confucian humanism', a philosophy which emphasised the need to base modernisation on the ethics of Confucius, including ideals of good government and social harmony, and Sun Yatsen's Three Principles of the People.[21] The result was a Kuomintang government that was almost the archetype of Chalmers Johnson's notion of 'soft authoritarianism'.[22]

Whether hard or soft, it was effectively a police state and remained so until the late 1970s. Martial law was not lifted and a free press was not permitted until 1987. A legitimate political opposition party, the Democratic Progressive Party, did not make its debut until 1987. The country was run along Leninist lines by a small elite consisting of the president, the premier and perhaps a dozen other individuals from key ministries, agencies or commissions, together with advisers from the Industrial Development Bureau and the Council for Economic Planning and Development, the Central Bank of Taiwan and the most important large public enterprises. This concentration of authority was conducive to the implementation of strategic planning and the maintenance of priorities in line with the national interest — in other words, the interests of the Kuomintang.[23]

The Kuomintang, often described as a Leninist party with power concentrated in the hands of a small elite, is in fact simply a reflection of the way things have always been in China. It was formed in 1912 to make revolution and fight wars, the ultimate aim of which was to reunify China and make it once again a great and powerful Middle Kingdom. The Kuomintang was born from struggle. It fought warlords, Mao's communists and the Japanese for several decades on the mainland and faced the threat of invasion from the mainland for several more decades after 1949. From the beginning, right through to the present time, the Kuomintang has had to face an enemy and therefore establish clear long-term national goals.

These goals transcended the rights and interests of individuals, at least until 1987, and were sharply focused on Taiwan's survival within the triangular dynamics of relations between the United States, Japan and China.

As well as being a political power, the Kuomintang dominated the Taiwanese economy. It inherited all of Japan's levers of economic power and was the receptacle for United States aid from 1949 to 1965. It was the island's biggest landowner and controlled more than half of Taiwan's main industries, including petroleum, energy, railways, steel, tobacco and spirits, shipbuilding, telecommunications and banking.

With such enormous economic and political power at its disposal, the Kuomintang could set the goals, change direction and assign the priorities for its program of nation-building. Basically, it could do as it pleased. It could engage in long-term centralised economic planning and decide on the allocation of resources without regard for what might be politically unpopular, as in a democratic society. In this respect, the Kuomintang was as powerful as the governments in socialist states like China, the Soviet Union and North Korea. The government's aim was to boost output, savings, education, human resources, infrastructure and productivity as quickly as possible so as to build an industrial base that would be strong enough to defend Taiwan and perhaps recover the mainland. These nation-building goals were not dissimilar to those pursued under the socialist flag by Mao Zedong.

However, the Kuomintang was able to do better in Taiwan than the communist regime on the mainland, partly because Taiwan was smaller and more easily managed and partly because Taiwan had United States aid and Japanese foundations. In addition, the Koumintang was an effective government that provided the Taiwanese with security, a powerful ally, financial stability, rapid economic growth, improving living standards and equal opportunities for education and upward mobility.[24]

Free marketism

The Kuomintang also did better on Taiwan because they adopted the capitalist values of the United States, the leading capitalist state and richest economy in the world. The Taiwanese embraced the role of material incentives and specialised in international trade with the United States and Japan. Taiwan was outward looking and increasingly competitive and responsive to international market indicators. In contrast, Mao's China looked inwards, pursued policies of economic self-reliance and egalitarianism and concentrated on building up its heavy industries.

In any event, the Kuomintang was forced through the United States aid program to accept American economic advice in such fields as taxation, housing, banking, investment, trade and foreign exchange.[25] In fact, there was agreement between Taipei and Washington on making Taiwan a showcase free market economy that would contrast with the mainland and serve as a model for other countries in the Asia-Pacific region.[26] That very objective presupposed government intervention to stabilise inflation, encourage savings, revitalise agriculture, start up new industries, attract foreign capital and technology and strengthen Taiwan's importance to the non-communist world.[27] It also presupposed a commitment to free enterprise and materialism.

Broad-based policy advice

The government did not rule by decree or implement policy on the basis of ideological principle. It consulted with United States advisers, drew on Taiwan's Japanese experience and made a virtue out of consulting closely with industry leaders and academic specialists. A glance through the Who's Who columns in the *China Yearbook* in any year since 1949 indicates that many of Taiwan's political leaders and most of the key officials in economic planning agencies have had dual careers in industry or academia. Kwoh-ting Li, for example, one of the architects of Taiwan's success, was president of the Taiwan Shipbuilding Corporation from 1951–53. He later became a member of the Industrial Development Commission and the Economic Stabilisation Board from 1953–58, Secretary General of the Council for United States Aid from 1958–63, Minister for Economic Affairs from 1965–69 and Vice Chairman of the Council for International Economic Co-operation and Development from 1963–73.[28]

Lee Huan was previously an academic at National Taiwan and National Sun Yatsen Universities from 1976–84 before becoming Minister for Education in 1984–87 and Premier of Taiwan from 1989–90.[29] Lien Chan, Taiwan's current premier, was a professor of political science at National Taiwan University from 1968–75 before he switched to government and politics.[30] Shirley W.Y. Kuo was a professor at National Taiwan University from 1966 before becoming vice chairperson of the Economic Planning Council in 1973, vice chairperson of the Council for Economic Planning and Development in 1977, deputy governor of the Central Bank of China in 1979 and Minister for Finance in 1988.[31]

The president, Lee Teng-hui, was an academic agricultural economist educated in Japan and the United States before he began his career in government in 1972. President Lee is a consensus-seeking leader who consults widely within Taiwan and also draws on the advice of foreign-trained Taiwanese academics such as Tien Hung-mao from the United States and C.L. Chiou from Australia.

As Saburo Okita noted, part of the explanation for the success of the NIEs was that the effectiveness of government policies was buttressed by close co-operative efforts between government, industry and academia.[32] This collaboration was and is very much a part of the Taiwanese approach to managing the economy and national politics.

Engineering approach

Many observers suggest that the government's style of economic management in Taiwan was due in large part to the cautious professional approach adopted by scientists and engineers.[33] In mainland China, the government disdained expertise and economic policy was often decided on political grounds. In Taiwan, in contrast, technical expertise has always been highly esteemed in government. Science and engineering courses at universities in Taiwan attract the top 5 per cent of high school graduates.[34] Ten of Taiwan's fourteen ministers of economic affairs between 1949 and 1985 were engineers.[35] Many other leaders were technocrats trained in the United States, Europe and Japan. They were fluent in English and familiar with foreign scientific and technical developments.[36] They had a style of thinking that convinced them of the efficacy of forward and backward linkages.[37] They 'concentrated on workable projects, rejected bureaucratic monopoly, favoured free market enterprise and readily accepted new knowledge and experience from the advanced nations of the world'.[38] They were interested in finding solutions in terms of 'enhanced technical efficiency and innovations in production' instead of being 'guided by the half-light of economic theory'.[39] They mapped out and implemented 'a strategy of promoting rational step by step development' in a process of 'orderly progression from labour intensive light industries to capital and technology intensive heavy ones'.[40]

K.Y. Yin (Yin Chung-jung), 'the moving spirit' behind Taiwan's industrial reform program in the 1950s, was an engineer.[41] His goal of an industrialised, independent and self-sustaining Taiwanese economy combined elements of the *laissez-faire* approach and state planning.[42] He strengthened designated parts of the private sector, including textiles, plastics, glass and plywood, and developed close relations with refugee capitalists from Shanghai.

K.T. Li (Li Kwoh-ting), Taiwan's chief economic planner and 'super-technocrat' from 1963 until the late 1980s, was trained in physics.[43]

Long-term planning and nation building

The government in Taiwan, like its counterpart in Beijing, was involved in ambitious, large-scale, long-term nation-building projects, especially in basic infrastructure, such as power, ports and transportation, and industries such as shipbuilding, steel, petroleum and petrochemicals. Systems and facilities to support exports were always high on the government's spending priorities. President Chiang Ching-kuo had highways, rail networks and deep-water ports built to facilitate the easy movement of raw materials to Taiwanese factories and the export of their finished products.[44] The government also devised long-term education, science and technology strategies with a time frame of ten years.

According to Li, central planning *per se* was vitally important for the formulation, promotion, co-ordination, follow up and evaluation of the government's long-term economic development plan.[45] It was conducive to consistency, long-term economic strategy, nurturing key industries and the construction of large-scale infrastructure projects. Setting national guideposts and giving purpose to the Taiwanese contributed political and economic stability in a threatening and uncertain world.

Planning agencies like the Economic Stabilisation Board, the Council of International Economic Co-operation and the Council for Economic Planning and Development were established to draw up strategic economic development plans and co-ordinate their implementation. Taiwan's economic history since 1949 is a history of long-term, centrally conceived economic blueprints. Beginning in 1953, the government drew up a series of four-, five-, six- and ten-year strategic economic development plans to upgrade the efficiency of transportation and communication networks, build new sources of power generation, improve housing and develop steel, shipbuilding and petrochemical industries.

The current six-year national development plan for 1991–96 envisages expenditure of over US$200 billion on 600 or more projects aimed at social and environmental refurbishment, housing and increased power generation. As with previous plans, there is heavy emphasis on transportation and communications, including tranportation grids that link up with new highways, high-speed railways and mass transit systems connecting all major uban centres (Taipei, Taiyuan, Hsinchu, Taichung, Tainan, and Kaohsiung).[46]

Starting up industries

As well as providing the infrastructure, the capital, the protection, the incentives and political and fiscal stability, the government also pioneered certain industries through a strategy of 'direct involvement' and 'active encouragement'. It shared with business the risks of doing business.[47] It set up large corporations (China Steel, Taipower, Taiwan Sugar Corporation, China Cement, China Airlines, China Shipbuilding and Chinese Petroleum) in strategic industries like banking, steel, fertilisers, electricity, shipbuilding, petroleum and gas, air transport and communications, and led the way in many others such as integrated circuit production, nuclear power and the aerospace industry. This involvement and government ownership gave Taiwan one of the largest public sectors in the world outside the communist bloc.[48] In 1952, 56.6 per cent of all industrial production was owned by the government and even though this had declined to 18 per cent in 1992, the government still controlled six out of the eight largest companies on Taiwan.[49]

The government supported such industries as textiles and synthetic fibres as start-up industries; later, it also supported automobiles, steel, aluminium, shipbuilding, copper smelting, petrochemicals, plastics, electrical and electronics industries.[50] In all these areas, the state played a crucial role through state-led negotiations for foreign (particularly United States) technology, state-owned industries, state-sponsored research and development, state-led co-ordination and supervision of particular industries, state financial assistance, control of foreign exchange, use of subsidies and tariff protection and local content requirements.[51]

Once key industries were established, however, the government gradually vacated the field. During the early 1950s, the government transferred Taiwan Cement Corporation, Taiwan Pulp and Paper Corporation, Taiwan Industrial and Mining Corporation and the Taiwan Agriculture and Forestry Development Corporation to private ownership. Industries remaining in the public sector include fuels, power, railroads, shipbuilding and iron and steel — in other words, capital-intensive strategic industries. But the trend has been towards a reduced government role as the economy picked up speed and sophistication. In 1952, government-owned corporations accounted for 56.6 per cent of industrial production, decreasing gradually to 48 per cent in 1960, 27.7 per cent in 1970, 21 per cent in 1980 and 18 per cent in 1992.[52]

Targeting industries

As well as basic industries like power and shipbuilding, the government targeted for development selected industries that had rapid growth and export potential. The government's choice as to which industries were favoured to receive special assistance was made in accordance with lists drawn up by the government's central economic planning agency, the Council for Economic Planning and Development.[53] Recent priorities have included electrical appliances, electronics, radios, electronic components, watches and clocks and other consumer durables.[54] In the electrical and electronics industry, the government formed an electronics working group to assist in marketing, co-ordinating production with the demands of foreign buyers, procuring raw materials, training personnel, improving quality and speeding up bureaucratic approval procedures.[55] By 1968, electrical and electronic goods were the second biggest export category after textiles. By 1984 they had overtaken textiles as Taiwan's leading export industry. Other export industries were favoured with concessions or privileges in taxation, customs, tariffs and access to foreign exchange.[56]

More recently, the government has supported electronics, computers and semiconductors. The government-funded United Microelectronic Corporation, set up in 1980 as Taiwan's only large-scale semi-conductor manufacturer, is now owned by private companies. The government also established the Taiwan Semiconductor Manufacturing Corporation, a chip fabrication company 48 per cent owned by the government and 27 per cent owned by Philips of Holland and 25 per cent local investors. It provided low-interest loans to other chip fabrication factories being built in the Hsinchu science-based park and trained computer engineers in chip design.[57]

This policy of industrial fostership was how most major new industries in Taiwan got started. The best known example was a polyvinyl chloride plastics factory that was constructed under government supervision and handed over to Y.C. Wang in 1957. Wang's Formosa Plastics

Group is now Taiwan's leading business enterprise and Y.C. Wang is Taiwan's richest man. The role of the state in developing new industries in Taiwan, says Wade in his definitive study on the subject, was 'the contrapuntal partner to the market system, helping to insure that resources went into industries important for future growth and military strength'.[58]

Protectionism and import-substituting industries

Taiwan was never an open economy accessible unconditionally to exporters from other countries. The Kuomintang had a powerful, secretive import control regime that rigorously applied a multiple exchange rate mechanism in the 1950s and tariff and non-tariff barriers thereafter to encourage import substituting and export oriented industries.[59]

Tariffs remained high until the mid-1980s. Taiwan's car industry, for example, was heavily protected with a ban on Japanese cars and a 65 per cent duty on cars from all other countries.[60] Tariffs on cars were 42 per cent in 1991 and 30 per cent in 1992. One consequence of Taiwan's tariff wall against imported Japanese cars was to force Japanese companies like Toyota, Subaru, Nissan and Honda into joint ventures with local car makers, but even then they had to satisfy a 70 per cent local content requirement.[61]

As well as tariffs, the government used non-tariff barriers such as restrictive quotas, over-valued exchange rates, licensing controls and simple prohibitions and preferential taxation to support certain industries, control external competition and otherwise protect existing industries and channel resources to new ones.[62] Prior to 1970, more than 42 per cent of all import items were subject to controls or prohibition, notably products made by state-owned monopolies, textiles, timber, agricultural and light industrial products.[63] According to Alice Amsden, Taiwan was little different from other Third World countries in implementing strict protectionist measures to guard its infant industries.[64] Between 1948 and 1955, the average nominal tariff rate for all imports more than doubled, from 20 to 45 per cent, but the effective tariff rate was substantially higher, especially for consumer goods, and was still around 31 per cent in 1980.[65] Such measures increased the profitability of import substitution and were partly responsible for the doubling of manufacturing production during the period 1950–58.[66] Items such as bicycles, sewing machines, paper, rubber, cement, leather and leather products, woollen yarn, cotton yarn, human-made fibres and chemical fertilisers were subject to tighter and tighter import controls in order to promote import substitution between 1950 and 1962.[67] Key industries like textiles, clothing, footwear, food processing, cement and light manufacturing were established during this period.

While measures that hindered Taiwan's export industries such as the multiple exchange rate system were simplified in 1959, protectionism as a policy tool remained intact up to the mid-1970s.[68] The number of imported commodities subject to import controls was 36.5 per cent of the total in 1953 and 41 per cent in 1970.[69]

Exporting as a way of life

The feature that most distinguishes government intervention in the Taiwanese economy from that of a similar style of government in China has been the focus on exports. According to Jui-meng Chang, Taiwan's government has 'consistently and persistently held to an outward-oriented trade policy' since 1958.[70] In that context, government intervention in Taiwan's domestic economy was always aimed at improving Taiwan's international export competitiveness — for example, by attracting modern Western technology, encouraging thrift, promoting Taiwan as a destination for foreign investment, investing in technical education, protecting infant industries and otherwise giving preferment to industries engaged in export trade.

Given the limits of Taiwan's domestic market, rapid economic growth could only be sustained by an export-oriented strategy, as in most East Asian economies.[71] While Taiwan's industrialisation strategy continued to nurture infant industries, it shifted in the late 1950s to export promotion and export efficiency.[72] The basis of the strategy was Taiwan's comparative advantage in low-cost labour, Taiwan's location at the crossroads of the Asia-Pacific region and its favoured commercial and strategic relationships with Japan and the United States.

The government initially concentrated on export industries that involved labour-intensive manufacturing such as food processing, agricultural products, textiles, clothing, plastic and rubber products and, by the mid-1960s, electrical appliances. These were all industries with characteristics that suited Taiwan's factor endowments: low investment requirements, simple processing, a rapid return on investment, labour intensity and expanding export markets, mainly in the United States.[73] Protectionist measures were then eased to encourage export-oriented industries and to improve the international competitiveness of domestic industries. In 1960 the NT$ was devalued from $NT15.55 to the US dollar to $NT40 and the multiple exchange rate system that inhibited export industries was scrapped. Tariffs were gradually reduced and import controls on components or materials used in export industries were liberalised. Access to foreign exchange for export enterprises was also liberalised. The 1961 Statute for the Encouragement of Investment gave export industries tax concessions such as a five-year tax holiday for machinery and equipment and tax exemptions on reinvested profits and foreign currency debts.[74] Other export-oriented measures included rebates on customs duty and commodity tax on imported materials used to make goods for exports; exemptions from business tax and lower stamp taxes for exporters; export loans at half the market rate for pre-shipment production financing and importation of raw materials; deductions of 2 per cent of annual export earnings from taxable income; tax rebates on the price of domestic inputs for export industries; deductions of 10 per cent tax for companies that exported 50 per cent of output (until 1970); export insurance by a government agency to minimise the exporter's risk; a right to retain foreign exchange earnings; formation of a trading organisation to control and synchronise production for export and eliminate competition amongst exporters; the introduction of export inspection, managerial, technical and trade consultation services and very detailed market research and support through organisations like the China External Trade Development Council (set up in 1970).[75] Export processing zones (EPZs) were established at Kaohsiung in 1965 and at Nantze and Taichung in 1970.

Cumulatively, these measures unleashed Taiwan's natural talents and became 'a powerful new force in the economy'.[76] They helped transform Taiwan from an inward-looking import-substituting economy to an outward-looking, export-oriented liberalised international market economy.[77] Exports became 'the driving force behind Taiwan's sustained and rapid economic growth' under the policy of 'everything is for export'.[78] Exports were given — and still have — top priority in Taiwan's economic and foreign policy agenda. The value of Taiwan's trade grew by a factor of almost 1000 between 1952 and 1992, with an average annual increase in total trade of 21 per cent between 1953 and 1989 and 27 per cent between 1959 and 1976.[79] Taiwan's foreign trade as a ratio of GNP was 23 per cent in 1951–53, rising to 81 per cent in 1971–73, 88 per cent in 1988, declining somewhat thereafter to 78.8 per cent in 1989 and 75.5 per cent in 1990.[80]

Export expansion became the engine driving Taiwan's rapid economic growth and was the primary source of its rapid industrialisation.[81] It underpinned rapid growth in labour-intensive manufacturing industries (See Table 7) and absorbed Taiwan's surplus rural labour. Exports were 8 per cent of GDP in 1952 and 53 per cent in 1983, while imports rose from 14.1 per cent to 41.7 per cent of GDP over the same period.[82] Export expansion accounted for 22.5 per cent of Taiwan's output growth in 1956–61, 35 per cent in 1961–66, 46 per cent in 1966–71 and 67.7 per cent by 1971–76.[83] By 1971, Taiwan had reached a situation of full employment leading to improved equity in distribution of income distribution as wages for lower-income groups increased and farmers had the opportunity of earning supplementary non-agricultural income.[84]

Taiwan's specialisation in exports of electronic applicances was due to a combination of cheap labour and direct foreign investment (DFI). In 1976, the average manufacturing wage in Taiwan was still less than 15 per cent of the wage in the United States and 20 per cent of the wage in Japan.[85] To exploit this resource, the Taiwanese actively wooed foreign investors by offering a very 'hospitable environment'.[86] Even from the early 1950s, there were no restrictions on foreign ownership; a broadly defined range of industry was open to foreign investors and used machinery and materials could be converted into capital. Firms engaged in exports were given preferential treatment such as subsidies, rebates, taxation rebates, investment incentives, soft loans, tariff protection and a range of other benefits and concessions.

In 1961, the Statute for the Encouragement of Investment gave generous tax incentives to export-oriented DFI (including a five-year tax holiday for suitable productive enterprises, tax exemptions on reinvested profits and foreign currency debts, tax deductions for exporters and reduced taxes on business), provided that the investment was to the long-term benefit of Taiwan's export trade, that it did not compete with certain selected strategic industries in Taiwan and that it raised the level of domestic technology.[87]

By the early 1960s, when Taiwan's future seemed less uncertain — thanks to United States military containment of mainland China and United States military aid and financial support for Taiwan — foreign investment began to gather strength.

Export Processing Zones (EPZs)

In 1965, the government established an EPZ in Kaohsiung to attract foreign investment and spearhead Taiwan's export drive. Other EPZs were opened in Taichung and Nantze in southern Taiwan in 1970. These were Asia's first tax and duty free industrial processing zones and were designed specifically for export and technology-oriented foreign investment. The EPZs provided smooth entry, established factory sites, cheap power and utilities, various tax concessions, preferential customs treatment, tariff protection against competition, guarantees against expropriation, easy access to ports and other incentives. They capitalised on Taiwan's central location, political stability and a cheap, skilled female labour force. The average monthly wages rates in the EPZs were much lower than those elsewhere in Taiwan.[88] The EPZs soon attracted a concentration of labour-intensive industries, especially in electronics, with the proportion of foreign investment reaching 23 per cent between 1966 and 1970.[89] Although it declined to 19 per cent by 1975 and 16 per cent by 1980 as investment opportunities outside the zones matched those inside, the EPZs had served their purpose in attracting competing foreign multinationals, boosting exports and raising the standard of local technology.

United States appliance makers like General Electrics were followed to Taiwan by other multinationals such as Philips, Grundig, Canon and Hitachi. All were seeking to maintain their competitive edge against each other. The United States sewing machine company Singer, for example, moved to Taiwan to try to beat competition from Japan for the sale of sewing machines in the United States market. By 1978, it had helped build a vibrant industry that had outstripped Japan in exports to the United States and the rest of the world and made Taiwan the world's largest producer of sewing machines.[90] Taiwan was in the right place at the right time: it offered cheap labour, location and facilities to American and European manufacturers of televisions and other electronic appliances seeking a base to compete against Japanese manufacturers. This in turn forced Japanese multinationals to set up factories in Taiwan in an effort to maintain their competitive edge.

After the opening of Taiwan's first EPZ in 1965, electrical and electronic exports grew at a rate of nearly 60 per cent per annum between 1966 and 1971.[91] Electronics and electrical machinery soon became the main manufacturing activity in the EPZs. Electrical machinery and apparatus accounted for 2.6 per cent of all exports in 1965, 12 per cent in 1970, 14.7 per cent in 1975, 18 per cent in 1980, 21 per cent in 1985 and 26.6 per cent in 1990.[92] Most output was exported to America, Europe and Japan by American, Japanese and European multinationals based in Taiwan.

Direct Foreign Investment (DFI)

Rival DFI from Japan and the United States played the dominant role in the supply of DFI to Taiwan, supplemented by investment from the overseas Chinese. For the overseas Chinese, Taiwan was Chinese and uncertainty about its future was removed by the 1954 Sino-United States Mutual Security Treaty. For United States companies like General Electrics and Westinghouse, Taiwan had a central East Asian base for manufacturing operations, the approval and support of the United States government, social and political stability, cheap labour, a well-developed infrastructure, the China connection and today, cheap computer engineers and surplus capital. For the Japanese, Taiwan was a former colony that was closer to Japanese society and culture than any other location in East Asia. It had hard-working, cheap labour, no social welfare or labour protection legislation and its security was guaranteed by the Americans. That is, Taiwan was a natural destination for American, Japanese and Chinese DFI. All the government in Taipei had to provide was political stability, cheap skilled (but docile) labour and the sites and utilities.

Initially, DFI was concentrated in labour-intensive light industries such as food, textiles and garments. Most DFI came after the government passed its 'Statute for the Encouragement of Investment' in 1960, completed key infrastructure projects, opened up export processing zones in the mid-1960s, and introduced a package of fiscal, financial and foreign exchange reforms.[93]

DFI was not important in Taiwan until the shift to labour-intensive export-oriented manufacturing occurred in the mid-1960s. DFI, however, was not a significant source of capital in Taiwan, although it must have helped plug the gap left by the cessation of United States aid in 1965.[94] DFI never exceeded 10 per cent of Taiwan's private fixed investment and never hired more than 6 per cent of Taiwan's total employees.[95] As a percentage of total capital formation, it reached a peak of 4.32 per cent between 1969 and 1972, but in all other periods was around 2 per cent or less.[96] Foreign capital has been complementary to local capital, not competitive, and the favoured avenue involves joint venture — for example, between Acer and Texas Instruments, British Aerospace and Taiwan Aerospace or Philips and Taiwan Semiconductor Manufacturing Corporation.

Initially, a substantial percentage of DFI (32 per cent) came from overseas Chinese, mainly from Hong Kong, in the period 1952–79 but they were soon replaced by investment from American and Japanese multinationals. Over the period 1952–92, the United States and Japan supplied, respectively, 25 per cent and 33 per cent, or around 58 per cent of all approved DFI in Taiwan (US$16.5 billion).[97] Of total DFI of US$16.5 billion over the period 1952–92, 28 per cent came from the United States, 29 per cent came from Japan, 15 per cent came from the Overseas Chinese (mainly in Hong Kong) and 15 per cent from Europe.[98]

The main role of DFI was to stimulate export industries and help in the transfer of technology, notably in the area of electronics and electrical machinery, when Kaohsiung and other EPZs were set up in the late 1960s. The electronics and electrical industry took most DFI (33 per cent between 1952 and 1979), followed by chemicals (11 per cent), services (10 per cent), machinery, equipment and instruments (6.6 per cent), basic metals and metal products (6.5 per cent) and garments and wood and paper products.[99] Chi Schive, after detailed examination of the activities of the Singer Sewing Machine Company, suggests that if modern economic growth is viewed as a continuous process of accumulation, application and the dissemination of scientific and technical knowledge, then direct foreign investment in Taiwan was a catalyst for Taiwan's subsequent economic development.[100] Technological improvements accounted for about 50 per cent of non-agricultural growth and 36 per cent of agricultural growth in Taiwan's economy between 1952 and 1979.[101]

United States investment in Taiwan in the early 1960s stimulated Japanese investment, especially in electronics and electrical appliances. The United States was the dominant source of foreign investment in the 1950s and 1960s, supplying around 90 per cent of the total in 1960 and 49 per cent in 1970.[102] To beat competition from cheap Japanese goods, United States firms had relocated to Taiwan to assemble goods, especially in consumer electronics, for export back to the United States. By 1980, the United States share had fallen to around 26 per cent and in 1990 it had dropped to 23 per cent.[103]

Japanese DFI, on the other hand, started later but soon caught up with and overtook the United States' share as Japanese companies, under the strategic guidance of MITI, Japan's Ministry of International Trade and Industry, sought to retain their competitive advantage by relocating their assembly or sub-contractor operations in Taiwan.[104]

The Japanese share of DFI in Taiwan was around 2 per cent in 1960, 20.5 per cent in 1970, 34 per cent in 1980 and 36 per cent in 1990.[105] Japan supplied 6.6 per cent of total foreign investment in the 1950s, 17 per cent for the period 1952–70 and 29 per cent, or $4.35 billion, for the period 1952–90.[106]

Most DFI over the period 1962–79 went into the manufacturing sector (85 per cent) and, of that, the biggest proportion (37 per cent) was directed to the electrical and electronics industry.[107] Most foreign firms in the electonics sector were Japanese or American. In 1976, they provided 40 per cent of all Taiwanese employment in this sector and exported most of the output, mainly to the United States.[108] It can be said, therefore, that as DFI was concentrated in the area of electronics and electrical appliances, Taiwan's leading export industry, DFI contributed directly to Taiwan's export-oriented growth.[109]

In 1992, exports of electrical machinery and apparatus totalled $US22 billion or 27 per cent of all exports.[110] In the same year, the United States took over 30 per cent of Taiwan's exports under the category of 'machinery and electrical equipment'.[111] That is, rival United States and Japanese firms were amongst the biggest investors in the electronics and electrical appliance industry in Taiwan. Their customers were mainly American or European and their suppliers were mainly Japanese.

In this sense, American and Japanese investment spawned the electronics and electrical appliance industries that became critically important to Taiwan's industrialisation, its rapid economic growth and its specialised trading niche between Japan and the United States. United States and Japanese-sourced DFI in the decade from 1965 to 1975 brought in the new technology and skills; it helped restructure Taiwan's economy and build new industries in electronics, electrical machinery, auto-parts and plastic products; it introduced new products and technologies; it was important in opening up channnels for marketing goods in the United States, the source of much of the DFI in the first place; and it helped polish Taiwan's global marketing orientation.[112] DFI also hitched Taiwan to the Japanese drive for exports to the United States. Taiwan became a nation of small subcontractors supplying cheap labour to assemble or manufacture goods for competing United States and Japanese corporations, mainly for export to the United States. The result was that Taiwan was bracketed most profitably between export dependency and a persistent trade surplus with the United States and import dependency and a recurrent trade deficit with Japan.[113]

In other words, United States and Japanese DFI and its concentration in the electronics and appliance sector, plus privileged access to the

United States market and a special relationship with Japan, were central to Taiwan's economic success. In the 1960s and 1970s, Taiwan was able to catch and ride what Ezra Vogel calls the fourth great wave of new technology in the world since the first industrial revolution — that is, the take-off in demand for consumer electronics and household appliances.[114] Electronics and electrical machinery were the destination of most DFI and became Taiwan's leading industrial sector by the mid-1980s.

With government assistance through projects like the Hsinchu Technology Park, the industry began to shift towards more technology-intensive electronic products in the 1980s and was thus well prepared to exploit Vogel's fifth great wave of computer, telecommunication and information technologies.[115]

Technology focus

Taiwan had been preparing to catch the fifth wave for some time with three consecutive long-term science development plans (1959–68, 1968–79, 1979–85 and 1986–95). Taiwan's National Science Council, responsible directly to the Executive Yuan, was developed in 1967 from the National Council on Science Development (founded in 1959). Its aim was to promote Taiwan's science and high-technology development through strategic planning, co-operation with scientific institutes in the United States, recruiting scientific personnel from overseas, giving rewards and subsidies for oustanding research, supporting research centres in particular disciplines, co-ordinating the S&T programs of various ministries such as Defence, Economic Affairs, Health, Communications and the Atomic Energy Council, developing science-based industrial parks and targeting selected areas for development, such as energy, materials, information and production automation, biotechnology and electro-optics.[116] The overall result has been that scientific research institutes in materials technology and processing are well endowed and well equipped, notably more so than, for example, their Australian counterparts.[117]

The government established the Industrial Technology Research Institute (ITRI) in 1973. Similar to Australia's CSIRO, ITRI has a staff of almost 6000, mostly scientists and engineers. ITRI conducts long- and medium-term research in industrial technologies. Under its umbrella are other institutes like the Electronic Research and Service Organisation, charged with acquiring core technologies to develop an information industry and produce semiconductors.

The Chung-Shan Institute of Science and Technology (CSIST) was set up in Taoyuan in 1979 to co-ordinate the government's defence-related research and development. It has 15 000 employees working on the integration of United States technology and the development of aeronautical systems, jet aircraft, missiles, early warning radars, stealth technology and electronics.

The Taiwan Aerospace Corporation (TAC), set up in 1991 with capital of $4 billion, is the basis of Taiwan's quest to build aircraft manufacturing and repair facilities and establish Taiwan as a regional aerospace centre. Aerospace is among the ten major new high-tech industries targeted for rapid development. TAC is 29 per cent owned by the government's Economic Co-operation and Development Fund, with state-owned China Steel Co. and Bank of Communication having 10 and 5 per cent shares respectively. It has a fifteen-year aerospace development plan involving joint ventures with advanced European and American companies. By the year 2000, aerospace is expected to contribute 2.2 per cent of Taiwan's GNP and Taiwan would then be the second largest aircraft and component manufacturer in (non-communist) Asia after Japan.[118]

While the budgetary resources allocated to R&D as a percentage of GNP have been relatively low in the past, they are being increased at a rate of up to 24 per cent per annum. The R&D budget rose from 1.06 per cent of GNP in 1987 to 1.38 per cent in 1989 and 1.7 per cent in 1991 (the same level as Japan in 1973),[119] with a target of 2.2 per cent by 1996 and 2.8 per cent by 2002.[120]

A notable feature of Taiwan's leading scientific laboratories and institutes is that they have tended to avoid original research and have instead concentrated on applying the results of foreign scientific research and on improving access to indigenous and foreign technology by Taiwan's 700 000 or so small to medium sized business enterprises.[121] To facilitate technology transfer between the laboratory and end-users, both ITRI and CSIST have industrial facilities that are capable of producing prototype components and products with commercial and defence applications.[122]

In 1980, a science-based industrial park was established at Hsinchu to develop Taiwan's base in more advanced technologies. Enterprises engaged in areas such as semiconductors, integrated circuits, electronic precision products, telecommunications equipment, computers, biotechnology, optoelectronics, automation, energy and environmental R&D were offered special tax incentives, low-interest loans, logistic support, a skilled workforce and strategic location. It was an attempt to keep Taiwan ahead of its competitors, with a view to the long term. According to some observers, it succeeded and was the catalyst for speeding up the restructuring of Taiwan's economy into relatively higher technology, science-based industries.[123]

Presently there are 134 firms in Hsinchu. Many are joint ventures between Taiwanese firms and foreign companies like IBM, Honeywell, AT&T and Ericson. Most are involved with computers and peripherals, integrated circuits, telecommunications, optoelectronics and automation. By 1996, it is estimated that Hsinchu will house 200 technology-intensive enterprises employing 50 000 people with a total annual output of US$6 billion.[124] Hsinchu enterprises produce 10 per cent of the world's output of personal computers, 50 per cent of the world's output of satellite television receivers and 70 per cent of the world's supply of hand-held scanners.[125]

There are other examples of government induced technology development through massive and direct state involvement, such as the science parks, or more indirectly, through tax concessions, subsidies, customs relief and financial incentives to foreign firms for bringing in new technology. A feature of the current Six Year National Development Plan (1991–96) is the focus on industrial technologies such as optoelectronics, computer software, industrial automation, materials applications, advanced sensing technology, biotechnology, resources development and energy conservation. The government aims to develop Taiwan as a regional technology centre in telecommunications, information, consumer electronics, semiconductors, precision machinery and automation, aerospace, advanced materials, speciality chemicals and pharmaceuticals, health care and pollution control.

Recruiting overseas Chinese scientists has also been a feature of Taiwan's long-term technology strategy ever since the first long-term plan was drawn up in 1959. Taiwan has targeted the large world pool of Chinese scientists and engineers from Taiwan or from the mainland who have received training in the United States or elsewhere in the West. Leading foreign-trained Chinese graduates in engineering, science, medicine and biotechnologies are listed on a Taiwanese 'databank of Chinese S&T talent residing overseas'.[126] They may be offered financial inducements to work in Taiwan or be invited to attend conferences and workshops sponsored by the National Science Council.[127] Through these and other interactions, Taiwan has built up a pattern of 'institutionalised consultation with overseas Chinese specialists on technological strategy' and co-operative linkages with prestigious scientific laboratories and academies in the United States and Europe, thereby circumventing its geographic and diplomatic isolation.[128] There has, in fact, been 'an unusually large interflow of human capital between Taiwan and the technologically advanced countries', mainly the United States and more recently with China (in areas such as communications, radio astronomy, astrophysics, nuclear power and aeronautics). This has yielded considerable returns for Taiwan in technology transfer.[129]

Today, Taiwan has a science and technology base that is currently ranked fifteenth in the world behind advanced countries like the United States, Japan, Germany, Britain, France, the Netherlands, Switzerland, Canada, Italy and Belgium.[130] Taiwan is well placed to take advantage of the globalisation of technology. It has surplus investment capital, location and networks in East Asia, a technologically advanced society with modern facilities such as the Hsinchu and Chang Hua science-based parks, strong government support and a skilled pool of United States trained electronics engineers and computer specialists available at salaries which are around 35–40 per cent of world levels. Taiwan has thus become a desirable joint venture partner for many multinationals seeking to combine their strengths with that of local Taiwanese firms. Mcdonnell Douglas and British Aerospace sought co-operative joint ventures with Taiwan Aerospace, Acer is involved in a joint venture with Texas Instruments to produce DRAMs and Taiwan Semiconductor Manufacturing Corporation is in a joint venture with Philips of Holland for to make computer chips. These trends have forced other multinationals, such as Sony of Japan in the case of computers, and Boeing and Rolls Royce in the case of aerospace industries, to compete for similar ventures in Taiwan.

Trading skills

As an exporting economy competing against exporters from other countries, Taiwanese manufacturers, politicians and bureaucrats have had to become highly skilled in the art of international trade. That imposed its own discipline on Taiwan's economic efficiency and policy formulation. It required responsiveness to market signals, adaptability, dexterity, efficiency in resource allocation, a constant improvement in technology and, above all, good marketing.[131] By the 1970s, international economic competitiveness and an export-oriented culture had replaced recovery of the mainland as Taiwan's principal national ideology. Strategic planning, export co-ordination and data analysis to support exports and exploit opportunities faster and better than competitors were the rules of the game. In the 1960s and 1970s, Taiwan developed what is, in a sense, a new comparative advantage that complemented its edge in cheap skilled labour *viz* international marketing skills and the ability to respond quickly to international market trends. This specialisation in trade has led to the saying that 'the business of Taiwan is business'.[132] A strategic approach to trade, careful collection and analysis of international trade data and the co-ordinating role played by Taiwan's China External Trade Development Council (CETRA) have been vitally important in supporting this specialised business.

Set up in 1970, CETRA has a network of international trade offices in virtually every corner of the globe. Its Taipei headquarters provides trade information, brings partners together, anticipates new market opportunities, publishes information on trade, organises trade exhibitions, promotes products and packaging, conducts overseas marketing surveys, sets up Taiwanese product and trade centres overseas, despatches trade missions abroad, trains businesspeople, helps Taiwan's small business enterprises penetrate foreign markets and designs appropriate marketing strategies.[133] It consults with businesspeople, academics and other experts in the shaping of national economic strategy through seminars, conferences and committees.

Taiwan's expertise in marketing its products and the use of English language material to promote Taiwan in general has become very sophisticated. This is partly due to the work and resources of government offices such as CETRA and the Government Information Office and Taiwan's long exposure to the English language and American consumer and cultural values. The result is that Taiwan is more competitive and more efficient than South Korea in monitoring and exploiting market trends.[134]

The Taiwanese skill in utilising borrowed foreign technology to make goods for export to world markets has become almost a way of life for Taiwanese entrepreneurs.[135] Taiwan's computer industry is a prime example of this niche strategy.[136] It has paid off handsomely. The Taiwanese mode of operation is to concentrate on manufacturing products that have a global market, adapting the foreign technologies, reducing production costs and marketing their product directly or as sub-contractors to United States and Japanese multinationals. Because of the previously mentioned tendency to avoid research and development, the Taiwanese put most of their effort into marketing and international trade fairs.[137]

This has meant a high degree of import dependency on Japan for new technology, components and machinery. Precision machinery, electrical components and equipment made up half Taiwan's imports from Japan in 1992 and contributed to a deficit of US$12.8 billion, three times what it was in 1986.[138] In an attempt to lessen dependency on Japan, the government has increased its funding for R&D and has tried to exploit foreign technology attracted to the Hsinchu science-based industrial park. One of Taiwan's leading microelectronic firms, Taiwan Semiconductor Manufacturing Corporation, was established in the Hsinchu science-based park in 1987 with 48 per cent government ownership, 27 per cent owned by Philips from the Netherlands and 25 per cent by local investors.[139] A third option has been piracy of foreign intellectual property, a practice for which Taiwanese entrepreneurs were notorious in the 1970s and 1980s. Even in 1989, Taiwan was the largest source of fake Japanese designs, industrial machines and transportation equipment. According to Japan's MITI, of 492 Japanese designs or trademarks pirated in 1989, Taiwan was responsible for 36 per cent of the total, compared with South Korea (14 per cent), Hong Kong (7.1 per cent), Thailand (5.7 per cent) and Singapore and Indonesia (2.8 per cent each).[140]

Part of a regional synergy

According to Bruce Cumings, much of the explanation of Taiwan's success lies in the fact that it was part of 'the fundamental unity and integrity of the modernisation of the whole Northeast Asian region'.[141] Ross Garnaut has also stressed the importance of Taiwan's location in Northeast Asia and its proximity to Japan, the region's industrialising pioneer.[142] As part of the Northeast Asia region, and formerly a Japanese colony,

Taiwan gained unique regional benefits in terms of the cost advantage of moving goods and technology across short distances and the spread of the virus of ideas and ambitions about rapid economic growth.[143] Taiwan, located in the centre of East Asia geographically, culturally, historically and politically, has absorbed and contributes to the synergy of regional economic growth, the regional division of labour and regional cross-investments. Taiwan's development has reinforced and is reinforced by the deepening interdependence in Northeast Asia that centres around Japan, the old NIEs, including Taiwan, and newly emerging NIEs, including different provinces in China and the ASEAN states. Taiwan and other East Asia NIEs successfully followed in the footsteps of Japan and as they graduated up a rung or two, regional economic growth began to accelerate. Other neighbouring states were drawn into the vortex of dynamic East Asian economic growth. This has created new opportunities for Chinese-connected, well-located, relatively experienced and wealthy international trading entities like Taiwan.

Taiwan's specialised mediating role between the United States, Japan and China has been further refined now that political barriers between China and Taiwan have been removed. Instead of fleeing from China to Taiwan to build factories to export to the United States, Taiwanese manufacturers have been flocking back to the mainland to build factories to export to the United States and the rest of the world. To supply the factories in China, the Taiwanese have had to expand their imports of components and technology from Japan. The result has contributed to a record surplus in China's trade with the United States (US$18.3 billion in 1992), an increased Taiwanese trade deficit with Japan (US$12.9 billion in 1992), a reduced surplus in Taiwan's trade with the United States (US$7.8 billion in 1992 after a peak of US$16 billion in 1987) and an increased surplus in Taiwan's trade with China/Hong Kong (US$13.6 billion in 1992). The net effect has been to sustain relatively high rates of economic growth in Taiwan, despite the recession in the rest of the world in the late 1980s, and add to Taiwan's large reserves of foreign exchange.

Conclusions

For Taiwan, the core of the formula for its impressive rise has been its pivotal location at the centre of a triangle of relationships between two constants (the United States and Japan) and one variable (China). From the United States came military protection, financial and material aid, capitalist ethics and advice, investment capital, technology, a huge market and strong political support. Japan provided markets, components, technology, investment and work and management practices. China supplied the political and cultural values, the Kuomintang leadership, the threat factor and, more recently, a huge new hinterland and market. The island of Taiwan supplied the central physical location, a defensible bastion and a cheap, skilled labour force. Fortunately, the Kuomintang applied the right economic policies at the right time, managed the variable — China — in a masterly way and specialised in exporting to Japan and the United States.

In the 1950s, Taiwan relied on Japan as an export market and the United States for imports. In the 1960s, the United States emerged as Taiwan's principal export market while Japan dominated Taiwan's imports. (See Tables 9 and 10). If exports were the engine of Taiwan's growth, then the United States economy and the United States market were the primary sources of that growth. In 1984 the United States took almost 49 per cent of Taiwan's exports. This proportion declined after Taiwan established its labour-intensive export-oriented factories in China and increased exports to Europe (where exports quadrupled between 1984 and 1990 to US$12 billion, about half the value of Taiwan's 1990 exports to the United States). Nonetheless, Taiwan still depends on the United States market for 30 per cent of its exports, a figure that would be much higher if Taiwanese exports to the United States from China were included. Despite its best efforts, Taiwan remains dependent on Japan, as it has since 1949, for 30 per cent of its imports. In 1993, Taiwan's deficit in trade with Japan was US$14.2 billion. However, the net balance in Taiwan's trade between the big three of Japan, the United States and China–Hong Kong favours Taiwan. It is a triangular economic dynamic in which centrally located Taiwan has been able to reap enormous profits, especially since 1981 (See Tables 8 and 9).

The role of the Kuomintang in deciding economic priorities, allocating resources, setting the timetable for political reform and managing relations with the United States, Japan and China has been an important factor in explaining Taiwan's ascendancy in East Asia. But, seen from the perspective of long-term economic and strategic trends in the Asia-Pacific, Taiwan has almost always been on the winning side in a three-cornered game: it was an ally of the United States in the struggle against communism in the 1950s and 1960s; it was a frontline state in the Cold War with China until the mid-1970s; in the 1980s, it prepared for the preoccupation of the post-Cold War world with spreading democracy and emphasising international trade. After 6 June 1989, Taiwan was widely perceived by the United States, Japan and China as the model for the transformation of Chinese communism and the modernisation of the Chinese economy.

In my view, the Kuomintang could not have transformed the economy and status of Taiwan without the historical, social, geographic and strategic circumstances — the critical setting — that it inherited and which prevailed in the decades after 1949. The interventionist role of the Kuomintang should not be overlooked but other countries could emulate Taiwan's success if they too were blessed with Taiwan's advantages in terms of location and the support, in one form or another, of the three most important states in the Pacific Basin.

Notes

1   The only other small countries to occupy the cultural, historical, strategic and economic crossroads between China, Japan and the United States are South Korea and Hong Kong.

2   Neil Jacoby, *United States Aid to Taiwan*, Praeger, New York, 1951, p. 241.

3   See, for example, Cal Clark, who suggests that because of the success of Japan and the even more spectacular transformation of the four little dragons, there must be a special East Asian formula to explain the puzzle of Taiwan's rapid growth: Cal Clark, *Taiwan's Development: Implications for Contending Political Economy Paradigms*, Greenwood Press, Connecticut, 1989, pp. 13ff. Also see Stephan Haggard, *Pathways from the Periphery: The Politics of Growth in the Newly Industrialising Countries*, Cornell University Press, Ithaca, New York, 1990.

4   James Riedel, 'Economic Development in East Asia: Doing What Comes Naturally', in Helen Hughes (ed.), *Achieving Industrialisation in East Asia*, Cambridge University Press, Cambridge, 1988, pp. 37, 38.

5   Alice Amsden, 'The State and Taiwan's Development', in Peter B. Evans, Dietrich Rueschemeyer and Theda Skocpol (eds), *Bringing the State Back In*, Cambridge University Press, Cambridge, New York, 1985, pp. 79, 98–99.

6   Bruce Cumings, 'The Northeast Asian Political Economy', *International Organization*, vol. 38, no. 1, Winter 1984, pp. 1, 28, 38.

7   Robert Wade, *Governing the Market: Economic Theory and the Role of Government in East Asian Industrialisation*, Princeton University Press, Princeton, New Jersey, 1990, p. 297.

8   Masato Hayashida, *Entrepreneurship in Taiwan and Korea: A Comparison*, IIGP Policy Paper 109, Tokyo, May 1993 p. 6.

9   See Jon Woronoff, *Asia's 'Miracle Economies'*, M.E. Sharpe, New York, 1986, pp. 167–70; Yuan-li Wu, 'Taiwan's Open Economy in the Twenty-first Century' in W. Klenner (ed.), *Trends of Economic Development in East Asia*, Springer Verlag Berlin, Heidelberg 1989, pp. 112, 114; Martin T. Daly, 'The Road to the Twenty First Century: The Myths and Miracles of Asian Manufacturing', paper, Department of Geography, University of Sydney, 1992. I am also comfortable with the eclectic approach of Ezra F. Vogel, *The Four Little Dragons: The Spread of Industrialisation in East Asia*, Harvard University Press, Cambridge, Mass., 1991.

10 Samuel C. Chu, 'The Three Principles of the People and Political Developments: Thoughts on Democracy in the Republic of China and the People's Republic of China', in Chang King-yuh (ed.), *The Impact of the Three Principles of the People on China*, Institute of International Relations, National Chengchi University, Taipei, 1988, pp. 1, 5.

11 See generally Chang, *The Impact of the Three Principles of the People on China*.

12 Woronoff, *Asia's 'Miracle Economies'*, p. 67.

13 Wade, *Governing the Market*, p. 96.

14 Stephen Fitzgerald, memo from Hong Kong, 6 August 1964, Department file No. 519/3/1: *Formosa: External Relations with Australia — General*.

15 Cheng Hsiao-shih, *Party–Military Relations in the PRC and Taiwan, Paradoxes of Control*, Westview, Boulder, Col., 1990, p. 23.

16 Wade, *Governing the Market*, p. 236.

17 Cheng, *Party–Military Relations in the PRC and Taiwan*, pp. 123–145.

18 ibid.

19 See Chapter 4.

20 Lucian Pye, 'The New Asian Capitalism: A Political Portrait', in Peter Berger and Hsin-Huang Hsiao (eds), *In Search of an East Asian Development Model 9*, Transaction Books, New Brunswick and Oxford, 1986, pp. 81, 83.

21 Thomas A. Metzger and Ramon H. Myers, 'Understanding the Taiwan Experience: An Historical Perspective', published by Shaw Yu-ming, Kwang Hwa Publishing Co, Taipei 1990, p. 10, reprinted from *Pacific Review*, vol. 2, no. 4, 1989.

22 Chalmers Johnson, 'Political Institutions and Economic Performance: The Government–Business Relationship in Japan, South Korea and Taiwan', in Frederic C. Deyo (ed.), *The Political Economy of the New Asian Industrialism*, Cornell University Press, Ithaca, 1987, pp. 136, 137.

23 Wade, *Governing the Market*, p. 195.

24 Samuel P. Huntington, *Political Order in Changing Societies*, New Haven, Yale University Press, 1968, pp. 12–31.

25 Jacoby, *United States Aid to Taiwan*, p. 132.

26 ibid., pp. 132–34.

27 Shirley W.Y. Kuo, Gustav Ranis and John C.H. Fei, *The Taiwan Success Story: Rapid Growth with Improved Distribution in the Republic of China 1952–1979*, Westview, Boulder, Col., 1981, p. 145.

28 *China Yearbook 1969–70*, China Publishing Company, Taipei, 1970, p. 589.

29 *The Republic of China Yearbook*, Government Information Office, Taipei, 1993, p. 598.

30 ibid., p. 605.

31 ibid., p. 594.

32 Saburo Okita, 'Pacific Development and its Implications for the World Economy', a keynote address at the PECC, Seoul, April 1985.

33 For example, Roy Hofheinz Jr and Kent E. Calder, *The Eastasia Edge*, Basic Books, New York, 1982, p. 58.

34 Report by the Australian Academy of Technological Sciences and Engineering, *Mission to Republic of Korea and Taiwan on Materials Technology*, 8–24 May 1991, p. 7.

35 A.P.L. Liu, *Phoenix and the Lame Lion: Modernisation in Taiwan and Mainland China 1950–1980*, Hoover Institution Press, Stanford, 1987,p. 51.

36 Vogel, *The Four Little Dragons*, p. 26.

37 Ian D. Little, 'An Economic Reconnaissance', in Walter Galenson (ed.), *Economic Growth and Structural Change in Taiwan*, Cornell University Press, Ithaca, 1979, pp. 448, 504.

38 Liu, *Phoenix and the Lame Lion: Modernisation in Taiwan and Mainland China 1950–1980*, pp. 61–62.

39 George Allen, 'Industry policy and innovation in Japan', in Charles Carter (ed.), *Industry Policy and Innovation*, Heinemann, London, 1981, cited in Wade, *Governing the Market*, p. 225

40 Kwoh-ting Li, *Economic Transformation of Taiwan, ROC*, Shepheard-Walwyn (Publishers) Ltd, London, 1988, p. 45

41 Haggard, *Pathways from the Periphery*, p. 88.

42 ibid., p. 89.

43 Vogel, *The Four Little Dragons* , p. 25.

44 Fredrick F. Chien, *Faith and Resilience The Republic of China on Taiwan Forges Ahead*, Kwang Hwa Publishing (U.S.A.) Inc., Houston, 1988, p. 275.

45 Li, *Economic Transformation of Taiwan*, p. 37.

46 Council for Economic Planning and Development, White Paper, *The Six Year National Development Plan for Taiwan, Republic of China 1991–1996, Macroeconomic Development Targets*, Executive Yuan, Taipei, January 1991.

47 Li, *Economic Transformation of Taiwan, ROC*, p. xiii.

48 Robert Wade, 'East Asia's Economic Success Conflicting Perspectives, Partial Insights, Shaky Evidence', *World Politics*, vol. 44, no. 2, January 1992, pp. 270, 282.

49 Council for Economic Planning and Development, *Taiwan Statistical Data Book (TSDB)*, Taipei, 1989, p. 89.

50 Wade, *Governing the Market*, pp. 92–112.

51 ibid., p. 138.

52 Council for Economic Planning and Development, *Taiwan Statistical Data Book (TSDB)*, Taipei, 1993, p. 84.

53 Wade, *Governing the Market*, pp. 166–68.

54 ibid., p.87.

55 ibid., p. 95.

56 ibid., pp. 159ff.

57 Linda Y.C. Lim and Pang Eng Fong, *Foreign Direct Investment and Industrialisation in Malaysia Singapore Taiwan and Thailand*, OECD Paris, 1991, pp. 135–36.

58 Wade, *Governing the Market*, p. 110.

59 See Jui-meng Chang, *The Determinants of Trade Policies in Taiwan*, Economic Monograph No. 18, Chung-Hua Institution for Economic Research, Taipei, 1987, Chapters 3, 5 and 6; and Li, *Economic Transformation of Taiwan*, p. 43.

60 Lim and Fong, *Foreign Direct Investment and Industrialisation in Malaysia Singapore Taiwan and Thailand*, pp. 160–61.

61 ibid.

62 Kuo, Ranis and Fei, *The Taiwan Success Story*, p. 26.

63 Chang, *The Determinants of Trade Policies in Taiwan*, pp. 154–55.

64 Amsden, 'The State and Taiwan's Development', in Evans et al., *Bringing the State Back In*, p. 364.

65 Yu-chi Tao, *The Tariff System of the Republic of China*, Taipei, 1969, pp. 175–78, cited in Samuel P.S. Ho, *Economic Development of Taiwan 1860–1970*, Yale University Press, New Haven, 1978, p. 191.

66 Kuo-shu Liang and Ching-ing Hou Liang, 'The Industrial Policy of Taiwan', in Hiromichi Mutoh, *Industrial Policies for Pacific Economic Growth*, Allen & Unwin, Sydney, 1986, pp. 104, 105.

67 Ho, *Economic Development of Taiwan 1860–1970*, p. 191

68 ibid., p. 198.

69 Rong I. Wu, 'Taiwan Industrialisation', in *Lessons from Taiwan, Pathways to Follow and Pitfalls to Avoid*, ISIS, Malaysia, 1986, pp. 42, 47.

70 Chang, *The Determinants of Trade Policies in Taiwan*, p. 171.

71 Hughes, *Achieving Industrialisation in East Asia*, p. xv.

72 Wu, 'Taiwan's Industrialisation', in *Lessons from Taiwan, Pathways to Follow and Pitfalls to Avoid*, p. 42, 46, 51; and Liang and Liang, 'The Industrial Policy of Taiwan', p. 105.

73 Chung-in Moon, 'Trade Friction and Industrial Adjustment: The Textiles and Apparel in the Pacific Basin', in Stephan Haggard and Chung-in Moon, *Pacific Dynamics: The International Politics of Industrial Change*, Center for International Studies, Inha University, Inchon/Westview, Col., 1989, pp. 185, 186.

74 Kuo, Ranis and Fei, *The Taiwan Success Story*, pp. 74–75; and Stephan Haggard and Tuan-jen Cheng, 'State and Foreign Capital in the East

Asian NICs', in Deyo, *The Political Economy of the New Asian Industrialism*, p. 116.

75 Yung-San Lee and Hong-Cheng Wang, 'Taiwan's Export Experience' in *Lessons from Taiwan, Pathways to Follow and Pitfalls to Avoid*, ISIS, Malaysia, 1986, pp. 89, 103ff; and Wu, 'Taiwan's Industrialisation', in *Lessons from Taiwan*, p. 50.

76 Ho, *Economic Development of Taiwan 1860–1970*, p. 198

77 Li, *Economic Transformation of Taiwan*, p. 402.

78 *Republic of China 1988: A Reference Book*, Hilit Publishing Company Ltd, Taipei, 1988, p. 231.

79 *TSDB*, 1993, p. 210

80 *China Post*, Taipei, 12 September 1991.

81 Kuo, Ranis and Fei, *The Taiwan Success Story*, p. 25.

82 *TSDB*, 1990, p. 43

83 Kuo, Ranis and Fei, *The Taiwan Success Story*, p. 110.

84 ibid., p. 145.

85 Bela Balassa, 'Development Strategy and the Six Year Plan in Taiwan', in Bela Balassa, *The Newly Industrialising Countries in the World Economy*, Pergamon, New York, 1981, pp. 381, 384.

86 Chi Schive, *The Foreign Factor: The multinational Corporation's Contribution to the Economic Modernisation of the Republic of China*, Hoover Institution Press, Stanford, 1990, p. 10.

87 Kuo, Ranis and Fei, *The Taiwan Success Story*, p. 75; Haggard and Cheng, 'State and Foreign Capital in the East Asian NICs', in Deyo, *The Political Economy of the New Asian Industrialism*, p. 249.

88 Wu, 'Taiwan's Industrialisation', in *Lessons from Taiwan*, p. 53.

89 Haggard, *Pathways from the Periphery*, p. 201.

90 Schive, *The Foreign Factor*, p. 60.

91 Wade, *Governing the Market*, p. 95.

92 *TSDB*, 1993, pp. 192–93

93 Jenn-Hwa Tu, *Direct Foreign Investment and Economic Growth: A Case Study of Taiwan*, Institute of Economics, Academia Sinica Monograph Series, No. 48, Taipei, December 1990, p. 8-10.

94 ibid., p. 11.

95 ibid., p. 2.

96 Schive, *The Foreign Factor*, p. 102.

97 *TSDB*, 1993, pp. 244–46.

98 Investment Commission, Ministry of Economic Affairs, *Statistics on Overseas Chinese and Foreign Investment, Technical Cooperation, Out-*

ward Investment, Outward Technical Cooperation, December 1992, pp. 1–4.

99 ibid., pp. 6–8.

100 Schive, *The Foreign Factor*, pp. 54, 66.

101 Kuo, Ranis and Fei, *The Taiwan Success Story*, p. 19.

102 Investment Commission, Ministry of Economic Affairs, *Statistics on Overseas Chinese and Foreign Investment*, December 1992, pp. 1–4.

103 ibid.

104 Thomas Gold, 'Entrepreneurs, Multinationals, and the State' in Edwin A. Winckler and Susan Greenhalgh (eds), *Contending Approaches to the Political Economy of Taiwan*, M.E. Sharpe, New York, 1988, pp. 175, 196.

105 Walden Bello and Stephanie Rosenfeld, *Dragons in Distress Asia's Miracle Economies in Crisis*, Food First, San Francisco, 1990, p. 245; and Tu, *Direct Foreign Investment*, p. 15.

106 American Institute in Taiwan, *Foreign Economic Trends and their Implications for the United States*, Taipei, various issues; and *Statistics on Overseas Chinese and Foreign Investment*, December 1992.

107 Tu, *Direct Foreign Investment*, p. 12.

108 Chi Schive, 'Cross Investment in the Asia-Pacific: The Case of Taiwan's Inward and Outward Investment', paper at the Taiwan Conference, The Fletcher School, Tufts University, Boston, 18–20 October 1991, p. 6.

109 Gold, 'Entrepreneurs, Multinationals and the State', in Winckler and Greenhalgh, *Contending Approaches to the Political Economy of Taiwan*, pp. 175, 179.

110 *TSDB*, 1993, pp. 192–93.

111 ibid., p. 214.

112 Lim and Fong, *Foreign Direct Investment and Industrialisation in Malaysia Singapore Taiwan and Thailand*, pp. 95–96; Schive, *The Foreign Factor*, p. 37.

113 Yuan-li Wu and Kung-chia Yeh, 'Taiwan's External Economic Relations', in Yuan-li Wu and Kung-chia Yeh (eds), *Growth Distribution and Social Change: Essays on the Economy of the Republic of China*, Occasional Papers No. 3, School of Law, University of Maryland, 1978, pp. 173, 188.

114 Vogel, *The Four Little Dragons*, pp. 6–7.

115 ibid.

116 *Republic of China Yearbook*, various editions, Taipei 1988, pp. 295ff; 1989, pp. 401ff; 1990–91, pp. 397ff; 1993, pp. 350ff.

117 Australian Academy of Technological Sciences and Engineering, *Mission to Republic of Korea and Taiwan*, pp. 4, 6.

118 Economics Minister, Vincent Siew, quoted in *Aerospace*, January 1992, p. 33

119 *TSDB*, 1989, p. 116; and *TSDB*, 1993, p. 108.

120 *China Post*,19 August 1992.

121 ibid., p. 4.

122 ibid., p. 6.

123 Lim and Fong, *Foreign Direct Investment*, p. 136.

124 *Doing Business with Taiwan ROC*, CETRA, Taipei, 1991, p. 37.

125 Philip Liu, 'Coming Home', *Free China Review*, December 1991, p. 41.

126 Li, *Economic Transformation of Taiwan*, p. 241.

127 ibid., p. 242.

128 ibid., p. 221; and Australian Academy of Technological Sciences and Engineering, *Mission to Republic of Korea & Taiwan*, p. 4.

129 Wu, 'Taiwan's Open Economy in the Twenty-First Century', in Klenner, *Trends of Economic Development in East Asia*, pp. 111, 122. The same conclusion was reached by the Australian Academy of Technological Sciences and Engineering, *Mission to Republic of Korea &Taiwan*, p. 4.

130 *New York Times*, 28 May 1991, cited in *China Post*, 2 July 1991.

131 Foreign trade and exposure to the international marketplace inevitably sharpen up resource allocation and the adaptability and dexterity of producers who must compete for markets with other producers if they wish to survive: S.B. Linder, *The Pacific Century: Economic and Political Consequences of Asia-Pacific Dynamism*, Stanford University Press, Stanford, 1986, pp. 33–34.

132 Australian Academy of Technological Sciences and Engineering, *Mission to Republic of Korea & Taiwan*, p. 3.

133 *The Republic of China Yearbook 1993*, Government Information Office, Taipei, 1993, p. 204.

134 Hayashida, *Entrepreneurship in Taiwan and Korea: A Comparison*, pp. 11, 12.

135 ibid, pp. 27–29.

136 Bello and Rosenfeld, *Dragons in Distress Asia's Miracle Economies in Crisis*, p. 267.

137 ibid., pp. 13, 15.

138 *TSDB*, 1993, pp. 196, 224.

139 Lim and Fong, *Foreign Direct Investment and Industrialisation in Malaysia Singapore Taiwan and Thailand*, p. 135.

140 Reported in *China Post*, 29 May 1992.

141 Cumings, 'The Origins and Development of the Northeast Asian Political Economy', p. 3.

142 Ross Garnaut, 'Asia's Giant', *Australian Economic Papers*, vol. 27, no. 51, December 1988, pp. 173, 175.

143 ibid.

6 Taiwan: Spreading South

The Lament on Going to Taiwan
Don't come to Taiwan
It's like the gate of hell
A thousand people go but none return
Alive or dead it's hard on us all.

Anonymous Hakka poet, Ch'ing Dynasty[1]

Taiwan has come a long way since the Ch'ing Dynasty. In terms of political stability, domestic prosperity and regional diplomatic influence, one might venture to say Taiwan is entering its first golden age. The island is more secure from external threat than at any time in the past five decades. Most Taiwanese regard themselves as part of an urbanised, well-to-do middle class. They are affluent, well educated, politically aware and well travelled. Of the 49 ethnic Chinese billionaires in the world, a quarter are Taiwanese.[2] In 1992, Taiwan had a GNP of US$211 billion compared with US$1 trillion for Britain, US$500 billion for Canada and US$425 billion for mainland China. Taiwan currently ranks 20th or 21st in the world in terms of GNP, up from 39th position in 1972 (see Table 1). At a growth rate of 7 per cent per annum, Taiwan's GNP is projected to reach around US$330 billion by the year 2000, which is comparable to Australia's GNP in 1992 of around US$300 billion.[3]

From being a primary producer exporting agricultural products to Japan in the early 1950s, Taiwan became an export-oriented industrial economy by the early 1970s (see Table 6). The sectoral share of agriculture in GDP declined from 31.2 per cent in 1952 to 12.2 per cent by 1972 and 3.5 per cent in 1992. Over the same period, the share of industry doubled from 19.7 per cent to 41.4 per cent.[4] Exports of industrial products rose from 8 per cent of total exports in 1952 to 95.7 per cent in 1992, whereas exports of agricultural products declined to just 4.3 per cent of the total, compared with 92 per cent in 1952 (see Table 6).[5] The ratio of foreign trade to GNP (exports plus imports to GNP) rose from 25.2 per cent in 1951 to 34.8 per cent in 1961, 67.5 per cent in 1971 and 102.9 per cent in

1981.[6] Taiwan, in short, ranks as one of the top 25 industrialised economies of the world.

Trade in manufactures has been Taiwan's 'engine of growth'.[7] In 1992, Taiwan's total trade was US$153 billion, making it then the twelfth largest trading state in the world after the United States ($999 billion), Germany ($837 billion), Japan ($573 billion), France ($476 billion), Britain ($413 billion), Italy ($342 billion), Canada ($265 billion), Belgium ($249 billion), Hong Kong ($240 billion), China ($166 billion) and South Korea ($159 billion).[8] In 1979, Taiwan was ranked 22nd as an exporting nation (see Table 2). Not surprisingly, the Taiwanese ports of Kaohsiung and Keelung are the third and sixth busiest in the Asia-Pacific region respectively.[9]

Taiwan's success as one of the world's leading trading states is reflected in its persistent trade surplus with the rest of the world in almost every year since 1971 (see Table 9). Ironically, 1971 was the year that Taiwan began to lose international diplomatic support as the Republic of China. While Taiwan was recognised by just a handful of states by the end of the 1970s, its accumulated foreign exchange reserves in 1995 amounted to about US$91 billion, the first or second largest such holdings in the world after Japan.[10]

This fortune was derived from Taiwan's skill in selling increasing quantities of desirable manufactured goods to people in the rest of the world 'at a price they are able and willing to pay'.[11] The Taiwanese make almost anything that sells on the world market, including hardware, watches, chemical products, bicycles, sewing machines, computers, 16M DRAM (dynamic random access memory) chips, compact motors and naval frigates. Taiwan is the only country in Asia manufacturing an indigenously designed modern jet fighter aircraft. After Japan, Taiwan is the most advanced economy in Asia in the area of electronics, telecommunications, integrated circuits and information technology. Taiwan is the sixth largest producer and exporter of computer equipment in the world. It is the world's biggest exporter of colour monitors, keyboards and image scanners and almost 70 per cent of the motherboards used in computers around the world are made in Taiwan. This manufacturing diversity has enabled Taiwan to weather worldwide recession and maintain above-average rates of economic growth.

As well as being an exporter of goods, Taiwan became an increasingly important market for agricultural and industrial raw materials, energy supplies, beef, grain, soybeans, prepared foodstuffs, chemicals, lumber, paper pulp, defence equipment and industrial machinery and components. In 1982, it was ranked amongst the top twenty export markets in the Asia–Pacific region. In 1992 it was among the top ten. Table 20 shows the rise in Taiwan's importance as an export market for most countries in the Asia-Pacific region over the decade 1982–92.

Even by the early 1970s, Taiwan was regarded as one of the world's most successful newly industrialising economies. Taiwan's GNP growth rate in the period up to 1965 (the year that United States aid ceased) averaged above 7 per cent per annum, higher than any other country in Asia except Japan.[12] Unemployment averaged just 2.2 per cent for the period 1961–91 and currently stands at around 1.5 per cent.[13] Taiwan's rate of inflation has also been low, averaging 3.8 per cent over the period 1960–89.[14] Foreign debt has been minimal.[15] According to a study made by Kuo, Ranis and Fei, the speed of Taiwan's industrialisation was faster than that attained by the United Kingdom, France, Italy, Germany, the former Soviet Union, the United States, Canada, Sweden and Japan (see Figure 3).[16] Taiwan's average annual growth rate in real GNP over the period 1960–89 was around 9 per cent, well above the average for the world's industrialised countries.[17] Today, Taiwan is a mature industrial economy and on the threshold of membership in the OECD.

Once criticised for its unrealistic foreign policies and repressive politics, Taiwan is widely regarded as being 'astoundingly successful in building a solid social and economic foundation for liberal democracy'.[18] It is 'a young dynamic nation, a model for the developing world' and a model for mainland China.[19] Senior Malaysian, Thai, Philippine and Vietnamese government leaders have expressed interest in the Taiwanese development formula. Indonesia's President Suharto, for example, spent most of his time in recent discussions with President Lee Teng-hui asking questions about Taiwan's agricultural reform and its success in providing employment opportunities.[20] Mainland leaders also regard Taiwan as a model for the economic development of China's southern provinces.[21] Other countries admire Taiwan's success and envy its wealth. Nearly all of them, including China, seek Taiwan's surplus investment capital.

The material rewards for the Taiwanese people have been substantial. In 1952, Taiwan's per capita GNP was one-thirtieth of GNP per capita in the United States whereas in 1992, it was one-third.[22] Per capita GNP more than doubled in the decade of the 1960s, rose by a factor of six in the decade of the 1970s and more than tripled again in the 1980s to reach US$8000 in 1991.[23] By March 1993, it was US$10 215, or 170 times the level of 1951, a figure that is fast approaching the per capita income of Ireland (US$11 000) and New Zealand (US$12 000). In per capita terms, Taiwan ranks amongst the 25 richest countries in the world.[24] On present trends, Taiwan's per capita income will reach around US$20 000 by the year 2000, which compares favourably with Canada's per capita GNP in 1990 of $21 972.[25]

There has been a marked improvement in other quality of life indicators (see Table 3). Rates of illiteracy dropped from 42 per cent in 1952 to 13.3 per cent in 1972 and 6.1 per cent in 1992.[26] The percentage of the population in secondary or higher education rose from 10.2 per cent in 1952 to 33 per cent in 1972 and 60.5 per cent in 1992.[27] Over the same period, the average life expectancy increased from 58.6 to 74.2 years and per capita daily calorie intake increased from 2078 to 3036.[28] Presently, one in three households owns a car, 80 per cent of households own their own house or apartment and most possess a motorcycle, a television set, a washing machine, telephone and refrigerator.[29]

Taiwan's record of rapid economic development has not been flawless. Prior to 1987, it was ruled by martial law.[30] The press was strictly controlled by the Kuomintang up until 1987 (see Table 14). Until recently, Taiwan was regarded as 'a centre for copyright piracy and trademark conterfeiting'.[31] It also has massive environmental problems with some of the dirtiest rivers and the worst urban pollution in the world. The island has been described as a 'big, putrid garbage tip' that had 'reached the

Figure 3
Speed of industrialisation:
Taiwan (1952–69) and other countries (1860–1913)

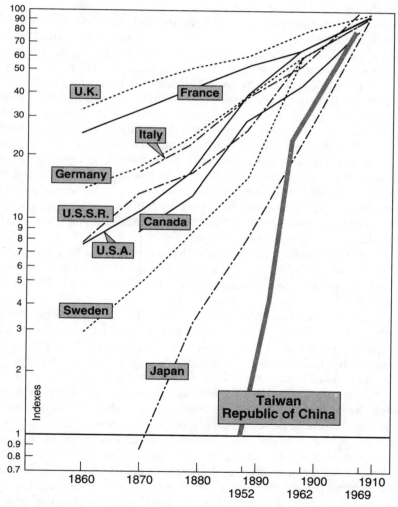

Source: Shirley W.Y. Kuo, Gustav Ranis and John C.H. Fel, *The Taiwan Success Story*, Boulder, Colorado: Westview Press, 1981, p. 9.

environmental limits of smokestack industrial growth'.[32] Of Taiwan's 17 000 tonnes of daily garbage (in 1989) only 10 000 tonnes was properly disposed of while the remainder was dumped at random.[33] Factory efflu- ent and human waste, much of which is untreated, is dumped in rivers. As a result, Taiwan has a high level of lead concentrate and chemical residue in its drinking water and the highest rate of hepatitis infection in the world. Taiwan's rivers are 'little more than flowing cesspools, devoid of fish, almost completely dead', while its air 'is contaminated by high levels of sulphur dioxide and nitrous dioxide'.[34] Air pollution in Taipei rose from 39 to 56 tons/square mile/month between 1959 and 1966.[35] Today, Taiwan's air has sulphur dioxide of 750 parts per million, or five times the limit applied in Los Angeles.[36]

Strong grassroots opposition to uncontrolled industrial development has been successfully exploited by the opposition Democratic Progres- sive Party. As well as environmental constraints on dirty industries, Taiwan's affluence has added to the cost of business. High growth rates and low unemployment have meant steadily rising wages (see Table 4). Democratic reforms have been accompanied by demands for better conditions. Wages rose by an average of 45 per cent per annum over the period 1987–89.[37] Despite the presence of up to 100 000 illegal workers from Southeast Asian countries, there is still a shortfall of 200 000 work- ers in labour-intensive industries such as textiles, food processing, iron and steel foundries, construction and restaurants. The shortage has been exacerbated by Taiwan's massive six-year public works develop- ment plan.[38] Meanwhile, the NT$ rose by 50 per cent against the US$ over the period 1986–92 (see Table 4). In July 1988, Taiwan lost its status in the United States as a developing country under the Generalised System of Preferences, which meant that exports from Taiwan, such as electric motors, were hit by tariffs of 25 per cent or more on entry to the United States, hitherto the main export destination for Taiwanese enterprises.[39]

To preserve Taiwan's international competitiveness, the government sought to diversify to new markets, new factory locations and new tech- nologies. It established the Hsinchu Technology Park in 1980 in an attempt to upgrade Taiwan's technology base and facilitate a shift away from labour-based industries to technology and capital intensive ones.[40] The government subsidised joint ventures between Taiwanese and United States companies such as Intel, AT & T, IBM, Hewlitt Packard, Zenith, RCA and Rockwell in an effort to tap into new technologies in information, communications, aerospace, precision ceramics, pharma- ceuticals, medicine, semiconductors, industrial design, consumer elec- tronics and precision machinery.[41] The government also tried to improve the competitiveness of Taiwanese enterprises by exposing them to international market forces through lower tariffs, the removal of non- tariff barriers and the removal of local content requirements and other protectionist measures.[42]

Manufacturers engaged in labour-intensive industries responded by moving offshore to locations where land and labour were cheaper and concern about the environment was less. As Chairman of China General Plastics, T.C. Chao, remarked, going international was an irreversible trend for many Taiwanese businesses because they faced tougher and tougher competition on international markets.[43] Most of Taiwan's cement, footwear and clothing industries have been exported to mainland China and Southeast Asia. Taiwan's footwear industry shrank from 2000 shoe factories to about 350. The value of its shoe exports dropped from US$3.7 billion in 1989 to US$2 billion in 1992.[44] Most of Taiwan's cement makers have also gone offshore — 'it was a matter of survival', said Chairman of the Taiwan Cement Manufacturers Association, Wang Lin-tai.[45] Taiwanese petrochemical firms face the same pressures. General Plastics Corporation opened naptha cracking plants in Malaysia (1988) and Louisiana in the United States (1991) in order to compete with another Taiwanese firm, Formosa Plastics, then building a plant in Texas and looking at another in China. Lee Shui-tu, Chairman of Sanfu Motor Industrial Company, said his company was investing in the mainland because 'intensified competition made it necessary', otherwise the 'business was just waiting to die'.[46] Wu Shun-wen, Chairman of Yue Loong, Taiwan's largest car maker, said the interests of his shareholders had led the company to move offshore.[47] Taiwan's camera makers were forced to build factories in China to try to maintain their competitive edge after Japanese camera companies — Ricoh and Canon — set up factories on the mainland to try to recapture the low end of the world camera market that they had earlier lost to the Taiwanese.[48] As Formosa Plastics Chairman Y.C. Yang said of Taiwan's petrochemical industry, the Taiwanese had to 'urgently move to exploit the mainland's cheap labour to beat competition from producers in South Korea and Japan'.[49]

As well as seeking competitive advantage and exporting sunset industries to developing economies, Taiwanese businesses moved offshore in order to sell products in host country markets, to get around third country trade barriers and quotas, to gain prestige in Taiwan, and to ensure access to modern technology.[50] These objectives are reflected in Taiwanese investment in Ireland (to gain a foothold in the European Community), in California (for technology) and Mexico (for a foothold in the North American Free Trade Area). In 1991, Taiwanese investment in Europe totalled US$350 million while for the United States it was US$298 million.[51]

The move offshore, especially after controls on foreign exchange were relaxed in July 1987, propelled Taiwan to ninth position amongst the world's capital-exporting countries (behind Japan, the United States, Germany, France, Britain, the Netherlands, Canada and Belgium).[52] In the period 1987–91, Taiwan supplied an estimated US$60 billion in foreign investment capital, the third largest amount in the world during that period after Japan (US$281.4 billion) and Germany (US$214.8 billion).[53]

Most of Taiwan's surplus capital flowed southward rather than north to Korea or Japan. The Taiwanese and the South Koreans, in particular, export similar products to the same markets in the United States and Europe and Taiwan's shift to non-energy intensive, non-polluting and technology-intensive activities like machine tools, semi-conductors, computers, telecommunications, robotics and biotechnology was in fact spurred by news that Korea was making progress in the same areas.[54]

'Looking southward' has evolved into a conscious government investment policy intended to make Taipei more politically influential in Southeast Asia. At the same time that Taiwan looked south for cheap labour and supplies of natural resources, countries in Southeast Asia, notably Malaysia, Vietnam and Indonesia, adopted a 'look east' policy.[55]

Like mainland China (discussed in the next chapter), Southeast Asia is a natural hinterland for a resource poor but industrially rich economy like Taiwan. Southeast Asia has natural resources and cheap labour. Taiwan, meanwhile, is a natural trading partner for the developing economies of Indochina and Southeast Asia. It has an enviable record in rapid economic development, appropriate levels of technology, surplus capital, global trading connections and a cultural affinity with the overseas Chinese communities of the Asia-Pacific. Overseas Chinese linkages give Taiwan important networks of influence that in many ways are more effective than orthodox levers of political and economic power, especially in Southeast Asia. Maintaining cultural solidarity with the 31 million overseas Chinese in the Asia-Pacific region is an important priority for Taiwan's Overseas Chinese Affairs Commission.[56] As Chi Schive suggests, Taiwanese businesses have key advantages in investing in ASEAN countries and China, including lower managerial costs, better understanding of the host country market, more appropriate technology, products that are better suited to host markets and better connections with local business.[57] Taiwan also appeals because it is a small, relatively innocuous country. Its businesses are mainly small to medium sized enterprises, unlike the powerful multinationals of Japan and the United States.

Overall, Taiwan is one of the largest sources of investment in the Asia-Pacific region. It is the third largest source of investment capital in the Asia-Pacific region after the United States and Japan.[58] It is the second largest source of investment capital in mainland China (after Hong Kong),[59] ranking first amongst foreign investors in Vietnam, second in the Philippines, second in Malaysia, third in Indonesia, fourth in Thailand and thirteenth in Singapore.[60] It is eleventh in the United States.[61] In 1992, 21.25 per cent of Taiwan's investment capital went to mainland China, 18.12 per cent to the United States, 14.63 per cent to Thailand, 11.5 per cent to Malaysia, 11.32 per cent to Hong Kong (most of which was reinvested in the mainland) and 5.05 per cent to Indonesia.[62]

Over 7000 Taiwanese companies are operating in Southeast Asia and Indochina and more than 26 000 have made investments in China. Previously the Taiwanese used to import intermediate manufactured goods from Japan for assembly and re-export, mainly to the United States. Now they are intermediaries in a burgeoning investment–trade relationship between Japan and the next rung down of developing economies in southern China, Southeast Asia and Indochina. As President Lee Teng-hui observed, trade has followed investment: the more that Taiwanese businesses invest in countries in the neighbouring region, the greater the volume of Taiwan's trade with those countries.[63] As a result, there has been a rapid expansion in Taiwan's exports of semi-finished components, machinery, materials and intermediate industrial goods to Taiwanese-owned or Taiwanese-managed factories and enterprises in southern China and Southeast Asia. This expansion, in fact, has been the engine driving the Taiwanese economy over the last decade. At the same time, however, increased exports from Taiwan to Taiwanese factories in East Asia have in turn been supported by increased imports of sophisticated machinery and components from Japan. This has contributed to the persistent deficit in Taiwan's bilateral trade with Japan (see Table 9).

Taiwan, said President Lee Teng-hui, was a wheel on the cart of Asia-Pacific economic integration while Japan was 'the chief navigator'.[64] In that sense, Taiwan is an intermediary between Japan and the developing economies of southern China, the ASEAN states and Indochina. Taiwan is in the second tier of industrialising states in East Asia, between Japan in the first tier with an emerging third tier comprised of the special industrial zones in Southeast Asia and coastal China.

The analogy with a wheel on a Japanese cart might be recast, however, to capture the idea of Taiwan being itself an important sub-hub of economic and political influence in the neighbouring region. Taiwan's intermediary role has been reinforced by its geographic location, its economic power and its human skills. It is disseminating a Taiwanese brand of economic, cultural and political influence in the Asia-Pacific region through trade, aid, investment, marketing services, Taiwanese technology and region-wide transport and aviation linkages. Increasingly, the Taiwanese are co-operating with Chinese from the mainland, and with the 31 million overseas Chinese in Hong Kong, Singapore, Jakarta, Manila, Bangkok and Saigon in a transnational web of financial dealings in southern China, Hong Kong and Southeast Asia. For example, Taiwan's Formosa Plastics group and wealthy Indonesian–Chinese interests (the Liem family) have proposed a huge banking and petrochemical complex in Xiamen in China's Fujian province.[65]

In establishing offshore manufacturing operations and industrial enclaves in Southeast Asia and China, the Taiwanese have enlisted the support of multinationals who in turn have sought alliances with leading Taiwanese corporations in their competition with each other. For example, aerospace companies such as McDonnell Douglas, Boeing and British Aerospace were competitors for a tie-up with Taiwan Aerospace Corporation in an effort to tap into Taiwanese capital and access the East

Asian aerospace market. Computer multinationals such as IBM and NEC formed strategic alliances with Taiwanese companies so that today Taiwan IBM Corporation competes with NEC Taiwan Ltd. Philips has a 27 per cent share of Taiwan Semiconductor Manufacturing Corporation while Acer has a chip manufacturing deal with Texas Instruments. In a similar fashion, vehicle makers like Toyota, Daihatsu, Isuzu, Honda, Mitsubishi, Ford, Renault, Nissan, Yamaha, General Motors and Vespa have formed local alliances to produce cars, motor cycles and engines for sale in Taiwan and for export within the region, including to China, North America and Australia. Honda, for example, produces components in Taiwan in conjunction with Sanyang Industry, Taiwan's fourth largest vehicle maker, and exports them to Canada; Ford America produces engines in Taiwan in conjunction with Ford Li Ho, the second largest car maker in Taiwan, for export to Ford Australia; Mitsubishi has a 25 per cent share in China Motor Co, Taiwan's third largest vehicle producer.[66] The car makers have been followed to Taiwan by auto parts makers.[67]

Government-initiated joint ventures between Taiwan and its neighbours are becoming more common. For example, a ministerial delegation from Singapore, Indonesia and Malaysia visited Taipei in September 1991 to discuss Taiwanese investment in the Growth Triangle Zone of Singapore, Malaysia's Johore and Indonesia's Batam and Riau islands. During a visit to Singapore on 4 January 1994, Taiwanese Premier Lien Chan proposed the joint development of petroleum and minerals in China's Hainan island with Prime Minister Goh Chok Tong, using finance from Taiwan, and management, processing and exporting carried out by Singapore.[68] In February 1994, President Lee Teng-hui led a 40-member delegation in talks with President Fidel Ramos at Manila airport on the redevelopment of Subic Bay. In April 1994, Vice Minister of Economics Lee Shu-jou discussed a proposal for a 1000-hectare industrial park for petrochemicals at Turban, near Surabaya, with Indonesian Vice President Try Sutrisno. At the same time, Taiwanese government and private interests have combined to develop export processing zones for labour-intensive industries such as plastic goods, textiles and electronics in Bandung in Indonesia and near Saigon in Vietnam. Such moves are designed to ease congestion in Taiwan, strengthen Taiwan's regional diplomacy and help preserve Taiwan's competitive edge in cheap labour manufacturing.

Taiwan's 'look south' policy is being actively encouraged by the government in an attempt to lessen Taiwan's growing reliance on mainland China as a market and investment destination.

Aggregate Taiwanese investment in Malaysia, Indonesia, Thailand and the Philippines over the period 1959–86 is conservatively estimated at around US$800 million.[69] Thereafter, the outflow of funds from Taiwan to Southeast Asia increased dramatically as the effects of rising domestic costs, an appreciating NT$ and the loss of GSP were felt by Taiwanese manufacturers (see Table 17). Between 1987 and 1993, the official amount of Taiwanese investment in Southeast Asia exceeded US$20 billion.[70]

However, as with all statistics on Taiwanese overseas investment, these figures grossly underestimate the real amount of Taiwanese cash flowing into Southeast Asia and southern China. In 1992, the government estimated that Taiwanese investment in Southeast Asia was over US$24 billion, which is substantially more than the officially declared amount.[71] In fact, according to Sanjaya Lall, officially acknowledged foreign investment from Taiwan is about one-tenth of the actual outflow.[72] Taiwan's Council for External Trade Relations (CETRA) also suggests the amount of capital flowing out of Taiwan may be as much as ten times greater than the official figures indicate.[73]

Taiwan's growing importance at the centre of a web of economic activity throughout the Asia-Pacific in the 1980s was enhanced by its trade performance. Its volume of imports has grown at an average rate of 24 per cent per annum over the last five years. By the late 1980s, Taiwan was of equal or greater importance as a trading partner than mainland China for most countries in the Asia-Pacific community. Taiwan's trade with the Philippines, Thailand, Malaysia, Indonesia and Singapore has grown by around 30 per cent per annum or more over the past five years, while for Australia the growth rate has been around 20 per cent per annum since 1986. By 1992, Taiwan was more important than China as an export market for Australia, Malaysia, New Zealand, the Philippines, Singapore and Thailand. For Japan, it was the second largest export market, up from tenth position in 1982. In 1992, Japanese exports to Taiwan were worth three times as much as Japanese exports to Australia, and were twice the value of Japanese exports to China, Britain, Korea, Singapore and Thailand (see Table 20). For the United States, Taiwan is a more important export market than China, India, Australia, Indonesia, Korea, Malaysia, the Philippines, Singapore, Thailand, and such European allies of the United States as France, Holland and Greece. In 1992, it was the sixth largest export market for the United States, up from fourteenth position in 1982.

By 1992, Canada and South Korea were the only countries in the Asia-Pacific region that did more business with China than with Taiwan. Even so, Taiwan was Canada's thirteenth largest export market in 1992, an improvement over twentieth place in 1982. For South Korea, two-way trade with Taiwan grew from US$490 million in 1982 to almost US$3.6 billion in 1992 and as an export market, Taiwan improved from nineteenth to seventh place over the decade 1982 to 1992.

At the same time, however, Taiwanese trade with China via Hong Kong grew by 25 per cent per annum over the period 1986–92, making Taiwan one of China's more important trading partners (to be discussed in the next chapter).

In 1992, Taiwan was the sixth largest trading partner for Australia and New Zealand, seventh for Canada, sixth for the United States, fourth for Japan, third for Hong Kong, fifth or sixth for China, fifth for Malaysia, Singapore and Thailand, sixth for Indonesia, and fourth for the Philippines. ASEAN as a bloc is Taiwan's largest trading partner after the

United States, Japan and Hong Kong. Trade with ASEAN was worth US$10.9 billion in 1990, US$12.74 billion in 1991 and almost US$15 billion in 1992, or an average growth rate of 18 per cent per annum.

Similar trends are apparent in Taiwan's trade with the countries of the European Community, mainly Germany, the United Kingdom, Holland, France and Italy. Taiwan is the eleventh largest trading partner of the European Community. In 1992, two-way trade between Taiwan and Europe reached US$26.4 billion compared with US$5.45 billion in 1985. The interest of the Europeans in business opportunities in Taiwan has reinforced the rise in Taiwan's political and economic status in the Asia-Pacific region, which, with the exception of the United States and Japan, is discussed below.[74]

Indonesia

Indonesia is particularly important for Taiwan's offshore investment strategy and its regional diplomacy. It is the senior state in ASEAN, a leader of the non-aligned group of countries, a key member of the APEC forum, and a foundation member of new regional forums, such as the East Asian Economic Caucus and the Committee for Security Co-operation in the Asia-Pacific. Conversely, Taiwan is increasingly important to Indonesia in terms of investment and trade, more so than China. Two-way trade between Taiwan and Indonesia quadrupled between 1982 and 1992 (see Table 19) and continues to be greater than two-way trade between China and Indonesia. Presently, Taiwan is the seventh largest supplier for Indonesia and its seventh largest export market. About 330 000 Taiwanese visited Indonesia in 1993 and spent close to US$400 million, making Taiwan the fifth largest source of tourism for Indonesia.

Indonesia accounts for a quarter of all Taiwanese investment in Southeast Asia.[75] In 1991, Taiwan emerged as the largest investor in Indonesia, with a total of $1.05 billion or 12.6 per cent of all foreign investment in that year (ahead of Japan with $836 million, Britain with $377 million, Singapore with $340 million, Switzerland and Korea with $307 million each, and the United States with $257 million). The figure for Taiwanese investment in Indonesia for the period 1967–93 was in excess of US$7 billion, most of it invested in paper-making, textiles, chemicals and mining. After Japan and Hong Kong, Taiwan is the third largest source of foreign investment in Indonesia and ranks ahead of the United States with US$2.195 billion, Holland with US$1.862 billion, Germany with US$1.853 billion, South Korea with US$1.666 billion, Singapore with US$993 million, and Australia with US$874 million.[76]

Taiwanese investment in Indonesia is likely to increase significantly in the next few years, given Taiwan's surplus funds, technology and regional marketing skills and its quest for cheap labour and natural resources. Economics ministers from Indonesia and Taiwan have held annual meetings since 1990. In 1991, Indonesia lifted its long-standing ban on Chinese publications and Chinese schools in Jakarta and permitted Taiwanese investors, technical experts and tourists to enter the country without a visa. A Taiwan desk was added to Indonesia's Foreign and Trade Ministries to develop Indonesia's burgeoning commercial relations with Taiwan.

Malaysia

As with Indonesia, Taiwanese businesses feel 'comfortable' about investing in Malaysia. The large overseas Chinese community, Malaysia's relatively low-cost land and labour, its oil, gas, rubber and timber resources and its preferential tariff treatment in the United States were very attractive to Taiwanese investors. At the same time, Taipei encouraged investment in Malaysia so as to diversify its trade and stabilise supplies of oil and rubber. In 1986, Taiwan supplied the smallest share of all foreign investment in Malaysia (after Singapore, Japan, Hong Kong and the United States). In 1987, it had risen to become the third largest after Japan and Singapore. By 1988, it was second after Japan, [77] and by 1991, it was in first place.

Taiwanese investment in Malaysia is concentrated in electronics, textiles, petrochemicals, computers, rubber products, wood and cane based industries and agriculture, with some large investments in chemical and petroleum projects. In 1988, Taiwan's China General Plastics invested US$400 million in a naptha cracking plant in Malaysia. In 1991, Taiwan's Chinese Petroleum Corporation took a 45 per cent share in a US$1.2 billion oil refinery in Binpulu in a joint venture with Malaysia's state oil company, Petronas. By 1993, the cumulative total for Taiwanese investment in Malaysia was US$7 billion or 43 per cent of all Taiwanese investment in Southeast Asia. At one stage a US$2.5 billion integrated steel mill was under consideration.[78]

Two-way trade between Malaysia and Taiwan grew from US$628 million in 1982 to over US$3.5 billion in 1992, or more than twice the volume of trade between Malaysia and mainland China (see Table 19). Most (80 per cent) of Malaysia's exports to Taiwan consist of logs or pulp and wood, petroleum, tin and rubber. Taiwan's exports to Malaysia consist mainly of machinery, electrical equipment, basic metals, textiles, clothing and processed foods.

In 1992, Malaysia exported materials and goods worth US$1270 million to Taiwan, more than twice the value of Malaysia's exports to countries such as Australia, France, the Philippines and Indonesia and five times the value of Malaysia's exports to New Zealand. In 1992, Taiwan was Malaysia's ninth largest export market after the United States, Singapore, Japan, the United Kingdom, Germany, Thailand, Hong Kong and Korea.

Malaysia values Taiwan as a source of surplus capital. Like Indonesia and other ASEAN states, Malaysia early on adopted a very pragmatic approach towards Taiwan: a Malaysia Friendship and Trade Centre (now called the Taipei Economic-Cultural Centre) was set up Taipei in 1979, two years ahead of a similar office established in Taipei by Australia; Prime Minister Mahathir has made several unpublicised visits to Taiwan since 1984; and a regular direct air service from Kuala Lumpur to Taipei began more than a decade before Australia and New Zealand established similar services. Malaysia perceives Taiwan to be an indigenous Asian model for economic development with 'delegation after delegation' of Malaysian government officials visiting Taipei since the 1960s in an effort to examine the Taiwanese formula that combined rapid economic development with political stability.[79]

The political relationship between Malaysia and Taiwan feeds off the reservations that both countries have about the big powers in the Asia-Pacific. Both fear mainland China, both are small regional market economies and their relationship has also drawn on their sense of a common Asian identity. Among the topics discussed during the December 1993 visit to Kuala Lumpur by Taiwanese Premier, Lien Chan, was Prime Minister Mahathir's proposal for a non-European organisation of East Asian countries (the East Asian Economic Group or Caucus) and Taiwan's wish to become an ASEAN dialogue partner.[80]

Singapore

After Taiwan was pushed out of the United Nations in 1971, it maintained a special relationship with only a few countries in the Asia-Pacific region. One of these exceptions was Singapore, which has maintained close political contacts with Taiwan and has quietly persisted in facilitating Taiwan's return to the mainstream of the Asia-Pacific community.[81] Singapore is a key member state in ASEAN and it was to Singapore that President Lee Teng-hui made his first major foray overseas in March 1989 and announced that in future it would be unimportant for Taiwan to care too much about its name (when he was introduced as the President of Taiwan rather than as the President of the Republic of China).[82]

Singapore has trained its armed forces in Taiwan for the last twenty years (the so-called Starlight Project) and has regular intelligence exchanges with security and defence agencies in Taipei. Taiwan, like Singapore, is a Chinese island state. While each has a sense of identity that is separate and distinct from mainland China, nonetheless both are conscious of their Chineseness. They are both small, capitalist-oriented island states that speak the same language and have a common Chinese culture. They support regional economic and political initiatives that are conducive to their speciality role as intermediary trading states. Singapore and Taiwan have a strategic interest in a stable transition for Hong Kong in 1997 and the gradual transformation of communism on the mainland. Singapore's Senior Minister, Lee Kuan Yew, has made more than twenty visits to Taipei and has played a bridging role between leaders in Taiwan and mainland China.[83] Prime Minister Goh Chok Tong visited Taiwan in September 1993 and met Premier Lien Chan in Singapore in January 1994 to discuss joint ventures in mainland China.

In 1994, Taiwan was Singapore's fifth largest trading partner after the United States, Japan, Malaysia and Hong Kong. China was in tenth place. Trade between Singapore and China exceeded trade between Taiwan and Singapore in 1982. While trade between China and Singapore grew by a factor of three between 1982 and 1992, trade between Singapore and Taiwan multiplied by a factor of five over the same period so that by 1992, Singapore's trade with Taiwan was worth about 25 per cent more than its trade with China (see Table 19). As an export destination for Singapore, Taiwan rose from eighteenth position in 1982 to ninth in 1992, whereas China improved from twenty-second to eleventh position (see Table 20).

Thailand

In 1992, Taiwanese investment in Thailand totalled about US$4.5 billion or 30 per cent of all Taiwanese investment funds in Southeast Asia. At the time, this made Thailand second after Malaysia as a destination for Taiwanese investment in Southeast Asia. Taiwan was the second largest investor in Thailand in 1992. Cumulatively, it is the fourth largest investor in Thailand after Japan, Hong Kong and the United States. Most of the Taiwanese investment is concentrated in small, export-oriented manufacturing enterprises numbering around 2000.[84]

Two-way trade between Taiwan and Thailand grew from US$322 million in 1982 to US$2866 million in 1992. By comparison, trade between Thailand and China grew from US$540 million in 1982 to US$1605 million in 1992. In other words, whereas China was a more important trading partner for Thailand in 1982, Taiwan became a much more important partner for Thailand by 1992 after a decade of growth at rates averaging over 25 per cent per annum (see Table 19). Most of the increase occurred in 1986–87, when controls on foreign exchange were lifted. As an export market for Thailand, Taiwan improved its position from sixteenth to tenth over the period 1982–92, whereas China slipped from seventh position to sixteenth (see Table 20). The measure of Taiwan's political influence in Thailand was reflected in the round of golf President Lee Teng-hui played with Thai Deputy Prime Minister Amnuay Virawan in Phuket on 15 February 1994 and King Bumiphol's decision to receive Lee in Bangkok on 16 February 1994, despite protests from Beijing.

The Philippines

The Philippines has always looked favourably on Taiwan, its closest neighbour. The Philippines voted consistently for Taiwan as the Republic of China at the United Nations and would possibly have abandoned the one China principle in 1986 had President Corazon Aquino not been restrained by the United States and vehement protests from Beijing.[85] Capital-starved and technology-poor, President Aquino's government was keen to develop a close relationship with Taiwan and any other country that could support national economic recovery policies with investment and aid.[86] The Philippines subsequently led the region in permitting 'private' ministerial visits to Taiwan. In 1988–89, a bill called the 'Philippine–Taiwan Relations Act' was presented to Congress. The bill, modelled on the United States *Taiwan Relations Act*, protected Taiwanese investors against government expropriation, gave legal status to Taiwanese entities in Manila, and expanded the consular powers of the Taiwanese representative office in Manila. The bill was passed despite objections from Beijing that it raised relations between Taiwan and the Philippines to an official level.[87] In fact, the Philippines Undersecretary of Trade and Commerce, Thomas Alcandara, said the agreement was an 'official-level' one, signed on behalf of the Philippines in Taipei in March 1992.[88]

The Philippines has attracted about US$2 billion, or around 12 per cent of all Taiwanese investment funds in Southeast Asia, and ranks fourth as a destination for Taiwanese funds after Malaysia, Thailand and Indonesia.[89] This level could increase significantly once the Taiwanese-sponsored Subic Bay industrial zone gets started. Taiwan is the third largest source of foreign investment in the Philippines after the United States and Japan.[90] Taiwanese investment in the Philippines has been complemented by aid donations and technical assistance with agriculture and fisheries.

As with other ASEAN states, Taiwan is a more important trading partner for the Philippines than China. In 1992, Taiwan was the Philippines' fourth largest trading partner after the United States, Japan and Hong Kong. It was the Philippines' sixth largest export destination, up from fifteenth position in 1982, whereas China slipped from eleventh to thirteenth position. In 1992, trade between Taiwan and the Philippines was worth US$1375 million, or more than four times the value of trade between the Philippines and China.

Vietnam

Vietnam has provided Taiwan with opportunities to develop its regional economic reach and political influence in Southeast Asia. Vietnam is an attractive location for Taiwanese investors because of its overseas Chinese community, its agricultural potential (sugar, rice and pigs), rich resources in timber, minerals, fisheries and offshore petroleum. It has enormous potential as a low cost export-oriented manufacturing base with labour costs that are a fraction of the rates in China, Thailand or Malaysia.

Taiwan and Vietnam, moreover, are natural allies *vis-a-vis* mainland China. Anti-communism and the American alliance system gave Taiwan and South Vietnam a common strategic interest up until the fall of Saigon in April 1975.[91] Taiwan has maintained close ties with the 960 000 overseas Chinese community in Vietnam, the majority of whom live in the South and retain their loyalty to Taiwan or Singapore rather than mainland China. Many have roots in Fujian and speak the same Chinese dialect as the Taiwanese. These connections have been resumed, particularly as Taipei is keen to encourage Taiwanese businesses to diversify investment away from the mainland. Since 1988, Taiwan has invested more than US$1.5 billion in over 600 projects in Vietnam. In May 1991, it was the largest source of direct foreign investment in Vietnam (ahead of Australia, Hong Kong, Japan and France).[92] Most investment (90 per cent) is concentrated in Saigon (Ho Chi Minh City), home for the majority of the Vietnamese overseas Chinese.

Presently, the Taiwanese provide 22 per cent of all foreign capital in Vietnam and constitute 50 per cent of all foreign arrivals in Saigon. Ministerial level talks have focused on aid programs for agriculture and fisheries and the establishment of a US$600 million industrial zone near Saigon.[93] Most investment in Vietnam is in labour-intensive industries and light manufacturing such as textiles, footwear, bamboo-ware, foodstuffs, construction, home appliances, motorcycles, hotels, golf courses and tourist services.

Australia

Relatively little Taiwanese investment has gone to Australia because of inefficiencies in infrastructure and the high cost of labour. Taiwanese investment in Australia between 1986 and 1992 totalled around US$850 million, which was about half the amount invested in Australia by mainland China over the same period. Most Taiwanese investment in Australia has been in retail property and real estate in Sydney and Melbourne, rather than in labour-intensive manufacturing as in Southeast Asia.

Australia, however, is an important supplier of raw materials, fuel and food for Taiwan. Australia's main exports to Taiwan include coal, aluminium, iron ore, beef, wool, seafood, zinc, cotton, dairy products, gold, hides, barley, nickel and petroleum products. Australia ranks as Taiwan's fourth most important source of imports, after Japan, the United States and Germany.

For Australia, Taiwan was one of Australia's fastest growing export markets, with a growth rate averaging more than 20 per cent per annum over the period 1972–92. Australian exports to Taiwan overtook Australian exports to China in 1983 (see Table 21). By 1986, Taiwan was Australia's third largest buyer of coal, the biggest market for its dairy products, second for cotton, sorghum and pulpwood, and third for beef, aluminium and zinc. Australia's self-interest clearly favoured some sort of reconciliation with Taiwan, a country which had been unceremoniously dumped by the Whitlam Labor government after Australia recognised the People's Republic of China on 22 December 1972.

In 1984, Professor Stuart Harris from the Australian National University was appointed Secretary of the Department of Foreign Affairs. Harris believed that Australian foreign policy ought to take more account of trade and international economic issues.[94] Harris was interested in broadening Australia's relations with Taiwan, within the constraints of Australia's recognition of Beijing, a view that was reflected in a departmental review of Australia's relations with China and Taiwan in late 1986. In 1987–88, after the amalgamation of the Departments of Foreign Affairs and Trade, international trade per se became a central element in Australia's regional diplomacy rather than, as it was hitherto, an issue often in dispute between rival government departments. The amalgamation set the stage for a greater flexibility and willingness by Australia to deal with Taiwan.

In 1989, Ross Garnaut published a report on Northeast Asia's economic importance for the Prime Minister, Bob Hawke.[95] Garnaut concluded that Australia 'must respond to the powerful and direct implications of Northeast Asian economic growth', including the rapid economic development of Taiwan, one of Australia's 'most important export markets and sources of tourism, business migrants and investment'.[96]

By 1991, Australia's approach to Taiwan matched that taken several years earlier by most of its Asian neighbours. In March 1991, the Taiwanese were allowed to open a 'Taipei Economic and Cultural Office' (TECO) in Canberra and were given regular access to officials in various government departments. Previously, they had been shunned by government and confined to offices in Sydney and Melbourne under the title 'Far East Trading Co'.[97] The Australia Foreign Minister, Senator Gareth Evans, explained that the name change was intended to indicate more clearly the actual role of the Taiwanese commercial offices in Australia and matched usage in other countries which had diplomatic relations with mainland China.[98] Or, as the then Leader of Australia's Opposition Liberal–National Party Coalition, John Hewson, observed, if a country like Australia wanted to participate in the major infrastructure development projects underway in Taiwan (with expenditure in the 'tens of billions of dollars'), then the Australian government would have to match the activities of competitors like France, Canada and Malaysia.[99] Direct airlinks were opened in September 1991. The Taiwanese were given exemptions on taxes and stamp duty for properties bought in Canberra.[100] From October 1992, diplomatic privileges and immunities were extended to TECO staff in Canberra using the 1963 *International Organisa-*

tions (Privileges and Immunities) Act.[101] 'Unofficially official' talks at ministerial level, the first in over twenty years, began in October 1992 and have
since become almost routine.

By 1992, Taiwan was taking 4.4 per cent of Australia's exports, compared with the United Kingdom's 3.9 per cent, China's 3.7 per cent,
Indonesia's 2.8 per cent, Thailand's 2.2 per cent, Malaysia 2.2 per cent,
Germany's 1.6 per cent, France's 1.4 per cent, Italy's 1.4 per cent, the
Netherlands' 1.4 per cent, Belgium's 1 per cent, the Philippines' 1 per
cent, Greece's 0.1 per cent and Brunei's 0.1 per cent.[102] Taiwan, in other
words, was a significantly more important export market for Australia
than closer neighbours in ASEAN and European countries that were traditionally well regarded by Australia. As of 1994, Taiwan was Australia's
sixth largest export market, up from ninth position in 1982.[103]

Oceania

New Zealand–Taiwan relations have followed the regional trend. New
Zealand severed diplomatic ties with Taiwan on 22 December 1972, the
same day as Australia. Thereafter, New Zealand — like Australia — pursued a policy that might be summed up as no official visits, no official
communications and no official visitors.[104] Taiwan, however, became
increasingly important for New Zealand. By 1990, Taiwan was a more
important export market for New Zealand than China, up from fifteenth
to sixth position between 1982 and 1992, whereas China had slipped from
seventh to tenth position (see Table 20). For New Zealand, Taiwan had
become an increasingly important source of tourists, capital and skilled
immigrants and was 'on course to rival even Britain in economic significance'.[105] As with Australia, direct flights between New Zealand and
Taiwan commenced and representative offices were upgraded from 'East
Asia Trade Centres' to 'Taipei Economic and Cultural Offices' in Auck-
land and Wellington.

The island countries of the South Pacific, too small to rate a mention as
Taiwanese trading partners or investment destinations, are nonetheless
important to Taiwan diplomatically. Of the 29 countries that formally
recognise Taiwan, four are in the South Pacific: Tonga (population
103 000), Tuvalu (population 10 000), Nauru (population 10 000) and the
Solomon Islands (population 360 000). Vanuatu (population 175 000)
recognised Taiwan as the Republic of China in December 1992 without
establishing formal diplomatic ties. As well, Taiwan has 'non-diplomatic
but official ties' with Fiji (the Taiwanese presence in Suva is designated
'the Republic of China Trade Mission' with consular privileges and
immunities) and Papua New Guinea (where the Taiwanese office in Port
Moresby is titled 'Trade Mission of the Republic of China on Taiwan').
Fiji's Prime Minister Ratu Sir Kamisese Mara and Papua New Guinea's
Sir Michael Somare have been regular visitors to Taiwan.

Small and economically vulnerable, the South Pacific island countries have been wooed with Taiwanese economic assistance such as civil aid, technical and development assistance, cash grants and large payments for fishing rights in direct competition with aid and interest-free loans from China.[106] In July 1991, the fifteen-member South Pacific Forum agreed that 'some mechanism had to be found to undertake consultations and exchanges of views with Taiwan, in view of its economic importance'.[107] Tonga, Tuvalu, the Solomon Islands and Nauru moved to have Taiwan recognised as a dialogue partner in post-Forum discussions along with other non-member nations including China, France, Canada, Britain, the European Community, the United States and Japan. Despite opposition from Beijing, the Forum countries agreed to give Taiwan status as dialogue partner at a separate meeting of the South Pacific Forum. This move, together with the 'non-diplomatic but official relations' accorded Taiwan by Fiji and Papua New Guinea, means the South Pacific is one of the few regions to practise a two-Chinas policy.

Taiwan's lures

In addition to trade and investment, Taiwan had two other important and attractive economic packages that it offered to the rest of world. One was the government's massive Six Year Development Plan (1991–96) announced in 1991. It envisaged expenditure of up to US$300 billion — roughly equivalent to Australia's 1992 GNP — on infrastructure development in Taiwan. Although subsequently downgraded to a more modest US$240 billion, the sums involved attracted enormous publicity and commercial interest around the world. Australian representatives in Taipei advised that the Plan presented a 'wealth of opportunities' for Australian companies in the 1990s 'in both traditional and new product/service areas', including transport and communications, environment protection, energy development, the information industry, medicine and health.[108] Additionally, Australia could hope to 'cash in' on selling the affluent Taiwanese more food products, fruit, seafood, beer, building materials and education and tourist services.[109] A record number of former prime ministers, presidents, finance and transport ministers, government advisers and important officials from leading industrialised economies joined a queue of visitors to Taipei to drum up business and investment opportunities.

The second package was Taiwan's ability to spend large sums on military equipment. Since the end of the Gulf War, Taiwan has placed orders for over US$20 billion in military equipment, making it the world's biggest spender in the global arms market since the end of the Gulf War for items such as warships, military aircraft and other high-value defence equipment. This attracted arms sellers and hence the attention of countries around the world, including Germany, the United States, Holland,

Britain, France and Russia. Australia, too, has been interested in selling defence technology to Taiwan.[110]

It was partly in recognition of Taiwan's growing importance in the world arms trade that France, for example, upgraded its office in Taipei along the lines of the American Institute. It subsequently secured contracts for the sale of Lafayette frigates (US$7.4 billion) and Mirage fighter aircraft (US$2.6 billion) and improved its chances of winning contracts for the construction of a high-speed train, a nuclear power plant and other infrastructure projects under Taiwan's Six Year Development Plan. As noted in Chapter 3, the United States made an unprecedented sale of 150 F-16 fighter aircraft to Taiwan in a deal worth almost US$6 billion.

As 'a very important economic power in the Pacific', Taiwan cannot be easily overlooked by states and multinationals competing for advantage in the world marketplace.[111] Inevitably, international economic interest in Taiwan — as a fast growing market, as a source of capital and as a regional technology base — has given Taipei leverage over countries thirsting to boost their exports and attract foreign funds. Taiwan's economic power is indeed the only real lever of influence available, given Taiwan's lack of diplomatic relations with most countries in the rest of the world and its non-membership of the United Nations and other key international organisations. Not surprisingly, the Ministry of Foreign Affairs co-ordinates its activities with ministries and commissions in charge of Taiwan's external economic affairs, the Overseas Chinese Affairs Commission, the Government Information Office and information centres in over 40 capital cities around the world so as to orchestrate Taiwan's foreign policy and maximise the benefits.[112]

Taiwan's international economic appeal has been supplemented by foreign aid. In 1989, Taiwan established an International Economic Co-operation Development Fund to give loans on concessional terms to needy economies including the Philippines (US$24 million), Nauru (US$9 million), Vietnam (US$45 million), Niger (US$20 million), Nicaragua (US$1 million) with smaller cash grants or aid in kind to others including Russia, Costa Rica, Panama, Ireland, Dominica, the Bahamas, Papua New Guinea, Saint Vincent, Malawi and Honduras and US$30 million for refugees from Kuwait living in Jordan, Turkey and Egypt. While modest by world standards (averaging 0.1 per cent of GNP compared with an average of 0.3 per cent for OECD countries), Taiwan's foreign aid program helps reinforce the message that Taiwan counts.[113]

Taipei aims to win acceptance, acknowledgement and, ideally, even recognition of its claim to be the Republic of China on Taiwan and as more and more countries pay attention to Taiwan, the Taiwanese in turn have become confident, willing and able to practise economic diplomacy. As Robert Wade concluded, the government plays an active role in the direction of Taiwanese foreign investment by including diplomatic considerations along with commercial ones in its process of decision-making, the ultimate object being an improvement in the political or legal treatment of Taiwan by the target country.[114] For example, in October 1989, the Taiwanese imposed a ban on Australian beef exports worth A$100 million, just when Australia was at a critical phase in its negotiations with Taiwan over direct air links. Whether deliberately timed or not, the effect was to reinforce pressure on Australia to acknowledge Taiwan's economic importance. Taiwanese officials explained that the ban was an attempt to 'bring to [Australia's] attention that good trade relations with Taiwan required a little more than the de facto recognition of Taiwan conceded by the Australian government'.[115]

In competing for Taiwanese investment, countries like Indonesia, Malaysia, Thailand, the Philippines, Australia and New Zealand have been forced to bid against each other to make conditions more attractive for Taiwanese investors. As many countries are competing for Taiwanese markets and Taiwanese capital, they risk losing 'a piece of the action' — whether an investment, a joint venture, a tender contract or a particular trade deal — if they fall behind regional trends in their treatment of Taiwan, its officials and its businesses. The country that is prepared to offer Taipei certain concessions may hope for a temporary advantage, although more often than not, the Taiwanese simply move on to another target. In December 1989, for example, China Steel announced it was looking for a site to build a US$2.5 billion integrated steel mill complex that would employ up to 6000 people.[116] The proposal was floated around the region to Malaysia, Canada and several states in Australia in a way that looked like a well-planned campaign, the true aim of which was to improve Taiwan's regional diplomacy.[117] The Australian government promptly passed the *Foreign Corporations (Application of Laws) Act* to guarantee protection of investments in Australia by states and governments not recognised by Australia — that is, a state like Taiwan.[118] Having persuaded Australia and Malaysia to pass investment guarantees protecting Taiwanese investment, the Taiwanese subsequently suggested that investment funds might begin to flow if Malaysia and Australia signed double taxation and other agreements that implied agreement between sovereign states. This bandwagon strategy can be likened to a game of Chinese checkers where the move of one supports the move of several. Investment guarantee agreements have subsequently been agreed to by Indonesia, Singapore, the Philippines, Vietnam and Thailand. Even mainland China passed a 'Law for Protecting Investments by Taiwan Compatriots' in March 1994 in an effort to encourage Taiwanese investment on the mainland.

The Chinese checkers strategy has been used in other areas. Most countries in the Asia-Pacific region have agreed to direct air links with Taipei. Most accept the practice of 'unofficial' ministerial visits, 'holiday' diplomacy and annual talks with senior foreign ministry officials from Taiwan. Senior ASEAN ministers in particular now meet frequently with their Taiwanese counterparts to discuss areas of possible economic and technical co-operation. Taiwanese officials serving at Taipei Economic and Cultural Offices have also been able to extract the right to privileges normally reserved for embassy staff. For example, staff at the Taipei Economic and Trade Centre in Bangkok have enjoyed diplomatic privileges since 1991.[119]

A similar situation exists with regard to use of the name 'Taipei Economic and Cultural Office' (TECO) as the title of Taiwan's representative offices. The argument from Taiwan is that because other countries in the region, such as New Zealand, Indonesia, Singapore, Canada or Vietnam, have given certain undertakings, other countries like Australia or Malaysia and Thailand should do likewise or risk being somehow disadvantaged in the race for Taiwan's dollars. An increasing number of countries have now been persuaded to allow the Taiwanese the right to incorporate the name 'Taipei' into the title of their representative offices. The Taiwanese offices in the United States, Indonesia, Japan, Malaysia, the Philippines, Thailand, Vietnam, Australia, New Zealand, Israel, Russia, Oman, Saudi Arabia, Turkey, Austria, Bulgaria, Czechoslovakia, Denmark, Finland, Germany, Greece, Switzerland, Macao, Canada and Mexico have become Taipei Economic and Cultural or Trade Offices. The most recent additions to the list of countries allowing TECO offices in their capitals include India and Cambodia. Sometimes the office is called Trade Mission of the Republic of China (as in Fiji, United Arab Emirates and Bahrain), or the Trade Mission of the Republic of China on Taiwan (PNG, Nigeria and Jordan), or the Commercial Office of the Republic of China (as in Jordan, Libya and Kuwait), Taipei Representative Office (Singapore) or Taipei Trade Office (Hungary). One exception is Hong Kong (Chung Hwa Travel Service).[120]

From Taiwan's perspective, such concessions amount to regional appreciation of Taiwan's respectability and its status as a Pacific economic power. Rather than publicising the success of its 'dollar diplomacy', and thereby provoking Beijing and embarrassing host countries, the Taiwanese have adopted a quieter, more mature style. As President Lee Teng-hui remarked following his February 1994 visit to the Philippines, Indonesia and Thailand, Taiwan should avoid engaging in 'promiscuous and improper acts just because we have tens of billions of dollars in our hands' and to concentrate instead on winning the respect of other countries 'because of our culture and moral standards'.[121]

Conclusion

The rapid rise in Taiwan's importance as a significant regional economic power was matched by a recovery in the international standing that Taiwan had lost in the decades of the 1970s. The mid-1980s can thus be seen as a transition decade in Taiwan's fortunes as regional thinking about Taiwan and China changed. Instead of constantly deferring to China over Taiwan, countries began to devise ways that recognised the reality of Taiwan and exploited the commercial opportunities it presented.

By the late 1980s, Taiwan was poised to re-enter the economic and political mainstream of the Asia-Pacific region. It had access to the United States market. It could count on the political and — to a degree — the tacit military support of the United States. It had a close relationship with Japan, the Asia-Pacific's number two power. Taiwan, in short, was engaged with two of the three leading great powers in the Asia-Pacific. It was a modern industrialised economy with a middle-class society and the trappings of democracy. It was also increasingly accepted by the majority of the Asia-Pacific community. It joined the non-government Pacific Economic Cooperation Conference in 1986. It was a natural member of the Asia-Pacific Economic Community when that group was proposed in January 1989. It is prospectively a member of other regional organisations such as the ASEAN Regional Forum and the South Pacific Forum. It is a desirable member of the World Trade Organisation and ultimately perhaps, a member of the United Nations.

Two key building blocks fell into place in the period between 1987 and 1992. These were, first, Taiwan's rapprochement with China, a development that is speeding up the transformation of Chinese communism (discussed in Chapter 7) but has been secured by Taiwan's military capabilities (discussed in Chapter 8); and second, the Tiananmen massacre in Beijing and its aftermath plus the consequences of the end of the Cold War (discussed in Chapter 9).

Notes

1   *Free China Review (FCR)*, March 1992, p. 32.

2   *Forbes Magazine*, cited in *China Post (CP)*, 16 July 1993.

3   *Economic and Trade Indicators, The Republic of China on Taiwan*, China External Trade Development Council, Taipei, 1991.

4   Council for Economic Planning and Development, *Taiwan Statistical Data Book (TSDB) 1993*, p. 42.

5   ibid., p. 194.

6   ibid., p. 183.

7   Rong-I Wu, 'The Distinctive Features of Taiwan's Development', in Peter Berger and Hsin-Huang Hsiao (eds), *In Search of an East Asian Development Model*, Transaction Books, New Brunswick and Oxford, 1986, pp. 179, 184.

8   *China News Service (CNS)*, Taipei, 3 June 1993.

9   Peter Rimmer, 'Taiwan's Future as a Regional Transport Hub', in Gary Klintworth (ed.), *Taiwan in the Asia-Pacific in the 1990s*, Allen & Unwin/Department of International Relations, ANU, 1994, p. 221.

10 Over half the reserves (57 per cent) are held in US dollars, 23 per cent in German marks and 15 per cent in Japanese yen. The reserves earn Taiwan around US$5 billion per annum in interest.

11 Jan S. Prybyla, 'Economic Developments in the Republic of China', in Thomas W. Robinson (ed.), *Democracy and Development in East Asia*, AEI Press, Washington 1991, pp. 49, 51.

12 Neil H. Jacoby, *US Aid to Taiwan*, Praeger, New York, 1966, p. 87.

13 *Yearbook of Labour Statistics, Republic of China*, 1981, 1986, 1987, 1990.

14 Shirley W.Y. Kuo, 'The Taiwan Economy in the 1990s', in Klintworth, *Taiwan in the Asia-Pacific*, Table 6.8, p. 110.

15 It was US$1.5 billion in 1988 and US$0.6 billion in 1992: *Asia Development Outlook 1991*, Asian Development Bank, Manila, 1991, p. 81.

16 Shirley W.Y. Kuo, Gustav Ranis and John C.H. Fei, *The Taiwan Success Story: Rapid Growth with Improved Distribution in the Republic of China 1952–1979*, Westview, Boulder, Col., 1981, pp. 8–9.

17 Kuo, 'The Taiwan Economy in the 1990s', in Klintworth, *Taiwan in the Asia-Pacific*, Table 6.5, p. 108.

18 Ross Munro, quoted by Lien Chan, 'The Republic of China on Taiwan Belongs in the United Nations', *Orbis*, vol. 37, no. 4, Fall 1993, p. 635.

19 *CNS*, 18 May 1992.

20 Lee Teng-hui, press conference, Taipei, 16 February 1994, in *Foreign Broadcast Information Service (FBIS) China*, Daily Report, 24 February 1994, pp. 58, 60.

21 For example, former President Yang Shangkun: reported in *Free China Journal (FCJ)*, 14 April 1992.

22 *FCJ*, 20 November 1992, p. 7.

23 *Taiwan Statistical Data Book (TSDB)*, Council for Economic Planning and Development, Taipei, 1993 p. 36.

24 Australia is ranked fifteenth.

25 *Economic and Trade Indicators, The Republic of China on Taiwan*, China External Trade Development Council, Taipei, 1991.

26 *TSDB*, 1993, p. 9.

27 ibid.

28 Kuo, 'The Taiwan Economy in the 1990s', in Klintworth, *Taiwan in the Asia-Pacific*, Table 6.2, p. 104.

29 ibid., Table 6.3, p. 106.

30 See Chapter 1.

31 United States Information Service, Wireless File, Canberra, 30 April 1992, p. 46.

32 Michael Stutchbury, 'Australia Opportunities as Taiwan Booms', *Australian Financial Review (AFR)*, 24 July 1991.

33 *The Six Year National Development Plan of the Republic of China*, Council of Economic Planning and Development, Taipei, April 1992, p. 41.

34 Walden Bello and Stephanie Rosenfeld, *Dragons in Distress: Asia's Miracle Economies in Crisis*, Food First, San Francisco, 1990, p. 202 and Chapter 12 in general. See also Jonathon Moore, 'Protests in This Green and Poisoned Land', *Far Eastern Economic Review*, 22 February 1988.

35 Samuel P.S. Ho, *Economic Development of Taiwan 1860–1970*, Yale University Press, New Haven, 1978, p. 230.

36 *The Economist*, 16 November 1991, p. 19.

37 *The Economist*, 14 July 1990, p. 20.

38 *FCR*, February 1991, p. 36.

39 *FCR*, February 1993, p. 29.

40 See previous chapter.

41 *CP*, 9 April 1992.

42 Jiann-Jong Guo and Raymond Chang, 'Taiwan's Economic Relations with the US', in Gary Klintworth (ed.), *Modern Taiwan in the 1990s*, Strategic and Defence Studies Centre, ANU, Canberra, 1991, pp. 106, 112.

43 *CP*, 8 April 1992.

44 *FCJ*, 14 April 1992.

45 *CP*, 15 May 1992.

46 *FCJ*, 14 April 1992.

47 ibid.

48 *CP*, 14 April 1992.

49 *CP*, 30 March 1992.

50 Chi Schive, *The Foreign Factor: The Multinational Corporation's Contribution to the Economic Modernisation of the Republic of China*, Hoover Institution Press, Stanford, 1990, pp. 86–91.

51 *Canberra Times*, 20 April 1992 and *FCJ*, 28 April 1992.

52 *CP*, 2 April 1992.

53 *CP*, 2 July 1993.

54 Robert Wade, *Governing the Market: Economic Theory and the Role of Government in East Asian Industrialisation*, Princeton University Press, Princeton, N.J., 1990, p. 98.

55 Lee, press conference, *FBIS China*, 24 February 1994, p. 58; and *CP*, 4 January 1994.

56 Government Information Office, *The Republic of China Yearbook*, Taipei, 1994, p. 184.

57 Schive, *The Foreign Factor*, p. 92.

58 Transnational Corporations and Management Division, *World Investment Report 1992: Transnational Corporations as Engines of Growth*, United Nations, New York, 1992, p. 24.

59 See the next chapter.

60 *CNS*, 22 February 1993.

61 *FCJ*, 4 December 1992.

62 *CP*, 18 July 1992.

63 Lee, press conference, *FBIS China*, 24 February 1994, p. 60.

64 Quoted in *CNS*, 11 May 1992.

65 *FCR*, June 1990, p. 58.

66 Linda Y.C. Lim and Pang Eng Fong, *Foreign Direct Investment and Industrialisation in Malaysia Singapore Taiwan and Thailand*, OECD, Paris, 1991, p. 162.

67 ibid., p. 161.

68 *CNS*, 4 January 1994.

69 Yuan-li Wu and Kung-chia Yeh, 'Taiwan's External Economic Relations', in Yuan-li Wu and Kung-chia Yeh (eds), *Growth, Distribution and Social Change: Essays on the Economy of the Republic of China*, Occasional Papers No. 3, School of Law, University of Maryland, 1978, pp. 173, 199; and Economic and Social Commission for Asia and the Pacific, *Transnational Corporations from Developing Asian Economies*, United Nations, Bangkok, 1988, p. 158.

70 Chung-hua Institute for Economic Research, cited in *CP*, 18 July 1992; *CP*, 1 January 1994.

71 *CNS*, 28 February 1992.

72 Sanjaya Lall, 'Emerging Sources of FDI in Asia and the Pacific', briefing paper for 'Roundtable on Foreign Direct Investment in the Asia-Pacific in the 1990s', East–West Centre, Honolulu, 26–28 March 1991, p. 1.

73 CETRA, quoted in CNS, 5 August 1992; see also Lim and Fong, *Foreign Direct Investment*, p. 68; Schive, *The Foreign Factor*, p. 82.

74 The role of the United States and Japan and their respective relationships with Taiwan are discussed in Chapters 2 and 3.

75 *CP*, 18 July 1992; *FCR*, February 1993; and *FCJ*, 27 August 1993.

76 *Monthly Statistical Bulletin*, Jakarta, January 1991, p. 65.

77 Malaysian Industrial Development Authority, cited in Lim and Fong, *Foreign Direct Investment*, p. 42.

78 In December 1992, China Steel made a decision to build the mill in Taiwan.

79 Afifuddin Haji Omar, 'Economic Cooperation between Malaysia and Taiwan', in *Lessons from Taiwan: Pathways to Follow and Pitfalls to Avoid*, ISIS, Malaysia, 1986, p. 21, and Craig C Wu, 'Economic Cooperation between the Republic of China and Malaysia' in ibid., pp. 30ff.

80 *CP*, 31 December 1993.

81 Kuo-hsiun Lee, 'The Republic of China and Southeast Asia: More than Economy', in Yu San Wang (ed.), *Foreign Policy of the Republic of China on Taiwan*, Praeger, New York, 1990, pp. 77, 93.

82 *Far Eastern Economic Review*, 22 March 1989.

83 For a useful discussion of Singapore's relations with Taiwan and China, and the ASEAN relationship with Taiwan and China in general, see Chen Jie, 'The Taiwan Problem in Peking's ASEAN Policy', *Issues and Studies*, vol. 29, no. 4, April 1993, p. 95.

84 *FCR*, February 1993, p. 29.

85 Chen Jie, 'The Taiwan Problem in Peking's ASEAN Policy', p. 116.

86 Aileen San Pablo-Baviera, 'Philippine–Taiwan Relations', in Theresa C. Carino (ed.), *China ASEAN Relations Political, Economic and Ethnic Dimensions*, The China Studies Program, De La Salle University, Manila, 1991, pp. 112, 114.

87 *South China Morning Post*, 14 March 1989.

88 *CP*, 29 February 1992.

89 *CP*, 18 July 1992; *FCR*, February 1993; and *FCJ*, 27 August 1993.

90 ibid.

91 Chiao Chiao Hsieh, *Strategy for Survival*, Sherwood Press, London, 1985, p. 162.

92 *Saigon Economic Times*, no. 24, June 1991.

93 *Indochina Digest*, 27 September 1991.

94 Stuart Harris, speech on Australia's trade policy, *Australian Foreign Affairs Record (AFAR)*, vol. 59, no. 5, 1988, pp. 195, 198; and see also Stuart Harris, 'The Amalgamation of the Department of Foreign Affairs and Trade', 17 March 1988, *AFAR*, vol. 59, no. 3, 1988, p. 71.

95 Ross Garnaut, *Australia and the Northeast Asian Ascendancy*, Australian Government Publishing Service, Canberra, 1989.

96 ibid., pp. 1–3 and *Annual Report*, Department of Foreign Affairs and Trade, Canberra, 1990–91, p. 20.

97 See Gary Klintworth, *Australia's Taiwan Policy 1942–1992*, Australian Foreign Policy Papers, ANU, Canberra, 1993.

98 Gareth Evans, Statement, Australian Foreign Affairs and Trade, 26 March 1991, p. 113.

99 John Hewson, 'Australian Trade Interests Boosted by Taiwan Visit', Media Release, 70/91, Canberra, 28 March 1991.

100 *Canberra Times*, 7 February 1992.

101 Section 7 of the Act provides that 'where a mission is sent by a country to Australia and it appears to the Governor-General that it is desirable that the diplomatic privileges and immunities (of the Act) should be applicable', the regulations may declare the mission to be a mission to which the section applies and the mission shall be entitled Section 7(2)a — to the privileges and immunities of an envoy

(defined as an envoy of a foreign sovereign power accredited to the Queen in Australia). The TECO office was gazetted as a mission under the Act on 26 August 1992. The privileges and immunities are set out in the schedules to the Act and include immunity from arrest and detention, immunity from suit or other legal processes, the inviolability of papers and documents, the right to communicate in code and to use sealed bags, privileges and immunities in respect of personal baggage as accorded to an envoy, and exemption from income and sales taxes, and customs duty on imported goods such as luxury cars. That is, TECO was declared to be a mission under the Act and granted the right to enjoy diplomatic immunities, exemptions and privileges normally accorded only to embassies and missions of other countries as set out in the Vienna Convention on Diplomatic Relations, Section 4, *Diplomatic Privileges and Immunities Act* No. 16, 1967. The Attorney-General's Department advised, however, that a country could be a country without being internationally recognised as a sovereign state and that therefore the TECO mission was not by the act of gazettal recognised by Australia as the mission of a sovereign state.

102 *Composition of Trade Australia 1992–93*, Department of Foreign Affairs and Trade, Canberra, October 1993.

103 China overtook Taiwan as a trading partner for Australia in 1993.

104 Steve Hoadley, *New Zealand and Taiwan: The Policy and Practice of Quasi-Diplomacy*, New Zealand Institute of International Affairs, Occasional Papers No. 7, October 1993, ibid., p. 15ff.

105 ibid., p. 1.

106 For a very useful study, see Thomas V. Biddick, 'Diplomatic Rivalry in the South Pacific: The PRC and Taiwan', *Asian Survey*, vol. XXIX, no. 8, August 1989, p. 800.

107 Forum spokesman, Ratu Sir Kamisese Mara, quoted in *The Age*, 31 July 1991.

108 Peter Osborne and Robert O'Donovan, *Taiwan in the 1990s: Opportunities for Australia*, ACC/Westpac Economic Discussion Papers 4/1991, pp. 1, 12, 13.

109 ibid.

110 In Australia's case, it was the technology involved in building the Collins-class submarine, the most lethal conventionally powered submarine in the world.

111 Robert Shih, Director of Taiwan's Department of East Asia and Pacific Affairs, Ministry of Foreign Affairs, quoted in the *Australian Financial Review*, 4 December 1989.

112 *FCR*, February 1993, p. 18.

113 Gerald Chan, 'Taiwan's Aid Diplomacy', paper for New Zealand Political Studies Association Annual Conference, University of Canterbury, August 1993.

114 Wade, *Governing the Market*, p. 157.

115 As explained to Bruce Crossing, the Vice-President of the NSW
     Farmers Association: *The Australian*, 30 October 1989.

116 Reported in *The Australian*, 4 December 1989.

117 *Australian Financial Review*, 20 October 1988.

118 The law, however, is unsatisfactory for Taiwan because it treats the
     Taiwanese as 'special domestic investors' rather than as foreign
     investors: *FCJ*, 18 March 1994.

119 *CP*, 7 September 1991.

120 Prior to 1990, host countries confined the name of Taiwanese repre-
     sentative offices to such vague designations as 'Far East Trading
     Company' (Australia), 'Association of East Asian Relations' (Japan),
     'Pacific Economic and Cultural Centre' (the Philippines), 'Far East
     Trade Office' (Thailand, the Netherlands and Greece), 'Chinese
     Chamber of Commerce' (Indonesia), 'East Asia Trade Centre' (New
     Zealand), 'Institute of Chinese Culture' (Austria), or the 'Sun Yat-sen
     Cultural Centre' (Spain, Switzerland, Belgium and Luxembourg).

121 Lee Teng-hui, press conference, *FBIS-China*, 24 February 1994,
     pp. 58, 62.

7 Greater China

Taiwan's linkages with Japan and the United States were discussed in previous chapters. This chapter focuses on the consequences of its rapprochement with China, the third of the three key components in Taiwan's history, culture and security outlook.

By the 1980s, Taiwan was a major economic power. It had claims to be part of a greater China with special ties to the 31 million overseas Chinese scattered throughout Southeast Asia, North America and Oceania.[1] It forged ahead in its competition with mainland China and Taiwanese investors were flooding into nearly all the economies of the Asia-Pacific region, including southern China, in search of new business opportunities. Taiwan, in short, had outgrown the physical and political dimensions of its island base, and was like a 'dancer with vitality in need of a wider stage to perform'.[2] It was ready for rapprochement with China, not least because Chiang Kai-shek and Mao Zedong, the chief protagonists in the Chinese civil war, had died in the mid-1970s.[3]

There were several other reasons for the Sino-Taiwanese rapprochement. First, the labour and resources of the mainland are a natural hinterland for an industrialised East Asian powerhouse like Taiwan. China has a plentiful Chinese-speaking labour force available at wages that are a fraction of the rates payable in Taiwan. In Xiamen, wages are up to seven times less than for workers on Taiwan, according to the manager of one Taiwanese electronics factory.[4] Land is much cheaper so, for example, Yulon Motor Co found that it would need US$200 million to set up a car plant on the mainland compared with US$400 million to set up the same plant in Taiwan.[5] China can supply cheap resources like coal, cement, cotton, uranium, steel, and agricultural and industrial raw materials.

Mainland coal, for example, is of a high quality and shipping costs are a fraction of the cost of shipping coal from Australia or North America. Taiwan's electricity company, Taipower, could therefore significantly lower its costs by tapping Shanxi coal and shipping it out through Qinhuangdao.[6] Harnessing China's cheap labour and resources would help preserve Taiwanese competitiveness. Second, the mainland is a new market of almost unlimited potential for Taiwanese–Chinese manufacturers. Third, by combining with China, Taiwan would be in a better position to compete with the United States, Japan and the EC in international trade. Fourth, Taiwan was in danger of being left behind by competitors in global industries like aerospace, automobiles and petrochemicals. Formosa Plastics Chairman, Y.C Yang, said Taiwan's petrochemical industry 'urgently needed to exploit the mainland's cheap labor to beat competition from producers in South Korea and Japan'.[7]

Fifth, in dealing with Beijing, the Taiwanese were increasingly confident of the strength of their military forces *vis-a-vis* PLA deployments on the other side of the Taiwan Strait. Taiwanese investors were also attracted to the mainland because of its less strict regard for the environment.[8]

In addition, the Taiwanese are Chinese. Mainland leaders can therefore call on the Taiwanese as Chinese 'to join hands with us in accomplishing the great cause of national reunification and the great goal of making China prosperous and strong, so as to win glory for our ancestors'.[9] Such patriotic appeals based on the notion of a greater China are not unattractive to the Kuomintang. Both Chinas have a common interest in the increased strategic leverage that would accrue from a united Chinese position on certain issues. For example, on Tibet, a senior Cabinet official, Chang Chun-yi, criticised the United States Congress for meddling in China's sovereign affairs by passing a resolution on Tibet.[10] Chang claimed that the United States and other foreign powers did not want a strong and unified China and were 'applying every possible means to sabotage the goal of reunification between Taiwan and mainland China'.[11] Both Taiwan and the mainland support the Chinese claim to islands and resources in the Western Pacific. They have supported each other against Japanese claims to the Senkaku Islands (Tiaoyutai) in the East China Sea and they agree that China's sovereignty over islands and resources in the South China Sea is non-negotiable.[12] At Bandung in July 1991, Taiwan and China joined forces to vote against Japanese participation in settlement of the latter dispute.[13]

As President Lee Teng-hui explained, 'we are all Chinese in terms of race, history and culture'.[14] Taiwan therefore claims it has a natural responsibility and a right to extend the Taiwanese model of economic and political development to the mainland.[15]

Increasingly, Beijing's view is that China should be prepared to give more leeway to Taiwan on the grounds that 'they are Chinese, after all'.[16] Taiwan, moreover, has assets such as its location, international networks, global trading skills, management knowhow, good technology and a proven modernisation formula. Taiwan's surplus capital and foreign exchange reserves are of particular interest.[17] As well, Taiwan retains close relations with the United States, Japan and Hong Kong, all vitally important contributors to China's modernisation. Any policy on Taiwan that threatened the regional peace, therefore, would be disastrous for China's economic development, its relations with the United States and Japan, its regional diplomacy in Southeast Asia and its desire to join international organisations like the GATT.

The rapprochement of the two parts of China after almost four decades of civil war was facilitated in particular by the radical changes wrought by Deng Xiaoping's decade of reform (1978–88). Those reforms, some would argue, stemmed directly from the contrast between a China impoverished by a decade of Maoism and the stunning success of Taiwan.[18] Deng, denounced during China's Cultural Revolution as the 'number two capitalist-roader' in China after Liu Shaoqi, simply took up where he had left off in the 1960s. When he resumed office in 1978, Deng almost immediately copied key aspects of the Taiwanese formula of rapid market-based economic development.[19] Deng preserved a repressive authoritarianism (as Taiwan had done until 1987). He dismantled the commune system and launched an agricultural reform program not dissimilar to Taiwan's land-to-the-tiller policies of the early 1950s. Material incentives, a household responsibility system bordering on leasehold land rights and decentralised free markets helped transform China's agricultural sector.[20] Economic self-reliance was abandoned in favour of an open door policy. Other features of the Taiwan model appeared, including the establishment of fully serviced export processing zones (or, as they were called in China, Special Economic Zones), an emphasis on light industry, preferential treatment for foreign investment, especially for Taiwanese Chinese, and the despatch of students to learn from the West.[21] In October 1980, Beijing made a special pitch for Taiwanese investment by designating Xiamen (in Fujian province opposite Taiwan) as a special economic zone for export-oriented manufacturing industries such as electronics, textiles, clothing and footwear. Xiamen became a duty free port in 1992. By then, Fujian was essentially a market economy joining the mainland to Taiwan.

Deng's policies would have been criticised for being counter-revolutionary during the Cultural Revolution. For the Kuomintang in Taiwan, however, this represented a light at the end of a long tunnel. Post-Mao China, it seemed, was abandoning communist principles of central planning and public ownership of property in favour of what Deng Xiaoping called 'socialism with Chinese characteristics'.[22] World Bank Vice President Attila Karaosmanoglu concluded that China was continuing with market-oriented reforms that 'were rather drastic and in economic terms, courageous'.[23]

From Taipei's perspective, Deng's reforms amounted to 'capitalism with Chinese characteristics' — in other words, a society and economy that was increasingly difficult to distinguish from the Taiwanese model. Such a convergence between adversaries who had fought each other, confronted each other, threatened each other and fought a bitter ideological battle that had lasted for several decades had been anticipated by some writers in their analysis of the contest between the Soviet Union and the United States.[24] Few foresaw a similar outcome to the Chinese Cold War but in any event, the phenomenon reaffirmed the Kuomintang's faith in the possibility that China could one day be reunified under Sun Yat-sen's Three Principles of the People.[25] China and Taiwan are basically similar societies with similar aspirations and values. They share the same language and the same cultural heritage. The only difference between them, as Lee Teng-hui observed, was their recent developmental experience.[26] If that difference is beginning to disappear, as would appear to be the case, then China may indeed become increasingly indistinguishable from Taiwan and Hong Kong. That goal could be achieved, said Kuomintang Party Secretary General James Soong, by promoting the Taiwan experience so that the mainland would undergo 'a peaceful evolution toward democratisation and liberalisation'.[27] If liberalisation and democratisation inevitably follow economic modernisation and the rise of a middle class, as was the case in the Taiwanese model, then Taipei has grounds for optimism about its future and that of China. However, as Richard Lowenthal observed in discussing totalitarian regimes in general, and as was the case with the Kuomintang which only lifted martial law in 1987, totalitarian regimes are not prepared for self-liquidation.[28]

Taipei's inclination towards pragmatism and compromise with Beijing was also encouraged by mainland statements that implicitly recognised the reality of Taiwan and the strength of its negotiating position.[29] Of course, the one China issue was a highly sensitive political issue for leadership elites in both Taipei and Beijing.[30] But, while China never renounced the use of force to recover Taiwan, its approach moved beyond threats of 'liberating Taiwan by force' to 'using peaceful means to liberate Taiwan'.[31] The bombardment of offshore islands ceased as of 1 January 1979.[32] Beijing Review noted that Deng Xiaoping had said in 1979 that 'we no longer use the phrase "liberate Taiwan" and so long as Taiwan returns to the embrace of the motherland, we will respect Taiwan's reality and its current system'.[33] In September 1979, China proposed 'one country two systems'.[34] Peaceful reunification could be achieved step by step, beginning with visits, trade, postal links and other confidence-building exchanges.[35] After reunification was achieved, Taiwan was promised 'a high degree of autonomy as a special administrative region' and the right to maintain its own armed forces and cultural and economic relations with foreign countries.[36] Taiwan's existing socio-economic system, lifestyle and foreign economic relations would remain intact for at least 50 years without mainland interference.[37] In fact,

Taiwan would have more freedom than Hong Kong, said Deng Xiaoping in talks with Helmut Schmidt.[38]

This package, including the possibility of 'one country, two systems', was a significant policy change by Beijing.[39] It comes close to matching the non-military confidence-building measures that China has proposed for relations between states in the Asia-Pacific region.[40] More recently, Beijing has appeared to be moving towards a policy of peaceful coexistence that accepts reunification as an eventual goal in the future (i.e. an acknowledgement that the government in Taipei is more than simply a local government with a different social and political system). Pending reunification, Taipei believes Beijing might be persuaded to accept the Taiwanese concept of one country, two governments, or one country, two areas, provided Taiwan remains committed to the 'one China' principle.[41] As President Jiang Zemin declared on 30 January 1995, mainland China would not use force against the Taiwanese, but it would not rule out the use of force to prevent 'foreign forces' interfering with China's reunification.[42] These and other indications that Beijing was prepared to stress mutual interdependence and economic complementarities rather than the use of force were 'all very heartening, to say the least' according to the *Free China Journal*.[43] The Kuomintang remains cautious, but concedes that the mainland has become slightly more positive and flexible.[44]

Nonetheless, China's good neighbour overtures and Taipei's appreciation of the historical significance of the capitalist road taken by Deng Xiaoping prompted the Taiwanese to review their China policy. By the early 1990s, both sides had reached a point where, as Guocan Huan observed, compromise is possible.[45]

However, although the Taiwanese have adopted a more flexible approach towards the mainland, their basic aim is to use Taiwan's economic and cultural influence to induce peaceful political change on the mainland.[46] As President Lee Teng-hui explained, Taiwan's goal was to use the Taiwan experience as 'a beacon of hope and a blueprint for the reconstruction of all of China'.[47] For that, said Lee, Taiwan 'must use peaceful economic and of course, cultural and artistic exchanges' to eliminate cross-Strait hostility and disseminate the Taiwanese modernisation experience.[48] By using its economic power and its Chineseness, Taipei could hope to hasten the pace of reform in post-Deng China and also influence its direction and possible outcomes.

Chalmers Johnson referred to the pressure on Communist regimes to relax their control if they wished to progress to a modern, specialised and complex socio-economic structure. In doing so, such regimes would open the door to the possibility of ever-rising demands for more change and more adjustment, leading to pressures on the leadership 'to consider dismantling certain controls that appear to be no longer desirable, and to begin experimenting with market mechanisms'.[49] Taiwan was the obvious socio-economic model for China to follow and, as far as the

Taiwanese were concerned, the revolution of rising expectations in China was manifest in the crisis that culminated in the massacre in Tiananmen in June 1989.

As well as change within China, there were dramatic political changes underway within Taiwan. The Taiwanisation policy that had been started by Chiang Ching-kuo in 1972 — partly out of foresight and partly from expedience — culminated in the lifting of martial law in 1987 and the legalisation of Taiwan's opposition Democratic Progressive Party.[50] Subsequent elections led to a more representative political system in Taiwan and the demise of the Kuomintang as a party that could claim to represent all of China. This democratisation of Taiwanese politics in turn forced the Kuomintang to revise its one China position and negotiate a new Taiwan–China relationship with Beijing. While the government in Taipei maintained that the idea of 'separating Taiwan from the mainland was illegal, irrational . . . and a betrayal of the people', President Lee Teng-hui announced that it was time Taiwan had the courage to recognise the fact that Taipei's administrative control was limited to Taiwan and that it did not exercise administrative sovereignty over the mainland.[51] In May 1991, Taiwan's acceptance of the reality and permanence of the Chinese Communist regime in Beijing was formally confirmed when President Lee Teng-hui declared an end to 'the state of war' with the mainland and an end to the Period of Mobilisation for Suppression of the Communist Rebellion. The announcement was greeted enthusiastically by Taiwanese businesses in anticipation of reduced bilateral tension and new opportunities for mainland trade and investment. It was also welcomed in Beijing as a move that would reduce hostility and help develop relations between the two sides.[52]

Taipei's declaration of peace, however, had serious implications for the one China principle, at least insofar as the notion of 'one China' was understood in Beijing. Its full import was subsequently explained by Taiwan's Economics Minister, Pin-Kung Chiang, at the Seattle APEC ministerial meeting in November 1993. Chiang said that until conditions were ripe for reunification with the mainland, Taiwan would 'pursue a step-by-step approach to a two China[s] policy'. Said Chiang:

> [T]here is but one China. Taiwan belongs to China geographically and culturally. Under the one China principle, we maintain that divided countries should coexist and we are pursuing a policy of one China by means of a two China[s] approach: [meanwhile] Taiwan and the PRC are two countries with independent sovereignty of their own.[53]

Chiang explained further that China was a 'neutral' name of geographical and historical reference and Taiwan was part of that China, but so was mainland China. However, the term China did not equate with the People's Republic of China and Taiwan therefore was not part of the PRC. The Taiwanese Foreign Ministry subsequently issued a statement elaborating on Chiang's remarks. It stated that while Taiwan was unwavering in its commitment to 'one China', it was also unwavering in its claim to be a sovereign and independent state. It was 'independently exercising exclusive sovereignty over territories under its effective control' and was not subordinate to the mainland.[54]

This thrust towards a one China–one Taiwan policy was not immediately and obviously apparent in the later 1980s and in any case, it has been balanced by Taiwan's open door policy towards the mainland.

Open door

The ban on Taiwanese travelling to the mainland was progressively eased from July 1987.[55] Indirect mail links began in April 1988 and indirect trade with the mainland was permitted in August 1988, although trade via Hong Kong was already a well-established fact from the early 1980s. In May 1989, Finance Minister Shirley Kuo attended a meeting of the Asian Development Bank in Beijing. Indirect telephone links began in June 1989. In October 1990, a National Unification Council was established to plan and advise on unification policy.[56] A Mainland Affairs Council was formally established in January 1991 to co-ordinate Taiwan's China policy. Channels for semi-official dialogue and negotiations on important policy issues were established.

The rapid development in Taiwanese–mainland exchanges helped Taiwan's former policy of three nos (no contacts, no compromise and no negotiations) give way to trade, tourism, telephone and links the exchange of mail and the three ifs:

1 if Beijing implemented political democracy and a free market system;
2 if it renounced the use of military force in the Taiwan Straits; and
3 if it did not interfere in the development of Taiwan's foreign relations on the basis of a one-China policy, then Taipei would be willing to consider establishing official channels of communication with Beijing.[57]

In the meantime, 'unofficially official' channels of communication between senior Chinese leaders and influential Taiwanese — for example, Shaw Yu-ming, formerly Director of the Government Information Office; Wego Chiang, President of the Society for Strategic Studies; Chao Yao-tung, a former Economics Minister and a national policy adviser to Lee Teng-hui; and former Transport and Communications Minister, Clement C.P. Chang — have become unexceptional.

In February 1991, Taiwan set up the Straits Exchange Foundation (SEF) as a non-official organisation to deal with commercial, legal and administrative matters arising from cross-Strait contacts. Beijing set up a counterpart Association for Relations Across the Taiwan Strait (ARATS) in November 1991.

The two bodies met in Singapore on 27 April 1993 and signed agreements on cross-Strait exchanges including strengthening economic ties, verification of documents and regularised channels of communications. Subsequent meetings were to be held every three months, alternating between Taipei and Beijing. They discuss topics such as the protection of Taiwanese investment rights, resource and energy co-operation, cultural, scientific and technology exchanges, repatriation of illegal immigrants from the mainland, settling fishery disputes, promoting economic exchanges and protecting intellectual property rights.[58] In December 1993, the first official-level delegation from China visited Taipei for cross-Strait talks between the mainland's ARATS and Taiwan's SEF.

In a sense, the first ARATS/SEF meeting was a cross-Strait summit. As the first high level contact between Taiwan and China since 1949, it was, said Lee Ching-ping, Deputy Secretary General of SEF, 'one of the historic moments of the century'.[59] It was historic because it symbolised the fundamental shift in the relationship between the two Chinas from one of confrontation between two sides engaged in an unfinished civil war (in which more than 50 million people had died)[60] to co-operative coexistence between complementary economies.

Equally important is the habit of dialogue inherent in regular SEF/ARATS meetings and through other informal channels. Such communication, often across a wide range of everyday practical issues, is conducive to the development of mutual trust and understanding and can therefore be important in controlling tension and defusing crises.[61] The ARATS/SEF talks take the Taiwan–China relationship beyond simple tension-reduction measures like the avoidance of sensitive airspace, prompt and practical responses to hijacking incidents, allowing fishing boats access to common waters and the cessation of provocative propaganda. Such meetings help focus the attention of both sides on the practical steps that can be taken to improve co-operation and mutual benefit. By building confidence and transparency between Beijing and Taipei, they will ensure that 'peace, prosperity and stability in the Taiwan Strait' will follow and that the possibility of 'China's unification may not be too far-fetched'.[62]

As Cheyne Chiu, Secretary General of the SEF observed, the policy of no contacts had 'fulfilled its historic mission' and should now 'bow out' since contacts between China and Taiwan were taking place.[63] In 1994, Economics Minister Pin-Kung Chiang advocated direct shipping links between designated cities and harbours on both sides of the Taiwan Strait.[64] Direct shipping links were commenced in May 1995.

Statistical data

According to the Mainland Affairs Council, over six million Taiwanese visited the mainland over the period 1987–95. Tourist figures for 1993 were estimated at 1.5 million.[65] Between 1988 and March 1991, the two sides exchanged over 30 million letters, 7.5 million telephone calls and 100 000 telegrams.[66] For 1992, the figures were 24.11 million items of mail, 14.72 million telephone calls and 62 000 telegrams.[67] On the basis that the Taiwanese speak to several mainlanders whilst in China and that these mainlanders then speak to their relatives and friends, knowledge of Taiwan's modernisation experience and appreciation of the contrast between Chinese consumer capitalism and Chinese socialism has been spread to perhaps 150 million mainlanders. The message, moreover, has been reinforced by the circulation in the mainland of Taiwanese songs and popular literature.[68] Popular culture from 'Gangtai' (Taiwan and Hong Kong) also encompasses film, television, advertising, decor and attire and it has, Thomas Gold argues, swept the mainland.[69] Ramon Myers suggests that the images of Taiwan that are being disseminated throughout China are compelling and powerful because they are Chinese and therefore easily understood by ordinary people and elite alike.[70] As an advertisement for the 'Taiwan way' to modernisation, they are creating new ways of thinking in China that are slowly but surely making mainlanders want fundamental change.[71] Many mainlanders share this viewpoint.[72]

Investment

Taiwan has emerged as one of the most important sources of investment funds in China and ranks second after Hong Kong and ahead of Japan and the United States. In fact, it may even be the largest investor in China since the funds attributable to Hong Kong are in fact often Taiwanese. Taiwanese investment in China has grown at the rate of 300 per cent per annum since 1987.[73] In 1993, China absorbed 66.52 per cent of Taiwan's total foreign investment, significantly increasing Taiwan's dependence on the mainland.[74] Most investment is in rubber and plastics manufacturing (23.9 per cent), followed by the electronics sector (18.5 per cent) and textiles (14.1 per cent).[75] According to Edward Chen, foreign investment is the reason why China's economic growth has been so rapid that it is projected to overtake the United States as the world's largest economic power by the year 2002.[76] Even if Chen's optimism is somewhat exaggerated and China simply confirms its position as the world's second or third largest economic power in 2002, it is clear that Taiwan has played and will continue to play a vital role in China's rise to great power status. While this seems rather ironic, given the civil war that divided China and Taiwan between 1949 and 1987, it is perhaps not so surprising. Taiwan in the mid-1980s was well equipped to deal with China: it was rich, industrialised, Chinese, close to the mainland and, militarily, almost impregnable to conventional attack (see below).

In addition, the failure to develop more technology-intensive industries meant that many labour-intensive Taiwanese businesses had to shift to the mainland to maintain their comparative advantage. With the price of China's labour is one-fifteenth of the rate payable in Taiwan, the move of one factory, especially in textiles, clothing and footwear, forced others to follow suit, close down or, as Economics Minister Pin-kung Chiang remarked, be 'choked to death'.[77]

More than half of Taiwan's footwear manufacturers have moved to China since 1987. They operate over 300 factories and employ more than 100 000 workers to produce famous brand name shoes such as Nike and Reebok for export to the United States and European Community. Taiwanese shoe exports dropped from 800 million pairs in 1987 to 370 million pairs in 1991 while exports of shoe parts to mainland China ballooned by almost 60 per cent in 1991. In 1991, 40 per cent of the 500 million mainland-made shoes sold in the United States were manufactured in Taiwanese factories in China and China replaced Taiwan as the biggest shoe supplier to the United States.[78]

More than 80 per cent of Taiwan's ceramic manufacturers, one-third of the plastics industry and a quarter of the toy and leather goods factories have also gone to China. One of Taiwan's largest toy makers, Union Toys and Garment Mfg Ltd, closed down its toy-making plants in Taiwan and moved to the mainland in 1992 because of an appreciating NT$ and labour shortages. At present, only five umbrella manufacturers remain in Taiwan, whereas 150 have gone to the mainland to set up operations in Guangdong and Fujian.[79] Most Taiwanese firms — about 70 per cent — have gone to Fujian and Guangdong where they can utilise networks of relatives.

Investment in the mainland started off in a small way, usually disguised through the 4000 Taiwanese companies operating in Hong Kong or invested through relatives in Canada and the United States. Most visitors to Hong Kong are Taiwanese.[80] Most Taiwanese investment in China has been in labour-intensive factories that produce textiles, ceramics, clothing, footwear, travel goods, toys, rubber and plastic goods and electronics.[81] The factories often use old plant and machinery shipped to China via Hong Kong. The majority of the output (up to 70 per cent) is exported to the United States and Europe with about 20 per cent sold on the mainland market and 10 per cent sold back to Taiwan.[82] Until recently, most Taiwanese investment (70 per cent) was concentrated in China's southern provinces of Fujian and Guangdong.[83] The Taiwanese soon became the largest source of foreign investment in Fujian province and the second largest in Guangdong. In Fujian, where many Taiwanese have their family roots, the bulk of Taiwanese investment went to Xiamen, Quanzhou, Fuzhou, and Zhangzhou.[84] In Guangdong, most Taiwanese investment went to Guangzhou and the SEZs of Shenzhen, Zhuhai and Shantou.[85] The result was to bring China's southern provinces, especially Fujian, into what is effectively a Taiwanese sphere of economic influence.

As Taiwanese confidence in China-based investments grew, the profile and destination of their investment began to change and a second wave

of Taiwanese investment in China is extending northwards from Guangdong and Fujian to the Yangtze Basin, the heartland of the Chinese economy. Taiwan's state-run China Steel and China Shipbuilding Corporation
is looking at setting up operations on the mainland.[86] In 1993, Shanghai
attracted more Taiwanese funds than Xiamen and Shenzhen with the Taiwanese making more substantial investments in technology and capital-
intensive enterprises such as precision machine tools, computers, car
parts, trucks, petrochemicals and heavy industrial plant.[87] Most of the
Taiwanese investment projects approved by the mainland authorities
now feature new production equipment.[88] The government, meanwhile,
is easing restrictions on Taiwanese investment in areas such as steel,
cement, glass and textile machinery. Sanfu Motors Industrial Co, for
example, is moving to establish a car manufacturing plant in Hunan
while Formosa Plastics is considering a US$6 billion petrochemical pro-
cessing complex in China's Yangtze River valley.[89] As many of the Taiwanese companies investing in China are medium and upstream manufacturers supplying small and medium enterprises (SMEs) in south
China with materials, components and spare parts, the upshot could be
the collective migration of entire sub-industries to China, as has happened with bicycles, umbrellas and shoes.[90]

The cumulative amount of investment in the mainland between 1981
and 1989 was estimated at around US$1 billion in 1000 projects. In 1990 it
was US$3 billion. In 1992, officially declared indirect investment in China
was estimated at US$9 billion — 20 per cent of all Taiwanese foreign
investment[91] — in over 10 000 to 15 000 enterprises.[92] However, the Mainland Affairs Council estimated the total capital outflow from Taiwan to
the mainland between October 1987 and December 1992 at around
US$19.4 billion.[93]

As with the figures for Taiwanese investment in Southeast Asia, the
real figure for Taiwanese investment in China is probably several times
greater when undeclared investments and reinvested profits are taken
into account.[94] Chinese tycoons from Taipei want their investment kept
secret, according to Zhang Zongxu, a vice-mayor of Xiamen.[95] Estimates
of the real amount of Taiwanese investment in the mainland since 1987
range between US$20 and US$50 billion. China also earned about
US$12–13 billion from expenditure by Taiwanese tourists in China.[96]
Remittances over the same period brought in a further amount estimated
at US$9–12 billion.[97]

When added together, this means that Taiwan was the source of
between US$40 and US$70 billion in foreign exchange flowing to China
over the period 1987–94. In a sense, therefore, while the mainland provided a life-raft for Taiwanese firms that might otherwise have gone
bankrupt, Taiwan helped rejuvenate post-Mao China: it provided huge
amounts of foreign exchange, a reassuring Chinese modernisation
model, management and marketing assistance and, increasingly, consumer technologies.

Trade

Since the Taiwanese industries relocating in China had to be serviced, Taiwan's trade with Hong Kong and the mainland grew dramatically in the 1980s (see Tables 8 and 9), repeating the pattern noted in the previous chapter of Taiwanese trade following investment in Southeast Asia. Taiwanese firms in China import, on average, 64 per cent of their raw materials and parts and 86 per cent of their production equipment and machinery from Taiwan.

Total trade between Taiwan and China was worth just US$321 million in 1980. Thereafter, as Taiwanese factories on the mainland started up, exports of Taiwanese materials, components and machinery to the mainland surged at an average annual growth rate of almost 70 per cent over the last decade while mainland exports to Taiwan have grown at a rate of more than 25 per cent per annum. By 1989, trade had risen tenfold to US$3.5 billion. By 1992 it had more than doubled again to US$7.4 billion. In 1993, it was officially about US$8.7 billion (Table 8) but, given that about 90 per cent of Taiwan's exports to Hong Kong are re-exported to China, it was actually at least US$14.7 billion (Table 9) and possibly more than that when trade through ports other than Hong Kong, such as Singapore and Guam, is taken into account.[98] In addition, there is a considerable volume of direct trade as most of the harbours on the Fujian coast are open to Taiwanese vessels.[99]

Hong Kong is important to Taiwan because trade with Hong Kong is essentially trade with the mainland. In 1992, Taiwan's trade with Hong Kong was worth US$17 billion with a balance in favour of Taiwan of $13.5 billion (see Table 9). Taiwan has had a surplus in its trade with Hong Kong in every year since 1954, with an accumulated surplus over the period of 1954–92 of around US$60 billion. In 1993, Taiwan's trade with Hong Kong rose by 35 per cent to US$23 billion, mainly because of Taiwan's trade with the mainland. Taiwanese make up the largest percentage of arrivals in Hong Kong (21.5 per cent in 1991), followed by Japan (20.9 per cent), Southeast Asia (16.8 per cent), Europe (13 per cent) and North America (13 per cent).[100]

Taiwanese goods sold to the mainland via Hong Kong include a wide range of consumer durables (electronic goods), artificial fibre materials (to the over 300 Taiwanese textile manufacturers operating factories on the mainland), semi-manufactured goods, chemical products, light industrial machinery, plastics, construction materials and electrical equipment. Taiwan imports mainland foodstuffs, medicines, minerals, agricultural products and raw materials for its textile factories.

With China emerging as Taiwan's fastest growing export market, Taiwan's top trade organisation CETRA (China External Trade Development Council) moved to consolidate the market by opening trade offices to promote Taiwanese products in 22 major mainland cities.

Taiwan's exports to the mainland as a ratio of total exports rose from

1.4 per cent in 1984 to 6.12 per cent in 1991, 7.72 per cent in 1992 and (using a method of calculation that takes account of the ultimate destination of Taiwanese exports to Hong Kong), 14.88 per cent in 1993.[101] On this basis, for 1992, China ranked as Taiwan's third largest export market after the United States (28.9 per cent) and Hong Kong (18.9 per cent), with Japan in third place (10.9 per cent). However, if Hong Kong and China are taken together as a Chinese economic entity — as will be the case after mid-1997 — then China is Taiwan's largest trading partner.

Taiwan and China are becoming more and more dependent on each other. China is an increasingly important export market for Taiwan, while Taiwan has become an important source of imports for mainland China. The ratio of Taiwan's commodity imports from the mainland to Taiwan's total commodity imports rose from 0.4 per cent in 1979, 0.5 per cent in 1984, 0.8 per cent in 1987, 1.3 per cent in 1990 and 1.67 per cent in 1991.[102] As a proportion of Taiwan's world trade, trade with China rose from 0.8 per cent in 1980 to 2.9 per cent in 1989, and 6 per cent in 1992. Meanwhile, the ratio of the mainland's commodity exports to Taiwan to the mainland's total exports increased from 0.43 per cent in 1980 to about 1.5 per cent in 1991 while the ratio of the mainland's imports from Taiwan to the mainland's total imports increased from 1.24 per cent in 1980 to almost 7 per cent in 1991.[103]

Both China and Taiwan are a little apprehensive about the implications of their growing interdependence. Taipei is concerned that it may become so dependent on the mainland that it will be vulnerable to pressure and manipulation from Beijing, as is the case in Hong Kong.[104] It also fears that Taiwanese technology and capital attracted by the mainland's 'candy and ants' policy will simply improve the latter's competitive edge in other products from Taiwan in the world market.[105] Beijing, for its part, is concerned about Taiwan's persistent trade surplus with the mainland. Total trade between 1980 and 1990 was US$15.8 billion, of which exports from the mainland were about 20 per cent and imports from Taiwan were 80 per cent, leaving China with a deficit in 1992 of US$12.9 billion and a cumulative deficit approaching US$30 billion by 1993 (although when tourism, remittances and investment are taken into account the balance may well be in China's favour). For its part, Beijing is also concerned about the impact on mainland socialism of 'sugar coated bullets' from Taiwan's bourgeois culture.

On the other hand, both sides have derived enormous economic benefit from the proliferation of cross-Strait exchanges, so much so that the incentive for transparency and confidence-building has begun to outweigh decades of distrust and the instinct to resist and confront. Both sides have found that they can work together in a constructive and pragmatic way to resolve issues relating to illegal immigration (over 10 000 were repatriated in 1988–90), hijacking, smuggling and other crimes, fishing disputes, customs matters, shipping, banking, investment guarantees, visas, marriages, death, copyright, dispute resolution and technology co-operation. Indeed, they have established a habit of dialogue through regular meetings between the ARATS and SEF in Singapore, Taipei, Beijing and Hong Kong.

Fundamentally, both sides have a growing interest in developing what has become a mutually profitable relationship. When Taiwan's exports to the rest of the world were growing at around 13 per cent, exports to China leapt by over 40 per cent per annum in the period 1981–91.[106] The mainland market supported strong growth in Taiwan's textile industry at a time when protectionist measures slowed growth in the United States and the EC and provided the largest market for Taiwanese machine tools. The China market has been equally important for Taiwan in the 1990s.[107] Meanwhile, investment from Taiwan, together with Hong Kong, has been perhaps the most significant factor behind China's export success in the 1980s.[108] As noted earlier, it is fuelling much of the extraordinary economic growth that is forecast to make China one of the world's largest economic powers by the year 2002.[109] For example, 200 million of the 500 million shoes exported to the United States from China in 1991 were manufactured in Taiwanese-owned mainland enterprises.[110] This practice has meant China often carries the blame for Taiwan when the United States complains about its trade deficit with China and, because Taiwan profits directly from Chinese exports to the United States, it favours an extension of United States Most Favoured Nation treatment for United States imports from China.

When China and Taiwan agreed to end their civil war — China in 1979, Taiwan in 1987 — they unleashed a natural synergy of economic and cultural forces.[111] This is driving them towards an economic interdependence and integration at a speed almost beyond the ability of either to control.[112] Taiwan and China are complementary economies subject to the law of comparative advantage once the barriers between them were removed. They are just 185 kilometres apart, they both need a peaceful environment and they share a Chinese vision of a greater China that combines the technology, capital, labour, resources, management skills and markets of the mainland, Taiwan and Hong Kong.[113]

Most Taiwanese businesses want direct contacts with China. Most have recouped their outlays, with one poll of 8000 Taiwanese investors showing that most (85 per cent) made a profit at a rate of 13 per cent, or twice what they were making in Taiwan.[114] In Fujian, profits were three times the rate that could be made in Taiwan, even though mainland labour is less efficient than that in Taiwan.[115]

Profits could be greater and time would be saved if there were direct links. For example, South Korean businesspeople can fly direct to Beijing and return to Seoul within a day, whereas it takes three times as long for the Taiwanese who must transit via Hong Kong. Similarly, the cost of transhipping a container to the mainland increased by US$300 because it went via Hong Kong, and since there were more than five million containers involved in Taiwan's China trade, the cost was over US$1.5 billion per annum.[116]

Many believe cross-Strait economic exchanges are 'an irreversible trend' and that the government's refusal to open up direct links is contrary to Taiwan's national economic interests. They argue that Taiwan should be exploiting its cultural and geographic advantages *vis-a-vis* the mainland at a time when other countries are scrambling to enter the market or take advantage of China's low-cost advanced technology.[117] Chao Yao-tung — a national policy adviser to President Lee Teng-hui — called for 'a great leap forward' in technical co-operation with the mainland so that the Chinese in Taiwan and China could compete more effectively with the Americans, the Japanese and the Europeans.[118] Proposals have been made for co-operation in aerospace, heavy-duty electrical engineering, bio-technology, photo-electricity, electronic information and other areas where the mainland has particular strengths.[119] In June 1992, scientists from China's Science Academy in the areas of genetics, laser chemistry, insulin and physics visited Taiwan as guests of the Academica Sinica, the first such exchange ever.[120] The first science and technology exchange seminar opened in Beijing in August 1992 to discuss co-operation in areas such as aviation, telecommunications, computers, nuclear engineering, biology, medicine, machinery and opto-electronics. Meanwhile, Taiwanese bans on imports of mainland Chinese technology have been eased and, to reduce reliance on Japan, Taiwanese companies have been allowed to hire mainland scientists and computer specialists and license mainland technologies in areas such as superconductivity, computers, lasers, biotechnology and high-definition television.[121] Taiwan's Industrial Technology Research Institute has set up an office in Beijing to promote technology co-operation between China and Taiwan.[122] There have been proposals for Taiwanese energy companies to join forces with mainland firms in joint ventures for offshore oil exploration and development in the East China Sea, the South China Sea, the Yellow Sea and the Gulf of Po Hai.[123] The Ministry of Economic Affairs plans to carry out a co-operative effort with Beijing over the next two to three years to explore mainland Chinese mineral deposits, including oil and coal. Taiwan's state-run Chinese Petroleum Corporation plans to look at onshore mainland wells such as Ta Ching and Sheng Li. Books about President Lee Teng-hui are on sale in Beijing.[124] In Taipei, Wego Chiang openly praised Deng Xiaoping and the practice of 'socialism with Chinese characteristics'.[125] In general, the government is cautiously positive. Taiwan's Economics Minister, Pin-Kung Chiang, for example, has foreshadowed the possibility of direct shipping links and closer co-operation to achieve a mutually profitable division of labour.[126]

These and other positive signals have contributed to an increasingly co-operative and uniquely Chinese-style relationship that is drawing Taiwan closer to the mainland and developing the first three stages in the Taiwanese plan for possible reunification:

First, exchanges and reciprocity to enhance understanding and eliminate hostility; solving disputes by peaceful means and move toward a phase of mutual trust and cooperation.

Second, in the medium term, develop mutual trust and cooperation, establish official communications on an equal footing, including direct postal, transport and commercial links, narrow the gap in living standards, work jointly in international organisations to assist each other and accept mutual visits by high ranking officials.

Third, in the long term, start a process of consultation organisation for unification, in which both sides (in accordance with the will of the people in both the mainland and Taiwan, and all the while adhering to the goals of democracy, economic freedom, social justice and nationalisation of the armed forces) jointly discuss the task of unification and map out a constitutional system to establish a democratic, free, equitable and prosperous China.[127]

Progress from one stage to the next would depend on a consensus being maintained in Taiwan, the renunciation of use of force against Taiwan by the mainland, the liberalisation of mainland politics and a change in China's policy towards Taiwan's international diplomacy.

In the meantime, Taiwan's economic integration with Hong Kong and China's southernmost provinces is proceeding apace, leading to the concept of a south China economic community[128] and for some, an even larger Chinese economic region.[129] This concept is built on the complementarity of:

(a) China's rich natural resources, plentiful cheap labour, huge potential in conducting basic research and large market;

(b) Hong Kong's speciality as a regional service centre with banking, finance, communications and technology standards of a world class and

(c) Taiwan's rich economy with a relatively sophisticated technological and industrial base.[130]

Exports from Taiwan, China and Hong Kong in 1992 were US$81.5 billion, US$80.5 billion and US$120 billion respectively, or a total of US$282 billion. This compares with Japanese exports in 1992 of US$340 billion and United States exports of US$448 billion. If China's 1992 trade of US$166 billion is added to Hong Kong's trade of US$240 billion and Taiwan's trade of US$153 billion, the total is US$559 billion, not far behind Japan's trade in 1992 of US$573 billion, but still well behind United States trade of US$1 trillion. The complementarities between the three Chinese economies are so favourable and their growth is so rapid that they could combine to become one of the largest and strongest trading blocs in the world.[131] Economics Minister Vincent Siew described the bloc as 'an industrial zone second to none'.[132] It could include Macao and, by incorporating the economic clout of the Chinese people further afield in Southeast Asia and the United States, it could constitute the world's fourth great economic bloc of 1.5 billion Chinese.[133]

The reintegration of Southeast China

There is a reintegration process underway that might be called the Tai-wanisation of China. The elements consist of the mainland, Taiwan, Hong Kong, Macao and the Chinese communities of Southeast China. But rather than China drawing Taiwan and Hong Kong inwards and reintegrating them with the mainland, Hong Kong and Taiwan, reinforced by the power of overseas Chinese communities in Southeast Asia, are pulling Guangdong, Fujian and coastal China into the mainstream of a prosperous East Asian economic community. Such a tendency has historical antecedents and is tacitly approved by the view of mainland officials that Taiwan is becoming a regional hub. It was reaffirmed by President Jiang Zemin in his reunification speech of 30 January 1995. Jiang said, *inter alia*, that China would enforce its laws protecting Taiwanese investments in the mainland. The mainland is now Taiwan's second largest export market after the United States, and Taiwan is the second largest source of mainland imports after Japan.

The prospect of a greater China has enhanced the interest of multinational corporations in Taiwan as a non-communist Chinese base, more secure than Hong Kong, that is located at the centre of the world's largest and fastest growing market. Multi-national corporations like Toyota, Renault, Ford, Vespa, IBM and NEC are seeking to entrench their positions in Taiwan both in their competition with each other and their scramble to tie up the China market. Nissan, for example, joined up with Yue Loong Motor Co and Renault joined up with Sanfu Motor Industrial Co to open production plants on the mainland.[134] In 1992, British Aerospace, McDonnell Douglas and other international aerospace corporations vied to establish a joint venture with Taiwan Aerospace to produce regional passenger jets, the main market for which is in China.[135] In some cases, mainland interests have joined the partnership, processing labour-intensive components such as gearboxes, engines and chassis with technology, capital and management from Taiwan and design by a European, Japanese or American partner. Taiwan's First International Computer Inc was joined by American Chinese and mainland Chinese interests to develop software with the United States side responsible for basic specifications, the mainland responsible for designing the program and Taiwan responsible for product testing, packaging and certification.[136]

New role

This vision of a greater China with Taiwan playing a pivotal role has a strong appeal for the Taiwanese. Since the mainland plus Hong Kong combination represents the locomotive of growth for Taiwan and, in many ways, is the key to its future, it is in the interest of the Taiwanese to work with, rather than to confront, mainland China. Such a policy defuses the only security threat faced by Taiwan and maximises economic gains in the world's fastest growing economy. Taiwan's mainland objectives thus eschew calls to overthrow the Chinese Communist Party. Taipei does not wish to see China disintegrate, as occurred after the collapse of the Communist Party of the Soviet Union in the former Soviet Union. Taiwan does not want the mainland thrown into turmoil, said Premier Hau Pei-tsun.[137] Nor would it 'sit back and wait for communism in China to collapse', in the words of President Lee Teng-hui.[138] Instead, Taiwan should do its best to seek a way out for China.[139] The Kuomintang's preferred option is to maintain the central authority of Beijing (i.e. the Chinese Communist Party). It has taken care to avoid challenging Beijing or creating unnecessary tension. Taipei, for example, refused to support the activities of the radio-broadcast ship *Goddess of Democracy* in May 1990.[140] It gave only modest publicity to the breakthrough in Taiwan's relations with the ASEAN states following Premier Lien Chan's visit to Singapore and Malaysia in January and that of President Lee Teng-hui to Indonesia, the Philippines and Thailand in February 1994. Mainland aircraft hijackers are not, as they once were, encouraged with monetary rewards, but are instead liable to the death penalty and are usually gaoled for up to ten years or more.[140]

Taipei has also consistently stressed a commitment to one China. President Lee Teng-hui said reunification was his ultimate goal 'at the earliest possible opportunity'.[141] However, it would not take place at the expense of 'the welfare of the entire Chinese people, nor will I sacrifice the security of the people in the Taiwan area'.[142] Previously, Taiwan had insisted that there would be no contact, no compromise and no negotiations with Beijing until it gave up its four cardinal principals (that is, adherence to the socialist road, the dictatorship of the proletariat, leadership by the Communist Party, and the key role of Marxist–Leninist–Mao Zedong ideology). In February 1995, after PRC President Jiang Zemin proposed to end the hostile standoff between the two sides, Taiwan's Premier Lien Chan said cross-Strait relations had entered an 'era of consultations'. He said Taipei was willing to increase exchanges and pursue unification, provided the mainland respected the fact that Taiwan and China were two equal political entities.[143] Then Taipei would be willing on the basis of equality to establish channels of communications with Beijing and open up academic, cultural, economic, trade, scientific and technological exchanges across the Taiwan Strait). Subsequently, when the gap in living standards between the mainland and Taiwan has been narrowed, Taipei would discuss reunification on the basis of two equal governments. Meanwhile, the policy is one of peaceful coexistence while working to bring about gradual and peaceful change in the mainland through trade, investment, tourism and other people-to-people exchanges, and aid offers of up to US$20 billion for infrastructure development.[144] Taiwan did not expect 'any magic or instant solution', said Lee Teng-hui.[145] In fact, it was preferable — 'prudent and responsible' — to advocate a gradual step-by-step approach to reunification based on the building up of 'mutual understanding, trust and goodwill'.[146] Lee said that, at the current stage, he was opposed to 'radical independence' and he was also against 'hasty reunification' or 'neo-isolationism'.[147] The influential former Premier and Defence Minister, Hau Pei-tsun, holds similar views.[148]

Reunification, nonetheless, is regarded by many, certainly in the Kuomintang, as an historical mission for which Taiwan had a Confucian-like moral responsibility, and those who advocated independence reflected a short-sighted and selfish attitude.[149] However, the Taiwanese goal 'to save China' has only become possible because of Taiwan's past.

As we saw in previous chapters, Taiwan's separation from China over the last century enabled it to thoroughly absorb foreign technology, an international trading culture and capitalist values. It was exposed to five decades of Japanese training, infrastructural development and preferential market access. This was followed by three decades of close association with the United States, the world's leading great power. Taiwan was given American aid, support, training, protection and preferential market access. Taiwan's Chinese values and the cumulative effects of its association with two of the great powers in the Asia-Pacific made Taiwan rich, successful and confident. These qualities meant Taiwan was well endowed to become the catalyst for change on the mainland once Deng Xiaoping resumed 'the capitalist road' in 1978.

Until then, Taiwan was technically at war with the mainland and the two sides were cut off from each other. Contact with the other side was considered an act of sedition. Limited contacts in the early 1980s became a flood after the ban was lifted in 1987. In its guise as a modernising agent, the government is trying to turn Taiwan into a regional operation centre and launching pad for investment and trade in China. Taiwan, in a sense, has resumed its old role of being an unsinkable aircraft carrier. This time, however, it is launching the virus of political, social and economic change in China. The Taiwanese, through Hong Kong, are best-placed for such intermediary operations because of their physical location in central East Asia, their wealth, their global networks and the fact that they have the same cultural heritage and language as the mainlanders. The Taiwanese — at least the Kuomintang — have also had the historical experience of co-operation with the CCP. In fact, it once ruled the mainland, and has a deep knowledge and understanding of the mainland, of Chinese culture, of communism and of the desires of ordinary Chinese.

The same logic applies to China and its views of Taiwan. China needs Taiwan. It needs peace in East Asia and it appreciates the gains that can be made by co-operating with rather than trying to isolate and corner Taiwan

in the international arena — hence China's willingness to give concessional bank loans and preferential tax treatment to Taiwanese investors
and its generally pragmatic approach to Taiwanese membership of
international economic organisations such as PECC (1986), APEC (1990)
and prospectively the GATT. China has been fairly relaxed about Taiwanese purchases of arms from France and the United States and China
did not suspend relations with Latvia in 1992 when Taiwan set up an
office in Riga using the name 'Republic of China'. These trends are
regarded in Taipei as indications that Beijing is becoming more tolerant of
Taipei's economic diplomacy.[150] As Premier Li Peng declared at the
National People's Congress in March 1992, China would strongly object to
Taiwan's policies of 'flexible diplomacy, dual recognition, two Chinas, one
China and one Taiwan or one China two governments', but it was 'not
against Taiwan developing economic and trade relations with other coun-
tries'.[151]

Conclusion

Rapprochement between the two Chinas has several important consequences.[152] One is that the linkages between Taiwan and Japan and
between Taiwan and the United States that had been built up over the
previous nine decades are now complemented by cross-Strait linkages
between Taiwan and China. As a result Taiwan, for the first time in its
history, is able to simultaneously trade, co-operate and manipulate its
relations with and between the three dominant powers in a tripolar Asia-
Pacific region (see Figure 3). This has enabled Taiwan to maximise its
diplomatic, economic and strategic influence generally and with regard
to mainland China in particular. This in turn has led to opportunities for
Taiwan to influence the pace and direction of reform in post-Mao China
and to position itself at the centre of an emerging greater Chinese economic community.

Opening up bi-coastal contacts with the mainland has served a broad
range of strategic, economic and political needs of Taiwan: it has reassured Beijing on reunification and shifted the focus of the relationship
from military confrontation to economic co-operation. It has postponed
the day of reckoning for Taiwan's old industries. It has opened up lucrative new market and investment opportunities for Taiwan. It has given
Taiwan new opportunities to become part of a greater China and to shape
the destiny of the mainland and Hong Kong. It has given Taiwan a bigger
voice in the world. And it has innoculated people in Taiwan against
reunification. The opening to the mainland is supported by a majority in
Taiwan, including business, public opinion and the opposition DPP.

But while trading with China has unleashed forces of integration and
defused the mainland threat, it has also allowed the Taiwanese scope to
build the basis for a bid to become a separate political entity within the con-

cept of one China.[153] This bid is based on an insurance policy that comprises Taiwan's links with Japan and the United States, the two dominant powers in the Asia-Pacific, Taiwan's membership in the broader Asia-Pacific economic community and, as a last resort, Taiwan's strong military capabilities.

Notes

1   See Wang Gungwu, 'Greater China and the Chinese Overseas', *China Quarterly*, no. 136, December 1993, p. 926.

2   Advertisement, *The Australian*, 25 March 1992.

3   Chiang Kaishek died in 1975; Mao Zedong died in 1976.

4   *South China Morning Post (SCMP)*, 9 September 1989.

5   *Free China Journal (FCJ)*, 18 September 1992.

6   Taiwanese Economics Minister, Vincent Siew, quoted in *FCJ*, 9 July 1990.

7   Quoted in *China Post (CP)*, 30 March 1992.

8   The environmental lobby in Taiwan was one of the main reasons why Formosa Plastics planned to invest US$7 billion in a petrochemical complex in Fujian province.

9   Ye Jianying, Chairman of the National People's Congress, in *Beijing Review*, no. 40, 5 October 1981, pp. 10–11.

10 Quoted in *CP*, 6 July 1993.

11 ibid.

12 *SCMP*, 21, 22, 30 October 1990; and *Far Eastern Economic Review (FEER)*, 5 May 1988. See also Chong-Pin Lin, 'The Role of the People's Liberation Army in the Process of Reunification: Exploring the Possibilities', in Richard Yang (ed.), *China's Military: the PLA in 1993*, Chinese Council for Advanced Policy Studies, Taipei, 1993, pp. 161, 163.

13 Taipei and Beijing have a common concern about Japan's revival as a great power: 'We hate to get Japan involved,' said a Taiwanese spokesman after China and Taiwan formed an alliance to oppose including Japan in talks aimed at settling conflicting claims to islands and adjacent seas in the South China Sea: *SCMP*, 18 July 1991; *CP*, 19 July 1991.

14 Lee Teng-hui, 'China Can Learn From Our Success', *Asian Wall Street Journal (AWSJ)*, 24 November 1989.

15 President Lee Teng-hui, 1992 National Day speech, in *CP*, 10 October 1992.

16 Sha Zukang, Deputy Director, Department of International Organisations, Ministry of Foreign Affairs, Beijing, personal communication, March 1994.

17 At a 1990 meeting of Taiwan's Commercial and Industrial Co-ordination Society of the Two Sides of the Strait and the mainland's Eco-

nomic and Trade Coordination Committee of the Two Sides of the Strait, 600 delegates from 23 mainland provinces met 650 Taiwanese investors and put forward proposals for 1400 investment projects worth around US$20 billion: *China Daily*, 4 July 1990.

18 In September 1979, Chinese Vice Premier Yu Qiuli reported that, whereas economic conditions in China and Taiwan had been similar in 1950, 30 years later, China was in economic crisis while the situation in Taiwan was just the opposite: quoted in Ramon Myers, 'Transferring the Republic of China's Modernisation Experience to the People's Republic of China', in Gary Klintworth (ed.), *Taiwan in the Asia-Pacific in the 1990s*, Allen & Unwin/Department of International Relations, ANU, Canberra, 1994, pp. 169, 180.

19 Robert Delfs, 'Little Dragon Model', *FEER*, 9 March 1989, p. 12.

20 See World Bank, *China: Long Term Issues and Options, Annex B, Agriculture to the Year 2000*, Report No 5206-CHA, 22 May 1985, and Robert F. Ash, 'The Evolution of Agricultural Policy', *China Quarterly*, December 1988, no. 116, p. 529.

21 *Guide to Foreign Investment in Quanzhou*, Fujian, April 1990. The Taiwanese are given preferential treatment in the form of tax holidays; exemptions from customs duties; the right to automatically sell locally up to 30 per cent of what they produce; and lower land leasehold rates for longer periods than other foreign investors. According to Philip Liu, 'Investment Slowdown', *Free China Review (FCR)*, January 1991, pp. 46, 48, a Taiwanese investor is given a three-year tax holiday on his or her business income, and then pays 7 per cent for years 4 to 6, and 10 per cent thereafter if the business is in exports, and 15 per cent for others. This is a substantial incentive in view of taxes averaging 25 per cent in Taiwan and 55 per cent for non-Chinese businesses in the mainland.

22 President Chiang Ching-kuo, address, 'China's Reunification and World Peace', at the opening of the Third Plenary of the Twelfth Central Committee of the Kuomintang, 29 March 1986, Taipei.

23 Quoted in *SCMP*, 12 June 1991.

24 See Alfred G. Meyer, 'Theories of Convergence', in Chalmers Johnson (ed.), *Change in Communist Systems*, Stanford University Press, Stanford, 1970, p. 313.

25 See for example, Samuel C. Chu, 'The Three Principles of the People and Political Developments: Thoughts on Democracy in the Republic of China and the People's Republic of China', in Chang King-yuh (ed.), *The Impact of the Three Principles of the People on China*, Institute of International Relations, National Chengchi University, Taipei, 1988, pp. 1, 17.

26 Lee Teng-hui, 'China Can Learn From Our Success', in *AWSJ*, 24 November 1989.

27 *China News Agency (CNA)*, (Taipei), 16 March 1992.

28 Richard Lowenthal, 'Development vs Utopia in Communist Policy' in Johnson, *Change in Communist Systems*, pp. 33, 69.

29 For an analysis of Beijing's evolving approach to Taiwan, see Qing-guo Jia, 'Changing Relations Across the Taiwan Strait', *Asian Survey*, vol. XXXII, no. 3, March 1992, p. 277.

30 No leader, whether in Beijing or Taipei, would risk being called a traitor to China by renouncing China's claims to Taiwan or calling for its independence: Chen Qimao, 'The Taiwan Issue and Sino-US Relations', *Asian Survey*, vol. XXVII, no. 11, November 1987, pp. 1161, 1168. Beijing has always maintained that it has the right to use of force to recover Taiwan, 'a piece of treasured Chinese territory from ancient times': Li Jiaquan, 'Taiwan Independence a Blind Alley', *Beijing Review*, 8–14 June 1992, p. 20. Taiwan's ruling Kuomintang holds similar views, with former Defence Minister, General Hau Pei-tsun threatening that the Taiwanese armed forces would not defend Taiwan if the mainland attacked the island in response to a Taiwanese bid for independence: quoted in the *FCJ*, 25 December 1989.

31 *Foreign Affairs Report*, Foreign Relations and Diplomatic Administration, Republic of China Foreign Ministry, Taipei, excerpted in *FCJ*, 9 April 1993.

32 For a useful overview of China's detente policy towards Taiwan, see Chong-Pin Lin, 'Beijing and Taipei: Dialectics in Post-Tiananmen Interactions', *The China Quarterly*, no. 136, 1993, pp. 770ff.

33 *Beijing Review*, 13–19 August 1990.

34 See Chien-min Chao, 'China's Policy Towards Taiwan', *Pacific Review*, vol. 3, no. 2, 1990, p. 125; and John Quansheng Zhao, '"One Country, Two Systems" and "One Country, Two Parties": PRC-Taiwan Unification and its Political Implications', *Pacific Review*, vol. 2, no. 4, 1989, p. 312.

35 Announced by Ye Jianying, Chairman of the National People's Congress, in *Beijing Review*, no. 40, 5 October 1981, pp. 10–11.

36 ibid.; reaffirmed in 'The Taiwan Question and Reunification of China', Taiwan Affairs & Information Office, State Council, People Republic of China, Beijing, August 1993, in Documents, *Beijing Review*, 6–12 September 1993.

37 Wen Qing, 'One Country, Two Systems', *Beijing Review*, 13–19 August 1990. Deng went so far as to suggest that Taiwan would be allowed to keep its socio-economic system unchanged for as long as 1000 years: quoted in the *New York Times*, 11 January 1979.

38 *CP*, 23 May 1990.

39 There have been reports (*CP*, vol. 28, 30 June 1992) of Beijing proposing a ceasefire pact with Taipei, which, if it ever eventuated, would signal Beijing's acceptance of the end of the civil war.

40 Qin Huasun, 'An approach to confidence-building in the Asia-Pacific region', in *Confidence-building Measures in the Asia-Pacific Region, Disarmament*, Topical Papers 6, United Nations, New York, 1991, p. 78. Qin, Director, Department of International Organisations and Conferences, Ministry of Foreign Affairs, Beijing, proposed *inter alia* non-

interference in the internal affairs of other countries, the development of mutually beneficial economic relations, the peaceful settlement of disputes and the promotion of exchanges and information flows.

41 *FCJ*, 17 January 1992.

42 Jiang Zemin's Reunification Speech', *Foreign Broadcast Information Service (FBIS)* — *China*, 30 January 1995, p. 84.

43 Editorial, *FCJ*, 25 February 1992.

44 While Taipei agrees that the possibility of the mainland using force to invade Taiwan in the near future is remote, it had to be 'alert at all times': *A Study of a Possible Communist Attack on Taiwan*, Government Information Office, Taipei, 1991, p. 12.

45 Guocang Huan, 'Taipei–Beijing Relations', *World Policy Journal*, Summer 1992, pp. 563, 564.

46 Secretary-General of the Kuomintang, James Soong, *CNA*, 16 March 1992.

47 Lee Teng-hui, 'China Can Learn From Our Success', *AWSJ*, 24 November 1989.

48 Quoted in *CP*, 21 May 1992.

49 Chalmers Johnson, 'Comparing Communist Nations', in Johnson, *Change in Communist Systems*, pp. 7, 23–26. See also Lowenthal, 'Development vs Utopia in Communist Policy' in Johnson, ibid., pp. 33, 111.

50 See C.L. Chiou, 'Democratising Taiwan: The 1990 National Affairs Conference', in Gary Klintworth (ed.), *Modern Taiwan in the 1990s*, Canberra Papers on Strategy and Defence No. 75, Strategic and Defence Studies Centre, ANU, Canberra, 1991, p. 39; and C.L. Chiou, 'Emerging Taiwanese Identity in the 1990s: Crisis and Transformation', in Klintworth, *Taiwan in the Asia-Pacific in the 1990s*, p. 21.

51 Second Plenary Session of the KMT Central Committee, June 1989: *FCJ*, 16 April 1990; and *FCJ*, 22 February 1990.

52 According to Beijing, while it was a decision that should have been made a long time ago, it was better late than never: *People's Daily*, 11 May 1991.

53 Quoted in *CP*, 23 November 1993.

54 Ministry of Foreign Affairs, ROC, Taipei, Press Release, 22 November 1993.

55 For summaries of Taiwan's opening to China, see the chapter on Mainland China and Hong Kong Affairs in the *Republic of China Yearbook 1990–91*, Government Information Office, Taipei, 1991. Also useful are Lu Yali, 'Current State and Future Prospects of ROC-PRC Relations', *China News Analysis*, 15 January 1990, no. 1402; and Ralph N. Clough, *Reaching Across the Taiwan Strait*, Westview Press, Boulder, Col., 1993.

56 The name of this body raises an ambiguity about Taiwan's status: reunification presupposes a rejoining of two parts that were once part of an original entity, whereas this meaning is absent in the term unification.

57 *Guidelines for National Unification*, Reference Paper, RR-91-02, Taipei, 5 March 1991.

58 *CP*, 30 April 1993.

59 Quoted in *CP*, 23 April 1993.

60 Edgar Snow, *The Other Side of the River*, Random House, New York, 1962, p. 353.

61 Bruce Russett, 'Politics and Alternative Security: Towards a More Democratic, Therefore More Peaceful World', in Burns H. Weston (ed.), *Alternative Security Living Without Nuclear Deterrence*, Westview Press, Boulder, Col., 1990, pp. 107, 129.

62 Or so it was claimed by the *CP*, 30 March 1993.

63 Quoted in *CP*, 23 March 1993.

64 Quoted in *CP*, 30 December 1993.

65 *FCJ*, 15 April 1994.

66 Mainland Affairs Council, *Public Opinion and the Mainland Policy*, June 1991.

67 Xinhua, Beijing, 15 February, in *FBIS — China*, 19 February 1993, p. 61. See also Fredrick F Chien, 'A View from Taipei', *Foreign Affairs*, vol. 70, no. 5, Winter 1991/92, pp. 93, 100.

69 Myers, 'Transferring the Republic of China's Modernisation Experience', in Klintworth, *Taiwan in the Asia-Pacific in the 1990s*, p. 177. See also Thomas B. Gold, 'Go With Your Feelings: Hong Kong and Taiwan Popular Culture in Greater China', *China Quarterly*, no. 136, December 1993, p. 907.

70 ibid., pp. 908–9.

71 Myers, 'Transferring the Republic of China's Modernisation Experience', in Klintworth, *Taiwan in the Asia-Pacific in the 1990s*, p. 193.

71 ibid., p. 194.

72 Survey of mainland students in Shaomin Li, 'What China Can Learn From Taiwan', *Orbis*, 1989, pp. 327, 333.

73 Yu Tzong-shian, 'The Two Sides of the Taiwan Straits: Economic Interdependence and Cooperation', paper presented to the International Conference on Trade, Investment and Economic Prospects in Mainland China, Hong Kong and Taiwan, Melbourne, 24 February 1992.

74 *CNA*, 28 February 1994, in *FBIS — China*, 2 March 1994, p. 62.

75 *CP*, 27 April 1992.

76 Edward Chen was speaking at the ANU's 1994 Asia-Pacific Insight Conference, reported in *The Australian*, 19 April 1994.

77 Quoted in *CP*, 8 July 1992.

78 *SCMP*, 22 February 1991; and *FCR*, February 1993 p. 30.

79 Taiwan nonetheless still controls around 75 per cent of the international umbrella market: *CP*, 30 September 1993.

80 *SCMP*, 30 May 1992.

81 *CP*, 27 April 1992.

82 ibid.

83 Li Fei, 'A Look at the Adaptability of Taiwanese Business Investment to the Prevailing Mainland System', *Taiwan Research Quarterly*, Xiamen, Feb/Mar 1990, p. 1 and Yu, 'The Two Sides of the Taiwan Straits: Economic Interdependence and Cooperation', conference paper, Melbourne, Table 3, p. 12-1.

84 Li Fei, 'A Look at the Adaptability of Taiwanese Business Investment to the Prevailing Mainland System'; see also Qi Luo and Christopher Howe, 'The Case of Taiwanese Investment in Xiamen', *China Quarterly*, no. 136, December 1993, p. 746.

85 Li Fei, 'A Look at the Adaptability of Taiwanese Business Investment to the Prevailing Mainland System'.

86 *CP*, 26, 30 March 1993.

87 *FCR*, June 1990, p. 61.

88 ibid.

89 *FCR*, June 1993 p. 47.

90 Ricky Tung, 'Taiwan and Southern China's Fujian and Guangdong Provinces', in Klintworth, *Taiwan in the Asia-Pacific in the 1990s*, p. 154.

91 *CP*, 27 April 1992.

92 Philip Liu, 'Mixed Diagnosis for Mainland Fever', *FCR*, September 1993, p. 42; *FCJ*, 15 April 1994; and *CNA*, 13 December 1993.

93 *CP*, 27 March 1993.

94 *SCMP*, 9 February 1990. See also Byron Weng, 'Taiwan's Mainland Policy Before and After June 4', in George Hicks (ed.), *The Broken Mirror: China After Tiananmen*, Longman, Essex (UK), 1990, pp. 257, 269; and Xinhua, Beijing, 4 January 1993, in *FBIS-China*, 19 January 1993, p. 70 and Office of Taiwan Affairs, Beijing, 5 February 1993, in *FBIS-China*, 9 February 1993, p. 9.

95 *AWSJ*, 4 June 1992.

96 Calculated at the rate of 6.7 million tourists spending $2000 per person. The figure of US$2000 was given in the *CP*, 27 March 1993.

97 Yu, 'The Two Sides of the Taiwan Straits: Economic Interdependence and Cooperation', conference paper, Melbourne. The Mainland Affairs Council gave a figure of about US$7 billion for remittances over the period 1987 to mid-1992: reported in *Sinorama*, September 1992, p. 21. A Japanese report said Taiwanese remittances to Hong Kong totalled US$15 billion in 1991 alone.

98 Philip Liu, 'Investment Slowdown', *FCR*, January 1991, pp. 46, 48.

99 Sueo Kojima, 'Economic Relations between China and Taiwan Enter a New Phase', Japan External Trade Organisation, *China Newsletter*, no. 76, October 1988, pp. 2, 7.

100 *SCMP*, 30 May 1992.

101 *FCJ*, 25 March 1994.

102 Yu, 'The Two Sides of the Taiwan Straits: Economic Interdependence and Cooperation', conference paper, Melbourne, Table 2, p. 11-1.

103 ibid.

104 Lin Bih-jaw, Director of the Institute of International Relations, quoted by Philip Liu, 'Mixed Diagnosis for Mainland Fever', *FCR*, September 1993, pp. 42, 44.

105 Premier Hau Pei-tsun, quoted in *CNA*, 11 March 1992.

106 Yu, 'The Two Sides of the Taiwan Strait: Economic Interdependence and Cooperation', conference paper, Melbourne.

107 Taiwan's Economics Minister, Pin-Kung Chiang, quoted in *CP*, 31 December 1993.

108 Yun-Wing Sung, 'The Re-integration of Southeast China', paper for the Conference on China's Reforms and Economic Growth, Australian National University, 11–14 November 1991. See also Yun-Wing Sung, *The China-Hong Kong Connection: The Key to China's Open-Door Policy*, Cambridge University Press, Hong Kong, 1991.

109 *FCJ*, 18 September 1992; FCR, February 1993, p. 30.

110 For an early prognosis, see Kojima, 'Economic Relations Between China and Taiwan Enter a New Phase'.

111 The result is a good example of what Keohane and Nye call the process of 'complex interdependence': Robert O. Keohane and Joseph S. Nye, *Power and Interdependence, World Politics in Transition*, Little, Brown and Company, Boston, 1977.

112 For a comprehensive analysis and discussion of a 'Greater China', see the *China Quarterly*, no. 136, December 1993, and in particular, Harry Harding, 'The Concept of Greater China: Themes, Variations and Reservations', pp. 660ff.

113 *CP*, 10 April 1992.

114 *SCMP*, 6 September 1989.

115 DPP legislator, Chen Shui-bian, reported in the *China Times*, 6 March 1992.

116 Yeh Wan-an, former Vice-Chairman of the Council for Economic Planning and Development and Wang Yu-yun, Chairman of Hua Eng Wire and Cable, quoted in Philip Liu, 'Mixed Diagnosis for Mainland Fever', *FCR*, September 1993, pp. 42, 47.

117 Quoted in *CP*, 19 May 1992.

118 *FCJ*, 20 March 1992. See also Xu Xinpeng, 'Taiwan's Economic Cooperation with Fujian and Guangdong the View from China', in Klintworth, *Taiwan in the Asia-Pacific in the 1990s*, pp. 142, 148.

119 *CNA*, 10 June 1992.

120 From *CP*, 8 April 1992 and 3 August 1993; *AWSJ*, 4 June 1992.

121 *CP*, 5 October 1993.

122 *CP*, 5 August 1993.

123   Chou Yu-kou, *A Thousand Days of Lee Teng-hui*, Xinhua, Beijing, 1993.

124   *CP*, 14 October 1993.

125   *CP*, 31 December 1993.

126   Taken from 'Bridges', *FCR*, July 1992, p. 53.

127   See, for example, *Southern China in Transition*, East Asia Analytical Unit, Department of Foreign Affairs and Trade, Canberra, 1992.

128   Also known as a CCM (Chinese Common Market); a CFTA (Chinese Free Trade Area); a Chinese Commonwealth; and a CEC (Chinese Economic Community). For a discussion of the prospect for a GCEA or 'Greater Chinese Economic Area' see Ricky Tung, 'Taiwan and Southern China's Fujian and Guangdong Provinces' in Klintworth, *Taiwan in the Asia-Pacific in the 1990s*.

129   Edward K.Y. Chen, 'The Hong Kong Economy in a Changing International Economic Environment', in Manfred Kulessa (ed.), *The Newly Industrialising Economies of Asia — Prospects for Cooperation*, Springer-Verlag, Berlin 1990, p. 105.

130   A view common to both sides: Minister for Economic Affairs, Vincent Siew, quoted by CNA, 6 November 1991; Fang Sheng, 'Economic Cooperation Between Mainland Taiwan and Hong Kong', *Beijing Review*, 25 November–1 December 1991, p. 24.

131   Quoted in *CP*, 9 April 1992.

132   ibid.

133   *FCJ*, 14 April 1992.

134   *CP*, 24 July 1993.

135   *CP*, 2 May 1992.

136   *CNA*, 28 February 1992.

137   *CNA*, 13 January 1992.

138   ibid.

139   *FEER*, 24 May 1990, p. 13.

140   *CNA*, 1 August 1993 and 23 October 1993.

141   *SCMP*, 19 May 1991.

142   ibid.

143   'Lien Chan says Mainland Links in "Era of Consultations"', *FCJ*, 24 February, 1995.

144   Three particular projects were mentioned: at Pudong near Shanghai; the Tumen River project in the Russian–Korean–Chinese tri-border area; and the Three Gorges project on the Yangtze River: *CNA*, 13 May 1992.

145   *SCMP*, 19 May 1991.

146   ibid.

147   *CNA*, 24 July, 28 November 1992.

148   Hau said while he was diametrically opposed to secessionist independence by the Taiwanese independence movement, he believed

Taiwan 'should not rush towards reunification' either: interview, *World Statesman* in *CNA*, 17 February 1993.

149 Editorial, *CP*, 2 September 1991.

150 *FCJ*, 14, 17, 21, 24 April 1992; Wu Xingdu, 'Taiwan dui dalu touzi de fenzi (Analysis of Taiwan's Investment in the mainland)', *Guoji Maoyi*, May 1991, p. 14; and Jia, 'Changing Relations Across the Taiwan Strait'.

151 Reported in *CP*, 21 March 1992.

152 See Lin, 'Beijing and Taipei: Interactions in the Post-Tiananmen Period', *China Quarterly*, p. 770.

153 In its 1993 Report on Foreign Affairs, Taiwan's Foreign Ministry declared that 'our government announced the end of the Period of Communist Rebellion [in May 1991] and regarded the Chinese Communist Party as a political entity. This shows that we have frankly accepted the fact of national separation. We hold that there is only one sovereign China. Prior to the realisation of national reunification, the ROC government and the Chinese Communist regime will coexist and each will rule the areas under their effective jurisdiction. Based on this viewpoint, both sides of the strait have the right to represent the Chinese people in their effective jurisdiction, to take part in various activities within the international community and to mutually respect one another's position in the international community': quoted in *FBIS-China*, 8 February 1993, p. 72.

8 The Survival of a Small State

T aiwan's rapid development as a small East Asian state followed a century of uniquely sequenced historical, geographic, social, economic and strategic factors. Successful development, however, always depended on one critical factor — the ability of Taiwan to keep itself or be kept at arm's length from the mainland. This independence in development stemmed in part from the fact that there was a sea barrier separating Taiwan from the mainland, and in part from the intervention of external powers — first Japan until 1945 and then the United States. China was deterred from attacking Taiwan in the 1950s, 1960s and 1970s by the United States commitment to defend the island. After the United States normalised relations with Beijing in 1979, the PLA may have planned to attack or at least use some form of military pressure against Taiwan. However, it was kept in check by the need to preserve a united front with the United States *vis-a-vis* the Soviet threat and the fact that, although the United States defence treaty with Taiwan had been abrogated in 1979, it had been replaced by similar commitments contained in the 1982 *Taiwan Relations Act*. For the Kuomintang, nonetheless, the period between the late 1970s and early 1980s was perhaps the most difficult in its postwar existence. Diplomatically, it had never been more isolated, while strategically it looked exposed and vulnerable to military and/or political pressure from the mainland. The United States, preoccupied with the Soviet challenge, was unwilling to alienate China for the sake of Taiwan. It refused to supply Taiwan with a new fighter aircraft and in 1982, President Reagan issued a communiqué stating that the United States:

> does not seek to carry out a long-term policy of arms sales to Taiwan, that its arms sales to Taiwan will not exceed, either in qual-

itative or in quantitative terms, the level of those supplied in recent years . . . and that it intends to gradually reduce its sales of arms to Taiwan, leading over a period of time to a final resolution.[1]

Taiwan turned to defence self-reliance. It built up its defence industries and sought to buy weapons systems such as submarines, frigates and fighter aircraft from European suppliers. Taiwan began to develop its own new fighter aircraft, a new main battle tank, powerful anti-ship and anti-aircraft missile systems, an integrated air defence system and phased surveillance and fire control radars. Its naval dockyards converted old World War II vintage destroyers into relatively modern warships equipped with anti-ship and ASW missiles, ASW sensors, ECM, CIWS and other anti-missile defences, five-inch guns and new propulsion systems.[2] The result was a significant improvement in Taiwan's indigenously produced weapons and defence equipment. At present, the mainland is being held at arm's length by Taiwan's strong defence capabilities and the emergence of an international coalition of interests that tacitly supports the preservation of Taiwan's independent status (see the next chapter). One consequence has been that China's reunification efforts have been consistently channelled towards what is fast becoming the only practical option — that is, peaceful integration by economic means.

Rather than Beijing being in a position to dictate the terms of a Taiwanese surrender, Taipei seeks to be in a position where it can negotiate reunification with Beijing as an equal, and yet fend off reunification pending the transformation of Chinese communism. In the next few years, Hong Kong will be returned to China, the succession to Deng Xiaoping will be decided and China's future direction will be determined after two decades of retreat from Maoism. The next five to ten years, therefore, will present Taiwan with its window of opportunity for the recovery of the mainland. However, while the Taiwanese — and indeed many on the mainland — are optimistic about the future of a reformed China and possible reunification, Taiwan has been careful to ensure that it can continue to keep China at arm's length pending an end to communism in the mainland. Taiwan's China strategy rests on the following elements:

1 a policy of constructive engagement with the mainland;
2 frequent and public reassurances to China;
3 a defence capability that is strong enough to deter; and
4 a strengthening in support for Taiwan from the United States and Japan, from the Asia-Pacific community and, ultimately, from organisations like the United Nations.

Taiwan's policy of conflict avoidance through constructive engagement was discussed in the previous chapter. The mainland reciprocated over the last decade with its own conciliatory policy approach towards Taiwan. The two sides have now progressed to the point where they hold almost routine talks on a broad range of bilateral issues including economic, cultural, legal, nuclear, environmental, fisheries, customs, academic and trade matters. Each side has become increasingly important to the other in terms of trade, investment and economic strategies for the future. At the same time, China's reform policies have created a social and economic system that has become much less objectionable to Taiwan.

This chapter will focus on Taiwan's conflict avoidance through a strategy that combines reassurance with deterrence based on a credible military capability and a readiness to staunchly resist any attack.

A policy that reassures and deters is a more sophisticated approach to conflict management than relying on simple deterrence or military guarantees from a large and powerful friend.[3] It is a particularly important survival strategy from small states facing a threat by larger, more powerful states.[4] Such reassurance contributes to conflict avoidance, especially when combined with a credible deterrent capability.[5] Deterrence is sometimes defined as 'a state of mind brought about by the existence of a credible threat of unacceptable counter action'.[6] But because it depends on 'a state of mind' and subjective judgments about the ability of one's opponent to strike back, deterrence is prone to misperception and misjudgment. By reassuring China on sensitive issues such as challenging Beijing's legitimacy, declaring Taiwan's independence and possessing nuclear weapons — matters which Beijing has frequently warned could trigger its use of force — Taiwan has minimised the likelihood of a mainland invasion.

Taiwan's first use of reassurance policy was to stop threatening to retake the mainland by force. President Chiang Kai-shek was still espousing the use of force against the mainland in 1967 when he told the Australian Prime Minister, Harold Holt, that Taiwan had a duty to attack and occupy bases in the mainland so as to rally support for the overthrow of communism.[7] But residual Kuomintang aspirations to recover the mainland dissipated with Chiang's death in 1975. The transition to recognition of the CCP's legitimacy and authority on the mainland started in the early 1970s. Chiang's son, Chiang Ching-kuo (premier from 1972 and president from 1978), implemented a program of Taiwanisation that led, after a tempestuous decade, to Lee Teng-hui becoming vice-president in 1984 and ultimately president in 1988. Apart from the domestic political significance of this move, it was an important signal to the Chinese Communist Party because it indicated the end of Taipei's challenge to Beijing's right to rule the mainland. In May 1990, tacit recognition of the mainland was formalised with President Lee Teng-hui's announcement that 'the state of war' with the mainland (i.e. the Period of Mobilisation for Suppression of the Communist Rebellion on the mainland) would cease, as from May 1991. Taiwan's new policy of non-provocative and peaceful coexistence with the mainland was reflected, for example, in Taipei's decision to refuse permission for the ship *Goddess of Democracy* to take on a radio transmitter at Keelung after the Tiananmen affair in June 1989.[8]

Other important reassurances given to Beijing by Taipei have been frequent and public reaffirmations of Taiwan's commitment to a one China policy and, after 1987, the relaxation of Taiwan's policy on exchanges with the mainland.

Cross-straits contacts served to placate Beijing on the one China principle at a critical time in the politics of both Taiwan and China. In Taiwan, the limits to support for self-determination and independence were being tested in a democratising society, leading Defence Minister General Hau Pei-tsun to warn that the Taiwanese armed forces would not defend the island if the mainland attacked in response to a Taiwanese bid for independence.[9] Hau claimed that reunification might take a long time, but most Taiwanese were opposed to independence.[10] This remains true, but the number of people in favour of independence is steadily increasing.[11]

Beijing, for its part, has never renounced the use of force to recover Taiwan.[12] It insists that Taiwan is 'a piece of treasured Chinese territory from ancient times that was stolen by Japan after a long period of humiliation'.[13] It has warned that attempts by 'a handful of seperatists . . . to make Taiwan break away from the large Chinese family is clearly against the will of all patriotic sons and daughters of China'.[14] Any suggestion or move that might be interpreted as supporting Taiwanese independence — no matter how tenuous the connection — invariably draws a shrill response from a leadership in Beijing predisposed to misperceive and distrust the Taiwanese on this particular issue.[15] Li Jiaquan, for example, described Taipei's 1990 move to give up claims to sovereignty over the mainland as 'a dangerous course' because it amounted to a bid for 'a separate independent status' under the guise of 'eventual reunification'.[16] In June 1990, the *People's Daily* stated that if Taiwan did try to separate itself from the mainland, China would 'not sit idly by with arms folded'.[17] In 1991, the *People's Daily* warned that 'the 1.13 billion people, including Taiwan compatriots and the Government of the People's Republic of China will never allow a very small number of the nation's scum to realise their plot of separating the treasured island of Taiwan from the motherland'.[18] In May 1991, a leaked report in Hong Kong said that senior PLA leaders were 'furious' with Taipei for setting unrealistic conditions for negotiations and failing to set a timetable for reunification.[19] The PLA proposed a partial blockade across the Taiwan Strait to remind Taipei that 'there should be no room for Taiwan to pursue any form of independence'.[20] In October 1991 there were reports that the PLA was preparing detailed options for the use of force 'to liberate Taiwan and achieve reunification with the mainland'.[21] Such campaigns of intimidation and the associated publicity, as in December 1994, are mainly targeted at advocates of independence on Taiwan, especially during Taiwanese election campaigns and so, in this sense, Beijing is working hand-in-glove with the Kuomintang.[22] At the same time, however, China would find it difficult to avoid a military response if Taiwan declared itself independent because such a move has implications for Beijing's hold on Tibet, Xinjiang and Inner Mongolia. There would also be a strong domestic reaction to any Chinese leader who acquiesced in an independent Republic of Taiwan.

While Chinese threats against an independent Taiwan have become a convenient tool for the Kuomintang to curb enthusiasm for the pro-independence Democratic Progressive Party, they are also taken seriously in Taipei.[23] The 1993 National Defence Report reaffirmed that China was Taiwan's top security threat and that it would probably attack if Taiwan declared itself independent.[24]

China is a large and powerful adversary, whereas Taiwan is one of the smallest countries in East Asia.[25] Taiwan's security outlook has become more uncertain because the Sino/Russian rapprochement and the collapse of the Soviet threat has meant the PLA, undistracted by a threat from the north, can concentrate on Taiwan and other small southern neighbours.[26]

Despite Taiwan's technological advantages, the PLA could defeat Taiwan by sheer weight of numbers if it was prepared to 'throw in the masses of men and materiel' necessary to overwhelm the island.[27] Next to China, Taiwan is a small, vulnerable state. China is armed with nuclear weapons, intercontinental missiles, an airforce with ten times as many fighter aircraft and a navy with at least ten times as many submarines as Taiwan (see Table 15). The People's Liberation Army has six times as many military personnel as Taiwan.[28] In relative terms, Taiwan has a small population, few resources and lacks strategic depth. But as the Iran–Iraq war demonstrated, there is often little correlation between forces and firepower and actual military outcomes and simple force ratio comparisons are a remarkably uncertain measure of military strength, both in terms of battles to be fought and in terms of the strength and weakness of a nation.[29] For example, sheer mass, whether in terms of weapons or personnel, is no substitute for military professionalism, clever battle management, superior technology, effective organisation, good command and control and defence engineering.[30]

Nonetheless, like all small states faced by powerful enemies, Taiwan cannot afford to go to war and, if it were to be attacked, it could not afford to lose the first battle.[31] Defence in depth is not a viable option.[32]

One alternative is to avoid providing the grounds for a conflict as well as preparing for the worst. The Taiwanese therefore have been trying to reassure the mainland on unification, the number one issue that could trigger a military response from the PLA. Taiwan 'should be sensitive about the mainland's paranoia about Taiwanese independence and not invite an invasion', said Defence Minister Sun Chen.[33] President Lee Teng-hui, often rumoured to favour independence for Taiwan 'in his mind', has been diligent in reaffirming his commitment to one China.[34] He established the National Unification Council in 1990 to demonstrate his determination in achieving the goal of one China.[35] Lee said the unification of China 'must come about as quickly as possible' and that it was his 'unshirkable duty to safeguard the country's territorial integrity'.[36] Such high-level reassurances have gone some way towards reassuring Beijing that Taiwan is not seeking independence, a goal that Beijing has often warned it will use all means — including force — to block.[37] While Lee Teng-hui might inwardly desire independence for Taiwan, he knows that, for the moment at least, it is out of the question, hence his lament to a Japanese journalist about 'the sorrows of being born a Taiwanese'.[38]

Beijing remains suspicious of domestic political trends in Taiwan, but recent comments about Taipei have been conciliatory.[39] Mainland leaders like Vice Premier Wu Xueqian have reaffirmed that the mainland would not use force against Taiwan.[40] Deng Xiaoping is reported to have advised the PLA that 'military force against Taiwan is the last thing we want' and that 'this is the national policy that cannot be hastily changed'.[41] Premier Li Peng concluded that 'relations between the two sides of the Straits had gone from tension and confrontation to gradual relaxation, from longstanding seclusion to mutual contact and were advancing in a direction favourable to reunification'.[42] The *People's Daily* commented that, while Lee Teng-hui's unification policy was belated, it was a welcome step that would help reduce hostility and develop relations between the two sides.[43]

Other facets of Taiwan's reassurance policy towards China appear in the practice of what in Europe was called the doctrine of non-provocative or defensive defence. Non-provocative defence is defined as 'the build-up, training, logistics and doctrine of the armed forces such that they are seen in their totality to be unsuitable for offence, but are unambiguously sufficient for a credible defence'.[44] According to Barry Buzan, non-provocative defence means making a country hard to attack, expensive to invade and difficult to occupy.[45] It means having strong denial forces which are not themselves suitable for long-range offensive action and do not therefore pose an offensive threat to other countries.[46] Taiwan has given up any plan it may once have had to recover the mainland through the use of force and it has, in consequence, steadily reduced the size of its army from 600 000 in 1961 to 370 000 in 1992, with further cuts of up to 170 000 scheduled over the next few years.[47] This defensive priority for Taiwan's armed forces — combined with Taiwan's technological edge — has been publicly documented to ensure that the correct signals are sent to Beijing. That is, instead of maintaining a large standing army that could be used to invade and occupy the mainland, Taiwan has concentrated on building up and maintaining a qualitative superiority in its air-force and navy. Defence Minister Sun Chien said that Taiwan would continue to reduce its army personnel, 'given positive trends in Taiwan's regional environment' (i.e. its relations with China).[48] In 1993, the defence budget was cut by 1.2 per cent to US$9.1 billion, or 24 per cent of total government outlays, the lowest percentage since 1949.[49] Meanwhile, the weapons systems that Taiwan is developing or buying from overseas do not threaten the mainland, at least not beyond the coastal areas immediately adjacent to Taiwan. They are clearly intended for the defence of the island of Taiwan and its approaches, not for waging war in China. For example, Taiwan has no long-range bomber aircraft or long-range missiles. Reports that Taiwan has ballistic missiles that could be used for pre-emptive strikes against ports and airfields along the mainland coast have been denied. Taiwan claims to have stopped producing offensive missiles such as the 'Chingfeng' surface-to-surface missile 'because the nation has changed from an offensive to a defensive strategy'.[50]

Taiwan has rejected the nuclear weapon option although it probably has the facilities and the technical capability to build nuclear weapons very quickly if it chose to do so.[51] The nuclear option was considered in the early 1970s, but was not pursued because it was felt that nuclear weapons could not be used against 'our own countrymen'.[52] Since then, Taiwan claims to have abandoned any 'intention whatsoever to develop nuclear weapons or a nuclear explosive device or to engage in any activities related to reprocessing purposes'.[53] Publicly, Taiwan's position is that it will 'never develop nuclear arms or conduct a nuclear test'.[54] Taiwan has placed all its nuclear facilities and materials under International Atomic Energy Agency (IAEA) safeguards and they are regularly visited by IAEA inspectors.[55] Premier Lien Chan reaffirmed Taiwan's non-nuclear stance in 1993. He claimed that Taiwan had 'never planned to develop nuclear weapons' and that its 'nuclear research projects were for peaceful and academic purposes only'.[56] These periodic disavowals of any interest in acquiring nuclear weapons are intended to satisfy another of Beijing's basic requirements for not threatening or using force against Taiwan (i.e. Taiwan must not develop a nuclear weapon capability).[57]

Taiwan's non-provocative defence has been combined with what Patrick Morgan calls the practice of general deterrence (i.e. a readiness posture and the maintenance of forces that succeed in deterring an opponent, over a long period of time, from ever moving to the point of seriously contemplating an attack.[58] This avoids immediate crises and instils a degree of stability in what is otherwise a hostile adversarial relationship.[59] Deterrence theory, used to analyse the nuclear stand-off between the two superpowers during the Cold War, is particularly relevant to the adversarial stand-off between Taiwan and mainland China, notwithstanding the rapprochement between them that was discussed in the previous chapter.

Deterrence is described as the prevention of aggressive war through the maintenance of a known and credible military capability.[60] The object of deterrence is to reduce the possibility of attack by threatening a potential adversary with the prospect of a net loss if they attack (i.e. the attacker will incur such unacceptable damage that they are deterred from launching an attack).[61] For deterrence to succeed, the target state must demonstrate a credible capability to fend off or repel an attack and possess the ability to retaliate, even after the other side has struck first.[62]

For the moment, Taiwanese specialists, PLA planning staff and informed Western analysts agree that an attack from the mainland is impractical, undesirable, too expensive and therefore unlikely. There are four main reasons for this conclusion. The Chinese armed forces are not strong enough to overcome Taiwan's defences; China has more important national and diplomatic priorities; the international strategic circumstances are increasingly unfavourable; and Taiwan and China are moving towards a practical state of rapprochement through their common economic interests.

At the height of the Korean War, the United States Defence Department estimated that China would need to transport at least 200 000 troops across the Taiwan Straits to successfully take the island.[63] In 1984, the United States Defence Intelligence Agency assessed that the PLA only had a sufficient number of conventional amphibious ships and craft to lift a force of about 30 000 troops and some equipment in a regional amphibious assault of less than 30 hours' transit.[64] In 1989, China was estimated to have about 40 amphibious assault ships and six attack transports which might be sufficient to take out small islands in the South China Sea but not Taiwan.[65] If China did succeed in obtaining a foothold on Taiwan, hundreds of merchant ships and thousands of motorised junks might then be used to carry support personnel and heavy equipment across the Strait. However, successful employment of such a force against a defended shore would require sustained air and naval superiority. China does not have these capabilities, a fact conceded on several occasions by Chinese leaders.[66] It has never previously fought or practised a multi-dimensional war against a well-defended island bastion. The Taiwan Strait is 142 kilometres wide at its narrowest point, or less than five hours by sea and a few minutes by fighter aircraft. However, it is five times wider than the English Channel, and as the Normandy landings on 6 June 1944 demonstrated, a successful invasion requires enormous preparation, a huge supporting fleet and control of the air. Military planners in Beijing's General Staff Department appreciate the degree of difficulty involved, which is why they concluded that the return of Taiwan was 'better resolved by peaceful means than by armed force'.[67]

China's PLA has numerical superiority over Taiwan, but geography and the limited capacity of airfields and ports in Fujian and Guangdong impose their own limits on the use of force.[68] The Taiwanese believe that the PLA could only despatch waves of 300 aircraft and five divisions to Taiwan at any one time.[69] This estimate is based on China having the capacity to transport five divisions but at present China's lift capacity is enough for one division, not five. This capacity is sufficient only for an assault on small lightly defended islands in the South China Sea, not an island fortress like Taiwan.

Even if China had the lift capability, an invasion would require the concentration of air and naval assets and an enormous logistic buildup in Nanjing Military Region. It would choke already overcrowded transport facilities and disrupt economic activity in China's most prosperous provinces. The impact on China's railways, ports and airfields would be quickly obvious, giving Taiwan ample warning time to prepare its defences. Taiwan could launch pre-emptive strikes from short range missiles such as the Tien Ma (range of 1000 kilometres).[70] Taiwan's new Mirage fighters (range 1500 kilometres) also have the capability of launching counterstrikes against airfields, ports, infrastructure and other military facilities in much of Nanjing and Guangzhou Military Regions. Although few in number, Taiwan's submarines add to mainland uncertainty as they possess the range to cover all of the ports on the mainland coast.[71]

The PLA was hard pressed to deal with Vietnam across a common land frontier in 1979. That war involved 300 000 troops supported by tanks and artillery for about three weeks after six months of preparation. It incurred heavy losses, was the subject of dissent amongst Chinese leaders and blew out the defence budget by 25 per cent or US$3 billion. The cost of an assault across the open sea against an island fortress defended by an airforce and navy qualitatively superior to the PLA would be many times greater. It would be fraught with uncertainty, militarily hazardous, financially disastrous and it might not succeed. Costs might include battlefield casualties, the destruction and depletion of arms and equipment, damage to national territory and the opportunity cost of diverting huge economic resources and national expenditures to wartime production.[72] It would also carry domestic political risks,[73] and could trigger United Nations intervention and intervention by the United States and/or Japan.[74]

There is, in any case, little evidence of Chinese preparations for the use of force against Taiwan. Rapprochement to the point of renewed defence co-operation between Russia and China has allowed China to revise its defence strategy and, if it chose, it could concentrate resources in the south. But there has been no sign of a major redeployment of forces southwards. There has been no buildup of forces adjacent to Taiwan, nor is there any indication of a program of construction of amphibious craft. On the contrary, China's priority has been domestic economic reform and modernisation. Since the mid-1980s, the strategic guidance for China's defence forces has swung away from preparing for war to 'the track of normal development in peacetime'.[75] In practice, this has meant severe constraints on defence expenditure, leading to complaints within the PLA that the technological gap between the PLA and 'the armies of countries on China's periphery' is steadily widening.[76] If China has a priority, it is in the South China Sea, where Taiwanese officials have said that Taiwanese forces would help the mainland defend Chinese claims to the Spratly islands against other claimants.

While estimates about the relative strengths and weaknesses of the military forces in China and Taiwan are prone to error, it is reasonable to conclude (as Chinese leaders and PLA planning staff have done) that, at present and for the next five to ten years, China does not have the strength or the incentive to invade Taiwan: China's military planners believe Taiwan's military forces are too strong.

While a PRC military attack against Taiwan is unlikely in the foreseeable future, there is a range of alternatives that could be used to threaten Taiwan. They include naval exercises in the Taiwan Strait; military manoeuvres in Guangzhou and Nanjing military regions; 'incidents' in the Taiwan Strait; an economic blockade; limited air and missile strikes against selected military bases on Taiwan; straddling Taiwan with a test firing of medium-range ballistic missiles and an assault on Taiwan's offshore islands of Matsu, Quemoy, Pratas and the Pescadores.

Taiwanese Defence Minister Chen Li-an said the possibility of harassment was greater than any large-scale military invasion of Taiwan.[77] He also listed refugees, mine warfare and the sealing of ports as possible ways China might try to debilitate the island's stability.[78]

The island of Taiwan has few natural resources and depends on access to the sea for imports of fuel, food and raw materials and exports of manufactured goods. Taiwan's port of Kaohsiung is the third busiest in the Asia-Pacific, while Keelung is ranked sixth. The most practical course for China seems to be a submarine blockade, or death by slow strangulation, a possibility referred to by several Chinese leaders.[79] Ironically, Taiwan's wealth, its modern industrialised economy and its dependence on international trade make it particuarly vulnerable to such pressure and interdiction. Taiwan's former Chief of Staff, Hau Pei-tsun, said that of the various war options open to China, the most likely was a blockade of the

Strait.[80] It would be a relatively low-risk, low-cost deniable operation that would exert maximum pressure without damaging the island's infrastructure.[81] It is the option that figures highest in Taiwan's present maritime force structure as the mere manifestation of a threat of mines and/or submarines (even obsolete ones like China's 40 or so old Romeo-class submarines) would undermine Taiwan's trading links with the rest of the world.[82] Even though Taiwan has reduced its dependence on imported energy by developing nuclear power stations, it still imports 90 per cent of its primary energy. Imported coal and oil account for 60 per cent of its electricity. Taiwan also depends, as we have seen, on trade with the rest of the world. In 1992, exports comprised 40 per cent of GDP (compared with 25 per cent for Indonesia, 7 per cent for China and 23 per cent for Korea).[83] Most of Taiwan's exports were manufactured from imported industrial raw materials and components. Taiwan's population is dependent on imported grain, soybeans and other foodstuffs. As Chief of Staff Admiral Liu Ho-chien observed, the sea lanes were Taiwan's life line.[84]

A strong, credible air and naval capability, therefore, is critical for Taiwan's survival. By demonstrating a capability to defeat a mainland invasion force, and creating sufficient uncertainty in the minds of planners in the PLA's General Staff Department about the likely success of use of force, Taipei's military planners hope, first, to deter the mainland from the threat or use of force and, second, to channel Beijing's reunification efforts towards a peacefully negotiated settlement. When the latter stage is assured, the Taiwanese plan to remain strong enough militarily to fend off unification until such time as they are satisfied that Chinese communism has been transformed. At that time, the credibility of Taiwan's military force will still be an essential insurance policy, this time to ensure that any negotiations that do take place are conducted on equal terms.

Taiwan has a relatively large army, navy and airforce (see Table 15) and spends disproportionately on defence. In relative terms, Taiwan spends much more on defence than, for example, a middle power like Australia. Taiwan's defence expenditure in 1980 was 60 per cent of the total government budget and 10 per cent of GNP. These ratios subsequently declined to around 28 per cent and 5 per cent respectively in 1992 (although they are still high compared with Australia, where defence expenditure is about 10 per cent of total government expenditure and 2 per cent of GNP). All males in Taiwan aged 19 are liable for two years' military service, and they remain on a reserve until age 45.[85] With army reserves totalling 1.6 million, Taiwan has a ready reaction armed force totalling two million, or 10 per cent of the population.

Taiwan's military forces have excellent support facilities, ports (Kaohsiung, Taichung, Hualien, Suao, Keelung), shipyards, airfields, transportation systems, a skilled workforce and an advanced R&D program.[86] They are amongst the best trained and best equipped armed forces in the world, with good conditions of service and a political commissar system to guarantee political loyalty.[87] By demonstrating resolve, high morale and preparedness to vigorously defend themselves, the Taiwanese have sought to eliminate one of the situations which might encourage China to resort to force (i.e. if and when Taiwan's armed forces became comparatively weak).[88]

Before China is in a position to launch an amphibious assault or impose a sea blockade against Taiwan, it must first gain air superiority over the Taiwan Strait. Taiwan's top priority, therefore, is air defence and the acquisition of sufficient numbers of modern high performance fighter aircraft. The second priority is sea defence and the development of a fleet of ships with anti-air and anti-submarine warfare capabilities.[89]

Taiwan's airforce is being modernised with the addition of 150 F-16 fighters, 60 Mirage 2000-5s and 130 domestically produced IDF fighters at a cost of close to US$18.3 billion. The first batch of F-16s — upgraded A/B models with advanced avionics, electronic countermeasures and greater mission capability — will not be delivered until 1996. The Mirages are to be delivered in 1998. They will have improved Thompson-CSF RDY multi-mode radar and fire control systems. However, over the next few years, Taiwan will acquire one of the most powerful and modern airforces in East Asia. It will be bolstered by the upgrading of 247 of the F5E fighter aircraft that are already in service, giving a total of more than 550 modern fighter interceptors.[90] Technologically, the Taiwanese airforce should be able to retain its superiority over mainland fighter aircraft.

Taiwan's next priority is naval strength, especially anti-submarine warfare (ASW) and mine counter-measures (MCM). It is re-equipping its navy with modern United States or European designed frigates in what is perhaps the biggest naval modernisation program in East Asia. The Kwang Hwa I program will build at least eight improved Perry-class frigates (4100 tonnes) with the possibility of a further eight.[91] United States companies are supplying the electronic and weapons suites, including ECM, ASW sonars, Mk-13 anti-aircraft launchers, Mk-32 ASW torpedo tubes and the SH-2F helicopters. Built by Kaman Corporation of Connecticut, the SH-2F is a light airborne multi-purpose system helicopter that can can detect and destroy submerged submarines. The ships will also be equipped with the Hsiung Feng II ASM, Italian 76mm OTO Melara Compact guns (range 11 kilometres), and Bofors (range 8 kilometres) and Phalanx CIWS. The American design was chosen over German and Italian competitors because of its anti-aircraft capabilities and its capacity to carry two ASW helicopters.[92] The first ship was launched in Taiwan in 1991, the second in 1992, the third in May 1993, with the eighth due by the late 1990s. In the interim, the United States has leased Taiwan six modernised Knox-class frigates (3000 tonnes).[93]

Taiwan is also building up to sixteen ASW frigates in the Kwang Hwa II program. This involves the assembly of six French Lafayette-class frigates (3200 tonnes) worth US$4.8 billion, with an option for a further ten.[94] The ships are being fabricated in France, minus weapons and electronic systems, and assembled in Taiwan. Separate contracts have been signed with French manufacturers for weapons systems to be fitted to the ships in Taiwan, including MM40 missiles, the MM100 cannon, and Thomson CSF Tavitac 200 combat systems. Taiwan has contracted with United States firms Raytheon and Litton Industries for 'the entire electronic combat suites' for the frigates, including radars and electronic countermeasures.[95]

Taiwan has a new multi-purpose support ship, the *Wu Yi*, commissioned in 1990 (26 110 tonnes loaded; equipped to carry a CH-47 helicopter and two S-70C Sikorsky helicopters) and an older workshop ship, the *Yu Tai* (14 490 tonnes loaded). These vessels give Taiwan's navy a blue water capability matched by few other navies in the Western Pacific apart from Australia. In 1992, the *Wu Yi* and a small naval task force were deployed to South Africa and in June 1993, a task force of two destroyers, accompanied by the *Wu Yi*, made a long-distance foray to the South Pacific. The cruise, of three months' duration, took in Honiara, Port Moresby, Surabaya and Manila.[96] The South African deployment means that it is the Taiwanese Chinese navy — rather than the mainland Chinese navy — that has undertaken the longest voyage by Chinese naval ships since the fifteenth century expeditions by Ming Admiral Cheng Ho.[97]

Taiwan recently purchased four coastal minehunters from Germany and four from the United States to supplement its fleet of 22 MCM ships. It has also been attempting to supplement its four-boat submarine fleet of two Dutch-built Zwaardvis II submarines (1870 tonnes, range 10 000 nautical miles, delivered in 1987–88) and two ex-United States Navy Guppy-class submarines of World War II vintage with an additional eight to ten modern diesel electric submarines.

Taiwan is looking to buy, or build under licence, further coastal patrol missile boats and corvettes to augment its existing fleet of about 80 small fast boats and upgrade their detection systems with FLIR technology. It needs to be able to police the Taiwan Strait and deal with the growing problems posed by arms and drug smugglers, mainland fishing boats and illegal immigration.

As well as defending Taiwan against a mainland assault, the navy has to resupply island fortresses of Quemoy, Matsu and the Pescadores in the Taiwan Strait and military garrisons on the Pratas and Taiping Islands in the South China Sea.[98]

Taiwan already has the capability to bottle up parts of the mainland Chinese fleet. Now it is acquiring a modern naval force of some 44 principal surface combatants. If it acquires the additional eight to ten submarines and ten new corvettes that it seeks, it will have one of the most powerful regional navies in the Western Pacific (see Table 15).

Taiwan's third defence priority is the construction of coastal defences to repel any mainland forces not destroyed by the airforce or the navy. Taiwan's land defences are based on layered missile coverage of the sea and air approaches over the Taiwan Strait. It has three coastal bases equipped with anti-ship missiles (including the Harpoon-like Hsiung Feng II which has a range reported to be between 80 and 160 kilometres). Taiwan has, or is in the process of acquiring from the United States, various helicopters for use as shore-based ASW, blockade busting and coastal patrol platforms. They include twelve Hughes 500MD Defender ASW helicopters and twelve Sikorsky S-70C Sea Hawk ASW helicopters. Reserve supplies of anti-ship missiles such as the Maverick and Bullpup air-to-surface missiles have also been stockpiled. In 1993, Taiwan's army bought 42 Bell Textron AH-1W Supercobra missile-equipped attack helicopters for coastal defence and 26 Kiowa OH-58D hunter-killer helicopters for day and night reconnaissance operations in the South China Sea and the Taiwan Strait.[99] The deal, worth US$1.2 billion, was a 'significantly boost for Taiwan's warfare capabilities', said President Lee Teng-hui.[100] American defence industries such as Raytheon Corporation are helping modernise Taiwan's land-based air defences, including the updating of the Hawk missile system, Taiwan's main air defence system.[101] In August 1992, Taiwan bought more than 200 Standard surface-to-air missiles.[102] In April 1994, Raytheon Corporation supplied 200 Patriot missiles worth US$377 million for the defence of northern Taiwan and missile components to upgrade the indigenously developed Sky Bow air defence missile batteries deployed around Taipei.[103] Stinger portable AAMs add to Taiwan's multi-layered missile defence system.

To improve warning time, Taiwan's armed forces have concentrated on intelligence gathering, early warning systems and electronic surveillance measures. Taiwan acquired four Grumman E-2T Hawkeye airborne early warning aircraft from the United States in 1993 to cover the Taiwan Strait and monitor possible staging areas on the mainland.[104] These aircraft can sit on station for up to five hours and detect fighter aircraft and shipping anywhere within an envelope of 150 000 square kilometres while simultaneously tracking up to 600 targets and controlling 200 airborne intercepts at any one time.[105] In addition, Taiwan has 32 Grumman S-2T Tracker ASW and maritime reconnaissance aircraft upgraded with turbo engines for longer range and endurance, improved acoustic systems, sensors and communications.[106] This early warning screen is backed up by the Chiang Wang or Strengthened Net, an integrated command, control and communications air defence system. Chiang Wang comprises an underground air operations centre near Taipei equipped with four large, very high speed computers. They co-ordinate phased array surveillance and fire control radars in Taiwan and on the offshore islands and Taiwan's airbases and missile and anti-aircraft artillery units.[107] The system, built by Hughes Aircraft Corporation, the Chung-shan Institute of Science and Technology and Taiwan International Standard Electronics Company, is one of the most sophisticated in the world. Because it can discriminate between Taiwanese and mainland aircraft and is a fully automatic, integrated air defence system, Chiang Wang gives the Taiwanese a significant detection and intercept capability in what would be a crowded air war environment.[108] The Taiwanese also maintain extensive intelligence networks in southern China and Hong Kong and retain informal links with the intelligence bureaucracy in Washington.[109]

A key element in deterrence theory is the concept of uncertainty. Where small states such as Taiwan, Switzerland, Israel and Singapore face larger opponents, creating uncertainty about whether an attack can succeed and raising the prospect of being able to inflict disproportionate costs by launching a crippling counterstrike is of critical importance.[110]

In the China–Taiwan context, the outcome of any conflict — pending external intervention or the use of nuclear weapons — will be decided by airpower and control of airspace over the Taiwan Strait. Apart from the 26 Su-27 long-range fighters bought and bartered from Russia in 1992–94, the majority of China's fighter aircraft are derived from MiG aircraft that first flew in the 1950s and 1960s. China's MiG-19, which makes up half the Chinese fighter aircraft inventory, first flew in 1964. They lack electronic countermeasures and modern missile systems.

Taiwan has a smaller but much more modern fleet of fighter aircraft. Its pilots are better trained and have more experience in aggressive overwater combat flying training than mainland pilots. So Defence Minister Chen Li-an's claim that 'once enemy planes came within . . . radar range, we should be able to maintain the upper hand' is probably true.[111] While Taiwan's defence strategy is based on achieving and maintaining command of the air over the Taiwan Strait and exposing mainland forces to piecemeal destruction, it can't afford to engage in a long, grinding air war.[112] With 5000 or so fighter aircraft, China has a quantitative advantage of the order of 10:1. Although the Taiwanese airforce managed to destroy 32 mainland aircraft for the loss of two of its own in 1958 — equivalent to a rate of 15:1 — it can't afford complacency.

For both sides, air superiority is best achieved through counter-air operations directed against aircraft on the ground, enemy airfields and facilities that support enemy air operations rather than through air-to-air combat.[113] Unless well protected from a surprise attack, most of Taiwan's airforce could be neutralised. To forestall that possibility, Taiwan relies on early warning indicators, such as the buildup of forces on mainland airfields and the option of launching pre-emptive strikes against mainland aircraft and mainland airfields if and when a war looks to be imminent. As Richard Betts observes, surprise is a force multiplier and by catching opposing forces unexpectedly, the attacker or defender can make the peacetime balance of forces almost instantaneously obsolete.[114] To forestall the possibility of being similarly caught out by a surprise attack, the Taiwanese have gone to great trouble and expense to protect their inventory of fighter aircraft.

Also relevant for Taiwan's air defence strategy are nuclear war fighting concepts relating to the importance of being first and maintaining a credible second-strike capability.[115] So too is the principle stressed by Sun Tzu and Mao Zedong that the basic aim in war is to hit and run (i.e. to preserve oneself and destroy the enemy by, for example, using safe base areas to sally forth and launch attacks or to retreat when the enemy force is too strong).[116] As Mao's Red Army Commander Chu Te explained, such bases were places where his troops could:

> return for rest, replenishment and retraining . . . with small arsenals, schools, hospitals . . . centred there. From these strongholds we can emerge to attack . . . garrisons, forts, strategic points, ammunition dumps, communication lines, railways. After destroying such objectives, our troops can disappear and strike elsewhere.[117]

Of particular interest in this area of surprise attacks, first strikes, retaliatory capability and sanctuary is Taiwan's recently constructed Chien An

No. 3 airbase at Chia-shan, near Hualien on the northeast coast. Chien An is the biggest and most modern underground air base in the Western Pacific.[118] It is also Taiwan's biggest and most sophisticated military installation.[119] It was literally built into mountainous terrain over a seven-year period with advice and assistance from Swedish engineers who drew on their experience in constructing bomb-proof runways and tunnels. Aircraft at Chien An are protected in underground sanctuaries and can be brought up by lift to tunnels that open on to a runway. The complex is protected by bombproof doors that can withstand the shock of all but a direct hit. Shielded by mountains of up to 3000 metres, the base cannot be hit by missiles fired from mainland China while hostile aircraft would be required to make difficult low-level attacks coming in from the east. With underground power generators, a microwave landing system to facilitate multiple landings and takeoffs and several months' supply of food, fuel and military stores, the base can protect and support the operation of up to 200 fighter aircraft, or about one-third of the Taiwanese airforce.[120] It offsets the limitations of small physical size, provides maximum protection for Taiwan's fighter aircraft and gives Taiwan a credible second strike or retaliatory capability. Eight other underground military bases are reported to be under construction around Taiwan.[121]

The credibility of Taiwan's defence capability has been reinforced by reports about the base published in magazines and journals available internationally and for an audience calculated to include the PLA's intelligence agencies.[122] Similar materials designed to communicate a message to Beijing about the preparedness of Taiwan's airforce and navy and Taiwan's willingness to defend its territory have been published in Taiwanese magazines.[123] Other information about Taiwan's defences, especially the range, altitude and capabilities of its missile systems, and details of new arms deals with the United States are nearly always announced in Taiwan's news media in the knowledge that such information will be read and digested in Beijing.

As well as the Chien An strategic base, Taiwan has a well-trained marine force of 31 000 personnel (two active divisions, and one reserve division) with a marine tank regiment and an amphibious fleet that includes two LSDs, 21 LSTs, 4 LSMs, 22 LCUs and 380 other landing vessels.[124] Six new Yuen Feng (3200 tonnes) attack transports, each capable of carrying 500–800 fully equipped combat troops, have recently been acquired.[125] Taiwan announced in May 1994 that it had signed a contract with the United States to lease several Newport-class LSTs, each capable of carrying 700 troops and 500 tonnes of equipment.[126]

Taiwan's marine force — six times the size of the PLA's marine brigade — is trained to launch a counter-landing, either on the mainland or to the rear of PLA forces trying to land on Taiwan or its offshore islands.[127]

Heavily fortified islands of Matsu, Quemoy and the Pescadores have a similar strategic function. Matsu, occupied by a force of 55 000 personnel, is 15 kilometres from Fuzhou. Quemoy, held by 18 000 troops, sits at the mouth of the Amoy river and is within 3 kilometres of Xiamen. The Pescadores are midway between the mainland and southern Taiwan. These Taiwanese-held islands straddle routes that might logically be taken by any seaborne force attempting to invade Taiwan from the mainland. As well as providing early warning of an impending assault, they could threaten the rear of any invasion.force and bombard or blockade Xiamen and Fuzhou, the two main ports of Fujian province.[128]

The fact is that China has a very limited ability to wage a modern air war across the open sea against a fortressed base like Taiwan. Taiwan is, metaphorically speaking, an unsinkable aircraft carrier. It is a fortified island with a powerful airforce, defended by coastal bases armed with Hsiung Feng II anti-ship missiles (range in excess of 80 kilometres); shore-based ASW helicopters (Hughes 500-MD and Sikorsky S-70C); and modernised Grumman Tracker ASW aircraft. It has a defence perimeter in the heavily fortified offshore islands of the Pescadores, Matsu and Quemoy.

Militarily, Taiwan is not simply a small state that is unable to defend itself. It is more properly listed in the same category of middle powers as Israel, Australia, Belgium, Sweden, Italy or even Canada.[129] Any state with financial resources and a high degree of technical competence can utilise new technologies as force multipliers to counter the threat of numerically superior forces. Precision-guided weapons, cruise missiles, electronic countermeasures, modern command and control systems and sophisticated surveillance and targeting technologies have transformed the battlefield so that even small powers can inflict disproportionate damage on or even defeat a larger power.[130] It is no longer sufficient to simply count the number of infantry divisions, ships and aircraft: military technology has obscured the clarity of distinction between small and great powers.[131]

The Taiwanese thus have worked very hard to build up a strong defence industrial base, especially in electronics.[132] By the early 1960s, Taiwan's defence industries were capable of making basic military equipment needed by the armed forces such as machine guns, M-14 rifles, artillery, mortars and ammunition. By 1970, they were making helicopters and in 1974 began co-production of the F-5E fighter with Northrop Corporation from the United States. Pressure to become self-reliant in modern conventional weaponry came with United States normalisation of its diplomatic ties with Beijing. By the late 1980s Taiwan's defence industries were producing long-range artillery, tanks, APCs, missiles, MRLs, ground attack and interceptor aircraft, missile boats, electronic communication facilities and anti-missile missiles. Taiwan's indigenous government-backed aerospace and defence industries are supported by state-owned institutes such as the Chung-Shan Institute of Science and Technology (CSIST) in Taoyuan. Founded in 1969, and controlled by the Defence Department, the CSIST has 15 000 employees. It co-ordinates the government's defence research and development of aeronautical systems, jet aircraft, missiles, early warning radars, stealth technology and defense electronics.

Taiwan Aerospace Corporation (TAC) was established in 1991, one of ten new high-tech industries targeted for rapid development. TAC is 29 per cent owned by the government's Economic Co-operation and Development Fund, with the state-owned China Steel Co and Bank of Communication owning another 15 per cent. TAC has a fifteen-year aerospace and defence industries development plan involving aircraft manufacturing and maintenance and joint ventures with advanced European and

American companies like Aerospatiale, Westinghouse, British Aerospace, Boeing, Pratt and Whitney, Rolls Royce, Deutsche Aerospace, Allied Signal, Dassault Aviation, Lockheed, Hughes, General Dynamics and General Electrics. TAC is building Pratt & Whitney PW4000 and CF6-80 engine parts and has signed contracts with Garrett for the TFE1042-70 jet engine and with British Aerospace and Airbus Industrie for engine maintenance.[133] It is negotiating with Aerospatiale for co-development of civilian and military versions of the Super Puma, Dauphin and Ecureuil helicopters, commercial aircraft and telecommunications satellites.[134] It is currently the only country in East Asia producing a modern lightweight twin-engine supersonic fighter aircraft (the IDF) and an advanced jet trainer (the AT-TC-3).[135] Present plans are to build 200 IDF fighters for export to gain a 12 per cent share of the global market for similar fighter aircraft.[136] By the year 2000, Taiwan will be the second largest aircraft and component manufacturer in non-communist Asia after Japan.[137]

As well as developing a local defence–industrial complex capable of producing modern missiles, fighter aircraft and frigates, Taiwan also buys advanced weapons and advanced defence technology from sellers in Europe and the United States. Since the Gulf War, Taiwan has emerged as the world's largest buyer of fighter aircraft, missiles, radars, naval ships and other defence-related equipment and technology.[138]

Buying from the United States has several objectives. It maintains a United States–Taiwan military relationship; it offsets Taiwan's trade surplus with the United States; and it gives Taiwan some of the world's best military technology. The United States is a vital source of technology for Taiwan's air and naval defence capabilities. Taiwan's IDF fighter aircraft was designed with technical assistance from General Dynamics and General Electrics and is equipped with advanced avionics from United States firms like Lear Astronics, Honeywell and Allied-Signal. The hulls of Taiwan's new 4100 tonne frigates (an improved version of the United States Perry class guided missile frigate), their ASW sonars and ASW SSM and AA weapons systems are made in the United States. The United States has sold Taiwan airborne early warning aircraft and a variety of helicopters and missile systems such as the Mk-46 ASW torpedoes.[139]

In 1992, the issue of whether or not such sales were caught by the 17 August 1982 Communiqué became academic. In August 1992, the Bush administration decided that, as China had acquired 'sophisticated systems from the Soviets' and as Taiwan's fighter aircraft (F-104s and F-5s) were 'stuff that was 35, 40 years old' they 'needed to be replaced' if Taiwan was to maintain its air defence capability.[140] Moreover, under the terms of the *Taiwan Relations Act*, the United States was required by law to provide Taiwan with sufficient military equipment to defend itself.[141] The United States State Department declared, in fact, that the 1979 *Taiwan Relations Act* was a law, whereas the 1982 Joint Communiqué was merely 'a statement of United States policy on the subject of arms sales to Taiwan'.[142] As a result, the United States agreed to sell Taiwan the F-16 fighter aircraft after having refused to do so for the previous decade on the grounds that Taiwan's air force was strong enough.[143] This shift in American policy on Taiwan has been of profound importance for Taiwan's confidence and its ability to continue to deter the mainland. This shift was followed by a major inter-agency review of United States–Taiwan relations.[144]

Taiwan is reaping the rewards of its remarkably successful political and economic development over the previous few decades and above all its possession of the world's largest reserves of foreign exchange.[145] Taiwan, in short, is well placed to exploit what has been described as the age of geo-economics in the Asia-Pacific in the 1990s.[146]

Taiwan's leverage in this regard is reflected in the number of senior trade officials, admirals and executives from multinational defence-related corporations like Bell Helicopters, Rolls Royce, Deutsche Aerospace, British Aerospace, Boeing and McDonnell Douglas who have flocked to Taipei. Taiwan had the cash to spend US$12.3 billion on 60 long-range Dassault Mirage 2000-5 and 150 General Dynamics F-16A/B intercepter fighter aircraft. It is negotiating to buy US$2.6 billion worth of naval weaponry including Exocet missiles, Crotale and Mistral anti-aircraft missiles, torpedoes, ECW equipment and CIWS from France.[147]

Despite pressure from Beijing, the Dutch, French and German governments have been considering their options in the light of recent multi-billion dollar deals for the Mirage and F-16 fighter aircraft. Taiwan's next big arms purchase — up to ten submarines and ten corvettes — is likely to be worth up to US$7.5 billion, a prospect that has attracted attention from Australia, Germany, Holland, France, Sweden, Argentina and the United States. Taiwan is still interested in buying the highly regarded German IKL/HDW Type 209 diesel attack submarine and the Blohm & Voss MEKO 140/200 corvette.[148] Although the bid was rejected by the German Federal Security Council, Taiwan remains hopeful.[149] Argentina, for example, manufactures German Type 209 submarines and Meko 140 corvettes under licence. France has offered Taiwan its Rubis-class of nuclear submarine, a small nuclear powered boat developed in the 1970s. The Dutch indicated that, rather than close their shipyards for lack of orders, it might allow the Rotterdamse Droogdok Mij (RDM) shipyard to sell additional Walrus-class submarines to Taiwan.[150] Sweden and Australia are similarly interested in selling submarine technology to Taiwan, possibly in a co-operative joint venture based on the Swedish-designed Collins-class submarines being constructed in Adelaide for the Australian navy.[151]

As well as engagement with, and the reassurance and deterrence of, the mainland, the fourth element in Taiwan's China strategy is to build a coalition of international support for Taiwan centred on the United States and Japan and the Asia-Pacific community generally. This issue is discussed in the next chapter.

Notes

1   *New York Times*, 18 August 1982, p. A12.
2   Admiral Tun Hwa Ko, a former Taiwanese Vice Minister of Defence: 'Taiwan as a Strategic Asset', *Global Affairs*, vol. IV, no. 2, Spring 1989, pp. 65, 77–78.

3   Richard Ned Lebow, 'The Deterrence Deadlock: Is There a Way Out?', in Robert Jervis et al., *Psychology and Deterrence*, The John Hopkins University Press, Baltimore, 1985, pp. 180, 226–27.

4   David Vital, *The Inequality of States*, Clarendon Press, Oxford, 1967, p. 12.

5   Lebow in Jervis, *Psychology and Deterrence*, p. 180.

6   Paul Dibb, *Review of Australia's Defence Capability*, AGPS, Canberra, 1986, p. 35.

7   Record of conversation between Chiang Kai-shek and Harold Holt, 6 April 1967, File 519/3/1, *Formosa — Relations with Australia: General*, Department of Foreign Affairs and Trade, Canberra, quoted in Gary Klintworth, *Australia's Taiwan Policy 1942–1992*, Australian Foreign Policy Papers, Australian National University, 1993, p. 48.

8   China News Agency (CNA), Taipei, 18 May 1990.

9   General Hau Pei-tsun was quoted in the *FCJ*, 25 December 1989.

10 *FCJ*, 3 September 1991.

11 Recent polls give a figure of 27 per cent in favour of independence, a record high, with 45 per cent opposed: (CNA), 18 April 1994, in *Foreign Broadcast Information Service (FBIS)-China*, 18 April 1994, p. 76.

12 See *A Study of a Possible Communist Attack on Taiwan*, Government Information Office, Taipei, June 1991.

13 Li Jiaquan, 'Taiwan Independence a Blind Alley', *Beijing Review*, 8–14 June 1992, p. 20.

14 ibid., p. 21. Also Li Jiaquan, 'On Taiwan's Elastic Diplomacy', *Beijing Review*, 26 February–4 March 1990, pp. 27, 31.

15 ibid.

16 Li Jiaquan, Deputy Director of the Taiwan Institute, Chinese Academy of Social Sciences, 'More on One Country, Two Governments', *Beijing Review*, 2–8 July 1990, pp. 13–17.

17 *Renmin Ribao Overseas Edition*, Beijing, 6 June 1990; *FBIS — China*, 7 June 1990, p. 63.

18 *People's Daily*, 3 June 1991.

19 *Mirror Monthly*, reported in *South China Morning Post (SCMP)*, 4 June 1991.

20 ibid.

21 *SCMP*, 4 October 1992.

22 The threats seem to have served their purpose because when the DPP ran on a pro-independence plank in election in December 1990, its popular vote dropped to 24 per cent compared with the 35 per cent it won in the previous year and it only recovered in subsequent elections after it moderated its calls for independence: C.L. Chiou, 'Emerging Taiwanese Identity in the 1990s: Crisis and Transformation', in Gary Klintworth (ed.), *Taiwan in the Asia-Pacific in the 1990s*, Allen & Unwin/Department of International Relations, Canberra, 1994, pp. 21, 33. A similar result occurred with the elections of December 1994.

23 Bih-jaw Lin, 'Taipei's Search for a New Foreign Policy', Conference Paper, Claremont Institute, Los Angeles, 7–8 April 1989.

24 *CNA*, 9 March 1994 in *FBIS-China*, 9 March 1994, p. 69. See also the *1992 National Defence Report*, Ministry of National Defence, Taipei (English trans.), Li Ming Cultural Entrprise Co., 1992, p. 53.

25 Small states have little margin for error in contests with larger states: Vital, *The Survival of Small States*, p. 12.

26 Admiral Liu Shu-hsi, President of Chung Shan Institute of Science and Technology, quoted in *Defence News*, 6–12 July 1992, p. 22.

27 According to Assistant Secretary of Foreign Relations John Holdridge, testifying before the United States Senate in August 1982: United States Congress, Senate, Committee on Foreign Relations, *US Policy Toward China and Taiwan: Hearings*, 17 August 1982, United States Government Printing Office, Washington, 1982, p. 27, cited in Richard Bush, 'Helping the Republic of China to Defend Itself', in Ramon Myers (ed.), *A Unique Relationship: The United States and the Republic of China Under the Taiwan Relations Act*, Hoover, Stanford, 1989, pp. 78, 96. On the other hand, according to State Department spokesman Alan B. Romberg, Taiwan could defend itself against the PLA and there was no military need for Taiwan to have an advanced fighter aircraft: cited in David Chou, 'The ROC and the Taiwan Relations Act', in Myers, *A Unique Relationship*, pp. 140, 151.

28 For an excellent discussion of the military balance between China and Taiwan, see Andrew Yang, 'Taiwan's Defence Build-up in the 1990s: Remodelling the Fortress', in Klintworth, *Taiwan in the Asia-Pacific in the 1990s*, p. 72.

29 Anthony H. Cordesman and Abraham R. Wagner, *The Lessons of Modern War Volume II: The Iran–Iraq War*, Westview Press, Boulder, Col., 1990, p. 591.

30 ibid., pp. 592–93.

31 Michael Handel, *Weak States in the International System*, Frank Cass, London, 1981, pp. 70–71.

32 Vital, *The Inequality of States*, p. 60.

33 Quoted in *China Post (CP)*, 29 March 1993.

34 Julian Baum, 'A Patriotic Stand', *Far Eastern Economic Review*, 18 October 1990, p. 36.

35 *FCJ*, 11 October 1990. It is interesting to note that the term 'unification', rather than 'reunification', is used. The latter connotes a return to the status quo ante (i.e. one nation that had been divided), whereas the former term implies a voluntary union between two parts with no judgment about the previous circumstance.

36 ibid.

37 Taiwan's first Defence White Paper of January 1992 listed several other scenarios in which the island might be attacked by the PLA: if political chaos erupted on Taiwan; if Taiwan's armed forces became comparatively weak and vulnerable; if foreign powers intervened in

Taiwan; and if Taiwan developed nuclear weapons: *1992 National Defense Report*, p. 55.

38 *Xinhua* Domestic Service, Beijing, 18 June 1994, in *FBIS-China*, 20 June 1994, p. 66.

39 For a review of recent exchanges between China and Taiwan, see Chong-Pin Lin, 'Beijing and Taipei: Dialectics in Post-Tiananmen Interactions', *The China Quarterly*, no. 136, pp. 771ff.

40 Although, as usual, Wu said China 'would not rule out the possibility of an invasion if the island was to become independent': *CP*, 2 July 1992.

41 *SCMP*, 4 June 1991. But see Deng's remarks to the contrary in *A Study of Possible Communist Attacks on Taiwan*, GIO, Taipei, 1991.

42 Li Peng, 'Report on the Work of the Government', 7th National People's Congress, *Beijing Review*, 16–22 April 1990.

43 *People's Daily*, 11 May 91, in *Beijing Review*, 20–26 May 1991, p. 8.

44 F. Barnaby and M. Ter Borg, *Emerging Technologies and Military Doctine: A Political Assessment*, Macmillan, London, 1986, p. 276. See also Thomas F. Lynch, 'The Military and Alternative Security: New Missions for Stable Conventional Security', in Burns H. Weston, *Alternative Security Living Without Nuclear Deterrence*, Westview Press, Boulder, 1990, pp. 7, 13.

45 See, for example, Barry Buzan, *An Introduction to Strategic Studies, Military Technology and International Relations*, Macmillan, London, 1987, pp. 276, 277–78.

46 ibid.

47 *CP*, 2 September 1991, 17 April 1992.

48 *Chung Kuo Shih Pao*, Taipei, 22 March 1994, in *FBIS-China*, 14 April 1994, p. 55.

49 *1992 National Defence Report*, p. 104. Defence expenditure as a percentage of government expenditure was around 34 per cent in 1988–89 and about 50 per cent for most of the previous four decades.

50 Han Lih-wu, *Taiwan Today*, Cheng Chung Press, Taipei, 1988, p. 56. Taiwan, however, has established an advanced space research program and plans to build a satellite ground station, develop space launch rockets and launch its own low-orbit satellites in 1997: *CNA*, 19 and 22 January 1992; and *Aerospace*, January 1992, p. 34. These systems could be converted to ballistic missiles carrying nuclear warheads if the need arose.

51 Even in 1977, Taiwan was credited with 'an extremely sophisticated scientific establishment, including theoretical and practical expertise in advanced electronics, heavy industry, nuclear physics, nuclear power and key military technologies': William Overholt, 'Nuclear Proliferation in Eastern Asia', in William H. Overholt (ed.), *Asia's Nuclear Future, Studies of the Research Institute on International Change*, Columbia University, Westview, Boulder, Col., 1977, pp. 139–40.

52 Premier Chiang Ching-kuo, quoted in Ralph Clough, *Island China*, Harvard University Press, Cambridge, Mass., 1978, p. 116, footnote 23.

53 Diplomatic note to the United States, cited in Clough, *Island China*, pp. 118–19. Taiwan may, of course, have a covert research program. In 1988, Chang Hsien-yi, a Taiwanese nuclear scientist and deputy director of the Nuclear Energy Research Institute, claimed that Taiwan had a nuclear weapons research program. United States officials later said that Taiwan had been secretly building a plutonium extraction plant but that it had been subsequently closed down: *Arms Control Reporter*, Section 602, 11 March 1988 and the *New York Times*, 23 March 1988. The reports were denied in Taipei: *Asian Wall Street Journal*, 25 March 1988. In 1990, Premier Hau Pei-tsun denied speculation that Taiwan had nuclear capabilities and said it was 'an absolute rumour' that Taiwan had an atomic bomb: quoted in *SCMP*, 12 October 1990.

54 Stated by Ma Ying-jeou, Vice Chairman of the Mainland Affairs Council, after China conducted a nuclear test in May 1992: *CP*, 23 May 1992.

55 Australian Nuclear Science and Technology Organisation, *Nuclear Developments in the Asia and Pacific Region*, July 1992, p. 29

56 *CNA*, 22 April 1993.

57 *1992 National Defense Report*, p. 55. This is not to deny, however, that Taiwan has the capability to develop nuclear weapons. It has considerable experience in nuclear power with four nuclear power plants and according to some, it has the technical capability to manufacture nuclear weapons within a month of a decision to do so: Dan C. Sanford, *The Future Association of Taiwan with the People's Republic of China*, China Research Monograph 22, Institute of East Asian Studies, University of California, Berkeley, 1981, p. 6. See also Clough, *Island China*, p. 117.

58 Patrick M. Morgan, *Assessing the Republic of China's Deterrence Situation*, Sun Yat-sen Centre for Policy Studies, Kaohsiung, Paper No. 4, April 1991, p. 2.

59 ibid.

60 Thomas F. Lynch, 'The Military and Alternative Security: New Missions for Stable Conventional Security', in Weston, *Alternative Security: Living Without Nuclear Deterrence*, pp. 7, 41. See also William W. Kaufmann, *The Requirements of Deterrence*, Center for International Studies, Princeton, 1954; Glenn H. Snyder, *Deterrence and Defence*, Princeton University Press, New Jersey, 1961; Alexander L. George and Richard Smoke, *Deterrence in American Foreign Policy: Theory and Practice*, Columbia University Press, New York, 1974; John Steinbruner, 'Beyond Rational Deterrence: The Struggle for New Conceptions', *World Politics*, vol. XXVIII, no. 2, January 1976, p. 223; Keith B. Payne, *Nuclear Deterrence in US–Soviet Relations*, Westview, Boulder, Col., 1982.

61 Glenn H. Snyder, *Deterrence and Defence*, Princeton University Press, New Jersey, 1961, p. 12. See also Steinbruner, 'Beyond Rational Deterrence', p. 225, which defined deterrence as follows: 'one player threatening his opponent with such severe retaliation to attack (i.e. a large negative pay-off with significant probability) that the rationally calculating opponent will always choose not to attack. Mutual deterrence exists when both players exercise such a threat against each other.'

62 See Patrick M. Morgan, *Deterrence: A Conceptual Analysis*, Sage Publications, Beverly Hills, Cal., 1977 and the informative discussion of his framework for deterrence in Peter Kien-hong Yu, 'Taipei's Perception of its Deterrence Situation from April to July 1989', in Richard Yang (ed.), *China's Military: The PLA in 1990/91*, Sun Yat-sen Center for Policy Studies, Kaohsiung, Taiwan, 1991, p. 63.

63 From Jon W. Heubner, 'The Americanisation of the Taiwan Straits', *Asian Profile*, vol. 13, no. 3, June 1985, p. 197. The Allied landing at Normandy on 6 June 1994 involved 7000 ships, 11 500 aircraft and more than 150 000 men in a battle that lasted for 77 days.

64 *Handbook for the Chinese People's Liberation Army*, Defence Intelligence Agency, Washington, November 1984, p. 59.

65 David G. Muller, 'China as a Maritime Power in the Year 2000', in Richard Yang (ed.), *SCPS PLA Yearbook 1988/89*, Sun Yat-sen Centre for Policy Studies, Kaohsiung, 1989, pp. 137, 144. In fact, the size of China amphibious landing force is about the same as, if not smaller than, Taiwan's more modern fleet.

66 See *A Study of Possible Communist Attacks on Taiwan*, GIO, Taipei, 1991, pp. 1–12.

67 Xiao Bing and Qing Bo, *Zhongguo Jundui Nengfou Daying Xia Yi Chang Zhanzheng* (Can the Chinese Army Win the Next War), Chongqing, June 1993, published by FBIS (JPRS CAR 94-024-L), 5 May 1994, p. 25.

68 General Hau Pei-tsun, Chief of General Staff, ROC armed forces, interview, *United Evening News Taipei*, 17 May 1988.

69 Tai Ming Cheung, *Far Eastern Economic Review*, 18 May 1989, p. 23.

70 *Military Technology*, April 1988, p. 78.

71 *FCJ*, 19 June 1989.

72 Paul K. Huth, *Extended Deterrence and the Prevention of War*, Yale University Press, New Haven, 1988, p. 15.

73 See Stephen P. Gilbert, 'Safeguarding Taiwan's Security', *Comparative Strategy*, vol. 8, no. 4, 1989, pp. 425, 441.

74 Section 2(b) of the United States *Taiwan Relations Act* of April 1979 states *inter alia* that 'it is US policy to declare that peace and stability in the area are in the political, security and economic interests of the US and are matters of international concern; to make clear that the US decision to establish diplomatic relations with the PRC rests upon the expectation that the future of Taiwan will be determined by

peaceful means; to consider any effort to determine the future of Taiwan by other than peaceful means, including by boycotts or embargoes, a threat to the peace and security of the Western Pacific area and of grave concern to the US; to provide Taiwan with arms of a defensive character; and to maintain the capacity of the US to resist any resort to force or other forms of coercion that would jeopardize the security or social or economic system of the people of Taiwan'.

Japan's position is a little more ambiguous, but there seems little doubt that it would seek to prevent China using force against Taiwan. In November 1969, then Japanese Prime Minister Eisaku Sato signed a joint communiqué with President Nixon declaring that Taiwan's security was vital to Japan and that Taiwan was 'within Japan's defence zone'; moreover Article 1 of the Japan–United States Treaty also refers to the deployment of United States land, air and sea forces in and about Japan 'to contribute to the maintenance of international peace and security in the Far East and to the security of Japan against armed attack . . . caused through instigation or intervention by an outside power or powers': from Chiao Chiao Hsieh, *Strategy for Survival*, The Sherwood Press, London, 1985, p. 275.

75 Chen Xiaogong and Liu Xige, 'Several Questions Concerning China's National Defence Policy', *International Strategic Studies*, (Beijing), no. 2, 1993, p. 1.

76 ibid., p. 3.

77 *FCJ*, 29 May 1992.

78 ibid.

79 The blockade option was referred to by Deng Xiaoping and Yao Yilin: see *A Study of Possible Communist Attacks on Taiwan*, p. 58. Former Chinese Party Secretary-General Hu Yaobang said that, while China did not have the strength to use military force against Taiwan, it might develop sufficient force in the 1990s and that 'if we have the strength to enforce a blockade and if Taiwan vehemently opposes reunification, we shall have to consider enforcing a blockade': interview *P'ai Hsing* magazine, Hong Kong, 25 December 1985.

80 Chief of Staff of the ROC Armed Forces, General Hau Pei-tsun, interview, *United Evening News*, Taipei, 17 May 1988.

81 See also Tai Ming Cheung, *Growth of Chinese Naval Power*, ISEAS, Pacific Strategic Papers, No. 1, Singapore, 1990, p. 14.

82 It is interesting to note that the strength of China's submarine fleet has been halved by the stroke of a pen. The *IISS Military Balance 1992–1993*, London, 1992, p. 146, gives China's submarine strength as just 46, half of what it was in the previous edition. The revised estimate was made because over half China's fleet — 49 Romeos — was considered non-operational.

83 Asia Pacific Economics Group, *Asia-Pacific Profiles 1993*, ANU Canberra, 1993.

84 *FCJ*, 20 October 1992.

85 Taiwan's reserves number about 1.6 million.

86 Tun Hwa Ko, 'Taiwan as a Strategic Asset', *Global Affairs*, vol. IV, no. 2, Spring 1989, p. 65.

87 On the political commissar system, see Cheng Hsiao-shih, *Party–Military Relations in the PRC and Taiwan*, Westview, Boulder, Col., 1990, p. 123.

88 *1992 National Defense Report*, p. 55.

89 Admiral Liu Shu-hsi, President of Chung Shan Institute of Science and Technology, *Defense News*, 6–12 July 1992, p. 22.

90 *Jane's Defence Weekly*, 16 January 1994, p. 14.

91 Anthony Leung, 'Taiwan's Shipbuilding Programmes' in *Naval Forces*, vol. XIII, no. III, 1992, pp. 28, 30.

92 'Overcoming Adversity on the Seas — The Navy Plans for the Future', *Sinorama*, vol. 16, no. 9, September 1991, pp. 83, 89.

93 *CP*, 7 July 1993.

94 *CP*, 9 March 1992; *Defense News*, 23–29 November 1992. Some reports mention a deal for up to sixteen of the frigates: *Jane's Defence Weekly*, 5 October 1993, p. 586.

95 *Los Angeles Times*, 27 April 1994.

96 *Far Eastern Economic Review*, 15 July 1993, p. 13.

97 The replenishment ship, *Wu Yi*, accompanied two of Taiwan's modernised destroyers on a recent voyage to South Africa: *Jane's Defence Weekly*, 16 January 1993, p. 24.

98 Taiwan recently announced that it would support naval patrols to protect Taiwanese fishing vessels, to study the feasibility of exploring for natural resources and to strengthen oceanographic research in the South China Sea: *China News Agency*, Taipei, 3 December 1992, in *FBIS-China*, 3 December 1992, p. 57.

99 *Defense News*, 23 March 1992.

100 *CP*, 16 November 1993.

101 *Jane's Defence Weekly*, 25 January 1992.

102 Pentagon News Release, Washington, 5 August 1992.

103 *FCJ*, 17 January 1992; and *FCJ*, 22 April 1994.

104 *Jane's Defence Weekly*, 18 April 1992, p. 643.

105 *The Almanac of Seapower*, Navy League of the US, Arlington, Virginia, vol. 33, no. 1, January 1990, p. 201.

106 Anthony Leung, 'Fortress Formosa — In Defence of Taiwan', *Military Technology*, vol. 8/90, pp. 19, 23.

107 Andrew Yang, 'Taiwan's Defence Build-up in the 1990s: Remodelling the Fortress' in Klintworth, *Taiwan in the Asia-Pacific in the 1990s*, pp. 72, 82.

108 ibid. Further details were revealed in *Lien Ho Pao*, 4 July 1994, in *FBIS — China*, 13 July 1994, p. 58.

109 The *Los Angeles Times*, for example, revealed that exchanges between Taiwanese and American defence officials are held annually: *FCJ*, 17 January 1992.

110 Vital, *The Inequality of States*, p. 154.

111 Interview, *Jane's Defence Weekly*, January 1991, p. 32.

112 Defence Minister Chen Li-an claimed on 29 October 1992 that Taiwan's airforce was strong enough to protect its airspace in the event of war, despite China's purchase of 24 or more Russian Su-27 long-range fighter aircraft. Chen claimed that Taiwan would have 'no problem repelling any invading mainland aircraft with its present fighters and missiles': *CN*, 2 November 1992.

113 Desmond Ball, 'The Future of Air Power in the Defence of Australia', in Desmond Ball (ed.), *Air Power: Global Developments and Australian Perspectives*, Pergamon-Brasseys Defence Publishers, Sydney 1988, p. 631.

114 Richard K. Betts, *Surprise Attack*, The Brookings Institution, Washington, 1982, p. 4.

115 On the principles of fighting a nuclear war, see Lawrence Freedman, *The Evolution of Nuclear Strategy*, Macmillan, London, 1988 (reprint).

116 Samuel B. Griffith, *Sun Tzu: The Art of War*, Oxford University Press, London, 1963, pp. 69, 80; *Selected Works of Mao Tse-tung, Volume II*, Foreign Languages Press, Peking, 1965, p. 81.

117 *CNA*, 19 December 1991.

118 *The Straits Times*, 19 January 1990.

119 Leung, 'Fortress Formosa — In Defence of Taiwan', pp. 19, 23; and Yu, 'Taipei's Perception of its Deterrence Situation', in Yang (ed.), *China's Military: The PLA in 1990/91*, Sun Yat-sen Center for Policy Studies, Kaohsiung, Taiwan, 1991, pp. 63, 66.

120 Lin, 'Beijing and Taipei: Dialectics in Post-Tiananmen Interactions', pp. 771, 793.

121 Details about the Chiashan base were published in *Military Technology*, vol. 8/90, p. 19; *Far Eastern Economic Review*, 29 September 1988, p. 41; Richard Yang (ed.), *China's Military: The PLA in 1990/91*, Sun Yat-sen Center for Policy Studies, Kaohsiung, Taiwan, 1991 p. 63, 66; and *The Journalist*, 26 February 1989, p. 16. Taiwan showed Chien An to Singapore's senior minister, Lee Kuan Yew, in January 1990. Lee, a frequent visitor to Beijing as well as Taipei, was probably shown the base so that, when next in Beijing, he could communicate the lengths to which Taiwan would go to defend itself when next in Beijing: *The Straits Times*, 19 January 1990.

122 Taiwanese journals such *Sinorama* and *Free China Review* frequently feature articles on Taiwan's defence forces. *Sinorama* of May 1991, for example, had a detailed cover story on the Taiwanese airforce, its aircraft, their equipment and the training and readiness of the pilots. *Sinorama* of September 1991 had a similar 18-page feature article on Taiwan's navy, its frigates, submarines and its fast missile boats.

123 *Weyers Rotten Taschenbuch (Warships of the World, Warship Documentation)*, Bernard and Graefe, Federal Republic of Germany, 1990/91, pp. 81, 83; and *Military Balance*, IISS, London, 1993–94, p. 169.

124 *Military Technology*, no. 8, 1990, p. 27, and no. 1, 1991, p. 238.

125 *CNA*, 26 May 1994.

126 See map published in *Lien-Ho Monthly*, May 1986, p. 22, reproduced in Yu, 'Taipei's Perception of its Deterrence Situation from April to July 1989', in Yang, *China's Military: The PLA in 1990/91*, pp. 63, 66.

127 George and Smoke, *Deterrence in American Foreign Policy*, p. 269.

128 Handel, *Weak States in the International System*, p. 23; and Vital, *The Inequality of States*, p. 8.

129 Erik Klippenberg, 'Strategy: The Impact of Technoloy', in Francois Heisbourg (ed.), *The Changing Strategic Landscape*, Macmillan, London, 1989, pp. 294, 296; and Richard Burt, *New Weapons Technologies: Debate and Directions*, Adelphi Papers No. 126, IISS London, 1976, p. 9.

130 Robert Rothstein, *Alliances and Small Powers*, Columbia University Press, New York and London, 1968, p. 18.

131 Robert Wade, *Governing the Market: Economic Theory and the Role of Government in East Asian Industrialisation*, Princeton University Press, Princeton, New Jersey, 1990, pp. 95–96.

132 *Aerospace*, January 1992, p. 33.

133 ibid., p. 34.

134 *CP*, 1 July 1993; and *Asian Wall Street Journal*, 27 April 1992.

135 *FCJ*, 24 June 1994.

136 *Aerospace*, January 1992, p. 34.

137 Taiwan has spent around US$20 billion: US$4.8 billion for the Lafayette frigates (France); US$250 million for the Knox-class frigates (US); US$1.2 billion for Cobra and Kiowa helicopters (US); US$126 million for the standard surface-to-air missiles (US); US$70 million for Harpoon missiles (US); US$377 million for the Patriot (US); US$6 billion for the F-16s (US); US$2.6 billion for the Mirages (US); US$4–5 billion for other weapons systems and equipment; and it is looking to spend US$7.5 billion to acquire six to ten attack submarines and ten corvettes. The United States defence industry has been the chief beneficiary.

138 USIS Wireless File, Canberra, 8 November 1993 and *CP*, 27 October 1993.

139 United States Secretary of State Dick Cheney, Interview, Indianapolis, USIS Wireless File, Canberra, 4 September 1992.

140 *Taiwan Relations Act*, Congressional Record — House 125 No. 38 March 16, 1979: H1668-70. See pp. 63, 222.

141 The Act provides in Section 3 that the United States 'will make available to Taiwan such defense articles and defense services as may be necessary to enable Taiwan to maintain a sufficient self-defence capability'.

142 State Department Report, 4 September 1992, USIS Wireless File, Canberra, 4 September 1992.

143 The deal, worth US$5.8 billion, includes 150 F-16 A/B models that have been upgraded with new mission computer and avionics systems (so that they can outperform the C/D model that Taiwan wanted).

144 On 7 September 1994, the Clinton Administration completed a lengthy, detailed inter-agency review of its policy towards Taiwan and China, the first in 22 years. Republican senators like Frank Murkowski, Charles Robb and Jesse Helms had sought to strengthen ties with Taiwan and, more specifically, recognise its achievements. Taiwan, they argued, was 'admirably more democratic, had grown to be one of America's most valued trading partners, and stood with the United States on an array of international issues'. Senator Robb said Taiwan was 'a good friend and a trusted ally that can be counted on for support'. Senator Murkowski said it was 'ironic and sad that the Clinton Administration was willing to risk the lives of American soldiers through restoring Aristide to power in Haiti in the guise of democracy, but it was not prepared to ruffle the PRC's feathers by rewarding democracy and human rights in Taiwan'.

In response, Assistant Secretary of State Winston Lord said relations with China were 'official and diplomatic', whereas relations with Taiwan were 'unofficial and strong'. He acknowledged that Taiwan was 'viscerally more attractive' than China. However, he claimed that the basic framework of United States policy towards China and Taiwan had been durable and productive over the last 22 years. It would, therfore, be a mistake to derail the 'delicately balanced' approach towards Beijing and Taipei that had been successfully maintained by previous administrations: it had been essential for maintaining peace, stability and economic development on both sides of the Taiwan Strait and it had buttressed the expansion of bilateral contacts between China and Taipei. Lord said, further, that the United States had made 'absolutely clear its expectation that cross-strait relations will evolve in a peaceful manner, that Taiwan's security is one of the most important aspects of United States policy, and that meeting the needs of Taiwan is critical not only for Taiwan, but also for peace and stability in the region'. The United States, said Lord, would continue to provide material and training to Taiwan to enable it to maintain a sufficient self-defence capability, as mandated by the *Taiwan Relations Act*. In addition, Taiwan's office in Washington was permitted to change its name from the Co-ordinating Council of North American Affairs to the more specific Taipei Economic and Cultural Representative Office, in line with the practice adopted by other countries in the Asia-Pacific region. Higher level United States government officials from economic and technical agencies were to be permitted to visit Taiwan and officials from Taiwan were permitted to meet their American counterparts in official settings 'rather than hotels and restaurants': transcript of Senate hearings,

United States Congress, 27 September 1994, from USIS Wireless File, Canberra, 28 September 1994.

In geo-political terms, the review reaffirmed the *Taiwan Relations Act* and significantly boosted Taiwan's political profile in Washington: United States policy on Taiwan had effectively changed tack.

145 Currently around US$85 billion.

146 Richard Solomon, Assistant Secretary of State, Presentation to the Pacific Rim Forum, San Diego, 15 May 1992, USIS Wireless File, Canberra, 14 May 1992, pp. 25, 26.

147 *CNA*, 23 October 1993.

148 *CP*, 8 September 1992. Chancellor Helmut Kohl turned the bid down in January 1993: *SCMP*, 29 January 1993, but other options were under consideration.

149 Over 130 German parliamentarians want the decision reversed so as to create jobs in Germany and negotiations are continuing: *CN*, 13 July 1993. Germany is Taiwan's largest trading partner in Europe with total trade in 1992 worth US$8 billion.

150 *Asian Defence Journal*, vol. 2/93, p. 20; *Far Eastern Economic Review*, 4 February 1993, p. 10.

151 Michael Richardson, 'Kockums' submarine set to penetrate regional markets', *Asia-Pacific Defence Reporter*, November 1990, p. 37.

9 Taiwan in the 1990s: Right Place, Right Time

One of the critical world events instinctively awaited by Taiwan was the end of the Cold War. The Kuomintang, in a sense, had been preparing for the collapse of communism and a crisis of legitimacy in China ever since 1949. Its bid to outperform communist China, indeed, provided the Kuomintang with much of the nation-building focus that gave it four decades of impressive economic development and the rationale to launch what was, with hindsight, a remarkably fortuitous program of political reform.

The shift in international attitudes towards Taiwan actually got underway in the mid-1980s. It was facilitated by Deng Xiaoping's revisionism in mainland China.[1] It gathered speed with the Gorbachev era that began in the Soviet Union in 1985 and gained momentum after the Tiananmen massacre in Beijing in 1989 and the collapse of the Soviet Union shortly thereafter.

Until the end of the 1980s, Taiwan was not accepted as a legitimate state actor by the world community. Most governments recognised China and took note of, respected or acknowledged the fact that Taipei was a Chinese provincial capital.[2] Taiwan is still recognised as the Republic of China by only 29 mostly small, marginally important, undeveloped countries in Latin America, the South Pacific and Africa.[3]

For those countries shifting diplomatic recognition to Beijing, Taiwan was an obstacle in the way of closer relations with China. The Australian government, for example, concluded that by opening an embassy in Beijing — 'the capital of China, of which Taiwan is a province' — Australia had come to terms with 'one of the central and inescapable facts of the region and redressed a serious imbalance and distortion in Australia's foreign policy'.[4] Thereafter, the policy of Australia — and most other governments in the world — was to have as little as possible to do with the government in Taipei, despite its clearly growing economic potential.[5]

The biggest blow to Taiwan's self-esteem came in December 1978, when the United States unceremoniously dumped Taiwan. President Carter announced the closure of the American embassy in Taipei as of 1 January 1979 and the abrogation of the United States–ROC Mutual Defence Treaty one year later.[6] The Kuomintang felt betrayed and disappointed. Premier Chiang Ching-kuo said the United States moves were 'tremendously adverse' and had 'seriously damaged' the people and government of Taiwan.[7] The United States Congress tried to reassure Taiwan by passing the *Taiwan Relations Act* of April 1979.[8] However, this was negated by the anti-Soviet priorities of the next United States President, Ronald Reagan, who, with advisers such as Secretary of State Alexander Haig, regarded the Soviet challenge as best met, *inter alia*, by the development of an alliance relationship with the PLA. This position was soon manifested in Sino-United States co-operation in support of rebel forces in Afghanistan and Cambodia and in monitoring Soviet missile tests from joint facilities in Xinjiang.[9] In 1982, the United States decided to help China modernise its navy and airforce. At the same time, President Reagan imposed limits on future United States arms sales to Taiwan.[10] In particular, the United States rejected Taiwanese requests to buy the F-16 fighter aircraft. Thereafter, according to Harvey Feldman, then Director of Republic of China Affairs in the United States State Department:

> Taiwan, and American concern about its fate, were simply embarrassments [in the way of the United States/China relationship and] the most elegant solution . . . would be reunification. If the terms of that reunification had to be those of the PRC, so be it.[11]

For other countries, such as Australia, there was no contest in the choice between Beijing and Taipei. China was seen to be the potentially larger, and therefore the more important, market for Australian wool, steel, iron ore, sugar and wheat.[12] Commercial considerations in Australia's case were supplemented by security concerns about the activities of the Soviet Pacific Fleet and its facilities in Cam Ranh Bay in Vietnam. Australian Prime Minister Malcolm Fraser found common ground with the government in Beijing in his opposition to Soviet expansionism.[13] Australia welcomed the August 1982 Sino-United States Joint Communiqué on Taiwan as an agreement that would enhance 'common interests of international peace and security' (i.e. Sino-United States opposition to the Soviet Union).[14]

Overall, the period from 1972 to the early 1980s was one of continued setbacks in Taiwan's foreign policy and diplomacy. Its deep sense of isolation and disappointment at being deserted by the international community, especially the United States, contributed to a decade of introspection and soul searching. In turn, however, these hard times forced the Kuomintang to review Taiwan's claim to be the Republic of China and led, eventually, to Premier Chiang Ching-kuo's survivalist move to construct a Taiwanese identity that was more appropriate to Taiwan's geopolitical circumstances. As a small state, Taiwan was, figuratively speaking, caught once more in the pull and push of two of the great powers that had always defined its place in the Asia-Pacific region: China and the United States. Because Taiwan could not accept the pull of reunification with China, its only option, once it was pushed away by the United States in 1979, was to try to establish an independent identity as the Republic of China on Taiwan (i.e. a compromise description that caught Taiwan's dilemma of being part of China — and threatened with war if it tried not to be — and an independent Taiwan).

A new Taiwanese identity flowed naturally from the consequences of Taiwan becoming rich, well educated, internationalised and middle class. As Taiwan's economy progressed in the four decades after 1949, there was a commensurate improvement in the conditions conducive to the development of a pluralist political system. As a trading state with modern transport and communication links to the rest of the world, Taiwan was immersed in international business, trade, languages, ideas, technology and culture — or what Jacoby called the 'seedbeds for the germination of democratic values'.[15] Other conditioning factors flowed from urbanisation, a system of compulsory universal education and a Western-trained bureaucratic elite.[16] These circumstances contributed to social diversity, variety, creativity, modernity and, ultimately, a readiness for political democratisation — or, as Premier Lien Chan described it, 'political liberalisation and democracy in a Chinese context'.[17]

Meanwhile, the Kuomintang's authoritarianism was mellowed and in due course transformed by the very prosperity it had created. With the idea of retaking the mainland looking more and more futile, and opportunities multiplying all the while on Taiwan, the Kuomintang began to look at Taiwan as a place that was more than just a temporary abode. This was especially so after the break with mainland China and with the past that was symbolised by the death of Chiang Kai-shek (in 1975) and Mao Zedong (in 1976), the two chief protagonists in the Chinese civil war.[18]

As well as international non-recognition of its claim to represent all of China and threats from Beijing to send the PLA to Taiwan in the event of a breakdown of law and order, the Kuomintang was also under pressure from the diminishing proportion of Taiwan's mainland-born population (down from 15 per cent in 1950 to 5.7 per cent in 1985). The native Taiwanese, furthermore, were increasingly active in their demands for a democratic political system that matched Taiwan's economic prosperity.[19] Sometimes this led to violent demonstrations, as in the nationwide anti-government rallies over ballot rigging and human rights at Chungli in November 1977 and Kaohsiung in December 1979.[20] These events, and the spectre of pro-democracy street unrest in neighbouring states such as

South Korea and the Philippines, helped the Kuomintang make up its mind.

Democratic reform was clearly in the Kuomintang's political self-interest: it provided a further point of contrast with mainland China; it helped broaden the Kuomintang's domestic political base and it was certain to win the approval of influential political bodies in the United States. President Carter's human rights agenda and critical Congressional comment about violations of human rights were additional considerations.[21]

The Nationalists, in any case, were ideologically committed to achieving democracy. The concept of *min-ch'uan*, or people's power, was one of Sun Yat-sen's Three Principles of the People. It envisaged incremental steps towards constitutional government and a fully democratic Taiwanese society after a period of military administration and one-party political tutelage.[22] To this end, the Kuomintang had held periodic elections for local magistrates and councils at the township, county and city level in the 1950s and 1960s. In 1969, 1972, 1973 and 1980, popular elections at the national level were held to fill vacancies left by mainlanders in the National Assembly. Additional seats for the National Assembly and the Legislative Yuan were filled through supplementary elections.[23]

At the same time, Taiwan had been subjected to several decades of American political influence. As a recipient of United States aid, protection, markets and education, Taiwan had been constantly exposed to American ideals, culture and tradition. Some graduate students returning from the United States, such as James Soong, Ma Ying-jeou and Shaw Yu-ming, became influential advisers to Chiang Ching-kuo when he was president from 1978–88.[24] Lee Teng-hui, appointed as Chiang's vice-president in 1984, had been trained in the United States in the 1950s and 1960s.

Finally, Kuomintang rivalry with, and its anticipation of, mainland China's looming political crisis gave a strategic rationale for undertaking democratic reform. According to Yu-ming Shaw, writing in 1985, the roots of Chinese communism were fundamentally weak, and China's traditional culture, exemplified by the success of Taiwan, was vastly superior. He forecast that:

> China's modernisation would produce a kind of revolution of rising expectations which would seriously shake the political and ideological foundations of the communist government, so much so that for its survival, the Chinese people and their communist leaders will have to look for other models of state building and government administration.[25]

In September 1987, the Secretary-General of the Kuomintang, Lee Huan, advocated that Taiwan should launch 'a political offensive' with the specific aim of bringing about a revolution in the mainland.[26] If the Kuomintang could seize the high moral ground as the world's first ever

Chinese democracy, this would then become Taiwan's window of opportunity — as, indeed, it proved to be.

All these considerations channelled Chiang Ching-kuo towards:

a domestic political reform and a quickening in the pace of Taiwanisation; and

b the decision to acknowledge the reality of the government in Beijing
   and its control of the mainland.

Chiang was also genuinely interested in reform. Despite his security
background, he was well known and well liked because of his habit of lis-
tening to the views of ordinary people.[27] He pushed through a policy of
radical political liberalisation that expanded the proportion of Taiwanese
on the Central Committee from 4:22 in 1976 to 9:27 in 1979 and 12:31 in
1984.[28] He appointed Lee Teng-hui, a Taiwanese, as vice president in 1984.
In 1987, non-mainlander Taiwanese were appointed to head the Judicial
and Control Yuans, key government positions that had previously been
held by mainland Taiwanese.[29] In July 1987, just before he died, Chiang
lifted martial law and the ban on opposition political parties.

Subsequently, the DPP and eleven other small political parties were
formed and their right to oppose the government and its policies was
accepted by the Kuomintang.[30] In October 1987, laws were passed guar-
anteeing the right of citizens to engage in public demonstrations. In January 1988, restrictions on the opening of newspapers were lifted. In 1990,
Lee Teng-hui, appointed caretaker president on the death of Chiang
Ching-kuo in January 1988, was elected president with his own mandate
to rule. Taiwan's transition to democracy came with elections held in
December 1989, when the Democratic Political Party (DPP) stood in
opposition to the Kuomintang and won 28 per cent of the popular vote.[31]
As C.L. Chiou observed, 'the snow had begun to melt'.[32]

Although the DPP vote was reduced to 23 per cent of the popular vote
in subsequent elections in 1991, the Kuomintang continued on the path of
political reforms. It accepted many of the economic and political
demands of the DPP — for example, on social welfare, private investment in state enterprises, environmental issues, reform of the judiciary,
institutionalising the democratic process, revising the Constitution,
ending confrontation with the mainland, reducing the size of the armed
forces, releasing political prisoners and promoting Chinese-Taiwanese
culture.

The Kuomintang's willingness to deal frankly with the 28 February
1947 massacre was an especially important step for the reconciliation of
mainlanders and local Taiwanese and the building of a new, cohesive Taiwanese identity. After having done its best to conceal the 1947 incident
for the previous four decades, the Kuomintang opened its records for
investigation in 1991 and published a report in February 1992 admitting
the government's responsibility. When President Lee Teng-hui, head
bowed, presided over a public remembrance ceremony for the events of

28 February 1947, he was effectively proclaiming a new Taiwan and a Tai-wanised Kuomintang that might legitimately and morally claim to repre-sent the wishes of the Taiwanese majority.

By December 1992, when the DPP won 31 per cent of the vote and established itself as a viable opposition political party, Taiwan's maturity as a Chinese democracy was complete.

Taiwan's domestic political reform was accompanied by a renaissance in Taiwanese art and a search of Taiwan's history for a truly Taiwanese identity.[33] Beginning in the 1970s when the study of Taiwan as a place with its own discrete history was first permitted, 'a new wave of Taiwan stud-ies' gained popularity in Taiwanese universities.[34] The relaxation of inter-nal security regulations that followed the lifting of martial law encour-aged Taiwanese scholars to examine their roots and the history of Taiwan as an island, areas that were once considered too sensitive for academics to research.[35] The new era of Taiwan-consciousness led to the publication of material previously banned because it suggested that Taiwan had a unique history that was not related to that of the mainland.[36] For example, James Davidson's 1903 book, *The Island of Formosa*, the best account of Taiwan's history at the turn of the century, and books and maps showing Taiwan in the seventeenth century under European rule were published. There was, said Yang Chung-sen, Director of Taiwan's National Central Library, 'a powerful burgeoning of native consciousness', so that 'at last, a new vogue. had been established in which the people of Taiwan were turning inward towards their roots with newfound nostalgia'.[37] Even gov-ernment publications began to probe Taiwan's origins, its prehistoric record, its European and Japanese interludes, its aboriginal culture, Tai-wanese folk culture, history, archaeology, sociology, anthropology and local literature, and the roots of a Taiwanese society that had evolved along with other Confucian 'dragons' in East Asia.

The Taiwanese, in short, were coming to grips with their non-main-land identity. They began to view themselves as a distinctive Taiwanese-Chinese society that was richer, more Western and more globally ori-ented than any previous Chinese society, apart perhaps from Hong Kong and Singapore. This has led, not surprisingly, to a growing debate over whether or not Taiwan is a Chinese society that can properly represent China and whether, to the contrary, Taiwan is different from the main-land, like Singapore.[38] Among the younger generation in Taiwan, includ-ing those whose parents may have been born on the mainland, 'identifi-cation with a China that includes the mainland was becoming an abstract notion and their primary concern was their own welfare on the island'.[39]

While there is a strong sense of Chinese nationality amongst Tai-wanese voters, there is little demand for reunification. This sentiment, based on 40 years of separation and a widening gap between the two Chinas, has been reinforced by the practice (since November 1987) of allowing Taiwanese to draw their own first-hand conclusions about mainland standards of living and lifestyle.[40]

Running parallel with the Kuomintang's domestic Taiwanisation program was a new mainland policy that aimed at a form of rapprochement with Beijing. The end of Taiwan's policy of no contacts with mainland China was intended to reassure the PLA and promote the common economic interests of both China and Taiwan (see Chapter 7). One of its effects, however, was to build a base for a one China, one Taiwan policy that upholds the principle of one China but claims that there are two sovereign parts to the notion of one China, and that 'both are entitled to the effective protection and representation of their fundamental rights in the United Nations'.[41]

Recognising the fact that the Chinese Communist Party ruled China was a major policy reversal for the Kuomintang, but it was a prerequisite for the move towards gradually developing a recognisable Taiwanese state. In May 1991, the Kuomintang terminated the 'Period of Mobilisation for Suppression of the Communist Rebellion', thereby acknowledging the reality of the People's Republic of China and Taiwan's separateness. For Taipei, the mainland's ruling Chinese Communist Party had ceased to be a rebel regime, which meant, in effect, that the Taiwanese 'conditionally recognised' the legitimacy of the Beijing government, its laws and its officials'.[42] While the move paved the way for negotiations between the two Chinas under the auspices of the newly formed National Reunification Council, it also paved the way for Taiwanese independence. In January 1992, Lee cut the last of Taiwan's symbolic ties with China by compulsorily retiring the remaining mainland-appointed parliamentarians (first appointed to the Legislative Yuan, the National Assembly and the Control Yuan in the 1940s). When Lien Chan took over the post of Premier in 1993, it meant that nearly all the top political posts in Taiwan had been filled by Taiwanese. A National Affairs Council was then established to seek a political consensus within Taiwan and further develop the Taiwanese identity.

Meanwhile, international attitudes towards Taiwan were beginning to change as indicators of Taiwan's raw economic power — notably the size of its foreign exchange reserves — came to be fully appreciated. In the early 1980s in Australia, for example, Ross Garnaut emphasised Taiwan's growing economic importance when he was economics adviser to the prime minister, Bob Hawke.[43] In 1984, the Secretary of the Department of Foreign Affairs and Trade, Professor Stuart Harris, also argued in favour of a closer relationship with Taiwan, a country that was increasingly acknowledged as one of Australia's 'most important export markets and sources of tourism, business migrants and investment'.[44] Although Australia cut diplomatic ties with Taipei in 1972, Taiwan expanded as an export market at a rate averaging 20 per cent per annum, making it one of Australia's fastest growing export markets.[45] By 1986, it was Australia's third largest buyer of coal, the biggest market for its dairy products, second for cotton, sorghum and pulpwood, and third for beef, aluminium and zinc. By 1988, Taiwan was buying significantly more from

Australia than mainland China. By 1989, it took 3.5 per cent of Australia's exports, well ahead of countries treated as important by the Australian government, such as Hong Kong, which took 2.6 per cent, Indonesia 2.6 per cent, China 2.5 per cent, Germany 2.3 per cent, Italy 2 per cent, Malaysia 1.9 per cent and France 1.5 per cent.[46] Ross Garnaut, predictably, recommended to the government in Canberra that Australia should expand its non-official links with Taiwan.[47]

Other countries made the same calculations about Taiwan's commercial merits and reached the same conclusions as Australia. Taiwan's steady ascendancy as a trading partner for countries in the Asia-Pacific region, compared with China, is shown in Tables 19 and 20. Improved political treatment of Taiwan inevitably followed. Australia, for example, reversed what had been a 20-year ban on ministerial contacts with Taipei in 1991.[48] Thereafter, 'unofficial' ministerial visits to Taiwan became an accepted part of the new Pacific diplomacy of countries such as the United States, Britain, France, Belgium, Germany, Austria, Indonesia, Canada, Singapore and Australia. It was truly a case of 'bandwagoning for profit'.[49]

While sensitive to the reaction from mainland China, most governments found it hard to resist sending a minister to join the queue of those seeking commercial advantage in Taipei. Most countries, indeed, began to move towards the policy espoused by former French Premier M. Rocard — that is, 'equal relations' with the three Chinas.

These developments weakened China's ability to control what other countries could or could not do *vis-a-vis* Taiwan. China's position, moreover, was being undermined by the normalisation of relations then taking place between the mainland and Taiwan, via Hong Kong, and the proliferation in their commercial exchanges (see Table 8). Taiwan, for its part, abandoned its claim to represent all of China and shifted from a position of no contacts and no negotiations to a pragmatic business-is-business approach (see Chapter 7). China, meanwhile, had become increasingly tolerant of non-official and non-publicised contacts between Taiwan and other countries.[50]

The biggest breakthrough in Taiwan's fortunes came with the political crisis in Beijing in 1989. A fundamental reappraisal of Taiwan was a foregone conclusion once images of pro-democracy demonstrations being crushed by tanks in Beijing were televised around the world. Attitudes towards China nose-dived. In the United States, Tiananmen stimulated the most intense and critical debate about United States policy towards China since the Sino-United States rapprochement of the early 1970s.[51] Instead of being well regarded as an ally or friend, China was perceived to be the last bastion of repressive communism and became the target of Western criticism over issues relating to democracy, Tibet, human rights, arms sales and, implicitly, its policy towards Taiwan.

Australia was no exception.[52] The Australian government expressed 'great outrage' at 'the barbarity practised in China by the Chinese government'.[53] Stephen FitzGerald, one of the architects of earlier China policy, called on Australia to give more attention to Taiwan.[54] Australia's Foreign Minister, Senator Gareth Evans, acknowledged that Tiananmen meant 'some countries, both inside and outside the region, that were already engaged in trade with Taiwan would feel less inhibited in increasing their contacts with Taiwan in other areas'.[55] That is precisely what happened. In effect, Taiwan's earlier well-timed moves in the area of 'freedom, democracy and prosperity' had become its 'most valuable and powerful assets'.[56]

However, few governments needed to be convinced about the importance of Taiwan, compared with a non-democratic mainland regime, when the former had its wealth and technical strengths factored into the balance. Taiwan's reputation as the country with highest or second highest foreign exchange reserves had already become an internationally recognised description — a trademark or instantly recognised logo — even before the massacre in Tiananmen in June 1989. Taiwan, however, has avoided emotional condemnation of China over human rights. In fact, Taipei prefers law and order in China, even under a communist regime, to the possibility of social instability and unrest.

Instead, Taiwanese propaganda has concentrated on promoting the Taiwan experience and knowledge of Taiwan's wealth in a world where the bottom line of most countries is 'of course, profits', as Foreign Minister Fredrick Chien astutely observed.[57] Governments have been subjected to a sophisticated public relations campaign organised by Taipei's Government Information Office (GIO). The GIO has a carefully targeted visitor program, especially for up and coming politicians and influential ex-politicians, such as George Bush, President Mikhail Gorbachev and Margaret Thatcher. It operates information centres in New York, London, Paris, Singapore and news and information offices in over 40 other international capitals. It airmails a range of well-written, beautifully illustrated, English-language publications around the world to promote 'the Taiwanese miracle'. It holds regular press conferences, invites journalists to Taiwan with all expenses paid and regularly advertises in leading newspapers — for example, *The Australian* in Australia, and the *New York Times*, *Los Angeles Times*, *Christian Science Monitor* and *Washington Post* in the United States. The Ministry of Foreign Affairs, meanwhile, carefully synchronises its work with the activities of departments and commissions involved in Taiwan's economic, cultural, educational and overseas Chinese affairs. The Minister of Foreign Affairs, Fredrick Chien, for example, calls the Minister for Economic Affairs, Vincent Siew, several times a week to co-ordinate Taiwan's 'dollar diplomacy'.[58]

Aid is an essential part of this effort, with offers of technical assistance in agriculture, fisheries, sugar milling, exploration of natural resources and industrial development all tailored to meet the needs of small dependent economies that might be swayed to vote for Taiwan on one issue or another. An Overseas Economic Co-operation Fund with capital of over

US$1 billion was established in 1988 to give financial aid or loans to developing nations in exchange for favours, such as support for Taiwan's GATT entry or its United Nations membership bid.[59] One of Taiwan's great strengths, as Tuan Y. Cheng notes, is its ability to exercise national resolve and solidarity in its use of economic power, skill in recognising opportunities and knowhow in organising international political support.[60]

Taiwan's aim, simply, is to underline its wealth, its minimal foreign debt and the extent of its cash flow. Statistical data on Taiwan's economic indicators — especially those relating to trade, foreign investment and Taiwan's US$90 billion in foreign exchange reserves — receive constant attention. Taiwan has also publicised a Six Year Development Plan (1991–96) that initially envisaged expenditure of US$300 billion, a huge amount by any standard. The plan, designed to make Taiwan one of the region's most advanced industrial economies by the turn of the century, was also intended to dazzle trade officials from countries interested in 'a slice of the Taiwanese action'. Even though the US$300 billion figure was later reduced to a more manageable US$240 billion, it generated enormous publicity and commercial interest. Ministers of Foreign Trade, Industry, Commerce, Public Works, Transport and Communications, ex-prime ministers, ex-presidents and ex-premiers went to Taiwan looking for 'a piece of the Six Year Plan pie'.[61] Australian trade officials, for example, claimed the plan presented a 'wealth of opportunities' for Australian companies in areas such as transport and communications, environment protection, energy development, the information industry, medicine and health.[62] Australian companies were urged to 'move both quickly and aggressively' if they did not want to be left in a market whose enormous potential had been realised by almost every other country in the world.[63]

Whether the measurement is profits or democratic reform, Taiwan's survival strategy has been to always identify squarely with the core values of the capitalist West. Thus it has tried to be a model low-tariff economy, it has introduced laws to protect intellectual property and endangered species and it has become environmentally sensitive. It has, in fact, become what Stephen Walt calls 'birds of a feather' — that is, it has adopted the political, cultural, ideological and economic traits of the West in general and the United States in particular.[64]

United States–Taiwan relations: The catalyst for change

As in the past, Taiwan's security and its place in the Asia-Pacific region are being determined by the ebb and flow of the Sino-United States relationship. Currently, the relationship is ebbing and it will continue to do so while China remains a non-democratic communist state.

America's antipathy towards anti-democratic societies has always been very strong. When Bill Clinton became president in 1992, the United States resumed its goal of supporting the spread of market-based democracies around the world (i.e. fostering a world environment in which American capitalism could survive and prosper).[65] The United States always had such a goal, according to Christopher Layne and Benjamin Schwarz, but it had been obscured by America's contest with the Soviet Union.[66] With the Soviet threat removed, the United States could concentrate on expanding 'the blessings of liberty'.[67] It was, therefore, 'working relentlessly' to promote the spread of democratic institutions, human rights and free markets in the Asia-Pacific.[68] Promotion of 'open societies and democratic values' was central to United States foreign policy because United States security was enhanced by democracies and threatened by dictatorships.[69]

Another consequence of the collapse of the Soviet Union was that it removed the only serious superpower challenge to United States global supremacy. This in turn changed the essence of the Sino-United States relationship. Instead of being tacit allies, China and the United States became potential enemies.

For many Americans, China is a dictatorship — it is one of the world's 'five remaining outdated repressive communist regimes'.[70] Americans could not forget Tiananmen Square, said Winston Lord, Assistant Secretary of State for East Asia.[71] Undesirable dictatorships in Asia, from the American perspective, are Vietnam, 'with a worse human rights record than Cuba's', North Korea, 'the worst troglodyte of all Stalinist regimes', and China.[72]

Such views about China meant that United States policy and attitudes towards Taiwan were destined to become much more positive. Madeleine Albright, United States Representative to the United Nations, for example, stipulated that United States post-Cold War foreign policy had four principal objectives: first, to strengthen ties with the major market economies (a priority that was applicable to Taiwan, rather than China); second, to help emerging democracies get on their feet (again, this applied to Taiwan and its attempts to democratise the mainland); third, to reform or isolate states that acted to undermine the stability and prosperity of the larger community (applicable, implicitly, to China); and fourth, to contain the chaos and ease the suffering in regions of greatest humanitarian concern (an area in which Taiwan has the financial resources and the incentive to make a substantial contribution).[73]

A concurrent post-Cold War United States aim, with direct implications for Taiwan, has been the expansion of exports and the revitalisation of America's national economic strength. Joan Spero, Under Secretary of State for Economic and Agricultural Affairs, explained that the United States had 'enormous economic, political and strategic stakes in the Pacific' a region that held 'terrific promise for job-creating exports of United States goods and services'.[74] Asia, said Winston Lord, was 'the key to the economic health of the US' and 'the most lucrative terrain for

American jobs and exports'.[75] Every billion dollars in exports created about 20 000 new American jobs.[76]

Defined in terms of jobs and democratic values, United States demands that China improve its human rights at 'a faster pace' and on 'a broader scale' were inevitable.[77] So too was a United States reappraisal of Taiwan and its economic significance.[78]

Taiwan is larger than China as an export market for the United States, and indeed, for many other countries. In 1991, Taiwan was America's ninth largest export market, whereas China was in sixteenth position. At a time when United States trade deficits were becoming a sensitive political issue in Washington, Taiwan proceeded to halve its trade surplus with the United States from a record US$16 billion in 1987 to US$7 billion in 1992, mainly by importing more products from the United States. In 1993, the United States exported twice as much to Taiwan (US$16.25 billion) as it did to China (US$8.7 billion) and in 1994, the Taiwanese signed a Trade and Investment Framework Agreement to further increase United States access to the Taiwanese market.

On the other hand, America's trade deficit with China skyrocketed to US$14 billion in 1991, up from US$6 billion in 1987. In 1992 it rose to almost US$20 billion (see Table 11) and was forecast to reach US$30 billion in 1993. China's trade surplus with the United States became a major source of friction that could not be sustained 'either politically or economically', according to United States Trade Representative Mickey Kantor.[79] This was especially so when issues like non-proliferation of weapons of mass destruction and strategic factors were added to the American calculus.

The non-proliferation of weapons of mass destruction is one of America's highest foreign policy priorities.[80] China, the world's fifth largest arms trading nation, has come under sustained criticism because of its alleged missile and nuclear technology transfers to Pakistan, Syria, Iran and Iraq. In this regard, one United States Congressmen described China as 'a rogue elephant in the world community with no regard for international stability'.[81] Joan Spero said the United States continued to have 'serious concerns about China's compliance with international standards on missile proliferation and nuclear testing'.[82] Taiwan, in contrast, does not export arms; it is a non-nuclear state; and it does not threaten America's strategic interests or offend its democratic values.

For the United States, predictably, Taiwan has become a model of how a Chinese state might best behave. Indeed, Spero declared that in a Pacific economic community based on shared prosperity, the expansion of market-oriented economies, a shared commitment to democratic values and respect for human rights, there were 'no better examples than Korea and Taiwan, where the democratic developments spurred by economic growth' were welcome for both humanitarian and practical reasons.[83] Such open, free market societies were desired by the United States elsewhere in East Asia on the rationale that such societies 'do not attack each other; they make better neighbours' and the result is 'a more secure and stable world'.[84]

While jobs and democracy have been important considerations for the United States in looking at the two Chinas, perhaps the most important factor arises from the modernisation of China as a great power and the present position of the United States as the world's only superpower.

Since the Soviet Union ceased to exist, there has been a reduction in forward-deployed United States air and naval forces in Pacific Asia. This has led to a perception of a power vacuum waiting to be filled by some ambitious regional power.[85] Of the possible contenders, China is seen to be the next state most likely to succeed in becoming a superpower and able, therefore, to disturb the regional and global equilibrium.[86] Some observers, such as Samuel Huntington, also fear that non-Christian and non-democratic China, with its tradition of anti-Western sentiment, will become overtly hostile to Western values once it becomes a strong, great power.[87]

In this regard, China's average annual GDP growth rate of 6 per cent between 1949 and 1978 jumped to 9 per cent over the decade 1979–89. In 1992–93, it was the fastest growing economy in the world, with a real GDP growth rate of nearly 13 per cent.[88] Assuming China can reconcile the rising expectations of its huge population with its resource scarcities and infrastructural bottlenecks, and provided it can maintain political stability and a program of incremental reform, it may be able to keep up a pattern of sustainable economic growth.[89] This could lead to a stable, relatively prosperous China that could spread positive economic benefits throughout the Asia-Pacific, especially if it can synergise with Hong Kong and Taiwan.

Yet it is the prospect of a strong, unified, relatively prosperous China that worries many security analysts.[90] Traditionally, China has often been the dominant power — the Middle Kingdom — in Pacific Asia. Physically, culturally and historically, China is a large country and large countries, we are reminded, tend to be ambitious and intent on increasing their power and influence.[91] Ironically, China's strategic and economic circumstances are more favourable than they have been for some time. It is more secure from external threats than at any other time in the last two centuries.[92] However, the collapse of the Soviet Union has lent weight to the view that China, unrestrained and unthreatened by a great power in the north, will be free to strike in the south. John Garver suggests that an overpopulated China is already embarked on a 'slow march south' to satisfy its need for energy resources.[93]

China, moreover, has disputed territory on the Sino-Indian border, the Sino-Vietnamese border, in the East China Sea where its claims are disputed by Japan and in the South China Sea where its claims are disputed by Vietnam, Malaysia and the Philippines. China supported insurgencies in Southeast Asia throughout the 1960s and 1970s and it retains ties with powerful overseas Chinese communities throughout Southeast Asia. It is due to recover control of Hong Kong in 1997 and Macao in 1999. It is continuing to test nuclear weapons and has what is claimed to be the fastest growing defence budget in the region. It is steadily developing its naval capabilities with new destroyers and frigates equipped with modern anti-ship and anti-aircraft missile systems.[94] It is training marine and airborne forces in amphibious landings and has increased its naval activities in the South and East China Seas, including the construction of an airstrip and berthing facilities on Woody Island in the Paracels, 400 kilometres south of Hainan Island.[95] China's B-6 naval bombers, equipped with Exocet-type C-601 anti-ship missiles (range 95 kilometres), can cover most of the South China Sea.[96] A full-length runway on Mischief Reef in the Spratly Islands further south would give China another stepping stone in the South China Sea. Meanwhile, China's recent acquisition of long range Su-27 fighter aircraft and Il-76 transport aircraft; its interest in inflight refuelling technology, Kilo-class submarines, aircraft carriers and other technology are seen as 'particularly menacing' because they give the PLA improved mobility, greater lift and longer reach.[97] These trends have added to concern about China's long-term great power ambitions.[98]

The result, not surprisingly, is considerable nervousness about China and its ability to project military force beyond its immediate borders into the western reaches of the Pacific Ocean.[99] As an emerging superpower, or simply the dominant power in the western Pacific, China is, *ipso facto*, a competitor of the United States. America's long-term strategic interest is to oppose the rise of China or 'any other potential future global competitor'.[100]

The corollary to this way of thinking is to look favourably on the potential of a country like Taiwan: it might be able to gradually democratise a communist China and it could contain a superpower China. Given its strategic location next to China (see Chapter 1) and its status as an important regional and global economic actor (see Chapter 6), Taiwan's strategic importance to the Asia-Pacific community has risen in inverse proportion to the post-Cold War re-evaluation of China as a potentially destabilising great power. Its importance has also been enhanced by the prospect of Hong Kong's return to China in 1997. Hong Kong, one of the world's leading trade and financial centres, has been under British control since 1842. Its imminent return to China has led to a widespread perception (unfounded, in my view) that it might be lost to the West. This disquiet has allowed Taiwan to present itself as a safe alternative base for many of the regional and China-related functions that are presently performed by Hong Kong. Like Hong Kong, Taiwan is a rich, Westernised Chinese enclave, located close to the China coast and in the centre of East Asia. However, it is far enough away and militarily strong enough to fend off any attempts at a takeover by Beijing.

Using Stephen Walt's analysis, Taiwan is a natural member of any group of states that has as one of its aims the need to balance and contain a state that is seen to be a rising great power.[101] Pending the rise of some third great power, such as Japan, or a rejuvenated Russia, requiring renewed strategic co-operation between China and the United States, Taiwan is a logical part of the array of forces that counter-balance and contain mainland China.

Taiwan, as we saw in Chapter 8, has a strong maritime and air force capability, a strong technical-industrial base and excellent ports and transport facilities. It still sits at the crossroads of overlapping interests between Japan, China and the United States. These assets make it an ideal base for supporting large-scale military operations in East Asia, especially with the closure of United States bases in the Philippines.

The result has been that Taiwan has been able to recover the strategic leverage it once enjoyed vis-a-vis China and the United States in the 1950s and 1960s. Taiwan's location on 'a strategic highway for great powers on the march' has remained unchanged.[102] As in the past, Taiwan is valued because it is located at the 'critical juncture' of busy sea lines of communications between Northeast Asia and Southeast Asia and between China and other countries in the Asia-Pacific region.[103] Container ships and tankers en route from Indonesian waters to the ports of Northeast Asia continue to transit either the Taiwan Strait or the Bashi Channel.[104]

Taiwan's location, its Chinese connections and its transportation and communications networks made it an important strategic launch pad during World War II. During the Korean War, when the West was set on containing China, Taiwan became 'an important anchor in the American defensive chain' in the Pacific.[105] Located a few minutes' flying time from the coast of mainland China, Taiwan was described as an unsinkable aircraft carrier, 'ideally located for . . . operations' against Chinese communism.[106]

Today, Taiwan is, metaphorically speaking, still an unsinkable aircraft carrier in the strictly military sense (see Chapter 8). But it is also an unsinkable aircraft carrier in an economic, political and cultural sense because it is contributing to gradual change in China. As vice-chairman of the Taiwan's Mainland Affairs Council, Ma Ying-jeou, commented, Taiwan is in an excellent position to contain and change the mainland.[107]

If China is to become, as Singapore's Senior Minister Lee Kuan Yew forecast, 'the biggest player in the recent history of the Asia-Pacific region',[108] then Taiwan's role in shaping its direction, its behaviour, its politics and its defence priorities could be critical. Knowledge of the Taiwanese modernisation experience is already spreading like a virus throughout the mainland, carried by an ever-increasing volume of visitors, telephone calls, fax messages and personal letters.[109] This penetration of the mainland consciousness is transforming Chinese communism gradually, effectively and peacefully. The effects on the region so far have been very positive. If Taiwan is one of the most critical factors in the peaceful evolution of communism in mainland China, its well-being as an independent political entity is of vital importance to the security and stability of the whole Asia-Pacific region. It is on the basis of this role, and regional concern about China, that Taiwan has offered to forge a new strategic alliance relationship with the United States, Japan and other APEC countries that have an interest in the future of China.[110]

The turnabout in international attitudes towards Taiwan is best illustrated by United States policy on arms sales to China and Taiwan (see Chapter 3). After Tiananmen, the United States cancelled sales of weapons and defence technology to China, including a contract for Grumman to upgrade Chinese F-8 fighter aircraft.[111] In November 1992, the United States, so to speak, switched sides — it began to help upgrade Taiwan's airforce with the sale of 150 F-16 fighter aircraft. The Taiwanese F-16s, said President George Bush, would 'help maintain peace and stability' in the Asia-Pacific region.[112] Coincidentally, the sale saved 3000 jobs at the General Dynamics F-16 plant in Fort Worth, Texas.[113] Bush claimed that the sale did not change United States commitments made to Beijing in the past.[114] In fact, the F-16 sale reversed the United States policy that had been established a decade earlier when, in 1982, President Reagan declared that the United States did not seek to carry out a long-term policy of arms sales to Taiwan and that it intended to gradually reduce its sales of arms to Taiwan, 'leading over a period of time to a final resolution'.[115] After the F-16 sale was announced, sales of United States weapons and defence technology to Taiwan increased rapidly, both in quantitative and qualitative terms.

Despite forecasts of its decline, the United States was, and is still, the strongest power in the Pacific.[116] It is likely to remain the only Pacific power that can protect small states and balance the ambitions of larger ones for at least the next few decades. American foreign and defence policies, therefore, are critically important in the China–Taiwan situation. As was the case in the 1970s, when other countries followed the United States lead on rapprochement with Beijing, the F-16 sale precipitated a significant shift in international attitudes towards Taiwan. Other countries, including France, Holland, Germany, Britain, Australia and Russia, tried to follow the American lead by offering to sell sophisticated defence equipment to Taiwan. At one stage, Taiwan had a choice between MiG-29s from Russia, F-16s and F-18s from the United States, the Lavi fighter from Israel and the Mirage 2000 from France. Many countries moved to upgrade their 'unofficial' relations with Taipei in recognition of Taiwan's importance as a market and source of investment funds, the reality of its independence from the mainland and the fact that the United States had effectively upgraded its relationship with Taipei. Today, Taiwan has 92 'Taipei Economic and Cultural Offices' in 60 countries compared with 66 in 43 countries in 1990. Many, including those in the United States, Australia, the Philippines, Singapore, Malaysia and Indonesia, receive diplomatic courtesies normally reserved only for embassies.[117] Taiwan, in other words, has been one of the chief beneficiaries of the gradual change in international diplomatic priorities that accompanied the retreat of communism and the end of the Cold War.

Beijing, meanwhile, has progressively relaxed its policy on relations between the rest of the world and Taiwan, to the point where, as we saw in Chapter 7, both sides of the Taiwan Strait are dealing with each other in a practical and confident way. Both participate in PBEC, PECC and APEC.[118] Taiwan is also a natural invitee to other regional forums, such as Malaysia's East Asian Economic Caucus; the security oriented roundtables organised by the ASEAN Institutes of Strategic and International Studies; the Indonesian-sponsored series of workshops on conflict management in the South China Sea; and the South Pacific Forum, where smaller aid-dependent island countries have sought to include Taiwan in their post-Forum dialogue. Taiwan's next goals are participation in the Conference on Security Co-operation in the Asia-Pacific (CSCAP), the various ASEAN forums, the OECD and the World Bank. While Chinese leaders have objected to Taiwan's membership of the ASEAN Regional Forum, they have stated that Taiwan can join the General Agreement on Tariffs and Trade (GATT), provided China is able to join first.[119]

For Taiwan, membership of APEC and GATT is a stepping stone to membership of the United Nations, an issue of profound importance to Japan, the United States and China. For both the United States and Japan, there are strategic advantages in keeping Taiwan separate from the mainland. Concerned about superpower China, they prefer to see Taiwan remain beyond the reach of Beijing on the grounds that a divided China equals a weaker China.[120] For China, the loss of Taiwan involves questions of face and domestic politics and it could be a reason to contemplate the threat or use of force.

Notes

1   See Parts II and III of Bih-jaw Lin and James T. Myers (eds), *Forces of Change in Contemporary China*, University of South Carolina Press, Columbia, 1993.

2   For details on the wording that different countries used in recognising Beijing, see Colin Mackerras and Amanda Yorke, *The Cambridge Handbook of Contemporary China*, Cambridge University Press, Cambridge, 1991, pp. 150ff.

3   They are the Bahamas, Belize, Burkina Faso (formerly Upper Volta), Costa Rica, Dominica, the Dominican Republic, El Salvador, Grenada, Guatemala, Guinea Bissau, Haiti, Honduras, Lesotho, Liberia, Malawi, Nauru, Nicaragua, Niger, Panama, Paraguay, Saint Christopher and Nevis, Saint Vincent and Grenadines, Saint Lucia, Swaziland, the Solomon Islands, Tonga, Tuvalu and Vatican City. Twelve of them have a population of less than 500 000 and a GNP of less than US$1 billion. The only important state that still recognises Taiwan is South Africa.

4   Prime Minister Gough Whitlam, statement on Australia's Foreign Policy, 24 May 1973, *Australian Foreign Affairs Record (AFAR)*, vol. 44, no. 5, 1973, pp. 335–37.

5   Gary Klintworth, *Australia's Taiwan Policy 1942–1992*, Australian Foreign Policy Papers, Department of International Relations, ANU, Canberra, 1993, pp. 50ff.

6   Hungdah Chiu, *The Taiwan Relations Act and Sino-American Relations*, Occasional Papers No. 5, School of Law, University of Maryland, 1990, p. 20.

7   Cited in Liang-tsai Wei, 'ROC–US Relations Since Shanghai Communiqué: A Critical Review of the Decade', in Yu-ming Shaw (ed.), *ROC–US Relations: A Decade After the Shanghai Communique*, The Asia and World Monograph Series, No. 31, Taipei, November 1983, pp. 11, 20.

8   The *Taiwan Relations Act* was intended by Congress to create a legal framework for continued trade, security and cultural ties between the United States and Taiwan in the absence of formal diplomatic recognition: Lin Bih-jaw, 'Taipei–Washington Relations: Moving Towards Institutionalisation', in Chang King-yuh (ed.), *ROC–US Relations Under the Taiwan Relations Act: Practice and Prospects*, Institute of International Relations, National Chengchi University, Taipei, 1988, pp. 40ff. See also Chapter 3.

9   Gary Klintworth, *China's Modernisation: The Strategic Implications for the Asia-Pacific Region*, AGPS, Canberra, 1989, pp. 87–89.

10 Joint Communiqué, 17 August 1982. See Chapter 3.

11 Harvey Feldman, 'Development of US–Taiwan Relations 1948–87', in Harvey Feldsman et al. (eds), *Taiwan in a Time of Transition*, Paragon House, New York, 1988, pp. 129, 156.

12 Klintworth, *Australia's Taiwan Policy 1942–1992*, p. 56.

13 ibid., pp. 61–62.

14 Australian Department of Foreign Affairs, *Annual Report 1982*, Australian Government Publishing Service, Canberra, 1983, p. 14.

15 Neil H. Jacoby, *US Aid to Taiwan*, Praeger, New York, 1966, p. 115.

16 Thomas Robinson, 'Democracy and Development in East Asia — Toward the Year 2000' in Thomas Robinson (ed.), *Democracy and Development in East Asia*, The AEI Press, Washington 1991, pp. 279, 282. For an overview of the effects of external factors on Taiwan's democratic development, see Martin L. Lasater, 'Taiwan's International Environment' in Robinson, ibid., pp. 91ff.

17 Premier Lien Chan, quoted in *China Post (CP)*, 12 May 1993.

18 Alice Amsden, 'The State and Taiwan's Economic Development', in Peter B. Evans, Dietrich Rueschemeyer, Theda Skocpol (eds), *Bringing the State Back In*, Cambridge University Press, Cambridge, New York, 1985, pp. 79, 100–101.

19 Ting Tin-yu, 'Sociocultural Developments in the ROC', in Robinson, *Democracy and Development in East Asia*, pp. 75, 80.

20 For an overview on early demands for democratisation in Taiwan, see Peng Ming-min, *A Taste of Freedom, Memoirs of a Formosan Independence Leader*, Holt Rinehart and Winston, New York, Chicago and San Francisco, 1972. On Taiwan's political transformation generally, see Tien Hung-mao, *The Great Transition: Political and Social Change in the Republic of China*, Hoover Institution Press, Stanford, 1989; and Tun-jen Cheng and Stephan Haggard (eds), *Political Change in Taiwan*, Lynne Rienner Publishers, Boulder, Col., 1992; Tien Hung-mao and Chu Yun-han, 'Taiwan's Domestic Political Reforms, Institutional Change and Power Realignment', in Gary Klintworth (ed.), *Taiwan in the Asia-Pacific in the 1990s*, Allen & Unwin/Department of International Relations, ANU, Canberra, 1994, pp. 1ff; C.L. Chiou, 'Emerging Taiwanese Identity in the 1990s: Crisis and Transformation', in Klintworth, ibid., p. 21; and C.L. Chiou, 'Democratising Taiwan: The 1990s National Affairs Conference', in Gary Klintworth (ed.), *Modern Taiwan in the 1990s*, Canberra Papers on Strategy and Defence No. 75, Strategic and Defence Studies Centre, ANU, Canberra, 1991, pp. 39, 41.

21 Taiwan's record on human rights often attracted bad publicity in the United States. Hearings were held in the United States Congress in 1981 on the surveillance, harassment and even murder in the United States of opponents of the KMT: *Taiwan Agents in America and the Death of Prof We-Chen Chen: Hearing before the Subcommittee on Asian and Pacific Affairs of the House Foreign Affairs Committee*, 97th Congress, 1st Session (1981) and *Murder of Henry Liu: Hearing Before the Subcommittee on Asian and Pacific Affairs of the House Foreign Affairs Committee*, 99th Congress, 1st Session (1985), both cited in Lori Fisier Damrosch, *The Taiwan Relations Act After Ten Years*, Occasional Papers in Contemporary Asian Series no. 4 (1990), School of Law, University of Maryland, pp. 15, 16.

22 Samuel C. Chu, 'The Three Principles of the People and Political Developments: Thoughts on Democracy in the Republic of China and the People's Republic of China', in Chang King-yuh (ed.), *The Impact of the Three Principles of the People on China*, Institute of International Relations, National Chengchi University, Taipei, 1988, pp. 1, 5.

23 Tien Hung-mao, 'Social Change and Political Development in Taiwan', in Feldman, *Taiwan in a Time of Transition*, pp. 1, 12.

24 Ting, 'Sociocultural Developments in the ROC', in Robinson, *Democracy and Development in East Asia*, pp. 75, 89.

25 Yu-ming Shaw, 'Taiwan: A View from Taipei', *Foreign Affairs*, vol. 63, no. 5, 1985, pp. 1062–63.

26 Quoted by An-chia Wu, 'Peking's Evaluation of Taiwan's Development Experience', in Lin and Myers, *Forces of Change in Contemporary China*, pp. 359, 360.

27 Lu Ya-li, 'Political Developments in the Republic of China' in Robinson (ed.), *Democracy and Development in East Asia*, p. 41.

28 The ratio increased to 14:31 in 1986 and 16:31 in 1988: Tien, 'Social Change and Political Development in Taiwan' in Feldman, *Taiwan in a Time of Transition*, p. 13.

29 ibid.

30 Today there are over 70 political parties in Taiwan.

31 Chiou, 'Democratising Taiwan: The 1990s National Affairs Conference', in Klintworth, *Modern Taiwan in the 1990s*, pp. 44ff.

32 ibid., pp. 45–59.

33 See the analysis by Jou-juo Chu, 'The Rise of Island-China Seperatism', in Klintworth, *Taiwan in the Asia-Pacific in the 1990s*, p. 44; and recent articles in Taiwanese government journals *Free China Review (FCR)* and *Sinorama*. The subject of Taiwan's identity was discussed in detail at the Conference on Taiwan's New Identities in the 1990s, Asia Research Centre, Murdoch University, 21–22 September 1993.

34 Historian Chang Yen-hsien, cited in Emma Wu, 'Local Scholars take a Closer Look at Home', in *FCR*, March 1992, pp. 5, 8.

35 ibid.

36 Special Section on Taiwan Studies, *FCR*, vol. 44, no. 2, February 1994, pp. 38ff.

37 Yang Chung-sen, Director of Taiwan's National Central Library, preface to Christine Vertente, Hsueh Chi-Hsu and Wu Mi-Cha, *The Authentic Story of Taiwan: An Illustrated History Based on Ancient Maps, Manuscripts and Prints*, Mappamundi Publishers, Knokke (Belgium), 1991.

38 A question raised by Chen Shao-hsin, of National Taiwan University in his 1979 book *The Population Changes and Social Changes in Taiwan*, cited in *FCR*, March 1992, p. 6.

39 Tien, 'Social Change and Political Development in Taiwan', in Feldman, *Taiwan in a Time of Transition*, p. 15.

40 Government officials or military personnel cannot visit China but they can invite their mainland relatives to visit them in Taiwan.

41 *The Participation of the Republic of China on Taiwan in the United Nations*, Mainland Affairs Council, Executive Yuan, Taipei, July 1994, p. 10.

42 Statute Governing Relations Between the People of Taiwan and the Mainland passed on 16 July 1992, *Free China Journal*, 21 July 1992.

43 Personal communication, 1 April 1993.

44 Stuart Harris, 'The Amalgamation of the Department of Foreign Affairs and Trade', 17 March 1988, *AFAR*, vol. 59, no. 3, 1988, p. 71 and *Annual Report*, Department of Foreign Affairs and Trade, Australian Government Publishing Service, Canberra, 1990–91, p. 20.

45 Along with China, which grew at an average of around 27 per cent per annum over the same period.

46 *Composition of Trade Australia 1990*, Department of Foreign Affairs and Trade, Canberra, 1990, pp. 16, 18.

47 Ross Garnaut, *Australia and the Northeast Asian Ascendancy*, Australian Government Publishing Service, Canberra, 1989, p. 279.

48 See Klintworth, *Australia's Taiwan Policy 1942–1992*, p. 111.

49 From the article by Randall L. Schweller, 'Bandwagoning for Profit', *International Security*, vol. 19, no. 1, Summer 1994, pp. 72–107.

50 *Free China Journal (FCJ)*, 28 July 1992.

51 Harry Harding, 'China's American Dilemma', *Annals, American Academy of Political and Social Science*, vol. 519, January 1992, p. 12.

52 See Gary Klintworth (ed.), *China's Crisis: The International Implications*, Canberra Papers No. 57, Strategic and Defence Studies Centre, Canberra, 1989.

53 Speech, Bob Hawke, 'Parliament Outraged at Events in China', 15 June 1989, *AFAR*, vol. 60, no. 6, 1989, p. 266.

54 *Australian Financial Review*, 4 December 1989, p. 14.

55 Gareth Evans, Speech, 'Asia-Pacific: An Australian View', 20 June 1989, *AFAR*, vol. 60, no. 6, 1989, p. 280.

56 Remarks by President Lee Teng-hui, reported in *SCMP*, 19 May 1991.

57 Quoted in *SCMP*, 2 May 1991.

58 Minister for Foreign Affairs, Fredrick Chien, interview, *FCR*, February 1993, pp. 16, 18.

59 In 1991, Taiwan's Vice President Li Yuan-zu gave low-interest loans of US$30 million to Honduras, $45 million to Costa Rica and $30 million to Nicaragua. These three countries, together with Panama, El Salvador and Guatemala, pledged support for Taiwan's GATT membership bid. All have diplomatic relations with Taiwan. Honduras and Costa Rica also pledged that they would not extend diplomatic recognition to Beijing. Nicaraguan President Chamorro said Nicaragua's economy was crippled economically and was in dire need of foreign investment, especially in agriculture. Vice President Li signed an investment agreement in Nicaragua for a multi-million dollar lumber investment that was expected to create 4000 new jobs: *Free China Journal*, 30 August 1991. Taiwan learned the value of well-pitched aid programs in Third and Fourth World countries in the 1960s. It was Taiwan's technical aid program in that decade that 'helped significantly in persuading African and Latin American states to maintain diplomatic relations with Taipei instead of Peking and to support the ROC on the Chinese representation issue in the United Nations': Ralph N. Clough, *Island China*, Harvard, Cambridge, Mass., 1978, p. 152.

60 Tuan Y. Cheng, *Economic Diplomacy in the Pacific Basin of the Republic of China on Taiwan*, Pacific Forum/CSIS, Hawaii, July 1992, p. 5.

61 Article, 'Contractual Relationships — Economic and Foreign Relations in the Six-Year Plan', *Sinorama*, February 1993, p. 21.

62 Peter Osborne and Robert O'Donovan, *Taiwan in the 1990s: Opportunities for Australia*, ACC/Westpac Economic Discussion Papers 4/1991,Canberra, 1991, pp. 1, 12, 13, 24.

63 ibid.

64 Stephen M. Walt, *The Origins of Alliances*, Cornell University Press, Ithaca, 1987, p. 33.

65 Christopher Layne and Benjamin Schwarz, 'American Hegemony — Without an Enemy', *Foreign Policy*, vol. 92, Fall 1993, p. 5.

66 ibid.

67 President Bill Clinton, Remarks aboard *USS George Washington*, Portsmouth, England, 5 June 1994, USIS Wireless File, Canberra, 7 June 1994.

68 United States Secretary of State, Warren Christopher, testimony, Senate Foreign Relations Committee, 4 November 1993, in USIS Wireless File, Canberra, 5 November 1993; and address, National Foreign Policy Conference 20 October 1993 in USIS Wireless file, Canberra, 21 October 1993.

69 ibid.

70 ibid.

71 Winston Lord, Confirmation Hearing Testimony, East Asia/Pacific Subcommittee, Senate Foreign Relations Committee, Washington, 31 March 1993, in USIS Wireless File, Canberra, 5 April 1993.

72 *Time Magazine*, 29 August 1994.

73 Madeleine Albright, speech to the National War College, Washington, 23 September 1993, USIS Wireless File, Canberra, 24 September 1993.

74 See, for example, Joan Spero, Under Secretary of State for Economic and Agricultural Affairs, speech at the Asia Foundation, San Francisco, 24 September 1993, USIS Wireless File, Canberra, 29 September 1993.

75 United States Assistant Secretary of State, Winston Lord, House Foreign Affairs Committee hearing, Washington, 15 June 1994, in USIS Wireless File, Canberra, 16 June 1994.

76 Admiral Charles R. Larson, Commander in Chief, United States Forces in the Pacific, address 'America's Pacific Challenge', Honolulu, in USIS Wireless File, Canberra, 15 October 1993.

77 US materials quoted in Guo Changlin, 'Sino–US Relations in Perspective', *Contemporary International Relations*, vol. 2, no. 7 (Beijing), July 1992, p. 8. See also Sa Benwang, 'Three Pillars of the Clinton Administration's Foreign Policy' in *International Strategic Studies*, no. 1, China Institute for International Strategic Studies, Beijing, 1993, p. 14.

78 Such a reappraisal occurred in mid-1994: United States State Department Report, 6 July 1994, in USIS Wireless File, Canberra, 8 July 1994. The review of United States policy on Taiwan led to an upgrading of Washington's 'unofficial' links with Taipei: reported in the *Sydney Morning Herald*, 11 August 1994.

79 Mickey Kantor, United States Trade Representative, National Foreign Policy Conference, Washington 20 October 1993 in USIS Wireless File, Canberra, 22 October 1993.

80 President Bill Clinton, address to the UN General Assembly, New
   York, 27 September 1993, USIS Wireless File, Canberra, 29 September
   1993.

81 United States Senator Joseph Biden, speech condemning China's
   arms sales to Middle East countries, reported in *SCMP*, 16 May 1991.

82 Spero, speech at the Asia Foundation.

83 Joan Spero, Under-Secretary of State, address, Korean Economic
   Institute of America, 19 October 1993, in USIS Wireless File, Canberra, 21 October 1993.

84 Winston Lord, Assistant Secretary of State for East Asian and Pacific
   Affairs, address, Washington, 12 October 1993 in USIS Wireless File,
   Canberra, 13 October 1993.

85 See, for example, 'End of the Cold War: Strategic Trends and Outlook', Appendix 1, in East Asia Analytical Unit, Department of Foreign Affairs and Trade, *Australia and North-East Asia in the 1990s:
   Accelerating Change*, Australian Government Publishing Service,
   Canberra, 1992, pp. 95–105.

86 See, for example, Barry Buzan, 'The Post-Cold War Asia-Pacific Security Order: Conflict or Cooperation', in Andrew Mack and John
   Ravenhill (eds), *Economic and Security Regimes in the Asia-Pacific*, Studies in World Affairs Series, Allen & Unwin, Sydney, 1994, pp. 130–51.

87 Samuel P. Huntington, 'The Clash of Civilisations', *Foreign Affairs*,
   vol. 72, no. 3, Summer 1993, p. 22.

88 *Asia-Pacific Profiles 1993*, Asia-Pacific Economics Group, Research
   School of Pacific and Asian Studies, ANU, Canberra, 1993, p. 63.

89 Peter Harrold, *China's Reform Experience to Date*, World Bank Discussion Papers 180, The World Bank, Washington, 1992, p. 38.

90 There are many pessimistic forecasts about China. See, for example,
   Paul Dibb, 'Asia's Security in the 21st Century', *Strategic and Defence
   Studies Newsletter*, March 1994, p. 1 and his article, 'Asia's Simmering
   Cauldron Could Soon Boil Over', *The Australian*, 19 November 1993.
   Articles with a similarly pessimistic viewpoint, certainly about
   China, include Denny Roy, 'Hegemon on the Horizon? China's
   Threat to East Asian Security', *International Security*, vol. 19, no. 1,
   Summer 1994, p. 140; and Barry Buzan and Gerald Segal 'Rethinking
   East Asian Security', *Survival*, Summer 1994, pp. 3–21.

91 Richard K. Betts, 'Wealth, Power, and Instability', *International Security*, vol. 18, no. 3, Winter 1993/94, pp. 34, 37; Christopher Layne,
   'The Unipolar Illusion: Why New Great Powers Will Rise', *International Security*, vol. 17, no. 4, Spring 1993, p. 5; and Samuel P. Huntington, 'Why Primacy Matters', *International Security*, vol. 17, no. 4,
   Spring 1993, pp. 68, 71.

92   Yan Xuetong, 'China's Security After the Cold War', *Contemporary International Relations* (Beijing), vol. 3, no. 5, May 1993, p. 1.

93   John Garver, 'China's Push Through the South China Sea: The Interaction of Bureaucratic and National Interests', *The China Quarterly*, no. 132, December 1992, p. 999.

94   'New Ships for the PLAN', *Jane's Defence Weekly*, 18 January 1992, p. 88.

95   Chang Pao-min, 'A New Scramble for the South China Sea Islands', *Contemporary Southeast Asia*, vol. 12, no. 1, June 1990, p. 27; and Sheng Lijun, 'China's Policy Towards the Spratly Islands in the 1990s', draft paper, with neibu documents, May 1994.

96   Duncan Lennox and Arthur Rees (eds), *Jane's Air Launched Weapons*, Jane's Information Group, Surrey, 1989, Issue 11; and IISS, *The Military Balance 1993*, Brassey's, London, p. 154.

97   Michael T. Klare, 'The Next Great Arms Race', *Foreign Affairs*, vol. 72, no. 3, Summer 1993, pp. 136, 141. These goals, however, have been long-standing ones for the PLA: see Gary Klintworth, *China's Modernisation and the Strategic Implications for the Asia-Pacific Region*, AGPS, Canberra, 1989, pp. 41ff.

98   See, for example, the remarks attributed to Derek da Cunha, Institute of Southeast Asian Studies, Singapore, reported in the *Straits Times*, 28 June 1994; and J.N. Mak, *ASEAN Defence Reorientation 1975–1992: The Dynamics of Modernisation and Structural Change*, Canberra Papers No. 103, Strategic and Defence Studies Centre, Research School of Pacific Studies, ANU, Canberra, 1993, pp. 45, 170.

99   Mak, *ASEAN Defence Reorientation 1975–1992*, p. 170.

100 'Excerpts from Pentagon's Plan: Prevent the Re-Emergence of a New Rival', *New York Times*, 8 March 1992, cited in Robert Jervis, 'International Primacy: Is the Game Worth the Candle?', *International Security*, vol. 17, no. 4, Spring 1993, pp. 52, 54.

101 Walt, *The Origins of Alliances*, p. 17. See also Robert Rothstein, *Alliances and Small Powers*, Columbia University Press, New York and London, 1968, pp. 52–53.

102 Michael Handel, *Weak States in the International System*, Frank Cass, London, 1981, p. 72.

103 See Chapter 1.

104 Tun Hwa Ko, 'Taiwan as a Strategic Asset', *Global Affairs*, vol. IV, no. 2, Spring 1989, pp. 65, 69.

105 United States Senate, Committee on Foreign Relations, Report on Mutual Defence Treaty with the Republic of China, 8 February 1955, Senate, 84th Congress, 1st Session, Executive Report No. 2, United States Government Printing Office, Washington, 1955, p. 8.

106 Department of External Affairs, Canberra, *Current Notes on International Affairs*,vol. 22, no. 7, 1951, p. 375.

107 Ma Ying-jeou, Vice Chairman of the Mainland Affairs Council, speech 'Regional Stability in East Asia: Implications of Taipei–Peking Relations', Munich, in *FCJ*, 19 February 1993, p. 7.

108 Lee Kuan Yew, Singapore's former Prime Minister, observed that 'it is not possible to pretend that [China] is just another big player. This is the biggest player in the history of man': quoted by Nicholas Kristof, 'China's Rise from Dinosaur to Dragon', *The Australian*, 29 November 1993, p. 11. See also Nicholas D. Kristof, 'The Rise of China', *Foreign Affairs*, vol. 72, no. 5, November/December 1993, p. 59; and William H. Overholt, *China: The Next Economic Superpower*, Weidenfeld and Nicolson, London, 1993.

109 Four million Taiwanese visited the mainland between 1987 and 1992, with the numbers now well over one million per annum. Over 25 million telephone calls were made and more than 56 million letters were posted to the mainland over the same period. Trade is flourishing almost exponentially while the Taiwanese have emerged as prolific investors throughout southern China and, more recently, throughout northern China as well: see Chapter 7.

110 Ministry of Foreign Affairs, Foreign Affairs Report — Foreign Relations and Diplomatic Administration, Taipei, 21 January 1993, cited in *FCJ*, 29 January 1993, p. 1. The report calls for interdependency between Asia-Pacific countries in the face of China's military buildup.

111 However, according to some observers, it suited China to have the deal cancelled because it was increasingly unattractive: Bin Yu, 'Sino-Russian Military Relations', *Asian Survey*, vol. XXXIII, no. 3, March 1993, pp. 302, 305.

112 Transcript, President George Bush, speech at the General Dynamics aircraft plant in Texas on 2 September 1992, USIS Wireless File, Canberra, 3 September 1992.

113 *Business Week*, 14 September 1992.

114 ibid.

115 ibid.

116 Samuel P. Huntington, 'The United States: Decline or Renewal', in Francis Heisbourg (ed.), *The Changing Strategic Landscape*, IISS, Macmillan, London, 1989, pp. 46, 57.

117 For Taiwanese offices in ASEAN countries, see Kuo-hsiun Lee. 'The Republic of China and Southeast Asia: More than Economy', in Yu San Wang (ed.), *Foreign Policy of the Republic of China on Taiwan*, Praeger, New York, 1990, pp. 77, 98.

118 Taiwan joined PBEC in 1980, PECC in 1986 and APEC in 1991. Membership of APEC gives Taiwan the right to be heard at ministerial level in the most important economic forum in the Asia-Pacific region. Other than the Asian Development Bank, Taiwan is not represented at ministerial level in any other international organisation.

119 Premier Li Peng, speaking to former Japanese Prime Minister Takeshita in Switzerland at the World Economic Council meeting, *Nikkei Weekly*, 8 February 1992. Taiwan has won wide support for its bid to join the GATT (as the 'Customs Territory of Taiwan, Penghu, Kinmen and Matsu' under Article XXXIII of the GATT regulations)

for the same reason that it was invited to join APEC: as a strong economic power, it simply cannot be excluded. However, at the inaugural meeting of the ASEAN Regional Forum on Security in Bangkok, Foreign Minister Qian Qichen said that Taiwan would not be allowed to join: *Bangkok Post*, 22 July 1994.

120 A similar rationale lies behind Western interest in supporting greater democracy in Hong Kong and a degree of independence for Tibet. In September 1993, for example, the United States Senate Foreign Relations Committee proposed a draft bill that described Tibet as 'an occupied sovereign country and stated that its true representatives are the Dalai Lama and the Tibetan Government-in-Exile': Senate bill, Washington, USIS Wireless File, Canberra, 20 September 1993.

10 The Republic of China on Taiwan

Taiwan has come a long way since the nineteenth century when it was merely an 'abode for outlaws, thieves, swindlers, and murderers who had been forced to fly from the mainland'.[1] It has emerged in the 1990s from its obscurity as an off-shore refuge after 50 years of Japanese colonial development, a quarter of a century of American aid and the overarching pressure of a threat of attack from mainland China. It is a modern, thriving industrial democracy poised to be recognised as the Republic of China on Taiwan. It is eminently recognisable because, economically, it is one of the most well-endowed middle powers in a post-Cold War world.

In the realm of competition between states, the measure of power and influence used to be deliverable nuclear weapons and numbers of aircraft, warships and tank divisions. Kenneth Waltz, for example, defined the power of a state 25 years ago as dependent on size of population and territory, resource endowments, economic capability, military strength, political stability, and competence.[2] However, the end of superpower rivalry and an easing of global tension changed the international criteria for political influence and standing amongst states.

Taiwan clearly lacks size when it is measured in terms of population, land mass and physical resources. But as Taiwan's Foreign Minister Fredrick Chien observed, a country's importance is no longer measured by the extent of its territory, the size of its army or the strength of its gross national product.[3] Instead of priority being given to strategic and security-based considerations, the criteria have been re-ordered to include progress on democracy, protection of human rights, financial strength, trading prowess, surplus investment capital, advanced levels of technology and international marketing skills. Military power is still important, but 'technological and commercial capabilities as much as military strength have become the defining elements of national power and influence'.[4] In the Asia–Pacific of the 1990s, power is measured by skills in marketing, mastery of information technologies, social stability, financial strength, international rank in terms of GNP, levels of trade, foreign exchange reserves, manufacturing technology and efficiency, effective public relations and ownership of foreign companies.[5] Geo-economics, to use a newly coined phrase, is in command in the Pacific and trading states like Taiwan are strongly advantaged. Taiwan in the 1990s, indeed, is a good example of how a small state can, with astute economic diplomacy, take advantage of its environment to maximise its international leverage.[6]

Richard Rosencrance suggests that trading states can achieve more through a strategy of economic development, aid, technology transfer, loans and trade leverage than bigger powers can through the old avenues of military power and intervention.[7] By using mechanisms of industrial-technological development and international trade, a small state can transform its position in international politics and win new rewards in an interdependent world.[8] It can become a middle power.

Taiwan is a prototype — even the archetypal — trading state. It has been able to pursue national advantage in the absence of diplomatic relations, through commercial exchanges, negotiations on aviation, investment and tourism agreements, aid programs, technical co-operation, participation in non-government international organisations, 'unofficial' official talks between high-ranking officials, golf course or vacation diplomacy between Presidents and Prime Ministers, investment delegations, agricultural trade missions and academic, cultural and educational exchanges.

Boundaries, territory, sovereignty, independence and military power remain key concepts. But so too are the elements of what Joseph Nye called 'soft power', such as management skills, leadership vision and resolve, effective communications and global marketing networks.[9] For Robert Gilpin, intangibles such as public morale, situational factors and the concept of prestige are also important.[10]

Taiwan has both 'soft power' and certain other intangibles. Its leadership has always had a long-term vision for Taiwan and China (see Chapter 4). Taiwan is politically stable, well led, well managed economically and it has gained in confidence from being a successful, newly industrialised Chinese market democracy. It has the situational advantages of being located, first, at the centre of the world's most economically dynamic region and, second, at the interface of the three greatest powers of Pacific Asia — China, Japan and the United States (see Figure 2, p. 9 and Figure 3, p. 145).[11] It draws power and prestige, in particular, from its location next to China.

Above all, however, Taiwan gains prestige from having the highest or second highest foreign exchange reserves in the world and being the world's seventh largest source of foreign investment capital. As Michael Armacost observed at a meeting of the International Monetary Fund in Osaka in 1991, the pool of savings held by countries like Taiwan was a critical asset to the world economy and 'the global struggle for access to it would be intense'.[12] Similarly, the Treasurer of the Asian Development Bank, Tomo Hayakawa, said that 'for the past 25 years, our major capital markets were Tokyo, New York, London, Frankfurt and Zurich. But now Taipei is where the money is.'[13]

Taiwan, furthermore, has been able to build coalitions of economic and cultural interests that are above and beyond the confines of orthodox diplomacy and the physical limits of state borders. It is operating in a borderless milieu of the kind envisaged by Kenichi Ohmae.[14] Taiwan, for instance, is fast becoming a hub for regional banking and finance, telecommunications, and air and sea transport. It is a base for American, Japanese and European multinational corporations operating regionally. To use Peter Drysdale's description, it has become a central part of 'the commingling of multinational corporations' and their global production and marketing strategies.[15] For the region, Taiwan is an essential participant in economic forums such as APEC and PECC; it has access to the China market and it has connections to the powerful overseas Chinese communities in Malaysia, Indonesia, the Philippines and Thailand.[16] For China, Taiwan is already contributing to what might yet become a greater Chinese economic community. For Singapore, Taiwan is a similarly small Chinese island state seeking an identity separate from the mainland, yet motivated by a sense of responsibility for China's future. For Australia, Taiwan is a major trading partner and source of tourism. For countries like Vietnam, Indonesia, Malaysia, the Philippines and Thailand, the value of Taiwan can be defined in terms of the level of its foreign investment and aid, and its role as a development model and as an exporter of certain medium-level technologies in the electronics industries. For the United States and Japan, Taiwan is a major trading partner but, more importantly, it offers a point of leverage *vis-a-vis* China. For them, Taiwan's new role as an investor and trading state and as a catalyst for change in China is too important to be snatched up by a communist China.

Being a rich Chinese island adjacent to the mainland, Taiwan's modernisation has led to inevitable comparisons with the often tumultuous development path taken by Beijing. If Taiwan had succumbed to threats from the mainland in 1949, it would have remained a stagnant island backwater for 40 years, like Hainan island. It could not have developed into an alternative model for China's modernisation, nor could it have become a constant and obvious reminder of the need for reform and change on the mainland. At present, the Taiwanese influences that are seeping into China from Taiwan are helping to peacefully transform Chinese communism. Deng Xiaoping in fact modelled many of his reforms on the lessons that could be learned from the Taiwanese experience.[17]

Deng may have described the results of changes he introduced to China as 'socialism with Chinese characteristics', but in reality it is a case of capitalism with Taiwanese characteristics. This impact led the Taiwanese to conclude with some justification that Taiwan has evolved from being 'a remote coastal region to a pivot capable of dominating China's future'.[18] If China's future, successful or otherwise, is destined to become one of the most important strategic issues in the early twenty-first century, then Taiwan's role — in bringing about reform and change in China, in shaping the direction of China, in maintaining security in the Taiwan Strait and contributing to stability in the Asia-Pacific region — is a matter of great strategic significance.[19]

This consideration is the basis for new thinking about Taiwan. It has been helped by two fundamental reassessments about China and Taiwan. First, China's threat to use force against Taiwan is regarded, even in Beijing, as being out of touch with the strategic and economic realities of the Asia-Pacific region in the 1990s. Second, there is little incentive for early reunification: the political, military, diplomatic, economic and ideological barriers are too great. Taiwan may be a part of notion of one China but only because Taiwanese leaders have stated that the island might be unified with the mainland at some time in the unspecified future. Otherwise the separation of Taiwan from mainland China (i.e. its de facto independence) is increasingly acknowledged as a hard fact by the rest of the world. The trick is to find a formula which can satisfy the aspirations of the Taiwanese and simultaneously leave Beijing reassured about Taiwan being part of one China.

Taiwan's Minister for Economics Affairs, Pin-Kung Chiang, tried to articulate such a formula at the Seattle APEC ministerial meeting in November 1993. Chiang said that until conditions were ripe for reunification with the mainland, Taiwan would 'pursue a step-by-step approach to a two China policy'. He said that the term 'China' was a 'neutral' name of geographical and historical reference. Taiwan was part of that China, and so was mainland China, but China did not equal the People's Republic of China and Taiwan was not part of the People's Republic of China. He said:

> There is but one China. Taiwan belongs to China geographically and culturally. Under the one China principle, we maintain that divided countries should coexist and we are pursuing a policy of one China by means of a two China approach: [meanwhile] *Taiwan and the PRC are two countries with independent sovereignty of their own* [italics added].[20]

Needless to say, Beijing was not reassured. The Taiwanese Foreign Ministry subsequently issued a statement elaborating on Chiang's remarks. It stated that while Taiwan was unwavering in its commitment to 'one China', it was also unwavering in its claim to be a sovereign and independent state. It was 'independently exercising exclusive sovereignty over territories under its effective control' and was not subordinate to the mainland.[21]

These evolving trends are still ill-defined, but they have changed international perceptions of China's claim to Taiwan, and Taiwan's claim for an independent voice in world and regional forums. They have contributed to a widespread upgrading of 'non-official' relations with Taipei and support for its entry into international organisations, such as APEC, 'the most powerful regional economy in the world' and, prospectively, Taiwanese membership of the GATT. The same groundswell of international support has convinced Taipei that the time is ripe to launch a campaign for membership of the United Nations.[22]

Taiwan's case for being the Republic of China on Taiwan

When the representative of the Republic of China walked out of the United Nations in 1971, few governments expected that the Nationalists would ever try to return as an independent member.

However, on 9 April 1993, President Li Teng-hui announced that Taiwan would 'actively seek membership in the United Nations' as the Republic of China on Taiwan. He said he hoped the international community would seriously consider Taiwan's bid over the next three years.[23] The Kuomintang claims that, as China has been divided into two areas that have been ruled for almost half a century by separate governments, there are two political entities in China existing alongside each other.[24] According to the Taiwanese, both accept the principle of one China, and, pending reunification, both are entitled to United Nations membership.[25]

Taiwan's initial foray ended rather ignominiously. It did not get listed on the agenda of the United Nations General Assembly's 48th session in September 1993. Predictably, for as long as China objects to any suggestion of one China and one Taiwan, most governments are extremely reluctant to give offence to Beijing. The preference of most countries is to wait until other governments make the first move to recognise Taiwan. Only if a sufficient consensus emerges will they then show their hand. In 1993, for example, 64 countries, including the United States and Britain, declined to comment when asked about their voting intentions on the Taiwanese issue.[26] That is, they adopted a typical 'sitting on the fence' approach, which is in fact very promising for Taipei. To succeed, Taiwan must try to win over China and reassure other governments that its United Nations bid is a precursor to China's reunification, not an attempt to create one China and one Taiwan.[27] Independence for Taiwan, said President Lee Teng-hui, was a dead end.[28] While the odds seem to be stacked against Taiwan joining the United Nations, the tide may yet turn, given Taiwan's favourable strategic and economic circumstances, together with persistent lobbying, carefully targeted dollar diplomacy and persuasive public diplomacy.[29]

The economic and strategic arguments that favour Taiwan's membership of the United Nations have already been addressed (see Chapters 6–9). Taiwan's bid also draws on difficult-to-refute principles of self-determination, basic human rights, the universality of UN membership and the reality of Taiwan as an entity that has never been ruled by Beijing.[30] It is also pitched at the common interest of the world community in finding solutions to environmental problems such as chlorofluorocarbon emissions and the disposal of hazardous waste. Most importantly, Taiwan has stressed its ability to contribute badly needed funds to an overstretched United Nations and to supply aid to developing countries via the United Nations and its agencies.

Taiwan should be entitled to United Nations membership on the basis of the principle of universal membership. United Nations Charter Article 4(1) provides that:

> Membership in the United Nations is open to all peace loving states which accept the obligations contained in the present Charter and in the judgement of the organisation, are able and willing to carry out these obligations.

Taiwan qualifies as peace loving. It meets all the established criteria for statehood, including possession of a defined territory, a permanent population that is larger than that of Australia, Singapore and many other members of the United Nations, a stable government with effective authority, consent of the people, political independence, a degree of permanency, an independent government and a willingness to obey international law. It also has a capacity to enter into diplomatic relations, with formal recognition by 5 per cent of members of the United Nations and de facto recognition by the remainder. It also has domestic political legitimacy.[31]

Article 4(2) provides that the admission of a state to membership in the United Nations will be effected by a decision of the General Assembly upon the recommendation of the Security Council. However, before the General Assembly can decide on the matter, the Security Council must first make a recommendation.

Because membership applications are a non-procedural matter, Article 27(3) requires that a decision to recommend as member must have the affirmative vote of nine members of the Security Council, including the concurring votes of the five Permanent Members.[32] As any one of the Permanent Members can veto a decision on a non-procedural matter, it would appear that any application by Taiwan to the Security Council would be doomed *ab initio*. However, United Nations Charter Article 27(3) provides that a party to a dispute shall abstain from voting on a non-procedural matter if it is involved in a dispute under Chapter VI or under Article 52(3) (both relating to pacific settlement of local disputes). Arguably, the rejection of Taiwan's 1993 United Nations bid demonstrated the existence of a dispute between China and Taiwan over Taiwan's right to participate, re-join or simply apply for membership. In any event, there is ample material available to show that China has a dispute with Taiwan that could lead to the threat or use of force. Taiwan, therefore, can claim that China should abstain in the vote on its application.[33]

As an interim step, Taiwan might seek participation in the United Nations as a non-member, a course taken by the Palestine Liberation Organisation and, earlier, by Austria and Italy (before the Soviet Union agreed not to veto their membership applications).[34] This possibility is the one favoured by Taiwanese Foreign Minister Fredrick Chien.[35] The provisions in Article 32 of the Charter on the participation of non-members call for approval from the General Assembly. A Permanent Member of the Security Council, such as China, cannot veto the participation of a non-member because it is a procedural matter and is listed as such in the United Nations Charter. According to Article 27(2), a decision on a procedural matter can be made on the affirmative vote of any nine of the Security Council's fifteen members. But participation as a non-member presupposes the existence of a dispute, which means the dispute *per se* must be listed on the agenda of the United Nations Security Council.[36] Again, however, selecting items for inclusion on the Security Council agenda is a procedural matter and no Permanent Member can exercise a right of veto.[37] This means Taiwan could raise an item for inclusion on the United Nations Security Council's agenda as a non-member, provided it receives at least the nine affirmative votes required under Article 27(2).

The non-member, however, must be recognisable as a state. It could, of course, be argued that Taiwan is not a state because it is only recognised by 29 out of 184 members of the United Nations and that this does not constitute a sufficient number of states. The practice of the United Nations in this regard, however, has been very liberal, as shown by the participation of the Palestine Liberation Organisation, despite doubts about its statehood and earlier, in 1947, in regard to the newly decolonised state of Indonesia.[38] In any event, lack of recognition or lack of diplomatic relations is not considered a valid reason for voting against a candidate applying for admission to the United Nations.[39] Recognition, indeed, is considered to be a political act, not a legal one, and merely declares the existence of a state.[40] According to Lauterpacht:

> it is a fundamental rule of international law that every independent State is entitled to be represented in the international sphere by a government which is habitually obeyed by the bulk of the population of that state and which exercises effective authority within its territory. To deny that right to a state is to question its independence ... When that government enjoys with a reasonable prospect of permanency the habitual and — though this is controversial — willing obedience of the bulk of the population, outside States are under a legal duty to recognise it in that capacity.[41]

Crawford similarly believes that, 'as a matter of general principle, any territorial entity formally separate and possessing a certain degree of actual power is capable of being, and *caeteris paribus*, should be regarded as a State for general international law purposes'.[42] He argues that a new state may exist despite claims to all or part of its territory — as, for example, with regard to Israel, Kuwait, Mauritania and Estonia.[43] If Taiwan is a state and recognisable as such in international law, the fact that it is part of the concept of one China should not be a bar to its membership of the United Nations. New states have been created from old states — with for example, Croatia and Bosnia-Herzegovina emerging from Yugoslavia and Pakistan from India — while divided states may reunite to form one state, as with the two Germanies and the two Yemens.

Article 35 provides, meanwhile, that any state which is not a member of the United Nations may bring to the attention of the Security Council or the General Assembly any dispute to which it is a party. For example, in 1950 the People's Republic of China, then not a member of the United Nations, had two items placed on the Security Council's agenda, despite objections from the Nationalist Chinese representative, whose government then held the China seat in the Security Council.[44] Taiwan, therefore, could argue to like effect in 1994: that it is a state, that because China refuses to allow Taipei to join the United Nations, contrary to the principle of universal membership, there is a dispute and that it should be discussed by the United Nations Security Council, notwithstanding objections from Beijing. Alternatively, Article 11 provides that the General Assembly may discuss any question relating to the maintenance of international peace and security brought before it by a member or a non-member of the United Nations, provided that it is not at the same time a matter under discussion before the Security Council (Article 12).

One of the most common reasons used by states for rejecting attempts to have certain disputes included on the agenda of the United Nations Security Council is that they are contrary to Article 2(7) of the Charter. Article 2(7) prohibits the United Nations from intervening in matters which are essentially within the domestic jurisdiction of any state. This has always been China's contention with regard to Taiwan — that, 'if we [China] . . . resort to non-peaceful means to solve the Taiwan issue, that is entirely China's internal affair' which other countries or the United Nations have 'no right to meddle in, let alone claim that it poses a threat to the peace and security of the Western Pacific area'.[45]

The future of Taiwan, however, is not simply a Chinese domestic political affair in which other states and international organisations like the United Nations can be unilaterally and unconditionally excluded. United Nations policy on what is and what is not a domestic affair has been significantly broadened by resolutions of the United Nations Security Council since the end of the Cold War. In 1991, for example, the Security Council ruled that the repression of the civilian population in Iraq had led to 'a massive flow of refugees towards and across international frontiers, thereby threatening regional peace and security'.[46] The United Nations claimed, therefore, that it had a right and an obligation to intervene under Chapter VII of the Charter relating to 'Acts with Respect to Threats to the Peace, Breaches of the Peace and Acts of Aggression'.[47] In 1992, the United Nations Security Council voted 13 to nil, with two abstentions (one of them being China), to use 'all necessary measures' to help suffering civilians in Serajevo on the grounds that there was a threat to the international peace and security posed by the situation inside Bosnia-Herzegovina.[48] A similar approach was used with regard to Haiti. The Security Council found that as the situation in Haiti constituted a threat to the regional peace, it authorised the use of 'all necessary force to facilitate the return of the legitimately elected President'.[49] The Haiti Resolution was passed by a vote of 12 to nil, with China again abstaining.[50]

In this light, therefore, any attempt by China to threaten or seize Taiwan by force or to try to starve Taipei into submission by, for example, a blockade would impact on the peace, security and stability of the neighbouring region. In view of Taiwan's de facto statehood, its ties with the rest of the world, its proximity to Japan and the fact that the United States is committed to help Taiwan under the terms of its 1982 *Taiwan Relations Act*, any threat to the independence of Taiwan posed by China or some other state would destabilise the East Asian region and could warrant United Nations concern and possible intervention under Chapter VII of the Charter.

Article 39 in Chapter VII of the Charter provides that the Security Council can determine if there is a threat to the peace or a breach of the peace and make recommendations or take appropriate measures. This was the route taken by the Security Council to circumvent any suggestion that it was intervening in the domestic affairs of Iraq, Bosnia-Herzegovina, Somalia and Haiti. Once the United Nations invokes Article 39, any question that might be violating Article 2(7) becomes irrelevant.

Dual representation, as in the case of the two Koreas, is a preferable initial course for Taiwan. It avoids a direct challenge to China's dignity because it conforms to the principle of one China.[51] Given a suitable formula, solid groundwork by Taipei and the acquiescence of Beijing, dual Chinese representation in the United Nations, if lodged under the one China principle and conditioned on eventual reunification, could attract widespread international support. Countries like Australia and the United States were sympathetic to such a solution in 1971 and would have tried to build a consensus in support of the idea if it had not then been rejected by Taipei.[52]

Another option stems from Articles 1, 55 and 73 of the United Nations Charter on the right to self-determination. There is a growing view that Taiwan is entitled to an act of self-determination free from any threat from China and that, in any case, China's concept of sovereignty over Taiwan and the notion of one state, two systems is outdated.[53] With the collapse of the Soviet Union and the breakup of states in Eastern Europe, there is an increasing tendency to accept that peoples of an identifiable culture have a right to an act of self-determination, especially if they were denied such a right in the past.[54] Gidon Gottlieb suggests that there is a clear need for a deconstruction and rearrangement of old rigid concepts of territorial borders, sovereignty and independence and that, in all cases, the interests of a population should be paramount.[55] Even if the concept is confined to colonial situations,[56] one could argue that the Taiwanese were entitled to an act of self-determination in 1945 because they had lived for the previous 50 years under Japanese colonial rule.

Taiwan never enjoyed an act of self-determination after World War II because Chiang Kai-shek had been promised Taiwan by the Allies. But any disposal of Taiwan agreed to during the war ought to have been subject to Charter Article 103 which provides that in the event of a conflict between the obligations of members under the Charter and any other international agreement, the obligations of members under the Charter 'shall prevail' (i.e. the Charter provisions on self-determination should have been given precedence over wartime agreements ostensibly returning Taiwan to China).[57]

More recently, the principle of self-determination has been broadened to apply to peoples in general.[58] For example, Part II of the 1993 Vienna Declaration on Human Rights recognises the right of peoples 'to take any legitimate action, in accordance with the Charter of the United Nations, to realise their inalienable right of self-determination', the denial of which was a violation of a fundamental human right. Chinese Premier Li Peng endorsed the principle in the context of the former Soviet Union. Premier Li Peng said, in answer to a question about China's policy towards the declaration of independence by the Soviet republics, that:

> it is up to the people of these republics to make the choice as to whether they will be independent. Should the republics gain independence, China is willing to develop normal friendly relations with them; should they remain in the union, or sign a new union treaty, China will also continue to develop normal ties with [the Union].[59]

Any suggestion of a right to break up a sovereign state, however, must take account of provisions in the 1970 United Nations General Assembly Resolution 2625, the 1993 Vienna Declaration on Human Rights and elsewhere to the effect that the right of self-determination cannot be construed 'so as to authorise or encourage any action which would dismember or impair, totally or in part, the territorial integrity or political unity of sovereign and independent states'.[60] On this particular point, however, it could be argued that Taiwan was not part of China since 1895 and that even before then, its links with the mainland were tenuous at best.[61] This view, predictably, is contested by Beijing, which claims that Taiwan has been 'an inalienable part of China since ancient times dating back 1700 years'.[62]

According to Beijing, 'the treasured island of Taiwan was stolen from China by a process of prolonged imperialist invasion that began with the Spanish, the Portugese, the Dutch and the Japanese'.[63] After World War II, Taiwan was returned to China but the civil war between the Communist and Kuomintang parties separated Taiwan from the mainland, a separation that was perpetuated by `aggressive foreign forces' (i.e. the United States).[64] According to Li Jiaquan, a leading mainland scholar working on Taiwan, it was 'universally accepted that Taiwan was an inseparable part of China' and various international agreements (including the 1943 Cairo and 1945 Potsdam Declarations) confirmed this stance.[65] When Japan surrendered, China took over the sovereignty of Taiwan and, having taken over the China seat in the United Nations, 'the Chinese government [therefore] is the sole legal government of China and Taiwan is an integral part of Chinese territory'.[66] In China's view, any action that attempted to establish a separate Taiwan violates Article 2(7) of the United Nations Charter concerning respect for the sovereignty and territorial integrity of member states.

Notwithstanding these views, there is persuasive legal argument to the contrary that has contributed to a bitter controversy as to whether Taiwan was and is part of China. The debate focuses on whether the Cairo and Potsdam Declarations effectively returned Taiwan to China, whether those Declarations were formal treaties and what the intentions of the signatories were, which authority represented all of China and whether Japan's renunciation of claims to Formosa and its subsequent peace treaties were sufficient to pass title to the Republic of China.[67]

The Peace Treaty signed between Japan and the Allies in San Francisco on 8 September 1951 and the Peace Treaty signed in Taipei between the Nationalist government and Japan on 28 April 1952 merely stated that Japan renounced its rights, claims and title over Formosa, but nowhere did they specify the beneficiary of the Japanese renunciation.[68] According to O'Connell, because the Allied powers could not agree on Taiwan's ultimate disposition, the matter was left ambiguous 'for time to resolve'.[69]

At the time, the British and Australian governments were of a similar opinion. For British Foreign Secretary Sir Anthony Eden:

> The Cairo Declaration . . . was a statement of intention that Formosa be retroceded to China after the war. This retrocession has in fact never taken place because of the difficulties arising from the existence of two entities claiming to represent China and the differences among the powers as to the status of these entities . . . Under the Peace Treaty of April 1952 Japan formally renounced all right, title and claim to Formosa and the Pescadores; but again this did not operate as a transfer to Chinese sovereignty, whether to the People's Republic of China or to the Chinese Nationalist authorities. Formosa and the Pescadores are therefore in the view of Her Majesties'

[sic] Government, territory the *de jure* sovereignty over which is uncertain or undetermined.[70]

Australian Prime Minister Robert Menzies likewise stated that 'the juridical status of Formosa remained to be determined and would no doubt be determined one day by UN machinery'.[71]

That time has arrived. In the meantime, however, the reality of Taiwan's existence as an independent and sovereign state is difficult to deny. It cannot be negated merely because a majority of countries have established diplomatic relations with the mainland and refuse to formally acknowledge the fact of Taiwan's existence. In any case, while most states recognise Beijing, they do not unambiguously endorse Beijing's claims to jurisdiction over Taiwan. Many governments made no mention of their position regarding Taiwan. Others, including Argentina, Australia, Belgium, Brazil, Canada, Chile, Fiji, Iceland, the Ivory Coast, Malaysia, New Zealand, Peru, Thailand and the United Kingdom, say they either take note of or acknowledge China's claim that Taiwan is an inalienable part of its territory, or is a province of China.[72] Japan and the Philippines recognise the PRC government as 'the sole legal government of China' and 'fully understand and respect' China's stand that Taiwan is an inalienable part of PRC territory. The United States recognises the PRC government as 'the sole legal government of China' and 'acknowledges the Chinese position that there is but one China and Taiwan is part of China' but it also affirmed that it would 'maintain cultural, commercial and other unofficial relations with the people of Taiwan'.[73]

It is this loophole that Taiwan is trying to exploit. If it succeeds at the United Nations, it will have effectively internationalised the Taiwan–China issue. This will increase the checks and balances on China and help neutralise the use of force as a viable option, provided, of course, there is a rational leadership in Beijing.[74] This, in turn, will strengthen Taiwan's position if and when unification becomes a matter to be negotiated.[75] If communism in China does not evolve into a variant of Chinese capitalism resembling Taiwan — as the Taiwanese hope, with their input, it will — then they will still be left with the benefits of United Nations membership, including the Charter's injunction against the threat or use of force to settle disputes. Taiwan will also have established a sound base to support its claim to be a state recognisable in international law, whether as the Republic of Taiwan, the Republic of China on Taiwan, Formosa or, perhaps, the State of Taiwan in a Commonwealth of China.

Whatever its future nomenclature may be, there are clearly some short-term risks for Taiwan. The United Nations bid will test Beijing's ability to think about solutions that move beyond any instinctive angry response and the threat or use of force. If the bid is handled sensitively, dual membership of the United Nations by the two Chinas could, like their dual representation in APEC, work to the benefit of both, provided the United States and Japan abide by the rules of the game.

Previously, Taiwan was caught up in the maelstrom of fiercely competing empires vying for territory, power and influence in the Western Pacific. Sometimes China, Japan and the United States went to war with each other; sometimes two of them were allies against the third. Peace, prosperity, security and independence for Taiwan only evolved after China, Japan and the United States each adjusted to the reality and power of the other two. Today, these three great powers have reached what is effectively a gentlemen's agreement about Taiwan. The arrangement between them brings to mind the idea of Hedley Bull and Adam Watson whereby a group of states 'establish by dialogue and consent, common rules and institutions for the conduct of their relations, and recognise their common interest in maintaining these arrangements'.[76] In Taiwan's case, the rules have been worked out by the three principal powers in the Asia-Pacific, after more than a century of rivalry, war and threats of war. Their understanding also suggests the 'principles, norms, rules, and decision-making procedures around which actor expectations converge in a given issue-area' that regime theorists have envisaged.[77]

One of the rules is that the threat or use of force against Taiwan by China is unacceptable, which is somewhat like the regime of common aversion suggested by Ernst B. Haas.[78] Another rule is that Taipei cannot depart from the one China principle and its pledge that Taiwan is a part of China. The third rule is that neither Japan or the United States should form a strategic relationship with Taiwan against China. Within those bounds, China is prepared to tolerate a very broad range of non-official contacts between Taiwan and the rest of the world and abide by the principle of non-use of force. It may even be prepared to consider some formula which allows Taiwan to enter the United Nations. One reason for China's pragmatism regarding Taiwan is its sense of security — it is not threatened by any of the great Pacific powers.[79] The three great Asia-Pacific powers, in other words, have reached a tacitly understood strategic accommodation that allows them all to pull back from Taiwan (see Figure 1, p. 4). This has given Taiwan room to move and operate as a country that is little different from South Korea, Hong Kong, Singapore or, indeed, any other member of the Asia-Pacific community.

Notes

1 *Taiwan (Formosa)*, Foreign Geography Information Series No. 5, Department of Mines and Technical Surveys, Ottawa, Canada, 1952, p. 1.

2 Kenneth Waltz, *Theory of International Politics*, Addison-Wesley Publishing Company, Reading, 1979, p. 131.

3 Foreign Minister Frederick Chien, speech in Boston, 20 November 1991, *China News Agency (CNA)*, 25 November 1991.

4   Richard Solomon, Assistant Secretary of State, Presentation to the Pacific Rim Forum, San Diego, 15 May 1992, USIS Wireless File, Canberra, 14 May 1992.

5   Samuel P. Huntington, 'Why International Primacy Matters' *International Security*, vol. 17, no. 4, Spring 1993, pp. 68, 73.

6   Maria Papadakis and Harvey Starr, 'Opportunity, Willingness, and Small States: The Relationship Between Environment and Foreign Policy', in Charles F. Hermann, Charles W. Kegley, James N. Rosenau (eds), *New Directions in the Study of Foreign Policy*, Allen & Unwin, Boston, 1987, pp. 409, 426.

7   Richard Rosencrance, *The Rise of the Trading State*, Basic Books Inc, New York, 1986.

8   ibid., p. ix.

9   Joseph S. Nye Jr, 'Soft Power', *Foreign Policy*, no. 80, Fall 1990, pp. 153ff.

10 Robert Gilpin, *War and Change in World Politics*, Cambridge University Press, Cambridge, 1981, pp. 13–14.

11 Waltz, *Theory of International Politics*, p. 163, states that there must be at least four great power states to create a stable balance, whereas Gilpin, *War and Change*, p. 29, suggests that just three will suffice, and that is borne out by Taiwan's situation between China, Japan and the United States.

12 Quoted in *South China Morning Post*, 4 June 1991.

13 *Time Magazine*, 13 January 1992.

14 Kenichi Ohmae, *The Borderless World: Power and Strategy in the Interlinked Economy*, Collins, London, 1990, p. xi.

15 Peter Drysdale, *International Economic Pluralism: Economic Policy in East Asia and the Pacific*, Allen & Unwin, Sydney, 1988, p. 204.

16 The 3.5 million overseas Chinese in Indonesia comprise 2 per cent of the population but control seventeen of the 25 biggest business enterprises and 75 per cent of the country's private domestic capital. In Malaysia, the Chinese comprise 37 per cent of the total population but control 60 per cent of the domestic economy. In Thailand the Chinese make up 8–10 per cent of the population but control half of Thailand's GDP. In the Philippines, the Chinese (1.5 per cent of the population) control two-thirds of the 67 largest companies: from *The Economist*, 16 November 1991; *The Guardian*, 22 July 1992; S. Gordon Redding, *The Spirit of Chinese Capitalism*, Waleter de Gruyter, Berline, 1990, p. 28; and Richard Robison, *Indonesia: the Rise of Capitalism*, Allen & Unwin, Sydney, 1986, p. 276.

17 See An-chia Wu, 'Peking's Evaluation of Taiwan's Development Experience', in Bih-jaw Lin and James T. Myers (eds), *Forces of Change*

in Contemporary China, University of South Carolina Press, Columbia, 1993, p. 359.

18 White Paper on Cross Straits Relations, reported in *Chung Kuo Shih Pao*, Taipei, 6 July 1994, in *Foreign Broadcast Information Service (FBIS) — China*, 11 July 1994, pp. 50–60.

19 ibid.

20 Quoted in *China Post (CP)*, 23 November 1993.

21 Press Release, Ministry of Foreign Affairs, Republic of China, Taipei, 22 November 1993.

22 A detailed study is in Gary Klintworth, 'Taiwan's UN Membership Bid', *Pacific Review*, vol. 7, no. 3, March 1994, pp. 283–95.

23 Quoted in *Taiwan Communiqué*, No. 59, September 1993, pp. 1–2.

24 Premier Lien Chan, 'The Republic of China on Taiwan Belongs in the United Nations', *Orbis*, vol. 37, no. 4, Fall 1993, pp. 633, 637.

25 Press Statement, Ministry of Foreign Affairs, Taipei, 22 November 1993.

26 *CNA*, 13 September 1993.

27 Fredrick Chien, interview, *Sinorama*, November 1993, pp. 85, 89.

28 Lee Teng-hui's remarks were reported in *CP*, 5 February 1993. See also Lien Chan's *CNN* interview, 11 March 1993, in *CP*, 12 April 1993. For Lin Bih-jaw, Director of the influential Institute of International Relations, it was suicidal: Bih-jaw Lin, 'Taipei's Search for a New Foreign Policy Approach', paper for the Conference on Taiwan–United States Relations, Claremont Institute, Los Angeles, 7–8 April 1989.

29 Taiwan currently has diplomatic relations with 29 countries or 'diplomatic allies' and aims to increase that number to between 40 and 50 in an effort to strengthen its next bid for United Nations membership: *Free China Journal*, 4 March 1994.

30 Jason Hu, Director General of GIO, gave ten reasons for Taiwan's United Nations bid as follows: Beijing could not properly represent the interests of the Taiwanese; Taipei wants to regain its international dignity; the United Nations could not afford to ignore Taiwan's political and economic achievements; the people of Taiwan want to participate in the United Nations; Taiwan wants to make its contribution to the common interests of mankind through the United Nations system; the United Nations could build upon the Taiwan experience to promote economic development elsewhere in the world; Taiwan's participation would be conducive to reunification and peace and stability in the Asia-Pacific region; the United Nations principle of universality of membership should apply to Taiwan; Taiwan's participation would reaffirm the United Nations' role in uniting divided nations; and Taiwan's participation would strengthen the Charter of

a post-Cold War United Nations system: Jason Hu, speech to the Atlantic Council, Washington, 17 September 1993, in *CP* 22–23 September 1993.

31 These criteria are discussed in James Crawford, *The Creation of States in International Law*, Clarendon Press, Oxford, 1979, p. viii.

32 Leland M. Goodrich, Edvard Hambro and Anne Patricia Simons, *Charter of the United Nations Commentary and Documents*, 3rd edn, Columbia University Press, New York, 1969, p. 223.

33 An interpretation on this issue could be sought by the General Assembly, or by Taiwan, from the International Court of Justice. Article 35 of the Statute of the Court allows states which are non-members of the United Nations to be parties to a case before the Court. However, as only states can be parties before the Court (Article 34), the Court may first have to determine whether or not Taiwan qualified as a state, a matter which in itself would be of vital importance.

34 Goodrich, Hambro and Simons, *Charter of the United Nations Commentary and Documents*, p. 248.

35 *Free China Journal*, 12 March 1993.

36 Goodrich, Hambro and Simons, *Charter of the United Nations Commentary and Documents*, p. 249.

37 ibid. p. 273.

38 ibid.

39 ibid., p. 78; see also D.W. Greig, *International Law*, 2nd edn, Butterworths, London, 1976, pp. 133–34.

40 H. Lauterpacht, *Recognition in International Law*, University Press, Cambridge, 1947, p. 41.

41 ibid., pp. 88–89.

42 Crawford, *The Creation of States in International Law*, p. 70.

43 ibid., pp. 37–38.

44 H. Lauterpacht (ed.), *International Law: A Treatise*, Vol. 1, 8th edn, Longmans, London, 1955, p. 129.

45 *Beijing Review*, 29 December 1980, p. 7. See also Taiwan Affairs Office, State Council of the People's Republic of China, 'The Taiwan Question and the Reunification of China', in *Beijing Review*, 6–12 September 1993, Documents I–VIII.

46 UN Security Council Resolution 688 (1991) UNSC 2982nd Meeting, New York, 5 April 1991.

47 See generally Gary Klintworth, 'A Right to Intervene in the Domestic Affairs of States', *Australian Journal of International Affairs*, vol. 46, no. 2, November 1992, p. 248.

48 UN Security Council Resolution 770, in USIS Wireless File, Canberra, 13 August 1992.

49 Text of UN Security Council Resolution 940, 31 July 1994, in USIS Wireless File, Canberra, 2 August 1994.

50 ibid.

51 Chang King-yuh, quoted in *Free China Journal*, 30 July 1993.

52 President Richard Nixon's News Conference of 16 September 1971, in *Public Papers of the Presidents of the United States*, Government Printing Office, Washington, 1972, p. 950 and statement by Prime Minister William McMahon, 16 July 1971, *Current Notes on International Affairs (CNIA)*, vol. 42, no. 7, Canberra, 1971, p. 389.

53 Quoted in Guo Changlin, 'Sino-US Relations in Perspective', *Contemporary International Relations*, vol. 2, no. 7, Beijing, July 1992, p. 3. The American official who said China's policy was unrealistic and outdated was James Lilley, former United States ambassador in Beijing, quoted in *Free China Journal*, 25 May 1993, p. 2.

54 Crawford Young, 'The Dialectics of Cultural Pluralism: Concept and Reality', in Crawford Young (ed.), *The Rising Tide of Pluralism: The Nation-State at Bay?*, University of Wisconsin Press, Wisconsin, 1993, pp. 3–36; and Ruth Lapidoth, 'Sovereignty in Transition', *Journal of International Affairs*, vol. 45, no. 2, Winter 1992, pp. 325, 336.

55 Gidon Gottlieb, 'Nations Without States', *Foreign Affairs*, vol. 73, no. 3, May/June 1994, pp. 100, 105.

56 UN Charter Articles 1(2) and 55 refer to self-determination of peoples generally, whereas Articles 73 and 76 suggest that self-determination only applies in a colonial situation.

57 In fact, Taiwan's situation seems to fit the scenario in which secession can be justified as a reappropriation of stolen property by the legitimate owners. Allen Buchanan argues that there may be a right to secede, as an act of self-determination, where the people seceding are the people who should have had title to the territory at the time of its unjust annexation: Allen Buchanan, 'Self-determination and the Right to Secede', *Journal of International Affairs*, vol. 45, no. 2, Winter 1992, pp. 347, 357.

58 Morton H. Halperin and David J Scheffer with Patricia L Small, *Self Determination in the New World Order*, Carnegie Endowment for International Peace, Washington, 1992.

59 Li Peng, interview with the *Hindustan Times* on 4 December 1991, in *FBIS China*, 9 December 1991, p. 12.

60 Declaration on Principles of International Law concerning Friendly Relations and Cooperation Among States, 24 October 1970, UNGA Res 2625(XXV), 25 UN GAOR, Supp. (No 28)) 121, UN Doc. A/8028 (1971).

61 See United States Departnment of State Publication 6844, *The Republic of China*, Far Eastern Series 81, October 1959, p. 8. cited in Frank P.

Morello, *The International Legal Status of Formosa*, Martinus Nijhoff, The Hague, 1966, p. 5; James W. Davidson, *The Island of Formosa Past and Present*, Macmillan and Co, London, 1903; Yosaburo Takekoshi, *Japanese Rule in Formosa* (trans George Braithwaite), Longmans Green and Co, London, 1907; Sophia Su-fei Yen, *Taiwan in China's Foreign Relations 1936–1974*, Shoe String Press Hamden, 1965 and Peng Ming-min, *A Taste of Freedom Memoirs of a Formosan Independence Leader*, Holt Rinehart and Winston, New York, 1972.

62   Taiwan Affairs Office, 'The Taiwan Question and the Reunification of China'.

63   Li Jiaquan, 'Taiwan Independence A Blind Alley', *Beijing Review*, 8–14 June 1992, pp. 20ff.

64   ibid.

65   ibid.

66   ibid.

67   See E. Lauterpacht, 'Effect of the Cairo and Postdam Declarations 1943 and 1946', *British Yearbook of International Law*, vol. 8, no. 1, January 1959, pp. 182, 186. Also L. Oppenheim, *International Law, A Treatise*, vol. 1 (ed. by H. Lauterpacht), London 1955, pp. 872–73 and D.P. O'Connell, 'Legal Aspects of the Peace Treaty with Japan', *XXIX British Yearbook of International Law 1953*, p. 423 at 427.

68   See Chapter 2, footnote 147.

69   D.P. O'Connell, 'The Status of Formosa and the China Recognition Problem' 50 *American Journal of International Law*, 1956, p. 405 at 406–7. A parallel can be found with regard to the disposal of the former Italian colonies in Africa after World War II. Under article 23 of the Treaty of Peace signed with Rome on 10 February 1947, Italy renounced all right and title to its former territorial possessions in Africa, namely Libya, Eritrea and Somaliland, with final disposal to be determined by a Council of Foreign Ministers of the United Kingdom, the Soviet Union, France and the United States. Since the Council of Ministers failed to reach agreement, the issue was referred to the United Nations. On 21 November 1947, the United Nations General Assembly recommended that the former Somaliland and Libya should become independent and Eritrea should become part of a federation with Ethiopia. Similarly with regard to Korea, which was not returned to China after World War II even though, like Taiwan, it was once a Chinese colony ceded to Japan by China at the turn of the century. As Mao Zedong once declared (in 1936), while it was China's purpose to regain its lost territories, that plan 'did not include Korea, formerly a Chinese colony', and China would 'help in their struggle for independence [and] the same thing applies for Taiwan': reported by Edgar Snow, *Red Star Over China*, rev. edn, Victor Gollancz, London, 1968, p. 110.

70 Sir Anthony Eden, Great Britain, Parliamentary Debates (*Hansard*), House of Commons, vol. 536, 4 February 1955, Col 159, cited in J.P. Jain, 'The Legal Status of Formosa', 57 *American Journal of International Law* (1963), pp. 25, 27–28. See also Hungdah Chiu, 'Taiwan in Sino-American Relations', in Hungdah Chiu (ed.), *China and the Taiwan Issue*, Praeger, New York, 1979, p. 155.

71 R.G. Menzies, quoted in 26 *CNIA*, Canberra, 1955, p. 176.

72 See Colin Mackerras and Amanda Yorke, *The Cambridge Handbook of Contemporary China*, Cambridge University Press, Cambridge, 1991, pp. 150ff.

73 ibid., pp. 151–55.

74 Of course, an irrational leadership in Beijing would be quite another matter.

75 One might interpret Taiwan's bid for membership of the United Nations as a consciously thought-out step that Taipei has taken preparatory to such negotiations.

76 Hedley Bull and Adam Watson (eds), *The Expansion of International Society*, Oxford University Press, Oxford, 1984, p. 1.

77 Stephen D. Krasner (ed.), *International Regimes*, Cornell University Press, Ithaca, 1983, but bearing in mind the scepticism about regimes expressed by Susan Strange, 'Cave! Hic Dragones: A Critique of Regime Analysis', in Krasner, ibid., p. 337.

78 Ernst B. Haas, 'Words Can Hurt You; or, Who Said what to Whom About Regimes', in Krasner, *International Regimes,* pp. 23, 27; and Arthur A. Stein, 'Coordination and Collaboration: Regimes in an Anarchic World', in Krasner, ibid., pp. 115, 125.

79 The biggest threat to Taiwan's security was in the 1950s and 1960s, a period when China felt threatened by the United States and its forward-based military posture in the Western Pacific.

References

Primary sources — Interviews

Australia

Eugene Bazhanov, Deputy Director for Research and International Relations, USSR Foreign Ministry, in Canberra

C.L. Chiou, Reader, Department of Government, University of Queensland

James C. Chu, Managing Director, Far East Trading Co. Pty Ltd, Melbourne

Stuart Harris, Professor, Northeast Asia Programme, ANU, Canberra

Francis C.R. Lee, Representative, Taipei Economic and Cultural Office, Canberra

Vladimir S. Miasnikov, Deputy Director, Institute of Far Eastern Studies, Academy of Sciences of the USSR, in Canberra

Ho Xuan Phong, Third Secretary, Embassy of the Socialist Republic of Vietnam, Canberra

Peter Rowe, Taiwan Section, Department of Foreign Affairs and Trade, Canberra

Bill Tweddell, Taiwan Section, Department of Foreign Affairs and Trade, Canberra

Thee Kian Wee, Head, Centre for Economic and Development Studies

(Indonesia), at the Department of Economics, Research School of Pacific Studies, ANU, Canberra

Fukang Xue, Chief, *Guangming Daily*, Canberra Bureau

Jerome C.H. Yen, Taipei Economic and Cultural Office, Canberra

Yu Jianzhong, Defence Attaché, Embassy of the People's Republic of China, Canberra

Taiwan

Thomas V. Biddick, Chief, General Affairs Section, American Institute in Taiwan, Taipei

King-Yuh Chang, President, National Chengchi University

Raymond J.M. Chang, President, Institute for National Policy Research, Taipei

B.C. Chew, Director, Malaysian Friendship and Trade Centre, Taipei

Antonio Chiang, Publisher, *Xin Xin Wen (The Journalist)*, Taipei

Kun-shuan Chiu, Associate Profesor, Institute of East Asia Studies, National Chengchi University, Taipei

James C.Y. Chu, Director, Department of Cultural Affairs, Kuomintang Central Committee, Taipei

Fujio Hara, Director, Interchange Association (Japan), Taipei

H. Steve Hsieh, Director General, Science Park Administration, Hsinchu

Hwang Yueh-chin, Professor of Law, National Chengchi University, Taipei

Gau-Jeng Ju, Caucus Whip, Democratic Progressive Party, Legislative Yuan, Taipei

Francias C.R. Lee, Deputy Director, Department of International Organisations, Ministry of Foreign Affairs, Taipei

Lee Kao Chao, Director of Economic Research, Council for Economic Planning and Development, Executive Yuan, Taipei

Lee Ming-Liang, Editor-in-Chief, *Free China Journal*, Taipei

Lin Bih-jaw, Director, Institute of International Relations, Taipei

Lin Yu-fang, Director, Graduate Institute of International and Strategic Studies, Tamkang University, Taipei

David T.C. Liu, Deputy Executive Director, Market Development, China External Trade Development Council, Taipei.

Robert O'Donovan, Australian Commerce and Industry Office, Taipei.

Joan M. Plaisted, Chief, Economic/Commercial Section, American Institute in Taiwan, Taipei

Robert C.J. Shih, Director, Department of East Asian and Pacific Affairs, Ministry of Foreign Affairs, Taipei

Tien Hung-mao, Chairman, Institute of National Policy Research, Taipei

Ching-lung Tsay, Institute of Economics, Academica Sinica, Taipei

Shih-Yuan Tsai, Deputy Secretary General, Democratic Progressive Party, DPP Headquarters, Taipei

David Y.S. Tzou, Director, Information and Protocol, Government Information Office, Taipei

K.M. Wei, Deputy Director, Trade Policy and International Organisations, Ministry of Economic Affairs, Taipei

Frank Wu, Manager, Second Department for Market Development, China External Trade Development Council, Taipei

Wu Wen-Cheng, Advisor, Government Information Office, Taipei

Andrew Nien-Dzu Yang, Secretary General, Chinese Council of Advanced Policy Studies, Taipei

Richard H. Yang, Chairman, Chinese Council for Advanced Policy Studies, Taipei

Laurence S. Yao, Legislator, Legislative Yuan, Taipei

Peter Kien-hong Yu, Sun Yat-sen Center for Policy Studies, Kaohsiung

Tzong-shian Yu, Vice-President, Chung-Hua Institution for Economic Research, Taipei

The Indonesian Chamber of Commerce to Taipei

China

Chen Jinyang, Senior Research Fellow, China Institute for International Strategic Studies (CIISS), Beijing

Kong-li Chen, Director, Taiwan Research Institute, Xiamen University, Xiamen

Gao Bing Tao, Manager, Xiamen San Teh Xing Industry Co, Xiamen

Han Qing-hai, Deputy Director, Taiwan Research Institute, Xiamen University, Xiamen

Hou Gang, Standing Council Member, CIISS, Beijing

Jiang Hongji, Standing Council Member, CIISS, Beijing

Lai Yong Cai, Deputy Secretary General of the Association for Promoting Economic and Cultural Contacts between Fujian and Taiwan, Fuzhou

Lan Hong Jie, Xiamen Foreign Affairs Office, Xiamen

Yuhong Lei, Political Department, Institute of Taiwan Studies, Chinese Academy of Social Sciences, Beijing

Li Jiaquan, Vice President, Institute of Taiwan Studies, Chinese Academy of Social Sciences, Beijing

Liu Guofen, Institute of Taiwan Studies, Chinese Academy of Social Sciences, Beijing

Liu Jiangyong, Director, East Asia Division, China Institute of Contemporary International Relations, Beijing

Lu Xiao Lan, Foreign Affairs Office of Fujian Province, Fuzhou

Pan Zhenqiang, Director, Institute for Strategic Studies, National Defence University of the PLA, Beijing

Igor A. Rogachev, Ambassador of the Russian Federation, Beijing

Song Deheng, Deputy Division Chief, Asian Department, Ministry of Foreign Affairs, Beijing

Song Zhongyue, Professor of Political Science, Academy of Military Science, Beijing

Sha Zukang, Counsellor, Department of International Organisations, Ministry of Foreign Affairs, Beijing

Te Li Geng, Vice President, Xiamen Economic Reform Committee, Xiamen

Tong Dalin, Director, Institute of Global Concern, Beijing

Wang Yi-fu, Associate Professor, Institute of Modern Taiwan Studies, Fujian Academy of Social Sciences, Fuzhou

Wei Zhongci, Director, Office of Taiwan Affairs, Fuzhou, Fujian province

Wu Neng-yuan, Vice President, Institute of Modern Taiwan Studies, Fujian Academy of Social Sciences, Fuzhou

Xu Xin Peng, Deputy Secretary-General, Taiwan Research Association, Taiwan Research Institute, Xiamen University, Xiamen

Ye Ru'an, Deputy Director, China Institute of International Studies, Beijing

Fang Sheng, Standing Committee Member, Council of Taiwan Studies, Chinese Academy of Social Sciences

Yu Gang, Senior Research Fellow, CIISS, Beijing

Zhang Hui Ling, Foreign Affairs Office, Quanzhou, Fujian

Zhu Chun, Council Member, CIISS, Beijing

Russia

Mikhail M. Bely, Deputy Director, Far East and Indochina Department, Ministry of Foreign Affairs, Moscow

Alexei V. Zagorsky, Centre for Japanese and Pacific Studies, Institute of World Economy and International Relations, Moscow

Eduard S. Grebenshchikov, Pacific Studies Department, Institute of World Economy and International Relations, Moscow

Vladimir I. Ivanov, Chairman, Pacific Regional Studies Department, Institute of World Economy and International Relations, Moscow

Andrei V. Kuzmenko, Counsellor, Far East and Indochina, Ministry of Foreign Affairs, Moscow

Anna Filatova, Leningrad Branch of the Soviet Peace Committee, Leningrad (St Petersburg)

Hong Kong

David Chen, Assistant Chief Editor, Asian Regional Development Projects Ltd

Susie Chiang, Director, Chung Hwa Information and Cultural Centre

Henry S.R. Kao, Professor, Department of Psychology, University of Hong Kong

John C.I. Ni, Managing Director, Chung Hwa Travel Service

Yen Ching-hwang, Professor of History, University of Hong Kong

Byron Weng, Professor of Government, Chinese University of Hong Kong

Japan

Chang Chin-Lin, Director, Far East Trade Service Centre, Tokyo

Ichiro Fujisaki, Director, Security Policy Division, Information Analysis, Research and Planning Bureau, Ministry of Foreign Affairs, Tokyo

Yasuto Fukushima, Professor, National Defence College, Tokyo

Hiroto Hirakoba, China and Mongolia Division, Ministry of Foreign Affairs, Tokyo

Hideki Ito, Deputy Director, Asian Affairs Bureau, Ministry of Foreign Affairs, Tokyo

Tadashi Imai, Director, Regional Policy Division, Asian Affairs Bureau, Ministry of Foreign Affairs, Tokyo

Tatsuaki Iwata, Senior Research Fellow, The Japan Institute of International Affairs, Tokyo

Nobuo Kobayashi, Development Economist, Japanese External Trade Organisation, Tokyo

Shigekatsu Kondo, Professor, National Institute of Defence Studies, Tokyo

Kyoichi Saitoh, Senior Analyst, Cabinet Research Office, Tokyo

Tomohisa Sakanaka, Professor of International Relations, Aoyama Gakuin University, Tokyo

Seizabro Sato, Director, International Institute for Global Peace, Tokyo

Takenaka Shigeo, Deputy Director General, Asian Affairs Bureau, Ministry of Foreign Affairs, Tokyo

Kameyoshi Tsuruta, Senior Analyst, Cabinet Research Office, Tokyo

Itaru Umezu, Acting Director, The Japan Institute of International Affairs, Tokyo

South Korea
Nai-Tsi Tu, Economic Counsellor, Embassy of the Republic of China, Seoul.

Primary sources — Government/official materials

Michael Armacost, Deputy Assistant Secretary, US Department of State, Hearings, Committee on Foreign Relations, US Senate, 96th Congress, US Government Printing Office, Washington DC, February 1979.

A Study of a Possible Communist Attack on Taiwan, Government Information Office, Taipei, 1991.

American Institute in Taiwan, *Foreign Economic Trends and their Implications for the US*, Taipei, various issues 1991, 1992.

Annual Report 1982, Department of Foreign Affairs, Australian Government Publishing Service, Canberra, 1983.

Asia Development Outlook 1991, Asian Development Bank, Manila, 1991.

Australian Foreign Affairs Record 1972–92.

Australia and North-East Asia in the 1990s: Accelerating Change, East Asia Analytical Unit, Department of Foreign Affairs and Trade, Australian Government Publishing Service, Canberra, 1992.

Australian Nuclear Science and Technology Organisation, *Nuclear Developments in the Asia and Pacific Region*, July 1992.

China: Long Term Issues and Options, Annex B, Agriculture to the Year 2000, Report No 5206-CHA, World Bank, New York, 22 May 1985.

Composition of Trade Australia 1990, Department of Foreign Affairs and Trade, Canberra, 1990.

Composition of Trade Australia 1992–93, Department of Foreign Affairs and Trade, Canberra, October 1993.

Council for Economic Planning and Development, *Taiwan Statistical Data Book*, 1989, 1990, 1991, 1992, 1993, 1994 editions, Republic of China, Taipei.

Council for Economic Planning and Development, White Paper, *The Six Year National Development Plan for Taiwan, Republic of China 1991–1996, Macroeconomic Development Targets*, Executive Yuan, Taipei, January 1991.

Current Notes on International Affairs, Department of Foreign Affairs and Trade, Canberra, 1950–71.

Declaration on Principles of International Law Concerning Friendly Relations and Cooperation Among States, 24 October 1970, UNGA Res 2625(XXV), 25 UN GAOR, Supp. (No 28)) 121, UN Doc. A/8028 (1971).

Doing Business with Taiwan R.O.C., China External Trade Development Council, Taipei, 1991.

Education and Training in Australia, Australian Bureau of Statistics, Cat. No. 4224.0, 1992.

Economic Statistics Annual (Taiwan Area) The Republic of China, Department of Statistics, Ministry of Economic Affairs, Taipei, 1992.

Economic and Trade Indicators, The Republic of China on Taiwan, China External Trade Development Council, Taipei, 1991.

Formosa — External Relations with Australia (General), File 519/3/1, parts 1–16, (1950–80), Department of Foreign Affairs and Trade, Canberra.

Guide to Foreign Investment in Quanzhou, Fujian, April 1990.

Guidelines for National Unification, Reference Paper, RR-91-02, Taipei, 5 March 1991.

Handbook for the Chinese People's Liberation Army, Defence Intelligence Agency, Washington, November 1984.

International Monetary Fund, *Direction of Trade Statistics Yearbook*, Washington DC, 1992, 1993 and 1994.

Investment Commission, Ministry of Economic Affairs, Taipei, *Statistics on Overseas Chinese and Foreign Investment, Technical Cooperation, Outward Investment, Outward Technical Cooperation*, December 1992.

Japanese Defence Agency, *Defence of Japan*, Tokyo, 1992.

Mainland Affairs Council, *Public Opinion and the Mainland Policy*, June 1991.

Military Situation in the Far East, Hearings before the Committee on Armed Services and the Committee on Foreign Relations, US Senate, 82nd Congress, 1st Session, Part III, US Government Printing Office, Washington, 1951.

Monthly Statistics of Exports and Imports (Taiwan Area), The Republic of China, Ministry of Finance, Taipei, December 1990.

Monthly Statistical Bulletin, Jakarta, January 1991.

National Defence Report, Ministry of National Defence, (English trans.), Li Ming Cultural Enterprise Co., Taipei, 1992 and 1994 editions.

Public Papers of the Presidents of the United States, Government Printing Office, Washington, 1972.

Report by the Australian Academy of Technological Sciences and Engineering, *Mission to Republic of Korea & Taiwan on Materials Technology, 8–24 May 1991*.

Republic of China Yearbook, Government Information Office, Taipei, various editions, 1970–94.

Southern China in Transition, East Asia Analytical Unit, Department of Foreign Affairs and Trade, Canberra, 1992.

Taiwan Relations Act, Congressional Record — House 125, No. 38, March 16, 1979: H1668-70.

'The Taiwan Question and Reunification of China', Taiwan Affairs & Information Office, State Council, People Republic of China, Beijing, August 1993, in Documents, *Beijing Review*, 6–12 September 1993.

The Participation of the Republic of China on Taiwan in the United Nations, Mainland Affairs Council, Executive Yuan, Taipei, July 1994.

Transnational Corporations and Management Division, *World Investment Report 1992 Transnational Corporations as Engines of Growth*, United Nations, New York, 1992.

US Senate, Committee on Foreign Relations, *Report on Mutual Defence Treaty with the Republic of China*, 8 February 1955, Senate, 84th Congress, 1st Session, Executive Report No. 2, US Government Printing Office, Washington, 1955.

US Department of Defence, *A Strategic Framework for the Asia Pacific Rim, Looking Towards the 21st Century*, Washington, 1990.

US Defence Department, *A Strategic Framework for the Asia-Pacific Rim*, Report to Congress, Washington, 1992.

US Department of State, *Foreign Relations of the United States, 1952–1954*, Vol XIV, US Government Printing Office, Washington, 1987.

US Department of State, *Foreign Relations of the United States 1955–1957*, Volume II, US Government Printing Office, Washington, 1987.

Weekly Compilation of Presidential Documents 1983, US Government Printing Office, Washington, 1983.

Yearbook of Labour Statistics, Republic of China, Taipei, 1981, 1986, 1987, 1990.

News media (1989–94)

The Age

Aerospace, January 1992

Arms Control Reporter, Section 602, 11 March 1988

Asia-Pacific Defence Reporter

Asian Defence Journal

Asian Wall Steet Journal

The Australian

The Australian Financial Review

Bangkok Post, 22 July 1994.

Beijing Review

Business Week, 14 September 1992

The Canberra Times

China Post (Taipei)

China Daily (Beijing)

China News Agency (Taipei)

Defence News (Washington)

The Economist

Far Eastern Economic Review

Foreign Broadcast Information Service — China (Daily Reports)

Free China Review (Taipei)

Free China Journal (Taipei)

Indochina Digest (Washington)

International Herald Tribune

Jane's Defence Weekly

Los Angeles Times, 27 April 1994

Military Technology

New York Times, 22 November 1969, 18 August 1982, 23 March 1988, 26 February 1992

Reuters Database

Saigon Economic Times, no. 24, June 1991.

Sinorama (Taipei)

South China Morning Post (Hong Kong)

The Straits Times (Singapore)

Sydney Morning Herald

Taiwan Communiqué (published by the International Committee for Human Rights in Taiwan, The Hague)

Time Magazine

United States Information Service Wireless File (East Asia) 1989–94

Articles

Alice H. Amsden, 'Taiwan's Economic History: A Case of Etatisme and a Challenge to Dependency Theory', *Modern China*, vol. 5, no. 3, July 1979, p. 341.

Robert F. Ash, 'The Evolution of Agricultural Policy', *China Quarterly*, December 1988, no. 116, p. 529.

Richard K. Betts, 'Wealth, Power and Instability: East Asia and the United States after the Cold War', *International Security*, vol. 18, no. 3, Winter 1993/94, p. 34.

Thomas V. Biddick, 'Diplomatic Rivalry in the South Pacific: The PRC and Taiwan', *Asian Survey*, vol. XXIX, no. 8, August 1989, p. 800.

Bin Yu, 'Sino-Russian Military Relations', *Asian Survey*, vol. XXXIII, no. 3, March 1993, p. 302.

H.W. Brands, 'Testing Massive Retaliation: Credibility and Crisis Management in the Taiwan Strait', *International Security*, vol. 12, no. 4, Spring 1988, p. 124.

Allen Buchanan, 'Self-determination and the Right to Secede', *Journal of International Affairs*, vol. 45, no. 2, Winter 1992, p. 347.

Barry Buzan and Gerald Segal, 'Rethinking East Asian Security', *Survival*, Summer 1994, p. 3.

Gerald Chan, 'Taiwan's Aid Diplomacy', paper for New Zealand Political Studies Association Annual Conference, University of Canterbury, August 1993.

Lien Chan, 'The Republic of China on Taiwan Belongs in the United Nations', *Orbis*, vol. 37, no. 4, Fall 1993, p. 635.

Gordon H. Chang, 'To the Nuclear Brink, Eisenhower, Dulles and the Quemoy–Matsu Crisis', *International Security*, vol. 12, no. 4, Spring 1988, p. 97.

Chang Pao-min, 'A New Scramble for the South China Sea Islands', *Contemporary Southeast Asia*, vol. 12, no. 1, June 1990, p. 27.

Chien-min Chao, 'China's Policy Towards Taiwan', in *Pacific Review*, vol. 3, no. 2, 1990, p. 125.

Chen Jie, 'The Taiwan Problem in Peking's ASEAN Policy', *Issues and Studies*, vol. 29, no. 4, April 1993, p. 95.

Chen Qimao, 'The Taiwan Issue and Sino-US Relations', *Asian Survey*, vol. XXVII, no. 11, November 1987, p. 1161.

Chen Xiaogong and Liu Xige, 'Several Questions Concerning China's National Defence Policy', *International Strategic Studies*, (Beijing), no. 2, 1993, p. 1.

Chi Schive, 'Cross Investment in the Asia-Pacific: The Case of Taiwan's Inward and Outward Investment', paper at the Taiwan Conference, The Fletcher School, Tufts University, Boston, 18–20 October 1991.

Fredrick F. Chien, 'A View from Taipei', *Foreign Affairs*, vol. 70, no. 5, Winter 1991/92, p. 93.

C.L. Chiou, 'The Uprising of 28 February 1947 on Taiwan: the Official 1992 Investigation Report', *China Information*, vol. VII, no. 4, Spring 1993, p. 1.

John Copper, 'Taiwan's Strategy and America's China Policy', *Orbis*, vol. 21, no. 2, Summer 1977, p. 261.

—— 'Ending Martial Law in Taiwan: Implications and Prospects', *Journal of Northeast Asian Studies*, vol. VII, no. 2, Summer 1988, p. 1.

Bruce Cumings, 'The Origins and Development of the Northeast Asian Political Economy: Industrial Sectors, Product Cycles and Political Consequences', *International Organization*, vol. 38, no. 1, Winter 1984, p. 1.

Martin T. Daly, 'The Road to the Twenty First Century: The Myths and Miracles of Asian Manufacturing', paper, Department of Geography, University of Sydney, 1992.

Lori Fisler Damrosch, *The Taiwan Relations Act After Ten Years*, Occasional Papers No. 4, School of Law, University of Maryland, 1990.

Gerald R. Ford, 'The US–Taiwan Connection', an address to the 13th Joint USA–ROC Business Conference, Honolulu, Hawaii, 18 November 1989, in *Sino-American Relations*, vol. XVI, no. 2, Summer 1990, p. 3.

Ross Garnaut, 'Asia's Giant', *Australian Economic Papers*, vol. 27, no. 51, December 1988, p. 173.

John Garver, 'China's Push Through the South China Sea: The Interaction of Bureaucratic and National Interests', *The China Quarterly*, no. 132, December 1992, p. 999.

Stephen P. Gilbert, 'Safeguarding Taiwan's Security', *Comparative Strategy*, vol. 8, no. 4, 1989, p. 425.

Thomas B. Gold, 'Go With Your Feelings: Hong Kong and Taiwan Popular Culture in Greater China', *China Quarterly*, no. 136, December 1993, p. 907.

Gidon Gottlieb, 'Nations Without States', *Foreign Affairs*, vol. 73, no. 3, May–June 1994, p. 100.

A. James Gregor, 'US Interests in Northeast Asia and the Security of Taiwan', *Strategic Review*, Winter 1985, p. 52.

Guo Changlin, 'Sino–US Relations in Perspective', *Contemporary International Relations*, vol. 2, no. 7, Beijing, July 1992.

Guocang Huan, 'Taipei–Beijing Relations', *World Policy Journal*, Summer 1992, p. 563.

Harry Harding, 'The Concept of Greater China: Themes, Variations and Reservations', *China Quarterly*, no. 136, December 1993, p. 660.

Jon W. Heubner, 'The Americanisation of the Taiwan Straits', *Asian Profile*, vol. 13, no. 3, June 1985, p. 197.

Samuel P. Huntington, 'The Clash of Civilisations', *Foreign Affairs*, vol. 72, no. 3, Summer 1993, p. 22.

—— 'Why Primacy Matters', *International Security*, vol. 17, no. 4, Spring 1993, p. 68.

J. Bruce Jacobs, 'Paradoxes in the Politics of Taiwan: Lessons for Comparative Politics', *Politics*, vol. 13, no. 2, p. 239.

J.P. Jain, 'The Legal Status of Formosa', 57 *American Journal of International Law* (1963), p. 25.

Robert Jervis, 'International Primacy: Is the Game Worth the Candle?', *International Security*, vol. 17, no. 4, Spring 1993, p. 52.

Qingguo Jia, 'Changing Relations Across the Taiwan Strait', *Asian Survey*, vol. XXXII, no. 3, March 1992, p. 277.

Michael T. Klare, 'The Next Great Arms Race', in *Foreign Affairs*, vol. 72, no. 3, Summer 1993, p. 136.

Gary Klintworth, 'Taiwan's United Nations Membership Bid', *Pacific Review*, vol. 7, no. 3, 1994, p. 283.

—— 'A Right to Intervene in the Domestic Affairs of States', *Australian Journal of International Affairs*, vol. 46, no. 2, November 1992, p. 248.

Koh Byong-ik, 'Confucianism in Asia's Modern Transformation', in *Korea Journal*, vol. 32, no. 4, Winter 1992, p. 61.

Nicholas D. Kristof, 'The Rise of China', *Foreign Affairs*, vol. 72, no. 5, November/December 1993, p. 59.

Sanjaya Lall, 'Emerging Sources of FDI in Asia and the Pacific', briefing paper for 'Roundtable on Foreign Direct Investment in the Asia-Pacific in the 1990s', East-West Centre, Honolulu, 26–28 March 1991.

Ruth Lapidoth, 'Sovereignty in Transition', *Journal of International Affairs*, vol. 45, no. 2, Winter 1992, p. 325.

Martin Lasater, 'The PRC's Force Modernisation: Shadow Over Taiwan and US Policy', *Strategic Review*, Winter 1984, p. 51.

E. Lauterpacht, 'Effect of the Cairo and Postdam Declarations 1943 and 1946', *British Yearbook of International Law*, vol. 8, no. 1, January 1959, p. 182.

Christopher Layne and Benjamin Schwarz, 'American Hegemony — Without an Enemy', *Foreign Policy*, vol. 92, Fall 1993, p. 5.

Christopher Layne, 'The Unipolar Illusion: Why New Great Powers Will Rise', *International Security*, vol. 17, no. 4, Spring 1993, p. 5.

Anthony Leung, 'Taiwan's Shipbuilding Programmes', *Naval Forces*, vol. XIII, no. III, 1992, p. 28.

Li Fei, 'A Look at the Adaptability of Taiwanese Business Investment to the Prevailing Mainland System', *Taiwan Research Quarterly*, Xiamen, February/March 1990, p. 1.

Li Jiaquan, 'On Taiwan's Elastic Diplomacy', *Beijing Review*, 26 February–4 March 1990, p. 27.

—— 'More on One Country, Two Governments', *Beijing Review*, 2–8 July 1990, p. 13.

—— 'Taiwan Independence a Blind Alley', *Beijing Review*, 8–14 June 1992, p. 20.

Shaomin Li, 'What China Can Learn From Taiwan', *Orbis*, 1989, p. 327.

Bih-jaw Lin, 'Taipei's Search for a New Foreign Policy', Conference Paper, Claremont Institute, Los Angeles, 7–8 April 1989.

—— paper 'Thinking about Taiwan's Experience', Institute of International Relations, National Chengchi University, Taipei, 1990.

Chong-Pin Lin, 'Beijing and Taipei: Dialectics in Post-Tiananmen Interactions', *The China Quarterly*, no. 136, 1993, p. 770.

Lu Yali, 'Current State and Future Prospects of ROC–PRC Relations', *China News Analysis*, no. 1402, 15 January 1990.

Ma Zongshi, 'China's Role in the Emerging Multipolar Asia-Pacific Scene', *Contemporary International Relations*, no. 6, China Institute of Contemporary International Relations, Beijing, February 1991.

Derek Massarella, Chinese, Tartars and *Thea* or a Tale of Two Companies: the English East India Company and Taiwan in the Late Seventeenth Century, unpublished paper, Princeton University, February 1993.

Thomas A. Metzger and Ramon H. Myers, 'Understanding the Taiwan Experience: An Historical Perspective', published by Shaw Yu-ming, Kwang Hwa Publishing Co, Taipei 1990, p. 10, reprinted from *Pacific Review*, vol. 2, no. 4, 1989.

Motoyuki Takamatsu, 'The United States and China: The Crises of 1954 and 1958', The China Academy, *Sino-American Relations*, vol. XIV, no. 1, Taipei, Spring 1988, p. 59.

Richard Nixon, 'Asia After Vietnam in Foreign Affairs', in *Foreign Affairs*, October 1967, p. 49.

Joseph S. Nye Jr, 'Soft Power', *Foreign Policy*, no. 80, Fall 1990, p. 153.

D.P. O'Connell, 'Legal Aspects of the Peace Treaty with Japan', *British Yearbook of International Law*, vol. XXIX, 1953, p. 423.

—— 'The Status of Formosa and the China Recognition Problem', 50 *American Journal of International Law*, 1956, p. 405.

Qi Luo and Christopher Howe, 'The Case of Taiwanese Investment in Xiamen', *China Quarterly*, no. 136, December 1993, p. 746.

Qin Huasun, 'An Approach to Confidence-building in the Asia-Pacific region' in *Confidence-building Measures in the Asia-Pacific Region, Disarmament*, Topical Papers 6, United Nations, New York, 1991.

Denny Roy, 'Hegemon on the Horizon? China's Threat to East Asian Security', *International Security*, vol. 19, no. 1, Summer 1994, p. 140.

Sa Benwang, 'Three Pillars of the Clinton Administration's Foreign Policy', *International Strategic Studies, No. 1*, China Institute for International Strategic Studies, Beijing, 1993, p. 14.

Saburo Okita, 'Pacific Development and its Implications for the World Economy', a keynote address at the PECC, Seoul, April 1985.

Randall L. Schweller, 'Bandwagoning for Profit', *International Security*, vol. 19, no. 1, Summer 1994, p. 72.

Yu-ming Shaw, 'Taiwan: A View from Taipei', *Foreign Affairs*, vol. 63, no. 5, 1985, p. 1062.

Sheng Lijun, 'China's Policy Towards the Spratly Islands in the 1990s', draft paper, Canberra, May 1994.

John Steinbruner, 'Beyond Rational Deterrence: The Struggle for New Conceptions', *World Politics*, vol. XXVIII, no. 2, January 1976, p. 223.

Sueo Kojima, 'Economic Relations Between China and Taiwan Enter a New Phase', Japan External Trade Organisation, *China Newsletter*, no. 76, October 1988, p. 2.

Yun-Wing Sung, 'The Re-integration of Southeast China', paper for the Conference on China's Reforms and Economic Growth, Australian National University, 11–14 November 1991.

Toru Nakakita, 'The Takeoff of the East Asian Economic Sphere', *Japan Review of International Affairs*, vol. 5, no. 1, Spring/Summer 1991, p. 62.

Tun Hwa Ko, 'Taiwan as a Strategic Asset', *Global Affairs*, vol. IV, no. 2, Spring 1989, p. 65.

Leonard Unger, 'Chiang Kai-shek's Second Chance', *Policy Review*, vol. 50, Fall 1989, p. 26.

Robert Wade, 'East Asia's Economic Success Conflicting Perspectives, Partial Insights; Shaky Evidence', *World Politics*, vol. 44, no. 2, January 1992, p. 270.

Wang Gungwu, 'Greater China and the Chinese Overseas', *China Quarterly*, no. 136, December 1993, p. 926.

Garry Woodard, 'Australian Foreign Policy on the Offshore Island Crisis of 1954–55 and Recognition of China', *Australian Journal of International Affairs*, vol. 45, no. 2, November 1991, p. 242.

Yan Xuetong, 'China's Security After the Cold War', *Contemporary International Relations* (Beijiing), vol. 3, no. 5, May 1993.

Paul T.K. Yen, 'Sino-American Relations in the 1980s: An Economic Review', *Sino-American Relations*, vol. XVI, no. 4, Winter 1990, p. 9.

Yu Tzong-shian, 'The Two Sides of the Taiwan Straits: Economic Interdependence and Cooperation', paper presented to the International Conference on Trade, Investment and Economic Prospects in Mainland China, Hong Kong and Taiwan, Melbourne, 24 February 1992.

John Quansheng Zhao, '"One Country, Two Systems" and "One Country, Two Parties": PRC-Taiwan Unification and its Political Implications', *Pacific Review*, vol. 2, no. 4, 1989, p. 312.

Books and monographs

G.C. Allen, *Japan's Economic Policy*, Macmillan, London, 1980.

The Almanac of Seapower, Navy League of the US, Arlington, Virginia, vol. 33, no. 1, January 1990.

Michael Armacost, Deputy Assistant Secretary, US Department of State, *Hearings, Committee on Foreign Relations, US Senate, 96th Congress*, US Government Printing Office, Washington DC, February 1979.

Asia Pacific Economics Group, *Asia-Pacific Profiles 1993*, ANU, Canberra, 1993.

Desmond Ball (ed.), *Air Power: Global Developments and Australian Perspectives*, Pergamon-Brasseys Defence Publishers, Sydney, 1988.

Joseph W. Ballantine, *Formosa*, The Brookings Institution, Washington, 1952.

George Barclay, *Colonial Development and Population in Taiwan*, Princeton University Press, Princeton, 1954.

F. Barnaby and M. Ter Borg, *Emerging Technologies and Military Doctrine: A Political Assessment*, Macmillan, London, 1986.

A. Doak Barnett, *China and the Major Powers in East Asia*, The Brookings Institution, Washington, 1977.

Bela Balassa, *The Newly Industrialising Countries of the World Economy*, Pergamon Press, New York, 1981.

Walden Bello and Stephanie Rosenfeld, *Dragons in Distress: Asia's Miracle Economies in Crisis*, Food First, San Francisco, 1990.

Peter Berger (ed.), *In Search of An East Asian Development Model*, Transaction Books, New Brunswick, 1988.

Mitchell Bernard, *Northeast Asia: The Political Economy of a Postwar Regional System*, Joint Centre for Asia Pacific Studies, Asia Papers No. 2, University of Toronto–York University, 1989.

Richard K. Betts, *Surprise Attack*, The Brookings Institution, Washington, 1982.

Zbigniew Brzezinski, *Power and Principle*, Farrer Straus, Giroux, New York, 1983.

Hedley Bull and Adam Watson (eds), *The Expansion of International Society*, Oxford University Press, Oxford, 1984.

Richard Burt, *New Weapons Technologies: Debate and Directions*, Adelphi Papers No. 126, IISS London, 1976.

Barry Buzan, *An Introduction to Strategic Studies*, Military Technology and International Relations, Macmillan, London, 1987.

Theresa C. Carino (ed.), *China ASEAN Relations: Political, Economic and Ethnic Dimensions*, The China Studies Program, De La Salle University, Manila, 1991.

William Henry Chamberlin, *Japan Over Asia*, Duckworth, London, 1938.

F. Gilbert Chan, *China's Reunification and the Taiwan Question*, Asia Research Service, Hong Kong, 1984.

Jui-meng Chang, *The Determinants of Trade Policies in Taiwan*, Chung-Hua Institution for Economic Research Economic Monograph No. 18, CIER, Taipei, 1987.

Chang King-yuh (ed.), *ROC–US Relations Under the Taiwan Relations Act: Practice and Prospects*, Institute of International Relations, Taipei, 1989.

—— *The Impact of the Three Principles on the People of China*, English Monograph Series No. 34, Institute of International Relations, National Chengchi University, Taipei, 1988.

—— *Ideology and Politics in Twentieth Century China*, English Monograph Series No. 32, Institute of International Relations, National Chengchi University, Taipei, 1988

Chen Cheng, *Land Reform in Taiwan*, China Publishing Co., Taipei, 1961.

Cheng Hsiao-shih, *Party–Military Relations in the PRC and Taiwan*, Paradoxes of Control, Westview, Boulder, Col., 1990.

Tun-jen Cheng and Stephan Haggard (eds), *Political Change in Taiwan*, Lynne Rienner Publishers, Boulder, Col., 1992.

Tuan Y. Cheng, *Economic Diplomacy in the Pacific Basin of the Republic of China on Taiwan*, Pacific Forum/CSIS, Hawaii, July 1992.

Fredrick F. Chien, *Faith and Resilience: The Republic of China on Taiwan Forges Ahead*, Kwang Hwa Publishing (USA) Inc., Houston, 1988.

Chi Schive, *The Foreign Factor: The Multinational Corporation's Contribution to the Economic Modernisation of the Republic of China*, Hoover Institution Press, Stanford, 1990.

Chiang Kai-shek, *China's Destiny and Chinese Economic Theory*, Dennis Dobson Ltd, London, 1947.

Hungdah Chiu, *China and the Taiwan Issue*, Praeger, New York, 1979.

—— *The Taiwan Relations Act and Sino-American Relations*, Occasional Papers No. 5, School of Law, University of Maryland, 1990.

Cal Clark, *Taiwan's Development: Implications for Contending Political Economy Paradigms*, Greenwood Press, Connecticut, 1989.

Ralph N. Clough, *Island China*, Harvard, Cambridge, Mass., 1978.

—— *Reaching Across the Taiwan Strait*, Westview Press, Boulder, Col., 1993.

O. Edmund Clubb, *China and Russia: The Great Game*, Columbia University Press, New York, 1971.

Conference on Successful Economic Development Strategies of the Pacific Rim Nations, Chung Hua Institution for Economic Research, Conference Series No. 10, Taipei, 1988.

John Copper, *Taiwan: Nation, State or Province*, Westview, Boulder, Col., 1990.

Anthony H. Cordesman and Abraham R. Wagner, *The Lessons of Modern War Volume II the Iran–Iraq War*, Westview Press, Boulder, Col., 1990.

Bruce Cumings (ed.), *The Origins of the Korean War: Volume II The Roaring of the Cataract*, Princeton University Press, Princeton, New Jersey, 1990.

James Crawford, *The Creation of States in International Law*, Clarendon Press, Oxford, 1979.

James W. Davidson, *The Island of Formosa Past and Present*, Macmillan and Co., London, 1903.

Department of Mines and Technical Surveys, *Taiwan (Formosa)*, Foreign Geography Information Series No. 5, Ottawa, Canada, 1952.

Frederic C. Deyo (ed.), *The Political Economy of the New Asian Industrialism*, Cornell University Press, Ithaca, 1987.

Paul Dibb, *Review of Australia's Defence Capability*, AGPS, Canberra, 1986.

—— 'Asia's Security in the 21st Century', *Strategic and Defence Studies Newsletter*, March 1994.

Peter Drysdale, *International Economic Pluralism: Economic Policy in East Asia and the Pacific*, Allen & Unwin, Sydney, 1988.

Kerry B. Dumbaugh, *China–US Relations in the 1990s: Issues for Congress*, Foreign Affairs and National Defense Division, Congressional

Research Service, the Library of Congress, Washington, 24 January 1992.

Hugh Dunn, *Conversations about Taiwan in Taipei and Beijing*, Australia-Asia Papers No. 47, Centre for the Study of Australia-Asian Relations, Griffith University, 1989.

Peter Evans, Dietrich Rueschemeyer and Theda Skocpol (eds), *Bringing the State Back In*, Cambridge University Press, Cambridge, 1985.

John C.H. Fei, Gustav Ranis and Shirley W.Y. Kuo, *Growth with Equity: The Taiwan Case*, Oxford University Press, New York, 1979.

Harvey J. Feldman et al. (eds), *Taiwan in a Time of Transition*, Paragon House, New York, 1988.

Andrew Fraser, *First Fruits of Empire: Japan's Colonial Administration in Taiwan 1895–1934*, Papers on Far Eastern History No. 38, Canberra, September 1988.

Lawrence Freedman, *The Evolution of Nuclear Strategy*, Macmillan, London, 1988.

Walter Galenson (ed.), *Economic Growth and Structural Change in Taiwan*, Cornell University Press, Ithaca, 1979.

Ross Garnaut, *Australia and the Northeast Asian Ascendancy*, Australian Government Publishing Service, Canberra, 1989.

Alexander L. George and Richard Smoke, *Deterrence in American Foreign Policy: Theory and Practice*, Columbia University Press, New York, 1974.

Gary Gereffi and Donald L. Wyman (eds), *Manufacturing Miracles: Paths of Industrialisation in Latin America and East Asia*, Princeton University Press, Princeton, 1990.

Robert Gilpin, *War and Change in World Politics*, Cambridge University Press, Cambridge, 1981.

Thomas B. Gold, *State and Society in the Taiwan Miracle*, M.E. Sharpe Inc., Armonk, 1986.

Leland M. Goodrich, Edvard Hambro and Anne Patricia Simons, *Charter of the United Nations Commentary and Documents*, 3rd edn, Columbia University Press, New York, 1969.

A. James Gregor and Maria Hsia Chang, *Essays on Sun Yat-sen and the Economic Development of Taiwan*, Occasional Papers in Contemporary Asian Studies No. 1, School of Law, University of Maryland, 1983.

D.W. Greig, *International Law*, 2nd edn, Butterworths, London, 1976.

Samuel B. Griffith, *Sun Tzu The Art of War*, Oxford University Press, London, 1963.

Stephan Haggard, *Pathways from the Periphery: The Politics of Growth in the Newly Industrialising Countries*, Cornell University Press, Ithaca and London, 1990.

Stephan Haggard and Chung-in Moon (eds), *Pacific Dynamics: The International Politics of Industrial Change*, CIS-Inha University Inchon/Westview, Col., 1989.

Morton H. Halperin and David J. Scheffer with Patricia L. Small, *Self Determination in the New World Order*, Carnegie Endowment for International Peace, Washington, 1992.

Han Lih-wu, *Taiwan Today*, Cheng Chung Book Company, Taipei, 1988.

Michael Handel, *Weak States in the International System*, Frank Cass, London, 1981.

Peter Harrold, *China's Reform Experience to Date*, World Bank Discussion Papers 180, The World Bank, Washington, 1992.

Francois Heisbourg (ed.), *The Changing Strategic Landscape*, Macmillan, London, 1989.

Han Herderschee, *Incentives for Exports: The Case of Taiwan*, Working Paper No. 91/9, National Centre for Development Studies (NCDS), ANU, Canberra, 1991.

—— *Protection and Exports: A Comparison of Taiwan and Thailand*, Working Paper No. 91/11, NCDS, ANU Canberra, 1991.

Charles F. Hermann, Charles W. Kegley, James N. Rosenau (eds), *New Directions in the Study of Foreign Policy*, Allen & Unwin, Boston, 1987.

George Hicks (ed.), *The Broken Mirror: China After Tiananmen*, Longmans, Essex (UK), 1990.

Samuel P.S. Ho, *Economic Development of Taiwan 1860–1970*, Yale University Press, New Haven, 1978.

Steve Hoadley, *New Zealand and Taiwan: The Policy and Practice of Quasi-Diplomacy*, New Zealand Institute of International Affairs, Occasional Papers No. 7, October 1993.

Roy Hofheinz Jr and Kent E. Calder, *The Eastasia Edge*, Basic Books, New York, 1982.

Chiao Chiao Hsieh, *Strategy for Survival*, The Sherwood Press, London, 1985.

Helen Hughes (ed.), *Achieving Industrialisation in East Asia*, Cambridge University Press, Cambridge, 1988.

Samuel P. Huntington, *Political Order in Changing Societies*, New Haven, Yale University Press, 1968.

Paul K. Huth, *Extended Deterrence and the Prevention of War*, Yale University Press, New Haven, 1988.

International Monetary Fund, *Direction of Trade Statistics Yearbook*, Washington DC, 1992, 1993 and 1994.

Neil H. Jacoby, *US Aid to Taiwan*, Praeger, New York, 1966.

Japanese Defence Agency, *Defence of Japan*, Tokyo, 1992.

Robert Jervis et al., *Psychology and Deterrence*, The John Hopkins University Press, Baltimore, 1985.

Chalmers Johnson (ed.), *Change in Communist Systems*, Stanford University Press, Stanford, 1970.

F.C. Jones, *Manchuria Since 1931*, Oxford University Press, London, 1949.

Herman Kahn, *World Economic Development: 1979 and Beyond*, Croom Helm, London, 1979.

William W. Kaufmann, *The Requirements of Deterrence*, Center for International Studies, Princeton, 1954.

Keiji Furuya, *Chiang Kai-shek His Life and Times*, St John's University, New York, 1981.

Robert O. Keohane and Joseph S. Nye, *Power and Interdependence, World Politics in Transition*, Little, Brown and Company, Boston, 1977.

George H. Kerr, *Formosa Betrayed*, Eyre & Spottiswoode, London, 1966.

Kiyoshi Kojima, *Japan and a New World Economic Order*, Tuttle, Tokyo, 1977.

W. Klenner (ed.), *Trends of Economic Development in East Asia*, Springer Verlag Berlin, Heidelberg 1989.

Gary Klintworth (ed.), *China's Crisis: The International Implications*, Canberra Papers No. 57, Strategic and Defence Studies Centre, Canberra, 1989.

—— (ed.), *Taiwan in the Asia-Pacific in the 1990s*, Allen & Unwin/Department of International Relations, ANU, Canberra, 1994.

—— *Australia–Taiwan Relations 1942–1992*, Department of International Relations, ANU, 1993.

—— *China's Modernisation and the Strategic Implications for the Asia-Pacific Region*, AGPS, Canberra, 1989.

—— (ed.), *Modern Taiwan in the 1990s*, Canberra Papers on Strategy and Defence, No. 75, Strategic and Defence Studies Centre, Canberra, 1990.

Stephen D. Krasner (ed.), *International Regimes*, Cornell University Press, Ithaca, 1983.

Manfred Kulessa (ed.), *The Newly Industrialising Economies of Asia — Prospects for Co-operation*, Springer-Verlag, Berlin, 1990.

Shirley W.Y. Kuo, Gustav Ranis and John C.H. Fei, *The Taiwan Success Story: Rapid Growth with Improved Distribution in the Republic of China 1952–1979*, Westview, Boulder, Col., 1981.

Martin L. Lasater, *US Interests in the New Taiwan*, Westview, Boulder, Col., 1993.

H. Lauterpacht, *Recognition in International Law*, University Press, Cambridge, 1947.

—— (ed.), *International Law: A Treatise*, 8th edn, vol 1, Longmans, London, 1955.

Lee Teng-hui, *Creating the Future: Towards a New Era for the Chinese People*, Government Information Office, Taipei, 1993.

Duncan Lennox and Arthur Rees (eds), *Jane's Air Launched Weapons*, Jane's Information Group, Surrey, 1989, Issue 11.

Lessons from Taiwan: Pathways to Follow and Pitfalls to Avoid, ISIS Malaysia, 1986.

Kwoh-ting Li, *Economic Transformation of Taiwan*, Shepheard-Walwyn, London, 1988.

Linda Y.C. Lim and Pang Eng Fong, *Foreign Direct Investment and Industrialisation in Malaysia, Singapore Taiwan and Thailand*, OECD, Paris, 1991.

Bih-jaw Lin and James T. Myers (eds), *Forces of Change in Contemporary China*, University of South Carolina Press, Columbia, 1993.

S.B. Linder, *The Pacific Century: Economic and Political Consequences of Asian-Pacific Dynamism*, Stanford University Press, Stanford, 1986.

A.P.L. Liu, *Phoenix and the Lame Lion: Modernisation in Taiwan and Mainland China 1950–1980*, Hoover Institution Press, Stanford, 1987.

Alan P.L. Liu, *The Political Basis of the Economic and Social Development in the Republic of China 1949–1980*, Occasional Papers No. 1, School of Law, University of Maryland, 1984.

Paul K.C. Liu, *Economic Development and Population in Taiwan since 1895: An Over-view*, The Institute of Economics, Academica Sinica, Taipei, 1972.

F.A. Lumley, *The Republic of China Under Chiang Kai-shek: Taiwan Today*, Barrie & Jenkins, London, 1976.

Andrew Mack and John Ravenhill (eds), *Economic and Security Regimes in the Asia-Pacific*, Studies in World Affairs Series, Allen & Unwin, St Leonards, 1994.

Colin Mackerras and Amanda Yorke, *The Cambridge Handbook of Contemporary China*, Cambridge University Press, Cambridge, 1991.

J.N. Mak, *ASEAN Defence Reorientation 1975–1992: The Dynamics of Modernisation and Structural Change*, Canberra Papers No. 103, Strategic and Defence Studies Centre, Research School of Pacific Studies, ANU, Canberra, 1993.

Mark Mancall, *Formosa Today*, Praeger, New York, 1964.

Masato Hayashida, *Entrepreneurship in Taiwan and Korea: A Comparison*, IIGP Policy Paper No 109E, International Institute for Global Peace, Tokyo, May 1993.

The Military Balance, Institute of International Strategic Studies, Brassey's, London, various issues.

Frank P. Morello, *The International Legal Status of Formosa*, Martinus Nijhoff, The Hague, 1966.

Patrick M. Morgan, *Assessing the Republic of China's Deterrence Situation*, Sun Yat-sen Centre for Policy Studies, Kaohsiung, Paper No. 4, April 1991

Akio Morita and Shintaro Ishihara, *The Japan That Can Say 'No'*, Kobunsha, Kappa-Holmes, 1990.

Steven W. Mosher (ed.), *The United States and the Republic of China*, Transaction Publishers, New Brunswick, 1992.

Hiromichi Mutoh et al., *Industrial Policies for Pacific Economic Growth*, Allen & Unwin, Sydney, 1986.

Ramon Myers (ed.), *A Unique Relationship: The United States and the Republic of China Under the Taiwan Relations Act*, Hoover, Stanford, 1989.

Ramon Myers and Mark R. Peattie (eds), *The Japanese Colonial Empire 1895–1945*, Princeton University Press, Princeton, 1984.

Ramon H. Myers and Adrienne Ching, 'Agricultural Development in Taiwan Under Japanese Colonial Rule', *Journal of Asian Studies*, vol. XXIII, no. 4, August 1964.

Peter Osborne and Robert O'Donovan, *Taiwan in the 1990s: Opportunities for Australia*, ACC/Westpac Economic Discussion Papers, 4/1991, Canberra, 1991.

Kenichi Ohmae, *The Borderless World: Power and Strategy in the Interlinked Economy*, Collins, London, 1990.

William H. Overholt (ed.), *Asia's Nuclear Future, Studies of the Research Institute on International Change*, Columbia University, Westview, Boulder, Col., 1977.

William H. Overholt, *China: The Next Economic Superpower*, Weidenfeld and Nicolson, London, 1993.

Keith B. Payne, *Nuclear Deterrence in US–Soviet Relations*, Westview, Boulder, Col., 1982.

Peng Ming-min, *A Taste of Freedom, Memoirs of a Formosan Independence Leader*, Holt, Rinehart and Winston, New York, Chicago and San Francisco, 1972.

Lucian Pye, *Asian Power and Politics*, Belknap Press, Cambridge Mass., 1985

Gustav Ranis (ed.), *Taiwan From Developing to Mature Economy*, Westview Press, Boulder, Col., 1992.

S. Gordon Redding, *The Spirit of Chinese Capitalism*, Walter de Gruyter, Berling, New York, 1990.

Edwin O. Reischauer, John K. Fairbank and Albert M. Craig, *East Asia: The Modern Transformation*, George Allen & Unwin, London, 1967.

Research Institute for Peace and Security, *Asia Security 1979*, Tokyo, 1979, 1980.

Richard Robison, *Indonesia: The Rise of Capitalism*, Allen & Unwin, Sydney, 1986.

Thomas W. Robinson (ed.), *Democracy and Development in East Asia*, AEI Press, Washington, 1991.

Richard Rosencrance, *The Rise of the Trading State*, Basic Books Inc., New York, 1986.

Robert Rothstein, *Alliances and Small Powers*, Columbia University Press, New York and London, 1968.

Selected Works of Mao Tse-tung, Volume II, Foreign Languages Press, Peking, 1965.

Selected Works of Deng Xiaoping, 1975–1982, Foreign Language Press, Beijing, 1983.

Yu-ming Shaw (ed.), *ROC–US Relations: A Decade After the Shanghai Communiqué*, The Asia and World Institute, Taipei, 1983.

Edgar Snow, *Red Star Over China*, rev. edn, Victor Gollancz, London, 1968.

—— *The Other Side of the River*, Random House, New York, 1962.

Glenn H. Snyder, *Deterrence and Defence*, Princeton University Press, New Jersey, 1961.

Saburo Okita, *Japan in the World Economy*, The Japan Foundation, Tokyo, 1975.

T.H. Shen, *Agricultural Development on Taiwan since World War II*, Cornell University Press, Ithaca, 1964.

—— *The Sino-American Joint Commission on Rural Reconstruction*, Cornell University Press, Ithaca, 1970.

Douglas C. Smith (ed.), *The Confucian Continuum: Educational Modernisation in Taiwan*, Praeger, New York, 1991.

Yun-Wing Sung, *The China–Hong Kong Connection: The Key to China's Open-Door Policy*, Cambridge University Press, Hong Kong, 1991.

Hung-chao Tai (ed.), *Confucianism and Economic Development: An Oriental Alternative?*, The Washington Institute Press, Washington, 1989.

Tai Ming Cheung, *Growth of Chinese Naval Power*, Institute of South East Asian Studies, Pacific Strategic Papers, No. 1, Singapore, 1990.

Takeshi Hayashi, *The Japanese Experience in Technology*, United Nations University Press, Tokyo, 1990.

Ssu-yu Teng and John K. Fairbank, *China's Response to the West: A Documentary Survey 1839–1923*, Atheneum, New York, 1969.

Tien Hung-mao, *The Great Transition Political and Social Change in the Republic of China*, Hoover Institution Press, Stanford, 1989.

Tran Van Tho, *Direct Investment and Technology: Japan and Northeast and Southeast Asia*, Japan Centre for Economic Research, Research Report Series No. 56, 1986.

Tsuneo Akaha and Frank Langdon (eds), *Japan in the Posthegemonic World*, Lynne Rienner, Boulder and London, 1989.

Jenn-Hwa Tu, *Direct Foreign Investment and Economic Growth: A Case Study of Taiwan*, Institute of Economics, Academia Sinica Monograph Series, No. 48, Taipei, December 1990.

US Department of State, *Foreign Relations of the United States 1955–1957*, Volume II, US Government Printing Office, Washington, 1987.

Christine Vertente, Hsu Hsueh-chi and Wu Mi-cha, *The Authentic Story of Taiwan*, Mappamundi Publishers, Knokke (Belgium), 1991.

David Vital, *The Inequality of States*, Clarendon Press, Oxford, 1967.

Ezra F. Vogel, *The Four Little Dragons: The Spread of Industrialisation in East Asia*, Harvard University Press, Cambridge, Mass., 1991.

Robert Wade, *Governing the Market: Economic Theory and the Role of Government in East Asian Industrialisation*, Princeton University Press, Princeton, New Jersey, 1990.

Stephen M. Walt, *The Origins of Alliances*, Cornell University Press, Ithaca, 1987.

Kenneth Waltz, *Theory of International Politics*, Addison-Wesley Publishing Company, Reading, 1979.

Yu San Wang (ed.), *Foreign Policy of the Republic of China on Taiwan*, Praeger, New York, 1990.

Wang Gungwu, *China and the Overseas Chinese*, Times Academic Press, Singapore, 1991.

Gordon White (ed.), *Developmental States in East Asia*, St Martin's Press, New York, 1988.

Edwin A. Winckler and Susan Greenhalgh (eds.), *Contending Approaches to the Political Economy of Taiwan*, M.E. Sharpe, New York, 1988.

Jon Woronoff, *Asia's 'Miracle Economies'*, M.E. Sharpe Inc., New York, 1986.

Yuan-li Wu and Kung-chia Yeh (eds), *Growth Distribution and Social Change: Essays on the Economy of the Republic of China*, Occasional Papers No. 3, School of Law, University of Maryland, 1978.

Xiao Bing and Qing Bo, *Zhongguo Jundui Nengfou Daying Xia Yi Chang Zhanzheng* (Can the Chinese Army Win the Next War), Chongqing, June 1993, published by FBIS (JPRS CAR 94-024-L), 5 May 1994.

Martin M.C. Yang, *Socio-Economic Results of Land Reform in Taiwan*, East West Center Press, Honolulu, 1970.

Richard Yang (ed.), *SCPS PLA Yearbook 1988/89*, Sun Yat-sen Centre for Policy Studies, Kaohsiung, 1989,

—— (ed.), *China's Military: The PLA in 1990/91*, Sun Yat-sen Center for Policy Studies, Kaohsiung, Taiwan, 1991.

—— (ed.), *China's Military: The PLA in 1992/93*, Chinese Council for Advanced Policy Studies, Taipei, 1993.

Sophia Su-fei Yen, *Taiwan in China's Foreign Relations 1936–1974*, Shoe String Press, Hamden, 1965.

Yosaburo Takekoshi (trans. George Braithwaite), *Japanese Rule in Formosa*, Longmans, London, 1907.

Crawford Young (ed.), *The Rising Tide of Pluralism: The Nation-State at Bay?*, University of Wisconsin Press, Wisconsin, 1993.

Yu San Wang (ed.), *Foreign Policy of the Republic of China on Taiwan*, Praeger, New York, 1990.

Burns H. Weston (ed.), *Alternative Security: Living Without Nuclear Deterrence*, Westview Press, Boulder, Col., 1990.

Appendix: Tables

Table 1 The Rise of Taiwan's Position in the Global Economy, 1972–91 (ascending order)

	1972	1981	1991
GNP	39	32	21
GNP/per capita	42	34	25
Total trade	25	22	14
Exports	23	16	12
Imports	27	22	17
Foreign reserves	27	14	1

Source: Yu Tzong-shian, 'Taiwan's Economic Position in East Asian regional restructuring', in Gary Klintworth, *Taiwan in the Asia-Pacific in the 1990s*, Allen & Unwin, Canberra, 1994, Table 15.1, p. 258.

Table 2 Taiwan's Rank as an Exporting Nation

1979		1992	
1	US	1	US
2	Germany	2	Germany
3	Japan	3	Japan
4	France	4	France
5	UK	5	UK
6	Italy	6	Italy
7	USSR	7	Netherlands
8	Netherlands	8	Canada
9	Saudi Arabia	9	Belgium
10	Canada	10	Hong Kong
11	Belgium	11	China
12	Sweden	12	Taiwan
13	Switzerland	13	Korea
22	Taiwan		

Sources: a *Composition of Trade Australia 1992–93*, Department of Foreign Affairs and Trade, Canberra, 1993, p. 41.

b GATT *Focus Newsletter*, no. 70, April 1994, p. 4.

Table 3 Taiwan: Quality of Life Indicators, 1966–91

Item

	1966	1991
1 Education	**1966**	**1991**
Literacy rate (of population 6 years old and older (%)	45.0[a]	93.6
Percentage of school-age children (6–11) in primary school	78.6[a]	99.9
Percentage of junior high-age youths (12–14) in junior high school	48.3	98.4
Percentage of senior high-age youths (15–17) in senior high and vocational school	28.3	91.0
Percentage of junior college- and university-age youths (18–21) in junior college and university	11.3	31.2
2 Sanitation	**1952**	**1991**
Crude death rate (per 1000)	9.9	5.2
Life expectancy (years)	58.6	74.2
Per capita daily calorie intake	2078.0	3036.0
Per capita daily protein intake (grams)	49.0	89.0
3 Transportation and communications	**1952**	**1991**
Automobiles (per 1000 population)	1	163
Motorcycles (per 1000 population)	0.2	449
Telephones (per 1000 population)	4	450
Correspondence posted (per capita)	7	85
4 Housing	**1952**	**1991**
Percentage of households with electric lighting	33.0[b]	99.7
Percentage of population with piped water	28.8	84.1
Living space per head (square metres)	4.6[b]	25.1[c]
Dwelling investment/GNP (%)	1.0	2.5

Source: Shirley W.Y. Kuo, 'The Taiwan Economy in the 1990s', in Gary Klintworth (ed.),
Taiwan in the Asia-Pacific in the 1990s, Allen & Unwin, Sydney, 1994, Table 6.2, p. 108.
   [a] 1946
   [b] 1949
   [c] 1990

Table 4 Indicators of Taiwan's Economy

Period	Foreign exchange $US million	Exchange rates $NT/$US	Unemploy-ment %	Economic growth %	GNP $US million	Per capita GNP $US	Gross savings % of GNP
1952	-	-	4.4	12.0	1 674	196	15.3
1955	-	-	3.8	8.1	1 928	203	14.6
1960	-	-	4.0	6.4	1 717	154	17.8
1965	245	40.05	3.3	11.0	2 811	217	20.7
1966	275	40.05	3.0	9.0	3 148	237	22.2
1967	335	40.05	2.3	10.6	3 637	267	23.1
1968	300	40.05	1.7	9.1	4 236	304	22.4
1969	361	40.05	1.9	9.0	4 915	345	23.8
1970	540	40.05	1.7	11.3	5 660	389	25.6
1971	617	40.50	1.7	13.0	6 589	443	28.8
1972	952	40.50	1.5	13.4	7 906	522	32.1
1973	1 026	38.00	1.3	12.8	10 727	695	34.4
1974	1 092	38.00	1.5	1.2	14 458	920	31.5
1975	1 074	38.00	2.4	4.4	15 429	964	26.7
1976	1 516	38.00	1.8	13.7	18 492	1 132	32.3
1977	1 345	38.00	1.8	10.3	21 681	1 301	32.6
1978	1 406	36.00	1.7	14.0	26 773	1 577	34.4
1979	1 467	36.03	1.3	8.5	33 229	1 920	33.4
1980	2 205	36.01	1.2	7.1	41 360	2 344	32.3
1981	7 235	37.84	1.4	5.8	47 955	2 669	31.3
1982	8 532	39.91	2.1	4.1	48 550	2 653	30.1
1983	11 859	40.27	2.7	8.7	52 503	2 823	32.1
1984	15 664	39.47	2.4	11.6	59 780	3 167	33.8
1985	22 556	39.85	2.9	5.6	63 097	3 297	33.6
1986	46 310	35.50	2.7	12.6	77 299	3 993	38.5
1987	76 648	28.55	2.0	11.9	103 200	5 275	38.5
1988	73 897	28.17	1.7	7.8	125 316	6 333	34.5
1989	73 224	26.16	1.6	7.3	150 283	7 512	30.8
1990	72 441	27.1075	1.7	5.0	160 913	7 954	29.2
1991	82 405	25.7475	1.5	7.2	179 763	8 788	29.5
1992	82 306	25.4025	1.5	6.1	210 886	10 215	28.0
1993	83 573	26.62	1.4	5.9	220 129	10 566	28.0

Source: Council for Economic Planning and Development, Taiwan Statistical Data Book, Taipei, 1994, pp. 1, 4, 16.

Table 5 Taiwan's GDP and Trade in Context (US$1000)

Country	GDP (US$ million)		Average annual Growth rate (%)		1990 trade (US$ million)		Average annual growth rate (%)			
							Exports		Imports	
	1965	1990	1965–80	1980–90	Exports	Imports	1965–80	1980–90	1965–80	1980–90
Republic of China	2 816	157 010	9.9	7.7	67 214	54 716	18.9	12.1	15.1	10.1
Australia	24 220	296 300	4.0	3.4	35 973	39 740	5.4	3.9	1.0	4.7
Canada	52 870	570 150	4.8	3.4	125 056	115 882	5.4	5.9	2.5	8.4
France	99 300	1 190 780	4.0	2.2	209 491	232 525	8.5	3.4	4.3	3.2
Germany	114 790	1 488 210	3.3	2.1	397 912	341 248	7.2	4.2	5.3	3.9
Hong Kong	2 150	59 670	8.6	7.1	29 002	82 495	9.1	6.2	8.3	11.0
Indonesia	5 980	107 290	7.0	5.5	25 553	21 837	9.6	2.8	13.0	1.4
Japan	91 290	2 942 890	6.4	4.1	286 768	231 223	11.4	4.2	4.9	5.6
Malaysia	-	42 370	7.4	5.2	29 409	29 251	4.6	10.3	2.2	5.6
Philippines	6 010	43 860	5.7	0.9	8 681	13 080	4.6	2.5	2.9	2.3
Republic of Korea	3 000	236 400	9.9	9.7	64 837	69 585	27.2	12.8	15.2	10.8
Singapore	970	34 600	10.0	6.4	52 627	60 647	4.7	8.6	7.0	6.7
Thailand	4 390	80 170	7.3	7.6	23 002	33 129	8.6	13.2	4.1	10.2
United States	701 380	5 392 200	2.7	3.4	371 466	515 635	6.4	3.3	5.5	7.6

Source: Council for Economic Planning and Development, *Taiwan Statistical Data Book*, Taipei, 1993, pp. 309, 311, 312–17.

Table 6 Taiwan's Gross Domestic Product by Kind of Activity (%)

Period	Total	Agriculture	Industries	Services
1952	100.0	32.2	19.7	48.1
1955	100.0	29.1	23.2	47.7
1960	100.0	28.5	26.9	44.6
1965	100.0	23.6	30.2	46.2
1966	100.0	22.5	30.5	46.9
1967	100.0	20.6	33.0	46.6
1968	100.0	19.0	34.4	46.5
1969	100.0	15.9	36.9	47.2
1970	100.0	15.5	36.8	47.7
1971	100.0	13.1	38.9	48.0
1972	100.0	12.2	41.6	46.1
1973	100.0	12.1	43.8	44.1
1974	100.0	12.4	40.7	46.9
1975	100.0	12.7	39.9	47.4
1976	100.0	11.4	43.2	45.5
1977	100.0	10.6	44.0	45.4
1978	100.0	9.4	45.2	45.4
1979	100.0	8.6	45.3	46.1
1980	100.0	7.7	45.7	46.6
1981	100.0	7.3	45.5	47.2
1982	100.0	7.7	44.4	47.9
1983	100.0	7.3	45.0	47.7
1984	100.0	6.3	46.2	47.5
1985	100.0	5.8	46.3	47.9
1986	100.0	5.5	47.6	46.8
1987	100.0	5.3	47.4	47.3
1988	100.0	5.0	45.7	49.3
1989	100.0	4.9	43.6	51.5
1990	100.0	4.1	42.5	53.4
1991	100.0	3.7	42.5	53.8
1992	100.0	3.5	41.4	55.1
1993	100.0	3.5	40.6	55.9

Source: Council for Economic Planning and Development, Taiwan Statistical Data Book, Taipei, 1994, p. 42.

Table 7 Taiwan's Composition of Exports

Period	Value (US$ million)				Percentage distribution (%)			
	Total	Agricultural products	Processed agricultural	Industrial products	Total	Agricultural products	Processed agricultural	Industrial products
1952	116.5	25.7	81.3	9.5	100.0	22.1	69.8	8.1
1955	123.3	34.7	75.8	12.8	100.0	28.1	61.5	10.4
1960	164.0	19.7	91.3	53.0	100.0	12.0	55.7	32.3
1965	449.7	106.2	136.6	206.9	100.0	23.6	30.4	46.0
1966	536.3	106.3	134.8	295.2	100.0	19.8	25.1	55.1
1967	640.7	97.2	148.7	394.8	100.0	15.2	23.2	61.6
1968	789.2	87.8	161.7	539.7	100.0	11.1	20.5	68.4
1969	1 049.4	98.1	174.9	776.4	100.0	9.3	16.7	74.0
1970	1 481.4	126.7	190.9	1 164.7	100.0	8.6	12.8	78.6
1971	2 060.4	163.0	230.5	1 666.9	100.0	7.9	11.2	80.9
1972	2 988.1	203.6	295.5	2 489.0	100.0	6.8	9.9	83.3
1973	4 483.4	337.6	351.7	3 794.1	100.0	7.5	7.9	84.6
1974	5 639.0	269.6	603.2	4 766.2	100.0	4.8	10.7	84.5
1975	5 308.8	295.7	572.5	4 440.6	100.0	5.6	10.8	83.6
1976	8 166.3	406.1	606.1	7 154.1	100.0	5.0	7.4	87.6
1977	9 360.7	502.3	669.6	8 188.8	100.0	5.4	7.1	87.5
1978	12 687.1	637.5	740.1	11 309.5	100.0	5.0	5.8	89.2
1979	16 103.4	703.0	819.6	14 580.8	100.0	4.4	5.1	90.5
1980	19 810.6	712.2	1 108.7	17 989.7	100.0	3.6	5.6	90.8
1981	22 611.2	580.2	1 042.0	20 989.0	100.0	2.6	4.6	92.8
1982	22 204.3	451.8	1 133.2	20 619.3	100.0	2.0	5.1	92.9
1983	25 122.7	485.3	1 215.4	23 422.0	100.0	1.9	4.8	93.3
1984	30 456.4	507.3	1 324.3	28 624.8	100.0	1.7	4.3	94.0
1985	30 725.7	491.9	1 386.7	28 847.1	100.0	1.6	4.5	93.9
1986	39 861.5	626.8	1 950.6	37 284.1	100.0	1.6	4.9	93.5
1987	53 678.7	689.6	2 559.1	50 430.0	100.0	1.3	4.8	93.9
1988	60 667.4	823.5	2 496.8	57 347.1	100.0	1.4	4.1	94.5
1989	66 304.0	477.8	2 579.3	63 246.9	100.0	0.7	3.9	95.4
1990	67 214.4	431.4	2 578.7	64 204.3	100.0	0.7	3.8	95.5
1991	76 178.3	524.5	3 045.5	72 608.3	100.0	0.7	4.0	95.3
1992	81 470.3	508.5	2 975.0	77 986.8	100.0	0.6	3.7	95.7
1993	84 916.6	471.1	3 013.0	81 432.0	100.0	0.6	3.5	95.9

Source: Council for Economic Planning and Development, *Taiwan Statistical Data Book*, Taipei, 1994, p. 194.

Table 8 Trade Between Taiwan and China in Hong Kong, 1978–94 (US$ million)

	Total	Exports	Imports	Balance
1978	46.8	0.1	46.7	-46.7
1979	77.1	21.3	55.8	-34.5
1980	320.7	242.2	78.5	163.8
1981	466.5	390.2	76.3	313.9
1982	298.1	208.2	89.9	118.2
1983	264.7	168.6	96.0	72.6
1984	553.4	425.6	127.7	297.9
1985	1 104.0	988.0	116.0	871.9
1986	925.2	811.0	114.2	666.9
1987	1 515.9	1 226.8	289.0	937.8
1988	2 717.4	2 239.3	478.1	1 761.3
1989	3 483.4	2 896.5	586.9	2 309.6
1990	1 829.4	3 278.3	765.3	2 513.0
1991	5 793.2	4 667.2	1 126.0	3 541.2
1992	7 406.9	6 287.9	1 119.0	5 168.9
1993	14 395.0	12 934.0	1 461.0	11 473.0
1994	16 510.0	14 650.0	1 860.0	12 790.0

Sources: ROC Board of Foreign Trade; Hong Kong Census & Statistics Department.

Table 9 Taiwan's Trade with Japan, the United States and Hong Kong (US$1000)

Period	Total trade			Japan		
	Imports	Exports	Balance	Imports	Exports	Balance
1952	187 215	116 474	-70 741	58 407	61 230	+2 823
1955	201 022	123 275	-77 747	61 235	73 322	+12 087
1960	296 780	163 982	-132 798	104 855	61 766	-43 089
1965	556 011	449 682	-106 329	221 319	137 599	-83 720
1966	622 361	536 270	-86 091	251 443	128 839	-122 604
1967	805 832	640 730	-165 102	325 050	114 648	-211 402
1968	903 280	789 189	-114 091	361 612	127 889	-233 723
1969	1 212 698	1 049 365	-163 333	535 863	157 578	-378 285
1970	1 523 951	1 481 436	-42 515	652 783	215 625	-437 158
1971	1 843 938	2 060 393	+216 455	827 023	245 029	-581 994
1972	2 513 502	2 988 123	+474 621	1 046 002	376 738	-669 264
1973	3 792 496	4 483 366	+690 870	1 427 697	823 784	-603 913
1974	6 965 757	5 638 993	-1 326 764	2 214 948	844 005	-1 370 943
1975	5 951 650	5 308 771	-642 879	1 812 220	694 234	-1 117 986
1976	7 598 931	8 166 340	+567 409	2 451 499	1 094 754	-1 356 745
1977	8 510 887	9 360 710	+849 823	2 642 984	1 120 070	-1 522 914
1978	11 026 931	12 687 140	+1 660 209	3 678 051	1 570 253	-2 107 798
1979	14 773 700	16 103 426	+1 329 726	4 561 431	2 248 576	-2 312 855
1980	19 733 135	19 810 618	+77 483	5 353 230	2 173 440	-3 179 790
1981	21 199 551	22 611 197	+1 411 646	5 928 525	2 478 738	-3 449 787
1982	18 888 375	22 204 270	+3 315 895	4 780 222	2 382 307	2 397 915
1983	20 287 078	25 122 747	+4 835 669	5 586 683	2 477 068	-3 109 615
1984	21 959 086	30 456 390	+8 497 304	6 441 861	3 186 462	-3 255 399
1985	20 102 049	30 725 662	+10 623 613	5 548 847	3 460 945	-2 087 902
1986	24 181 460	39 861 504	+15 680 044	8 254 741	4 559 809	-3 694 932
1987	34 983 380	53 678 748	+18 695 368	11 840 566	6 986 014	-4 854 552
1988	49 672 800	60 667 362	+10 994 562	14 825 440	8 771 697	-6 053 743
1989	52 265 326	66 303 952	+14 038 626	16 031 015	9 064 862	-6 966 153
1990	54 716 004	67 214 446	+12 498 442	15 998 428	8 337 715	-7 660 713
1991	62 860 545	76 178 309	+13 317 764	18 858 256	9 188 897	-9 669 359
1992	71 976 553	81 470 250	+9 493 697	21 766 639	8 893 655	-12 872 984
1993	77 061 203	84 916 602	+7 855 399	23 186 059	8 964 099	-14 221 960

Source: Council for Economic Planning and Development, *Taiwan Statistical Data Book*, Taipei, 1994, pp. 196, 197.

Table 10 Taiwan's Import and Export Dependency on Japan and the United States (%)

	US			Hong Kong	
Imports	Exports	Balance	Imports	Exports	Balance
85 566	4 065	-81 501	16 797	8 980	-7 817
95 543	5 400	-90 143	3 045	6 779	+3 734
113 108	18 853	-94 255	4 726	20 658	+15 932
176 372	95 680	-80 692	5 766	27 904	+22 138
166 335	115 885	-50 450	7 535	32 949	+25 414
247 302	167 815	-79 487	12 164	51 142	+38 978
239 494	278 194	+38 700	12 890	72 307	+59 417
291 752	399 047	+107 295	18 958	93 057	+74 099
363 839	564 174	+200 335	27 262	135 877	+108 615
408 159	859 200	+451 041	39 191	160 071	+120 880
543 424	1 251 317	+707 893	59 689	229 105	+169 416
952 533	1 677 106	+724 573	99 542	295 976	+196 434
1 679 905	2 036 638	+356 733	117 031	338 334	+221 303
1 652 129	1 822 737	+170 608	74 795	363 020	+288 225
1 797 540	3 038 699	+1 241 159	101 409	610 369	+508 960
1 963 852	3 636 250	+1 672 398	200 303	638 439	+438 136
2 376 063	5 010 378	+2 634 315	152 708	857 705	+704 997
3 380 797	5 652 243	+2 271 446	205 361	1 140 352	+934 991
4 673 486	6 760 300	+2 086 814	249 921	1 550 610	+1 300 689
4 765 763	8 163 099	+3 397 336	308 912	1 896 959	+1 588 047
4 563 266	8 758 918	+4 195 652	307 398	1 565 348	+1 257 950
4 646 433	11 333 713	+6 687 280	298 892	1 643 628	+1 344 736
5 041 650	14 867 717	+9 826 067	370 361	2 087 134	+1 716 773
4 746 273	14 773 373	+10 027 100	319 677	2 539 718	+2 220 041
5 432 594	19 013 878	+13 581 284	378 655	2 921 305	+2 542 650
7 647 962	23 684 790	+16 036 828	753 785	4 123 315	+3 369 530
13 006 725	23 467 169	+10.460 444	1 922 086	5 587 070	+3 664 984
12 002 788	24 036 214	+12 033 426	2 205 206	7 042 278	+4 837 072
12 611 827	21 745 853	+9 134 026	1 445 867	8 556 243	+7 110 376
14 113 788	22 320 844	+8 207 056	1 946 753	12 430 520	+10 483 767
15 771 032	23 571 604	+7 800 572	1 781 388	15 414 978	+13 633 590
16 722 624	23 484 496	+6 761 872	1 728 757	18 444 257	+16 715 500

Source: Council for Economic Planning and Development, Taiwan Statistical Data Book, Taipei, 1994, pp. 201, 203.

Table 10 Taiwan's Import and Export Dependency on Japan and the United States (%)

Period	Imports			Exports		
	Total	Japan	US	Total	Japan	US
1952	100.0	31.2	45.7	100.0	52.6	3.5
1955	100.0	30.5	47.5	100.0	59.5	4.4
1960	100.0	35.3	38.1	100.0	37.7	11.5
1965	100.0	39.8	31.7	100.0	30.6	21.3
1966	100.0	40.4	26.7	100.0	24.0	21.6
1967	100.0	40.5	30.7	100.0	17.9	26.2
1968	100.0	40.0	26.5	100.0	16.2	35.3
1969	100.0	44.2	24.1	100.0	15.0	38.0
1970	100.0	42.8	23.9	100.0	14.6	38.1
1971	100.0	44.9	22.1	100.0	11.9	41.7
1972	100.0	41.6	21.6	100.0	12.6	41.9
1973	100.0	37.7	25.1	100.0	18.4	37.4
1974	100.0	31.8	24.1	100.0	15.0	36.1
1975	100.0	30.6	27.8	100.0	13.1	34.3
1976	100.0	32.3	23.7	100.0	13.4	37.2
1977	100.0	31.1	23.1	100.0	12.0	38.8
1978	100.0	33.4	21.5	100.0	12.4	39.5
1979	100.0	30.9	22.9	100.0	14.0	35.1
1980	100.0	27.1	23.7	100.0	11.0	34.1
1981	100.0	28.0	22.5	100.0	11.0	36.1
1982	100.0	25.3	24.1	100.0	10.7	39.4
1983	100.0	27.5	22.9	100.0	9.9	45.1
1984	100.0	29.3	23.0	100.0	10.5	48.8
1985	100.0	27.6	23.6	100.0	11.3	48.1
1986	100.0	34.1	22.5	100.0	11.4	47.7
1987	100.0	33.8	21.9	100.0	13.0	44.1
1988	100.0	29.8	26.2	100.0	14.5	38.7
1989	100.0	30.7	23.0	100.0	13.7	36.3
1990	100.0	29.2	23.0	100.0	12.4	32.4
1991	100.0	30.0	22.4	100.0	12.1	29.3
1992	100.0	30.2	21.9	100.0	10.9	28.9
1993	100.0	30.1	21.7	100.0	10.6	27.7

Source: Council for Economic Planning and Development, *Taiwan Statistical Data Book*, Taipei, 1994, pp. 201, 203.

Table 11 Asia-Pacific Trade with China, Hong Kong and Taiwan, 1992 (US$ million)

	China		Hong Kong		Taiwan	
	Exports	*Imports*	*Exports*	*Imports*	*Exports*	*Imports*
Australia	1 351.0	1 695.0	1 699.0	590.0	1 863.0	1 533.0
Brunei	4.7	11.3	.7	36.1	70.5	8.2
Canada	1 808.0	2 041.0	691.0	940.0	787.0	2 042.0
India	164.0	174.0	685.0	363.0	199.0	191.0
Indonesia	1 613.0	518.0	869.0	808.0	1 345.0	1 335.0
Japan	11 967.0	16 972.0	20 779.0	2 046.0	21 166.0	9 449.0
South Korea	2 654.0	3 725.0	5 909.0	794.0	2 262.0	1 315.0
Malaysia	772.0	975.0	1 549.0	905.0	1 270.0	2 245.0
New Zealand	192.5	242.9	217.9	119.2	236.9	244.8
Philippines	146.0	243.0	425.0	1 203.0	283.0	1 091.0
Singapore	1 124.0	2 232.0	4 591.0	3 443.0	1 545.0	2 752.0
Thailand	385.8	1 219.5	1 506.7	492.9	618.2	2 247.9
United States	7 470.0	27 413.0	9 069.0	10 266.0	15 205.0	25 806.0
former USSR	3 526.0	2 958.0	63.0	270.0	494.0	72.0
Vietnam	66.0	116.7	135.1	1 034.6	130.6*	72.5*

Source: International Monetary Fund, *Direction of Trade Yearbook 1993.*

Note: * 1991.

Table 12 Foreign investment in Taiwan (US$1000)

Period	Total		Overseas Chinese		US	
	Case	Amount	Case	Amount	Case	Amount
Total (1952–92)	6 573	16 491 409	2 326	2 485 388	943	4 063 152
1952	5	1 067	5	1 067		
1955	5	4 599	3	176	2	4 423
1960	14	15 473	6	1 135	5	14 029
1965	66	41 610	30	6 470	17	31 104
1966	103	29 281	51	8 377	15	17 711
1967	212	57 006	105	18 340	18	15 714
1968	325	89 894	203	36 449	20	34 555
1969	201	109 437	90	27 499	30	27 862
1970	151	138 896	80	29 731	16	67 816
1971	130	162 956	86	37 808	17	43 736
1972	166	126 656	114	26 466	17	37 307
1973	351	248 854	201	55 166	29	66 876
1974	168	189 376	85	80 640	21	38 760
1975	85	118 175	44	47 235	13	41 857
1976	98	141 519	53	39 487	8	22 236
1977	102	163 909	52	68 723	17	27 833
1978	116	212 929	50	76 210	18	69 765
1979	123	328 835	50	147 352	19	80 375
1980	110	465 964	39	222 584	15	110 093
1981	105	395 757	32	39 463	25	203 213
1982	132	380 006	50	59 720	33	79 606
1983	149	404 468	49	29 086	35	93 294
1984	174	558 741	74	39 770	41	231 175
1985	174	702 460	67	41 757	42	332 760
1986	286	770 380	80	64 806	56	138 428
1987	480	1 418 796	117	195 727	74	414 061
1988	527	1 182 538	89	121 377	60	134 726
1989	548	2 418 299	70	177 273	54	343 002
1990	461	2 301 772	85	220 115	61	540 367
1991	389	1 778 419	65	219 462	61	587 661
1992	411	1 461 374	73	312 146	71	183 820
1993	323	1 213 467	62	123 501	50	207 970

Source: Council for Economic Planning and Development, *Taiwan Statistical Data Book*, Taipei, 1994, pp. 244, 246.

Japan		Europe		Others	
Case	Amount	Case	Amount	Case	Amount
2 074	4 626 442	520	2 436 167	710	2 880 260
-	-				
-	-	-	-		
3	309	-	-		
14	2 081	1	43	4	1 912
35	2 447	2	746		
76	15 947	4	1 872	9	5 133
96	14 855	2	1 762	4	2 273
75	17 379	4	36 311	2	386
51	28 530	4	11 694	2	1 125
17	12 400	4	66 135	6	2 877
26	7 728	4	6 842	5	48 313
92	44 599	14	33 874	15	48 339
50	38 901	3	14 761	9	16 314
22	23 234	2	4 193	4	1 656
26	30 760	2	32 796	9	16 240
20	24 145	3	28 001	10	15 207
43	50 336	1	4 468	4	12 150
39	50 462	2	19 766	13	30 880
35	86 081	11	14 428	10	32 778
27	64 623	9	13 196	12	75 262
24	152 164	11	46 570	14	41 946
33	196 770	7	20 746	25	64 572
28	113 978	15	92 242	16	81 576
32	145 236	12	100 011	21	82 696
88	253 596	24	139 642	38	173 908
207	399 240	38	234 332	44	175 436
212	431 867	75	206 236	91	288 332
233	640 552	85	531 420	106	726 052
179	826 800	66	348 350	70	366 140
138	526 183	54	221 736	71	223 377
117	417 776	58	203 763	92	343 869
88	272 512	39	209 974	84	399 519

Table 13 Private Foreign and Overseas Chinese Investment in Taiwan, 1952–92 (US$1000)

Industry	Total		Overseas Chinese		Private foreign	
	Case	Amount	Case	Amount	Case	Amount
Total	6 573	16 491 409	2 326	2 485 388	4 247	14 006 021
1 Agriculture and forestry	21	6 002	17	4 410	4	1 592
2 Food and beverages	252	702 317	116	66 910	136	635 407
3 Electronic and electric products	896	4 028 752	170	127 902	726	3 900 850
4 Fisheries and livestock	62	30 790	53	22 710	9	8 080
5 Textiles	326	392 073	202	169 773	124	222 300
6 Paper and paper products	59	109 400	36	55 125	23	54 275
7 Chemicals	847	3 038 532	284	146 440	563	2 892 093
8 Non-metallic mineral products	214	560 816	102	292 762	112	268 054
9 Metal products	496	1 121 023	102	108 310	394	1 012 713
10 Machinery, equipment and instruments	376	1 330 091	66	51 873	310	1 278 218
11 Transportation	138	369 874	86	127 391	52	242 483
12 Construction of buildings	207	179 129	157	95 458	50	83 671
13 Banking and insurance	153	1 163 241	34	452 200	119	711 041
14 Foreign trade	1 255	1 138 714	426	89 086	829	1 049 629
15 Services	843	1 996 018	257	594 643	586	1 401 375
16 Others	428	324 637	218	80 395	210	244 240

Source: Council for Economic Planning and Development, *Taiwan Statistical Data Book*, Taipei, 1993, p. 247.

Table 14 Taiwan: Number of Newspapers and News Agencies

End of year	Newspapers	News agencies
1952	30	28
1955	34	39
1960	30	42
1965	31	43
1966	31	43
1967	31	43
1968	31	43
1969	31	43
1970	31	43
1971	31	43
1972	31	44
1973	31	44
1974	31	44
1975	31	44
1976	31	44
1977	31	44
1978	31	44
1979	31	44
1980	31	44
1981	31	43
1982	31	44
1983	31	44
1984	31	44
1985	31	44
1986	31	44
1987	31	44
1988	124	131
1989	197	158
1990	209	178
1991	234	188
1992	272	204
1993	274	231

Source: Council for Economic Planning and Development, *Taiwan Statistical Data Book,* Taipei, 1994, p. 271.

Table 15 Military Forces: Taiwan and its Neighbours

	Total armed forces	Principal warships	Submarines	Combat aircraft
ROC	360 000	41*	4	486
China	3 030 000	54	46	5 850
India	1 100 000	28	15	720
Japan	246 000	64	4	470
North Korea	1 132 000	3	26	732
Australia	67 900	11	5	157
Indonesia	283 000	17	2	99
Malaysia	127 500	4	-	69
Singapore	55 500	-	-	192
Thailand	283 000	8	-	192
Vietnam	857 000	7	-	185

Source: The Military Balance 1992–1993, International Institute for Strategic Studies, London, 1992.
Note: * Includes 25 destroyers, ten frigates, and six ex-US Navy Knox-class frigates.

Table 16 Taiwan's 1992 Trade with Asia and Australia (% of Taiwan's total imports/exports)

	Japan	Korea	Hong Kong	Australia	Singapore	Philippines	Thailand	Indonesia	Malaysia
Imports	30.2	3.2	2.5	2.9	2.4	0.4	1.1	2.0	1.7
Exports	10.9	1.4	18.9	1.8	3.1	1.3	2.2	1.5	2.7

Source: Council for Economic Planning and Development, Taiwan Statistical Data Book 1993, pp. 201–4; International Monetary Fund, Direction of Trade Statistics Yearbook 1993.

Table 17 Taiwan's Investments in Southeast Asia (unit $m)

	Permitted by Southeast Asia		Permitted by Taiwan	
	Amount	Case	Amount	Case
Thailand				
1986	70.00	21	5.81	3
1987	300.00	102	5.36	5
1988	842.00	308	11.88	15
1989	871.00	214	51.60	23
1990	761.00	144	149.39	39
1991	567.57	69	86.43	33
1992	-	-	83.29	23
1993	-	-	109.16	19
Malaysia				
1986	4.07	15	-	-
1987	91.00	37	5.83	5
1988	313.00	111	2.70	5
1989	815.00	191	158.64	25
1990	2 383.00	270	184.88	36
1991	1 314.21	182	442.01	35
1992	-	-	155.72	17
1993	-	-	64.54	18
Philippines				
1986	0.35	8	0.07	1
1987	9.04	43	2.64	3
1988	109.87	86	36.20	7
1989	148.69	190	66.31	13
1990	140.65	158	123.60	16
1991	11.61	109	1.31	2
1992	-	-	1.21	3
1993	-	-	6.50	12
Indonesia				
1986	18.00	-	-	-
1987	9.00	3	-	-
1988	913.00	17	1.92	3
1989	158.00	50	0.31	1
1990	618.00	94	61.34	18
1991	1 056.50	57	160.34	25
1992	-	-	39.93	20
1993	-	-	25.93	11
Singapore				
1986	43.95	49	0.43	3
1987	0.02	-	1.30	-
1988	0.63	-	6.43	3
1989	0.54	1	5.20	6
1990	3.16	3	47.62	10
1991	23.73	4	12.54	13
1992	-	-	8.79	11
1993	-	-	69.47	12

Source: Statistics on Overseas Chinese and Foreign Investment, Investment Commission, Ministry of Economic Affairs, Taipei, September 1994, p. 55; and Investment Commission, Ministry of Economic Affairs, Outward Investment Analysis Report, Taipei, 1991.

Table 18 Foreign Direct Investment Approvals in Southeast Asia, 1986–89 ($ million)

To	Indonesia		Malaysia		Philippines		Thailand	
	1986–88	1989	1986–88	1989	1986–88	1989	1986–88	1989
Japan	369	769	265	993	49	158	1 522	3 524
NIEs	663	1 197	315	1 335	63	323	815	2 012
Hong Kong	157	407	57	130	21	133	211	562
Korea	78	466	7	70	1	17	41	171
Singapore	116	166	112	338	1	24	157	411
Taipei China	312	158	139	797	40	149	406	868
Asia	1 032	1 966	580	2 328	112	481	2 337	5 536
World	2 231	4 719	1 112	3 194	239	804	3 279	7 996

Source: *Asia Development Outlook 1991*, Asian Development Bank, Manila, p. 48.

Table 19 Regional Trade Patterns, 1986–91 (US$ million)

	1982		1992	
	With Taiwan	With China	With Taiwan	With China
Australia	1 176	1 157	3 396	3 046
Canada	790	2 829	1 170	3 849
Indonesia	638	245	2 680	2 131
Japan	6 682	8 838	30 615	28 939
South Korea	490	-	3 577	6 379
Malaysia	628	387	3 515	1 747
New Zealand	138	152	482	435
Philippines	288	327	1 375	389
Singapore	881	1 121	4 297	3 356
Thailand	322	541	2 866	1 605
United States	13 954	5 414	41 011	34 883

Source: International Monetary Fund, *Direction of Trade Yearbook, 1982–1985, 1986–1992*.

Table 20 Rank of Taiwan and China as APEC Export Markets, 1982–92

	Exports to Taiwan		Exports to China	
	1982	1992	1982	1992
Australia	9th	7th	5th	9th
Canada	20th	13th	6th	5th
China*	-	7th	-	-
Hong Kong	8th	6th	2nd	1st
Japan	10th	2nd	12th	8th
Indonesia	12th	6th	29th	4th
Korea	19th	7th	-	6th
Malaysia	9th	9th	18th	11th
New Zealand	15th	6th	7th	10th
Philippines	15th	6th	11th	13th
Singapore	18th	9th	22nd	11th
Thailand	16th	10th	7th	16th
United States	14th	6th	18th	15th

Source: IMF, *Direction of Trade Statistics Yearbook 1989;*
    IMF, *Direction of Trade Statistics Yearbook 1993.*
Note: * estimate

Table 21 Australian Exports to Taiwan and China 1973–93 (A$ million)

	To Taiwan	To China
1973	68.9	97.7
1974	87.0	218.3
1975	99.2	245.68
1976	116.0	214.4
1977	157.0	413.47
1978	230.1	422.7
1979	321.8	696.2
1980	371.1	700.9
1981	409.5	554.8
1982	495.1	766.2
1983	648.2	467.3
1984	737.4	871.2
1985	995.7	1 271.0
1986	1 126.7	1 587.2
1987	1 267.7	1 526.0
1988	1 493.3	1 101.6
1989	1 720.8	1 201.6
1990	1 801.6	1 294.7
1991	2 324.0	1 500.5
1991–92	2 536.8	1 456.6
1992–93	2 676.1	2 269.1

Source: Direction of Trade Time Series Australia 1972–90, and *Composition of Trade Australia 1992–93,* Department of Foreign Affairs and Trade, Canberra.

Table 21 Australian Exports to Taiwan and China 1973–93 (A$ million)

Index

aboriginal tribes, 5, 7
ADB, 3
aerospace industry, 150
agriculture
  development under Japan, 32–33
  development under US, 60
  under Kuomintang, 84
aid, 237–38
  from US, see under United States
air links, 163
  with China, 184
  with Japan, 28
aircraft hijackers, 188
airforce, 210
  airpower, 213–14
Albright, Madeleine, 239
Americanisation, 54, 232, 238
anti-China policy, of US, 14
APEC, 3, 18, 164, 257, 259
  export rank in, 319
architecture, 18
Armacost, Michael, 257
arms, 240
  European sales, 217
  sales to Taiwan, 20, 161
  US sales of, 65, 69–70, 216–17, 230, 244

ASEAN, 148
  Regional Forum, 19, 164, 245
Asia-Pacific Economic Co-operation, 19
Asia-Pacific region
  acceptance by, 163–64
  as centre of, 9
  as export market, 132
  as mediator in, 132
  role in, 1, 68, 131–32, 238, 267
  trade, 311
Asian Development Bank, 177, 257
Association for Relations Across the Taiwan Strait, 19, 177–78, 184
Association of East Asia Relations Office, 43
Australia
  export links with, 235–36
  exports to Taiwan and China, 319
  investment in, 157–59
  non-official links with, 236
  policy towards, 23
  trade with, 157–59, 238, 316
banking
  Kuomintang monopolisation of, 86
  hub for, 257
Basic Labour Standards Law, 88
Beijing massacre, see Tiananmen affair
Bush, George, 237, 244